Irish Stereotype in American Cinema

Studia Imagologica

Series Editors

Hugo Dyserinck[†]
Joep Leerssen (*University of Amsterdam*)

VOLUME 29

The titles published in this series are listed at *brill.com/imag*

Irish Stereotype in American Cinema

Stories of Violence

By

Piotr Szczypa

BRILL

LEIDEN | BOSTON

Cover illustration: "The riot on St. Patrick's Day - the attack on the police at the corner of Grand and Pitt Streets, New York City"; First published in Frank Leslie's illustrated newspaper, v. 24, 1867 April 6; Courtesy of the Library of Congress Prints and Photographs Division Washington, D.C. 20540 USA, LC-USZ62-121400.

The Library of Congress Cataloging-in-Publication Data is available online at http://catalog.loc.gov
LC record available at http://lccn.loc.gov/2021027190

Typeface for the Latin, Greek, and Cyrillic scripts: "Brill". See and download: brill.com/brill-typeface.

ISSN 0927-4065
ISBN 978-90-04-46796-5 (hardback)
ISBN 978-90-04-46797-2 (e-book)

Copyright 2021 by Koninklijke Brill NV, Leiden, The Netherlands.
Koninklijke Brill NV incorporates the imprints Brill, Brill Nijhoff, Brill Hotei, Brill Schöningh, Brill Fink, Brill mentis, Vandenhoeck & Ruprecht, Böhlau Verlag and V&R Unipress.
All rights reserved. No part of this publication may be reproduced, translated, stored in a retrieval system, or transmitted in any form or by any means, electronic, mechanical, photocopying, recording or otherwise, without prior written permission from the publisher. Requests for re-use and/or translations must be addressed to Koninklijke Brill NV via brill.com or copyright.com.

This book is printed on acid-free paper and produced in a sustainable manner.

To Ola, Adaś, and Jerzyk for their love, unwavering support, and patience

∵

Contents

Acknowledgements   IX

Introduction: Violence and the Irish   1

1 **An Irish Colony across the Atlantic Ocean**   10
  1   The Irish in Colonial America   11
  2   The American War of Independence   14
  3   The Great Famine Period   17
  4   Irish Americans in the 20th Century: Divided We Stand   26
  5   Irish Americans and Irish Nationalism   28
  6   The Second World War: The Irish Fall from Grace   33
  7   The Troubles   34
  8   The Irish in American Popular Culture   37

2 **The Irish on the Silver Screen**   42
  1   Irish Film Characters of the Silent Film Era   46
  2   The Classical Period since 1930   54
     2.1   *Violent Ways: The Irish as Gangsters*   55
     2.2   *Against Violence: Irish American Catholic Priests*   64
     2.3   *Irish Police Officers*   72
     2.4   *Destroyed by Violence: Irish Boxers*   76
     2.5   *IRA Films*   92
     2.6   *The Irish and Union Violence*   97
     2.7   *Irish American Combatants*   101

3 **The Irish in New Hollywood**   110
  1   Don Siegel's Dan Madigan and Harry Callahan   113
  2   Ted Post's *Magnum Force* and James Fargo's *The Enforcer*   124
  3   Jimmy "Popeye" Doyle: *The French Connection*   131
  4   Union Violence   136
  5   Gangsters and Boxers: Old and Tired   138
  6   Other Representations of the Irish in New Hollywood   142

4 **Contemporary Hollywood: The Irish as Outlaw Heroes**   147
  1   Irish Cops: Labeled as Irish   150
     1.1   *The Twilight of* Dirty Harry   150
     1.2   *The Dawn (and Twilight) of John McClane*   153
     1.3   *The Irish Killing Machine:* RoboCop   159

2	Northern Irish Republicanism	167
3	Irish Gangs: The Great Return	180
4	Irish American Vigilantism	203

5 Contemporary Hollywood: The Irish as Official Heroes 214

1	Irish American Law Enforcement	214
2	Firefighters in the Irish American *Bildungsroman*	218
3	New Boxers in Irish America	225
4	Other Violent Characters	237
5	The Irish Ethnotype in Contemporary American Cinema	238

Conclusion 244

Filmography 251
Works Cited 262
Index 270

Acknowledgements

I would like to express my sincerest gratitude to Professor Christopher Garbowski (Maria Curie-Skłodowska University). Without his continuous mentorship, this book would never be possible.

I would also like to thank Professor Marek Paryż (University of Warsaw) and Professor Paweł Frelik (University of Warsaw) for the valuable input they have provided.

INTRODUCTION

Violence and the Irish

There is a quotation usually attributed to William Butler Yeats, although more probably used by an unknown person to refer to that poet, which runs: "Being Irish, he had an abiding sense of tragedy, which sustained him through temporary periods of joy."[1] Regardless of the real source of the quotation, the sentence seems to be an accurate description of a general national characteristic, as, because of the history of their country, the Irish are accustomed to painful and tragic moments. The history of Ireland, even when given but a cursory look, abounds in events that put the nation's strength and determination to the test. Due to the turbulent situation in their homeland, the Irish began seeking refuge in the colonies established in North America quite early on. In time, when the colonies became the United States, immigrants from Ireland constituted one of the major groups of Europeans striving to find a new life in the newly formed country.

Even though the 20th century saw the Irish emerge as one of the most numerous and prosperous ethnic groups in the USA, their new homeland initially did not treat them well. Uneducated Catholic immigrants from then underdeveloped Ireland occupied the poorest neighborhoods of the country's emerging cities dominated by the affluent White Anglo-Saxon Protestant majority. Therefore, it should not be a surprise that the Irish, living in poor conditions, started to epitomize everything America could not accept. Not only were they considered backward, but their communities were believed to be a reservoir of diseases, such as cholera[2] and typhoid,[3] and, above all, a source of violence. Back in their homeland, the Irish had organized themselves in gangs and tended to resort to violence against British oppressors.[4] When they moved to the U.S., they brought with them their gang culture and their disrespect for oppressive authority. Thus, they frequently turned against the owners of businesses where they worked.[5] When the Irish achieved success, their violent image was reinforced by the financial support they offered to

---

1   Robert Emmet Meagher and Elizabeth Neave, *Ancient Ireland: An Explorer's Guide* (Northampton: Interlink Books, 2004), 33.
2   Timothy J. Meagher, *The Columbia Guide to Irish American History*, The Columbia Guides to American History and Cultures (New York: Columbia University Press, 2005), 78.
3   Kevin Kenny, *The American Irish: A History* (London: Routledge, 2014), 187.
4   Meagher, *The Columbia Guide to Irish American History*, 88.
5   Kenny, *The American Irish*, 67.

© KONINKLIJKE BRILL NV, LEIDEN, 2021 | DOI: 10.1163/9789004467972_002

their compatriots fighting for Ireland's independence and later for the independence of its Northern part.[6]

American cinema quickly took an interest in the Irish, transforming the violent stereotypes associated with them into patterns of cinematic representation. Thus, stereotypical Irish violence became a narrative motif employed by Hollywood in the creation of Irish characters. Early filmmakers often chose violence as an Irish national characteristic, which their films often addressed mockingly. Later productions explored it in more developed and complex plots, putting the Irish in America in the roles of gangsters and boxers using violence for personal gain. These characters were quickly linked with Irish American Catholic priests and Irish American women who opposed crime in a non-violent way. Such non-violent, or even anti-violent representations showed the Irish in the context of values desirable for American society, e.g., their devotion to the family and community. In time, it became apparent that violence remained the kernel of the representation of the Irish, the critical ingredient in the construction of Irish characters, linked inextricably to the inveterate Irish stereotype existing in American culture. However, this violence was not necessarily perceived as a negative feature; guided and controlled, it was sometimes necessary as a means of serving and protecting the community and society.

This book examines the evolution of the stereotypical representation of the Irish in American cinema on the assumption that violence, understood widely as a usually deliberate and harmful violation of a person's physical or emotional equilibrium,[7] is the central part of the stereotype. The analysis begins in the pre-Hollywood era, follows through Classical Hollywood (about 1927 – 1967), the short and stormy time of New Hollywood (roughly 1967 – 1982), and concludes with contemporary cinema. Irish and Irish American characters are present in all three of the periods American cinema is usually divided into. Depending on the plot and character construction, their Irish origins are foregrounded or only signaled to the viewer, and they are presented in the context of violence more often than not. They may be extremely brutal, or they might oppose violence and lead a crusade against it, but violence is present in their lives because of their professions and the social roles they usually perform. The ubiquity of Irish characters in various genres of American films means that there are also productions that do not show violence but still include Irish characters. Although such films do not form the core of the present analysis, they may attest to the changing attitude of American cinema to Irishness, taking into account the time when they appeared.

---

6 Meagher, *The Columbia Guide to Irish American History*, 166.

7 W. James Potter, *On Media Violence* (Thousand Oaks: SAGE, 1999), 80.

The films selected for the analysis reflect the evolution of the Irish ethno-type in American cinema with violence as the constant, most prevalent part of the stereotype. However, the selection of films produced between 1903 and the present by no means exhausts the stock of American films featuring Irish characters. Therefore, the reader may notice that some films they might have expected to be a part of this book are not here. On the other hand, there may be several titles whose presence here will be surprising, as the selected films include not only productions which explicitly address their characters' Irish origins but also those in which the characters are given an Irish surname, as this seems to prove the existence of an association between violence and the Irish and may attest to the conscious or subconscious activation of ste-reotypes.[8] The selection includes some of the most critically acclaimed pro-ductions of the American cinema, as well as poorly received films, some of which are virtually forgotten. The characters in the films studied here all pertain to the stereotypical view of the Irish deeply rooted in American cul-ture and stemming from the history of the Irish in America. These stereo-types are usually connected to the professions or social roles performed by the characters and include gangsters, police officers, Catholic priests, box-ers, members of trade unions, Northern Irish republicans, combatants, and vigilantes, all representing the most common types of Irish characters in American cinema.

Taking into account the types of characters and the development of their representations, a clear tendency to abandon straightforwardly negative Irish characters in favor of more positive ones is visible in classical American cinema. This seems to coincide with the growing acceptance of the Irish by American society. As a period of social uncertainty, New Hollywood reimagines the char-acter of the Irish American police officer, providing the viewer with the overly brutal but ultimately positive figure of "Dirty" Harry Callahan. The violence connected with this character is freed from the Production Code's restraints imposed on filmmakers in the 1930s but is shown as a necessity and duty that the Irish American cop is ready to accept. The period also re-evaluates the old classic characters of Irish American gangsters, boxers, and trade unionists, drawing inspiration from their earlier incarnations. The contemporary period returns to the classic versions of Irish American gangsters, boxers, and anti-vi-olence police officers focused on family values and devotion to American law, but also to New Hollywood's excessively violent Irish cops believing in retrib-utive justice. It also introduces new types of leading Irish characters, such as

---

8 Matthew S. Eastin, *Encyclopedia of Media Violence: One-Volume Set* (Los Angeles: SAGE Publications, 2013), 302.

firefighters—one of the quintessential Irish professions—and Irish vigilantes, whose most recent incarnation appears as a curious combination of violent gangster, cop, and priest. Regardless of these developments, violence remains the critical ingredient in the representation of the Irish.

However, at this point, it is necessary to signal that violent characters in the films studied are predominantly men. In most cases studied, Irish and Irish American women are anti-violent characters. Two reasons for this suggest themselves. Firstly, violent stereotypes seem to apply to men rather than to women as violence, associated with physical strength, has usually been portrayed as a masculine rather than feminine feature. Even in contemporary American cinema, in which female characters, especially in action genres, are often presented as violent, the type of violence they engage in, i.e., highly destructive and with the use of weaponry, is identified as predominantly masculine.[9] Secondly, Irish American women in America, unlike men, often worked in professions not associated with violence.[10] Therefore, they may have been perceived as an opposition to the Irish men; hence, their frequent anti-violence role in the plots analyzed. Admittedly, there are exceptions in which Irish American women are assigned stereotypically male professions and social roles. Notably, the typical representation of Irish American women as non-violent and Irish women in Ireland as intimate with violence may have served an ideological purpose, acknowledging the stereotype's roots but pointing to the difference between Irish and American culture.

As a study of a national and cultural stereotype—understood here as the perceived character of the Irish preserved in American culture and displayed in the texts produced by this culture—this book belongs to the tradition of imagology. Originating in literary studies, imagology focuses on "images of foreigners," or "strangers," in narrative texts, influenced by specific clichés, myths, and stereotypes existing in a given culture.[11] In this context, the book is based on the assumption that violence is perceived as an integral and inextricable element of the Irish stereotype in American culture, as expressed in American cinema. This stereotype's expression exists as the most typical representation of Irishness in American cinema, i.e., its ethnotype.

---

9   Katy Gilpatric, "Violent Female Action Characters in Contemporary American Cinema," *Sex Roles* 62, no. June 2010 (March 7, 2010): 743, https://doi.org/10.1007/s11199-010-9757-7.

10   Kenny, *The American Irish*, 186.

11   Małgorzata Świderska, "Comparativist Imagology and the Phenomenon of Strangeness," *CLCWeb: Comparative Literature and Culture* 15, no. 7 (West Lafayette: Purdue University Press, 2013): n. pag.

One of the core ideas of imagology is the existence of the "auto-image," i.e., the image of the Self, and the "hetero-image," the image of the Other.[12] The two images stand in opposition to each other and play a role in the process of identification. A nation's auto-image may be influenced or even constructed on the basis of the contrast with the hetero-image of another nation. Such an opposition existed, for example, in the perception of the Irish by the British, and also by Americans. The cross-national dynamics between the three were based on stereotypes and prejudices.

Generally, the stereotypes and prejudices attributed to a given nation influence the formation and development of the representation of the perceived national character, i.e., the ethnotype. In texts of culture, ethnotypes exist in the form of narrative themes and formulas[13] and serve as an explication of the behavior of the characters.[14] In this case, when the Irish became stereotypically perceived as violent, the ethnotype of the violent Irishman was formed. With the birth of the cinema, violence became an intrinsic element of the representation of the Irish on the screen. Importantly, there is a contrast between an ethnotype and a general perception of a given nation. More precisely, "[n]ot everything that can be said of a given nation or country can count as ethnotype" but only those features that differentiate a given nation.[15] Therefore, prior to studying a particular ethnotype, it seems vital to determine whether a given characteristic or a pattern of behavior is, in fact, readily attributed to a nation and stands out as one of its defining features. Thus, in the next section, an account of the history of Irish immigration to America is presented in order to see how the stereotype of the violent Irishman came into existence, how it determined the perception of the Irish by Americans, and why it has apparently dominated the Irish ethnotype in American cinema.

Various stereotypes pertaining to the same nation may exist in different cultures and may result in different ethnotypes. This is based on the perceived cultural distance on the Self vs. the Other axis, i.e., between the nation's auto-image and its hetero-image of a different group of people. Therefore, the stereotype of the violent Irishman existing in America and rooted in the idea of White Anglo-Saxon Protestant (WASP) dominance transferred to America from Britain, does not necessarily have to exist in Continental Europe.

---

12   Joep Leerssen, "Imagology: On Using Ethnicity to Make Sense of the World," in *Les Stéréotypes Dans La Construction Des Identités Nationales Depuis Une Perspective Transnationale*, ed. Géraldine Galéote, vol. 10 (Paris: Revue Iberic@l, 2016), 16.

13   Leerssen, 16.

14   Joep Leerssen, "The Rhetoric of National Character: A Programmatic Survey," *Poetics Today* 21, no. 2 (June 1, 2000): 268, https://doi.org/10.1215/03335372-21-2-267.

15   Leerssen, "Imagology: On Using Ethnicity to Make Sense of the World," 17.

Moreover, ethnotypes evolve together with the stereotypes in which they are rooted. In fact, as noted by Joep Leerssen, since the Middle Ages, the Irish have been perceived in many contradictory ways, but on the whole, their image had been negative for a very long time.[16] Often ridiculed, they were considered fierce, savage, unintelligent, and evil. This hetero-image was contrasted with the English, whose auto-image was that of civilized, righteous, and intelligent people. The stereotypical perception of the Irish by the English was reflected by the ethnotype of the "Stage Irishman," an epitome of the stereotype, which was the dominant representation of the Irish until the middle of the 18th century, when a sentimental, more positive view of the Irish became more pronounced in Europe.[17] The positive image of the Irish in Europe was rooted in the nation's deep religiousness, as well as its Celtic culture, considered spiritual, mysterious, and mystic, and reinforced by Irish authors and poets.[18]

Today, there seems to be a dissonance between the perception and representation of the Irish in Continental Europe and in America. The hetero-image of economically successful and socially forward-looking Ireland is in Europe combined with the sentimental and mystic image of the country, promoted especially by the popularity of Irish music, an inextricable element of the ubiquitous Irish pub culture.[19] In America, however, although the ethnotype of the Irishman has evolved, violence is still the feature most readily associated with the Irish in cinema.

In the context of the Irish in America and their representation in American cinema, the stereotype based on prejudice against them may be seen as a self-fulfilling prophecy. As described by McGarty et al.,

> Stereotypes may affect the ways the members of one group treat another and that in turn may lead to changes in behaviour of the stereotyped group. Perceiving the members of some group as violent and dangerous may, for example, lead to hostile treatment of that group which may in turn lead to a violent response from the stereotyped group.[20]

---

16   Joep Leerssen, "Nationality: Irish," Imagologica, accessed May 2, 2020, https://imagologica. eu/ethnotypology.

17   Leerssen.

18   Leerssen.

19   Desi Wilkinson, "Euro-Paddy Land," The Journal of Music, accessed May 9, 2020, https://journalofmusic.com/focus/euro-paddy-land.

20   "Social, Cultural and Cognitive Factors in Stereotype Formation," in *Stereotypes as Explanations: The Formation of Meaningful Beliefs about Social Groups*, ed. Craig McGarty, Vincent Y. Yzerbyt, and Russell Spears (Cambridge: Cambridge University Press, 2002), 10,

VIOLENCE AND THE IRISH

In a certain way, the concept of the stereotype as a "self-fulfilling prophecy" is related to Johan Galtung's three levels of violence: cultural, structural, and direct.[21] Structural violence is the central part of the three levels; it refers to the repression or exploitation of a group by another group and is indirect. Cultural violence is symbolic and legitimizes the use of structural violence by giving the perpetrators of violence a justification for their actions.[22] Although structural violence is indirect, it may lead to a response from the persecuted group, which is only able to respond with direct violence.[23] As Galtung states, "The underlying assumption is simple: 'violence breeds violence.'"[24] Thus, the connection between the "self-fulfilling prophecy" and Galtung's division of the types of violence lies in the fact that the persecuted group responding with direct violence may become stereotypically perceived as violent.

As some researchers point out, "[i]f there is one medium that has produced the most brutal, macabre, bloody and excessive scenes of violence, and to which controversy about such representations inevitably returns, it is film."[25] The apparent omnipresence of violence on the screen may be explained by the audience's psychological need to feel "control over the source of fear—through information and narrative resolution."[26] Cinematic violence is usually portrayed in connection with certain types of characters in various film genres. Thus it may serve as one of the defining features in the construction of a given character or a group of characters—in this case the Irish in American cinema—in contrast with a non-violent or less violent context in which they are presented. What is more, the ubiquity of cinematic violence is the reason for the variety of its forms represented on the screen. This, in turn, corresponds to various attitudes the audience may have to violent film characters and is based on other elements used in such characters' construction. In other words, violence does not necessarily have to be presented in a negative way as everything depends on the way it is shown to the viewer. In the classical films analyzed here, it quickly becomes apparent that violence represented in connection with the Irish is negative when it serves selfish purposes as a means of achieving quick success but positive when used for a greater good.

---

21   Johan Galtung, *Peace by Peaceful Means: Peace and Conflict, Development and Civilization* (Los Angeles: SAGE, 1996), 2.

22   Galtung, 2.

23   Galtung, 200.

24   Galtung, 200.

25   Cynthia Carter and C. Kay Weaver, *Violence And The Media* (Buckingham: Open University Press, 2003), 6.

26   Alison Young, *The Scene of Violence: Cinema, Crime, Affect* (London: Routledge, 2010), 2.

This also applies to Irish republican fighters, presented in a positive way when fighting for freedom, and negatively when pursuing selfish agendas. Moreover, beginning with the classical period, selfish violence seems to have been more readily presented in connection with Irish outsiders, or less-integrated Irish Americans; as such, it appears to be a part of the hetero-image of the Irish who do not belong or are rejected by American society. By contrast, assimilated Irish Americans tend to use violence in a socially acceptable way—when they are not non-violent or even anti-violence. This tendency is present in the New Hollywood and contemporary eras.

Moreover, even though violence is the central element of the representation of the Irish in American cinema, it is not the only feature commonly associated with them. The Irish stereotype and the Irish ethnotype in American cinema are not straightforward, uniform cultural constructs; on the contrary, they should be treated as complex categories encompassing various stereotypes and ethnotypes associated with the Irish. Positively represented Irish are people devoted to the sense of duty towards their community and society in general, for which they are ready to put their lives in danger, often leading to the ultimate sacrifice. They possess a sense of justice making them do what they see as fair, even when it means being at odds with the established American or international legal order. Regardless of their portrayal, they seem to be influenced by their fathers, real or adoptive, usually in a positive way; hence the analysis also focuses on the importance of the father figure in the construction of characters, where such a motif is used.

This book is divided into five chapters. The first presents the historical context for the study, giving an account of the Irish in America from the Colonial Era. This serves as context for a short analysis of the changing social position of the Irish, not only in the U.S. but also in Ireland and Northern Ireland. The chapter focuses on the combination of historical and social reasons contributing to the birth of the violent Irish stereotype in America. Chapter two presents an analysis of the representations of the Irish in classical American cinema, including the pre-Hollywood period and silent Hollywood era, and focusing on the fully mature Classical Hollywood films made between 1930 and the 1960s. The third chapter contains an analysis of the motif of violence in New Hollywood cinema (1967 – 1982). Chapters four and five focus on Irish characters appearing in contemporary American cinema. Since contemporary Hollywood presents a broad spectrum of such characters, they are divided into two categories, based on the division proposed by Robert Ray.[27] The first category,

---

27   Robert Beverley Ray, *A Certain Tendency of the Hollywood Cinema, 1930–1980* (Princeton, N.J.: Princeton University Press, 1985), 58–63.

presented in chapter four, involves outlaw heroes, i.e., those who use violence for reasons that although not always selfish run counter to the American vision of law and order; therefore, they are labeled as "unlawful." In the study, such characters are not necessarily assimilated; they feel more Irish than American and are more frequently referred to as Irish by other characters. Examples include gangsters, vigilantes, and Irish republican fighters, but also some violent police officers, labeled as "Irish cops." The second category, presented in chapter five, involves characters designated as "lawful" or "official heroes," who serve American law, attesting to their high degree of assimilation into American culture. These include police officers, boxers, and firefighters.

Because of their large numbers and the weight of the social baggage they carried, the Irish have left a lasting mark on American culture. They were perceived as distant from the American self-perception, which meant their image was distorted by prejudices and stereotypes, with violence becoming their most iconic stereotypical feature. This book is the story of how this violent national stereotype became entrenched in the American consciousness, how it found its place in the American cinematic industry and survived through various periods of the history of Hollywood.

CHAPTER 1

An Irish Colony across the Atlantic Ocean

The United Kingdom finds its "special relationship" with the United States a matter of the utmost importance in its international politics. The two countries are closely linked by shared history, language, tradition, and military partnership.[1] However, there is one European country whose links with America seem more reliable than the abovementioned "special relationship:" links created by ordinary people who traveled to the wild New World because the unknown waiting there was easier to accept than the bitter reality of the place where they lived. It is Ireland that became one of the most important countries in the history of the United States, even before the latter came into existence.

The Irish were among the most numerous groups of people who crossed the Atlantic Ocean during the American Colonial Period. As stated in the introduction to *The Columbia Guide to Irish American History*:

> The first Irishman came to America in 1584 as part of Sir Walter Raleigh's ill-fated expedition to the Outer Banks of North Carolina. The last Irish man or woman has not yet arrived and may never come, because few things have been as constant in the histories of Ireland and America as Irish immigration to the United States. There may never be a last Irish immigrant as long as Ireland and the United States exist.[2]

Thus, the presence of the Irish in America is inextricably connected to American history and culture. The Irish came to America in search of religious freedom, to escape from persecution, disease, hunger, and violence. However, Americans were influenced by British culture and, it follows, a British worldview in which the Irish were considered brutal savages.[3] It was not only the fact that the Irish were Catholics—outcasts in the colonies dominated by Protestants of various denominations. It was also because the Irish, after literally centuries of foreign domination of their homeland, were mostly poor and uneducated. However, the reality of America in the colonial period, and immediately afterward, was brutal and violent. The colonists had to fight for survival

---

1 John Oakland, *British Civilization: An Introduction* (London; New York: Routledge, 2010), 124.

2 Meagher, *The Columbia Guide to Irish American History*, 3.

3 Edward G. Lengel, *The Irish Through British Eyes: Perceptions of Ireland in the Famine Era* (Westport: Greenwood Publishing Group, 2002), 36.

© KONINKLIJKE BRILL NV, LEIDEN, 2021 | DOI:10.1163/9789004467972_003

AN IRISH COLONY ACROSS THE ATLANTIC OCEAN   11

far from western civilization; they fought against nature, the Native Americans, and frequently against each other in the struggle for control and power. Subsequently, they participated in the bloodshed of the Revolutionary War, helping to establish the United States of America. Afterward, the new country fought continuously, pushing the frontier further to the west, and then, divided into the North and the South, submerged itself in the Civil War. During all this time, the Irish were there to fight. The history of Ireland is the history of violence and the struggle for independence. The history of American-Irishmen is similar, and wars were just a part of the lives of Irish Americans, as the Irish organized themselves in gangs and fought against each other, bringing old feuds to the New World.

1   The Irish in Colonial America

Setting aside the misfortunate expedition in 1584, the question of the first Irish colonists in America is slightly problematic. *Eagle Wing*, the first America-bound ship carrying a group of people from Ulster, set sail in 1636 but heavy storms disrupted the voyage, and the would-be colonists had to turn back. Thus, the first colonists from Ireland began to settle in America in the Chesapeake region in the 1680s.[4] Among the settlers from Ireland arriving in America were not only Catholics but also Presbyterian Scotch-Irish, the descendants of Scots who started to settle in Ulster in the seventeenth century, encouraged by the English who wanted to drive the Irish out of Ulster.[5] Therefore, it is difficult to say whether the first Irish colonists in America were actually Irish or Scottish, and opinions regarding this matter are divided. However, the Scotch-Irish constituted a considerable number of settlers originating from Ireland in the eighteenth century, outnumbering "all others sailing across the Atlantic, with the notable exception of those bound to the New World in slave ships."[6]

Having come from Ulster, the Scotch-Irish quickly gained a reputation for being a fierce and brutal people. It was believed that, in Ulster, they formed "a human buffer between so-called 'civilization' and 'savagery'."[7] The colonies also needed such a buffer against Native Americans. Therefore, the Scotch-Irish

---

4   Lengel., 24.
5   Philip S. Robinson, *The Plantation of Ulster: British Settlement in an Irish Landscape, 1600–1670* (Belfast: Ulster Historical Foundation, 2000), 52–55.
6   Patrick Griffin, *The People with No Name: Ireland's Ulster Scots, America's Scots Irish, and the Creation of a British Atlantic World, 1689–1764* (Princeton, N.J.: Princeton University Press, 2001), 1.
7   Kenny, *The American Irish*, 29.

were welcome on the frontier, where they soon gained fame as cruel and violent fighters, "slaughtering and being slaughtered in gruesome numbers."[8] What is more, they quickly lost their attachment to Ireland.[9] This runs counter to the idea that the Irish are a people who always remember the country of their ancestors. These people, or their ancestors, were colonists in Ireland and so they were ready to move on to another colony without much regret about leaving Ireland.

As for the reasons they left Ireland, it is generally believed that the migration occurred due to the following factors. Firstly, the Presbyterians, although in an undoubtedly better position than Catholics in Ireland ruled by Protestants, were also dependent on English landlords. The Scots who were encouraged to settle in Ireland in the seventeenth century were given preferential conditions in terms of the rents they had to pay to the landlords. However, with more and more immigrants settling in Ireland, landlords began to raise the rents. Given that, the lure of the New World, with land for the taking, seemed like an exciting option to many Presbyterians.[10] Secondly, the next wave of Ulster Presbyterians left Ireland In the 18th century, when Ireland was struck by the Famine of 1740—perhaps as serious as the later Great Famine. Although it is difficult to estimate the exact number of people who died during *Bliain an* Áir, as it was referred to, it is generally agreed that there were between 200,000 and 400,000 casualties.[11] Thirdly, the economy of Ulster at the time was based on the linen industry, which was unstable and subject to fluctuations depending on the demand for linen, mainly in Britain. The periods of Presbyterian emigration to America coincided with drops in the sale of linen.[12]

The other significant group of colonists from Ireland was made up of members of the Church of Ireland, a part of the Anglican Church. This group was composed of the descendants of English colonists who had settled in Ireland and the Irish who converted from Catholicism to Protestantism.[13] It is important to remember that members of the Anglican Church enjoyed more privileges than Presbyterians, not to mention Catholics. Therefore, although most Protestants emigrated to America because of the economic situation, some of them—the members of the gentry—moved to the New World in order to form the ruling class of the colonies.[14]

---

8   Kenny, 29.
9   Meagher, *The Columbia Guide to Irish American History*, 41.
10   Meagher, 25.
11   Meagher, 25, 29.
12   Meagher, 26.
13   Meagher, 26.
14   Meagher, 26.

AN IRISH COLONY ACROSS THE ATLANTIC OCEAN

Notwithstanding the above, there were also Catholic-Irish colonists in America in the seventeenth and eighteenth centuries. However, the colonies were an extension of the Empire, and, similarly to Britain, the ruling class of British colonies in the New World was composed of the privileged Protestants and followed the customs and traditions of the mother country in order to emphasize their *esprit de corps* and identification with the British aristocracy. Therefore, Irish Catholics trying to escape one oppressive regime by choosing immigration to the New World, usually as indentured servants, which meant they had to work for a predetermined time in exchange for the voyage, inadvertently found themselves in a place that strove to be a part of Great Britain, with all the anti-Catholic sentiments that characterized the motherland. Others were transported against their will—as prisoners. This forced migration to America served as a substitution to imprisonment or the death penalty.[15] Both groups were considered outcasts and were unable to form successful and thriving Catholic communities. The situation of more disadvantaged Irish migrants did not change when they arrived in America. As for the more affluent Irish and Catholics in general, they had to convert to Anglicanism if they wanted to achieve success in the colonies.

Admittedly, there were exceptions from this rule as there were, in fact, Catholics in America who were successful. One such exception was the case of the Catholic family of George Calvert, the First Lord of Baltimore, who named the colony formed in America to honor Henrietta Maria—the Catholic wife of Charles I.[16] An example of a very successful Irish Catholic family were the Carrolls of Annapolis in Maryland. Charles Carroll, named "the Settler" by his descendants, traveled to America in 1688, following his motto "Anywhere So Long As There Be Freedom."[17] Although wealthy, he must have been considered, not without reason, a violent Irishman, as he is reported to have been arrested twice for assaulting Protestant officials.[18] Soon, he became the wealthiest landowner in Maryland.[19]

The Carrolls of Annapolis remained one of the most influential Irish American families in the colonial period. The descendants of the Settler remained faithful Catholics despite the religious bias still present in the colonies. Charles

---

15   Meagher, 27.

16   Richard Middleton and Anne Lombard, *Colonial America: A History to 1763* (New York: John Wiley & Sons, 2011), 74–74.

17   Scott McDermott, *Charles Carroll of Carrollton: Faithful Revolutionary* (New York: Scepter, 2002), 25.

18   Ronald Hoffman, *Princes of Ireland, Planters of Maryland: A Carroll Saga, 1500–1782* (Williamsburg: UNC Press Books, 2002), 45.

19   Hoffman, 71.

14   CHAPTER 1

Carroll's son, also named Charles, was an advocate of Catholic rights, while the
Settler's grandson, Charles Carroll III, was one of Maryland's signatories of the
Declaration of Independence, while another Carroll, John, was in 1790 ordained
the first Catholic bishop in the USA.[20] The history of the Carrolls of Annapolis
stands in sharp contrast to the stories of the majority of Irish settlers, who did
not have a chance of a normal life in the colonies, especially outside Maryland.
The only other place in which Catholics were able to practice their faith openly
was Pennsylvania. In all the remaining colonies, Catholics were in danger of
being tried and executed, as Protestants literally hunted them.[21]

2   The American War of Independence

Before the War, the journey from Ireland to America was difficult but possible
for the Irish. In the seventeenth century, Ireland started supplying provisions,
mainly beef, to the colonies in the Caribbean. Later, the trade extended to the
mainland colonies in America. Ships to Ireland carried flax seed and returned
with linen cloth and immigrants. Still, the cost of such a trip was too much
for most people. It is estimated that thirty-six percent of the Irish who emigrated to the colonies in the eighteenth century were indentured servants.[22]
The journey took about seven weeks. When the War of Independence started,
the voyage became more dangerous than before because of naval warfare.
However, the immigrants "feared not only enemy warships and privateers,"[23]
as they also faced the possibility of impressment into the British army. Forced
impressment caused protests in Ireland.[24]

Nevertheless, at the beginning of the Revolutionary War in America, the
Irish remaining in their motherland saw the conflict as an opportunity for
themselves to show their loyalty to the king. Thus, the Irish elite encouraged
lower-class Irish Catholics to join the fight on the British side. They hoped
that the king would return the colony of Maryland to Catholics.[25] The war in
America became a theme for ballads, which described Americans as black

---

20   MichaePadden and Robert Sullivan, *May the Road Rise to Meet You: Everything You Need to
      Know about Irish American History* (New York: Plume, 1999), 65.
21   Meagher, *The Columbia Guide to Irish American History*, 31.
22   Meagher, 32.
23   Kerby A. Miller, *Emigrants and Exiles: Ireland and the Irish Exodus to North America* (New
      York: Oxford University Press, 1988), 169.
24   Miller, 170.
25   Miller, 180–81.

savages whose only aim was to expel the Irish from the colonies.[26] Still, as the war progressed, the Irish began to identify with the colonists, who, like them, were oppressed by the British and stood against this oppression. This was true especially for lower-class Irish Catholics, the most downtrodden social group in the British area of influence. Moreover, the Irish expected that America's allies, France and Spain, which were also allied with Ireland, would invade Britain, granting the Irish their freedom.[27] The pro-American attitude was also seen in Irish literary works of the period, in which, again as quoted by Miller, the British were "arrogant robbers" who "were wounded" by the success of the Revolution, and George Washington was enumerated in the same breath with Irish heroes such as Brian Boru.[28] What is more, it is estimated that despite the enormous difficulties in traveling to America, 25,000 men left Ireland in order to join the fight against the British.[29] Some of them were undoubtedly conscripted into the British army, but others managed to reach the revolutionary forces in America. Therefore, there were Irish fighting on both sides of the American War of Independence. This sometimes carried tragic implications. For instance, Patrick Carr, an immigrant who had recently arrived from Ireland, was one of the victims of the Boston Massacre. He was wounded with a musket ball by one of the British red-coat troops of the 29th British Regiment, five of whom came from Dublin.[30]

According to some sources, 1,492 officers and twenty-two generals fighting in the American War of Independence were of Irish origin.[31] One British officer, Captain Joshua Pell, described the revolutionary forces as being "chiefly composed of Irish redemptioners and convicts, the most audacious rascals existing."[32] However, it is essential to remember that most of them were Irish Presbyterians, or in other words, the descendants of the Scots who emigrated from Ulster. The reason for that was simple: although many Irish Catholics went to America in the colonial period, they were still a minority among all the Irish immigrants.[33]

Nevertheless, the Irish in America took an active part in the Revolutionary War. As stated by Padden and Sullivan: "They were seeking something that had seemed to be an elusive dream back home: if they couldn't be free as Irish

---

26   Miller, 181.

27   Miller, 181.

28   Miller, 181.

29   Padden and Sullivan, *May the Road Rise to Meet You*, 59.

30   Padden and Sullivan, 59.

31   Padden and Sullivan, 59.

32   Meagher, *The Columbia Guide to Irish American History*, 39.

33   Meagher, 41.

living in Ireland, they would be free as Irish living in America."[34] When the war was over, they suddenly found themselves citizens of a free country. However, the concept of Irishness was slightly different at the time of the Revolutionary War than it is today. Irish Americans of the time were not interested in Ireland, as they were mostly Presbyterians or Protestants of a different denomination. They lived mostly in the South and were farm laborers.[35]

What is more, Irish fascination with the war in America had a strong influence on Ireland. The colonists were "battling the hereditary enemy"[36] so in 1791, in Dublin and Belfast, the Society of United Irishmen was created, seeking to establish a free Irish republic based on universal suffrage, similarly to the United States.[37] Soon, they joined the Defenders, a Catholic organization, and allied with France, which was going to help the Irish in regaining their freedom. However, although they treated France as their most important ally, the Irish felt intimately connected to the colonists fighting in America.[38] Britain could not accept this. Protestants loyal to the Crown were organized into Orangemen and started pre-emptively persecuting the United Irishmen. Although the rebels were decimated, in the so-called "dragooning of Ulster," in 1798, influenced by America, the United Irishmen in Ireland rebelled against Britain.[39] The rebellion was aided by France when 1,100 troops arrived in County Mayo. However, the allies arrived too late, and they were not enough to help peasants in the war against a well-trained army. Soon, in the same year, the rebellion was finished. The persecution of the United Irishmen intensified, forcing some of them to emigrate.[40] In the United States, the exiles were welcome as brothers in arms, fighting for the same cause as Americans.[41] They brought the ideals of republican freedom and democracy. What is more, they strongly influenced American culture, becoming editors of newspapers, authors of plays and histories. Finally, they emerged as radically republican political leaders, such as, for example, James McHenry—George Washington's secretary of war. They propagated an image of an Ireland free and driven by republican ideals. These were not just words, as they took measures to include Catholics in the life of the Society of United Irishmen and American society as a whole.[42]

---

34   *May the Road Rise to Meet You*, 64.

35   Meagher, *The Columbia Guide to Irish American History*, 41.

36   Miller, *Emigrants and Exiles*, 181.

37   Miller, 182–83.

38   Miller, 183.

39   Miller, 184.

40   Meagher, *The Columbia Guide to Irish American History*, 48.

41   Miller, *Emigrants, and Exiles*, 189.

42   Kenny, *The American Irish*, 41.

AN IRISH COLONY ACROSS THE ATLANTIC OCEAN

The United Irishmen's presence in the United States and their quest to unite the feuding sectarian groups influenced the image of the Irishman in America. The stereotypical Irishman of that time was "a blundering, ignorant, comic peasant"; however, the same Irishman was "capable of redemption in the wholesome and free environment of the new American republic."[43] Also, at that time, Ireland was romanticized as a country of "dead heroes, moody rural landscapes, and lost loves."[44] However, some Americans, mainly Federalists, were still apprehensive about accepting the "Wild Irish" into their country.[45]

3 The Great Famine Period

With the emergence of the independent United States of America, new waves of Irish people emigrated to the New World. Irish immigration to the USA reached its peak in the nineteenth century due to several reasons.

After the rebellion of 1798, the situation in Ireland worsened both for Protestants and for Catholics. The persecution led by the Orangemen was aimed not only at the United Irishmen but also at Catholics, including those who had not taken part in the rebellion. Quoting an anonymous Irish Catholic rebel, Miller mentions murdered women and children and even "infants dashed against the walls."[46] The Catholics organized themselves and responded with violence. Catholic mobs, sometimes even led by priests, murdered Protestants. The victims of such attacks were not necessarily Orangemen, but rather Protestants in general. Thus, the Protestants turned to the Crown, and, in 1801, the Protestant-led Irish Parliament ceased to exist as the country was incorporated into the United Kingdom of Great Britain and Ireland. However, this did not stop the eruption of sectarian violence. Militant Irish Catholic groups terrorized Protestant landlords, who responded with violence.[47] In these circumstances, people continued to emigrate to America, escaping the persecution. Here they took part in another conflict between the United States and the United Kingdom in the War of 1812. Among those who fought was the future first president of the United States to be a descendant of Irish Presbyterians, Andrew Jackson.[48]

---

43   Meagher, *The Columbia Guide to Irish American History*, 50.
44   Meagher, 49–50.
45   Miller, *Emigrants and Exiles*, 188.
46   Miller, 187–88.
47   Miller, 186.
48   Padden and Sullivan, *May the Road Rise to Meet You*, 69.

This new wave of migrants arriving in the nineteenth century was dominated by Catholics. This was due to several reasons, the most important being the fact that the trail for them had been blazed by the United Irishmen, who—as exiles—were inscribed in the tradition of political banishment, already present in Irish history. They suggested an alternative to Europe: the New World, where they propagated the republican values of equality among all Irishmen and offered protection and guidance for recent immigrants. The position of the Irish grew in America, culminating with Andrew Jackson's election in 1828.[49] However, this does not mean that living conditions in America improved for ordinary Irish people. They were given jobs nobody else wanted to take, and—what is striking, even in this context—they were used as cheap substitutes for African slaves.[50] This does not mean that the Irish in America were enslaved, but that it was cheaper to pay an Irishman than to buy a slave. Moreover, when an Irishman was injured or killed while doing his or her duties, their employer could replace them with other Irishmen, without any financial loss. Poverty and, it follows, violence and criminality were widespread. For instance, the Five Points district in New York was a place where Irish Americans and free African Americans lived next to each other in appalling conditions. They occupied an old brewery converted into housing for the poorest and surrounding tenements. The brewery was home for several hundred people, while the tenements were occupied by about a hundred residents each. Five Points was also the place where Irish gangs operated.[51] When it comes to Irish women, they performed domestic services, and also worked in the so-called "needle trades"—in the production of clothes and ornaments, while those who could not find any job would often turn to the streets.[52]

As the Irish in American lived close to African Americans, the relationships between the two groups were often complicated. To American society, the two groups were very similar and, therefore, were similarly downtrodden. The Irish and Africans shared neighborhoods and frequently had children together.[53] Also together, they engaged in criminal activity, with Irish business owners buying stolen goods from African slaves whom they paid with alcohol.[54] To American society, the two groups constituted the same source of social problems. The perception and the social status of the Irish was affected by the social position of African Americans. This is visible also in racial slurs used at

---

49   Miller, *Emigrants and Exiles*, 189.
50   Kenny, *The American Irish*, 63.
51   Kenny, 61.
52   Kenny, 63.
53   Noel Ignatiev, *How the Irish Became White* (New York; London: Routledge, 1995), 40.
54   Ignatiev, 41.

the beginning of the 19th century, when African Americans were referred to as "smoked Irish," while the Irish people were named "niggers turned inside out."[55] With the improving social standing of the Irish, the two ethnicities began drifting apart. The Irish were accepted into mainstream society much earlier than African Americans.

Although in the 19th century the Irish in America lived in appalling conditions, they still believed America was a land of opportunity. Thus, the main reason for Irish immigration to America in the nineteenth century was economic. To start with, during the Napoleonic wars, England required Irish agricultural products. The majority of the Irish population at that time—as much as four-fifths, according to Reginald Byron—lived in the countryside, and the largest occupational group was formed by farm laborers who did not own their land.[56] The survival of this group was based on irregular earnings and the *conacre*—a traditional system by which Irish peasants were allowed to use one acre of their employer's land to grow potatoes—a cheap, reliable, and relatively nutritional crop.[57] Thus, the potato became the basis for the diet of the most impoverished Irish farmers. The remaining groups were formed by tenant smallholders, small farmers, and commercial farmers. The last group had enough land to employ laborers—mainly the landless workers under the *conacre* system. However, the members of all these groups were heavily dependent on their landlords and could be evicted from the land for economic reasons or on their landlords' whim.[58] As the wars ended in 1815, the demand for Irish crops decreased, and people living in rural areas were left without jobs. At this point, they began to leave their homeland in the hope of finding a new home in Britain, Canada, even Australia, but most of them in the USA. About 40,000 Irish immigrated to the U.S. from 1815 until the end of 1816. In the early 1820s, between 5,000 and 10,000 people emigrated every year. In the 1830s, the process turned into mass migration, with 50,000 people moving to America every year.[59] Importantly, emigration was state-assisted and thus available even to the poor. As David Boyce points out:

> There was simply no alternative for the people except the precarious existence available to them from their simple diet and their small patches of land; none, that is, except emigration. Between 1815 and 1845, over a

---

55   Ignatiev, 41.

56   Reginald Byron, *Irish America: Oxford Studies in Social and Cultural Anthropology* (Oxford: Oxford University Press, 1999), 39.

57   Byron, 39.

58   Byron, 39.

59   Meagher, *The Columbia Guide to Irish American History*, 52.

million inhabitants left Ireland, and one of the remedies frequently suggested for the Irish rural problem was state-assisted emigration rather than workhouse relief. Nevertheless, emigration in itself, while possibly a palliative, was not a cure since the fundamental problem—that of a society in which most people did not have the money to buy alternative means of subsistence if their staple crop failed—remained untouched.[60]

The problematic situation of Irish landless farmworkers was ignored by landlords and, thus, the situation in Ireland was a catastrophe waiting to happen.

The worst thing possible took place in 1845 when the infamous potato blight struck. The culprit—the parasitic fungus *Phytophthora infestans*—was first observed in September 1845 in Leinster, in the east of Ireland, and its range was quite restricted. However, by 1846 the blight had spread across the country, destroying up to eighty percent of the harvest and nearly all of the crops one year later.[61] The situation continued until 1851. The poor wandered from farm to farm, looking for anything to eat. They ate farm animals that could not be replaced due to the farmers' lack of income. The relatively rich sold their herds, knowing that the animals would be eaten by the starving if they were kept. However, one of the most curious and tragic aspects of the Famine was that Ireland did not stop exporting its agricultural products.[62] Undoubtedly, the export was not as high as during the Napoleonic Wars, but it continued throughout the whole period of the Great Famine. Importantly, foreign aid was given to the starving and grain was imported to Ireland from Europe and the USA.[63]

However, the aid failed due to the following reasons. Firstly, such was the loss of the crops that the import could not replace the potato losses. Secondly, the imported food included grain, wheat flour, and maize.[64] The grain and flour were of no use for homeless people with no access to grindstones and ovens. Moreover, the aid rarely reached those in need because, in most cases, it was inhibited by bureaucracy. As for the maize, the Irish were unfamiliar with it.[65] All this emphasizes another aspect of the tragedy that struck Ireland: there was sufficient food to meet the needs of the starving Irish; it was just the method of distribution that failed.

---

60   David George Boyce, *Nineteenth-Century Ireland: The Search for Stability* (Dublin: Gill & Macmillan, 2005), 113.

61   Meagher, *The Columbia Guide to Irish American History*, 62.

62   Meagher, 67–68.

63   Byron, *Irish America*, 46.

64   Byron, 46.

65   Byron, 46.

A tremendous number of ninety thousand people starved to death, and about nine hundred thousand died of illnesses appearing as a direct result of the Famine.[66] Disease raged as malnutrition affected the people's immunological systems. Those who sought to help the poor also contracted diseases carried by fleas and lice. For all these reasons, the total number of Irish people who died during the Great Famine ranges from five hundred thousand to one million. The discrepancy stems from the fact that many of those who died were quickly buried in mass graves. The highest mortality occurred in Connaught: forty percent of the dead. Thirty percent of the dead were from Munster, twenty percent from Ulster, and the remaining 10 percent from Leinster. In such circumstances did Irish emigration reach its peak with about 1,200,000 emigrants. As a result of all these combined reasons, the population of Ireland shrunk by 1,600,000 – 2,000,000 from 1841 to 1851.[67] There is little doubt that most of those who emigrated blamed the United Kingdom for the tragedy that struck the nation.

The country needed time to heal its wounds. The remainder of the century and the beginning of the next one saw the continuous immigration of the Irish to the USA. The majority of Irish immigrants of the Famine period arrived in New York. It is estimated that 848,000 chose this city as their destination. Some of them settled there, others moved on, but New York became the home of the largest Irish communities in the United States. They constituted from one-fifth to one-third of the city's population, depending on the neighborhood that they occupied.[68] There, they lived in the complete chaos of New York in the nineteenth century, often with other ethnic groups as neighbors. That is to say, the immigrants lived wherever they could, in harsh conditions. As mentioned by Timothy Meagher, the first case of cholera was diagnosed among a family of Irish immigrants, the Gilligans, in 1849.[69] Although they lived in appalling conditions, they still supported each other, and it was family and friends that helped the newly arrived immigrants. This is also illustrated by the fact that most of them married within the community, choosing partners from among the immigrants from the same county as their own.[70] They remained in groups originating from the same regions in Ireland, among people often bearing the same surname, and cherished the traditions of the Old Country.[71] Many of the

---

66   Byron, 50.
67   Byron, 49.
68   Meagher, *The Columbia Guide to Irish American History*, 77.
69   Meagher, 78.
70   Meagher, 87.
71   Miller, *Emigrants and Exiles*, 327.

Irish living in New York suffered nervous breakdowns when, having escaped from the hell of starvation and disease, they found themselves in a similar situation in their supposed promised land. This may account for the fact that they constituted sixty percent of all the people treated at the New York Lunatic Asylum.[72] They were also unskilled and could not find any work that would allow them to sustain themselves and their families. As quoted by Meagher, "the scattered debris of the Irish nation" were referred to as "the poorest and most wretched population that can be found in the world" by an Irish immigrant from Tyrone—Archbishop John Hughes.[73]

The Irish then started moving to other American cities, mostly to Boston in New England. However, the city was unprepared for the massive influx of immigrants, and the conditions there were even worse than in New York. Apart from the appalling conditions in which the immigrants had to live, the biggest problem was recurring cholera epidemics. Although most of the city was affected by the disease, the highest death rate was among the poorest, that is, the Irish.[74] Other New England towns offered similar conditions: poor accommodation meant that people lived wherever they could, and diseases such as cholera and tuberculosis decimated the Irish population.[75] Another problem was violence. Irish gangs, such as the "Corkonians," "Connaughtmen," "Munstermen," and the "Far Downers,"[76] fought each other, and crime was widespread, often leading to violent riots, such as the one on Palm Sunday in 1847 on the streets of Worcester, Massachusetts,[77] or, later, in 1863, in New York.[78]

Some of the Irish decided to go west, where they found a good place to live in San Francisco. The Irish population in the city numbered 4,000 in 1852. It was also in San Francisco that the Famine immigrants found white-collar jobs and soon turned into the city's elite.[79] Similar conditions, although not as good as in San Francisco, were offered by Detroit, where they could find jobs, and in Milwaukee, Natchez, and Memphis.[80]

The Famine generation of Irish immigrants was seen in sharp contrast to earlier ones. Even though the previous wave of Irish Catholic immigrants to the United States were considered inferior, they were still seen as being better than

---

72   Meagher, *The Columbia Guide to Irish American History*, 78.
73   Meagher, 79.
74   Meagher, 80.
75   Meagher, 80.
76   John W. Blake, *The Ulster American Connection* (Ulster: New University of Ulster, 1981), 29.
77   Meagher, *The Columbia Guide to Irish American History*, 81.
78   Miller, *Emigrants and Exiles*, 327.
79   Meagher, *The Columbia Guide to Irish American History*, 85.
80   Meagher, 86.

those who arrived as a result of the Famine. This was because the later arrivals were mostly Gaelic-speaking peasants for whom America was too modern.[81] The Irish were accustomed to violence, and, arguably, it was the necessity for a violent response to the harsh conditions in which they lived that started to bring their community together in the broader sense, i.e., not only within the network of family and friends but within the whole minority. In pre-famine years, they used violent acts such as sabotage, which would be referred to as terrorism today, against their landlords; there was also a great deal of sectarian violence among the various Christian denominations. When members of opposing groups moved to America, where they were forced to live next to each other, they continued to fight against each other. The aforementioned Irish gangs were, thus, the first sign of the Irish forming some sort of social groups outside their families. They also formed secret societies reminiscent of the groups that existed in Ireland, such as the Whiteboys and Ribbonmen.[82] Importantly, in pre-famine years, the Irish gained ill-fame for preferring to use violence against their employers, rather than going on strike.[83] The Irish arriving in America in the nineteenth century were no longer treated like the United Irishmen, as heroic freedom fighters in political exile, but as people who were inferior to the WASP elite. This stereotype was reinforced by the attitude the Irish had towards property and leadership.[84] In Ireland, those in power, usually Protestants, were considered the oppressors. When the Irish who emigrated from Ireland in the wake of the Famine reached the New World, they brought with themselves deep prejudice against the rich in general and wealthy Protestants in particular. They gathered in militant secret societies and fought both against their new "masters" and each other.[85]

However, as mentioned by Kevin Kenny, when these violent "traditions" were "transplanted" to America, they were adjusted to the reality of a more industrial society.[86] Soon, the Irish were leading figures in trade unions, constituting, for example, the majority of the officers of New York's Tailors' Trade Association. They also managed to take control of the waterfront of New York City, as—having driven out black workers—they formed the "racially exclusive" Longshoremen's and Laborer's United Benevolent Society.[87] What is more, some of the Irish were members of the Fenian Brotherhood, an organization

---

81   Miller, *Emigrants and Exiles*, 326.

82   Kenny, *The American Irish*, 65.

83   Kenny, 66.

84   Miller, *Emigrants and Exiles*, 327.

85   Miller, 327.

86   *The American Irish*, 111.

87   Kenny, 112.

founded in 1858 in New York by John O'Mahony. This was an American branch of the Irish Republican Brotherhood, formed in Dublin by James Stephens, also in 1858.[88] One such person was Thomas Masterson, a shoemaker who, together with Robert Blissert, a tailor, became the leader of the Irish working on the waterfront.[89] This might have meant that the trade unions led by the Irish had connections with Irish nationalists. Suffice it to say that the Irish dominated American trade unions in the nineteenth century. However, their presence in such organizations was an extension of their violent response against landowners in Ireland and their employers in America.

With the massive influx of Irish (and German) Catholics, Catholicism became the largest Christian denomination in America, with 4.5 million believers in 1870. Comparisons started to be made between the Irish and the Puritans, who fled Europe in search of religious toleration, thus suggesting that they were "Perfect Americans."[90] Nevertheless, in the eyes of the nineteenth century Protestants living in America, the Irish were anti-American. This view was rooted primarily in the fact that the Irish preferred parish schools run by the Roman Catholic Church to the conventional school system. The most important group of Protestants in the anti-Irish movement were the old Scotch-Irish immigrants.[91] They formed the Nativist movement and opposed immigration in general. They did not want to be confused with poor Irish Catholics flooding America. According to Kenny, this was when they started to refer to themselves as "Scotch-Irish."[92] Sometimes, the opposition to the newly arrived Irishmen turned into violent pogroms, especially in the South, where Irish Catholics were not welcome due to the large population of Scotch-Irish. The 6 August 1855 is known as the Bloody Monday, as several Irish Catholics, including a priest, were killed in a violent rally in Louisville, Kentucky. A similar event took place in the city in which the Irish had been able to live relatively well—San Francisco—in 1856. Finally, in 1857, nativists set fire to a quarantine hospital in New York, on Staten Island, in order to kill the Irish who were there.[93]

The Famine generation did not find a comfortable life in the USA, and the further construction of their identity also involved violence, as they fought in American wars. The first of them was the Mexican-American War (1846–1848). Kevin Kenny states that roughly half of the American forces in the war were

---

88 Eoin Neeson, *Myths from Easter 1916* (Aubane, Ireland: Aubane Historical Society, 2007), 17.

89 Kenny, *The American Irish*, 112.

90 Kenny, 112.

91 Kenny, 113.

92 87.

93 Padden and Sullivan, *May the Road Rise to Meet You*, 102.

composed of recent immigrants; half of this group were the Irish.[94] The officers of the American army bore a deep prejudice against the immigrants, especially those who came from Ireland, which was one of the reasons why more than a hundred soldiers deserted and joined the Mexicans. They were led by John Riley, an Irishman, and the group itself consisted of about forty Irishmen. The deserters used Irish symbols, "a crudely drawn figure of St Patrick, a shamrock and a harp" on their flag.[95] Thus, the Irish involvement in the war did not have a positive effect on their feeling of belonging to American society. It is said that the only two official organizations which were open to the Irish were the Catholic Church and the Democratic Party.[96]

In the post-Civil War period, the Irish in America were still defined by their allegiances to Christian denominations, which contributed to perpetuating divisions within the Irish community. These divisions took the most violent form in 1870 and 1871, during the Orange and Green Riots in New York. The riots were started by Catholics objecting to the Orangemen's parade. The Orange Lodges, acknowledged and supported by the Grand Orange Lodge of Ireland, were made up of Scotch-Irish Presbyterians. On 12 July 1870, the Catholics attacked the marching Orangemen. The following year, the situation was repeated, but with more casualties—during the first riot, nine men were killed; one year later, the number of casualties reached sixty.[97]

The last important aspect of the development of Irish American identity in the nineteenth century was the growth of Irish nationalism in America. First, there was the Young Ireland movement, whose members opted for "a return to the tradition of physical force republicanism" and complete independence, in opposition to the views and strategy of the important Irish political leader, Daniel O'Connell, and his political quest for Irish autonomy.[98] The Fenians, operating both in Dublin and in New York, aimed at regaining Irish rule over Ireland with the aid and financial support of Americans. Eventually, they set up an Irish republican government in Philadelphia.[99] The Fenians even saw a chance for their cause in the conflict between Britain and America. In order to start a war between the two countries, they planned to invade Canada. Simultaneously, they organized a transport of weapons to Ireland. However, the invasion of Canada failed and the transport was intercepted by cooperating British and US navies.[100]

---

94 Kenny, *The American Irish*, 121.
95 Kenny, 121–22.
96 Kenny, 82.
97 Kenny, 129.
98 Kenny, 126–27.
99 Kenny, 128.
100 Kenny, 129.

4 Irish Americans in the 20th Century: Divided We Stand

Between the end of the Famine period and the emergence of the Irish Free State, three million people migrated from Ireland to America.[101] However, only 339,065 of them came between 1901 and 1910, with 146,181 in the following decade.[102] This wave of immigrants was slightly different from the previous ones. First of all, most of them were young single women. In typically large Irish families living in still poor Irish rural areas, only a son could inherit a farm, and only the oldest daughter could expect a dowry. This forced young people, deprived of other perspectives, to emigrate.[103] The members of the new wave were no longer the unruly crowd that had flooded the shores of the New World in the nineteenth century.

These new Irish immigrants were still poor but they also reflected the changes that had taken place in Ireland after the Famine. First of all, they were better educated, as, at the end of the nineteenth century, the literacy rate in Ireland was one of the highest in Europe. Secondly, they were disciplined members of the Catholic Church, modernized in the wake of the Devotional Revolution.[104] What is more, with the growing numbers of eastern Europeans immigrating to the USA, the Irish suddenly started to appear "quite normal in comparison" to this group.[105] This helped especially the native-born Irish Americans reach a higher rung on the social ladder, which was reflected primarily by the fact that they started doing skilled and better-paid jobs. Some of them, about 6 percent, even managed to become members of the middle class, working as salesmen, bookkeepers, and clerks.[106|107] Irish women of the second generation worked as stenographers, secretaries, and nurses, but, first and foremost, as schoolteachers.[108] Finally, the native-born Irish Americans started moving out of the poorer districts where they were born and into new districts and suburbs.[109] However, this sudden acceptance by American society did not seem to extend to the new wave of immigrants. They still belonged to the working class and had to do unskilled jobs, and it was almost impossible for them to achieve any form of economic success. At the beginning of the

---

101 Kenny, 131.
102 Kenny, 180–81.
103 Meagher, *The Columbia Guide to Irish American History*, 101.
104 Meagher, 101.
105 Kenny, *The American Irish*, 181.
106 Meagher, *The Columbia Guide to Irish American History*, 103.
107 Kenny, *The American Irish*, 185.
108 Kenny, 186.
109 Meagher, *The Columbia Guide to Irish American History*, 105.

twentieth century, twenty-three percent of men who emigrated from Ireland to the US worked as day laborers. In comparison, 55 percent of women worked as domestic servants, much like the female members of the Famine generation of immigrants.[110] Finally, they still tended to remain within their group. For these reasons, the new immigrants could not play an essential role in the development of Irish American identity in the twentieth century. Thus, the most important role in this process fell to the descendants of the Irish who arrived in the United States during the Great Famine. What is also essential for this study, the beginning of the twentieth century was a time when old Irish stereotypes in America were re-evaluated, and in some cases reinforced, while new stereotypes were created.

The twentieth century saw the further development of trade unions in which second or even third-generation Irish Americans played the dominant role. Their traditional tendency to fight against people in authority, stemming from violence directed at landlords in Ireland, developed into their participation in trade unions. At the beginning of the twentieth century, there were about a hundred trade unions in the USA, fifty led by Irishmen.[111] These labor organizations still turned to violent acts, as when, for instance, over eighty buildings were destroyed by, presumably, the McNamara brothers, who were members of the Union of Bridge and Structural Iron Workers.[112] They also had connections with Irish nationalists; James Connolly, the author of *Labour in Irish History*, published in 1910, was one of the leaders of the Irish uprising in 1916 and was executed by the British as a result.[113] What is more, the Irish-led trade unions were still radical. Probably the best example of such an organization was the IWW (Industrial Workers of the World), an anarcho-syndicalist organization. It was established by James "Big Jim" Larking, one of the founders of the American Communist Party, and by James Connolly. Finally, they were still racially exclusive, but this time, the discrimination was also aimed against white workers from Eastern Europe.[114]

Thus, the trade unions in which Irish Americans played the dominant role were not significantly different from those that had existed in the previous century. Even though the position of Irish American workers was better, they were still associated with violence. However, this was beginning to change as some union leaders began abandoning radicalism in favor of less violent action. Two

---

110   Meagher, 101.
111   Kenny, *The American Irish*, 188.
112   Kenny, 188.
113   Kenny, 188–89.
114   Kenny, 188–89.

examples of such leaders were P.J. McGuire, one of the originators of America's Labor Day, and Samuel Gompers, an anti-socialist.[115] What is more, not only Irish men but also women played an essential role in American trade unions. Among them was Agnes Nestor, leader of the International Glove Workers Union; Julia O'Connor, a member of the International Brotherhood of Electrical Workers, who headed the department of telephone operators; and Leonora O'Reilly, a member of the board of the National Women's Trade Union League.[116] For the remainder of the century, the Irish continued to play an important role in the American labor movement.

However, as stated before, there was a yawning gap between the established and the newly arrived Irish immigrants. This was seen especially in the sphere of labor, as the latter were often discriminated against. The most famous example of this is the founding of the Butte Miners' Union in Butte, Montana. The town was the world leader in copper mining and had a significant Irish minority, as "26 percent of the residents were either Irish-born or the children of Irish-born," mostly from county Cork, where there were also copper mines.[117] The Miners' Union in Butte advocated, among other things, "the exclusion of 'new immigrants,'" which led to the outbreak of strikes and violence.[118] Thus, once again, the Irish resorted to violent actions in response to a difficult situation.

5   Irish Americans and Irish Nationalism

Until the twentieth century, relations between America and Ireland were based on the following pattern: America, at least in theory, offered land and opportunities and the Irish chose to settle in the New World, usually during crises, thus providing a steady influx of people. The actions of Irish nationalists in America were restricted and usually easily thwarted by both Britain and America. However, in the twentieth century, the situation began to change, as Irish immigrants and their descendants grew in wealth and influence, and both the nature of Irish nationalism and the situation in Ireland has changed forever.

The history of Irish nationalism in America can be traced to the first Catholic exiles from Ireland, the United Irishmen (1791). Fifty years later, the Repeal movement sought to annul the Act of Union. In the 1860s, the Fenians tried to

---

115   Kenny, 189.
116   Kenny, 190.
117   Kenny, 190.
118   Kenny, 191.

AN IRISH COLONY ACROSS THE ATLANTIC OCEAN 29

use America's power to free Ireland.[119] Later, in 1867, there appeared another nationalist organization—Clan na Gael, which became the heir of the Fenians.[120] The end of the nineteenth century saw the further development of Irish nationalism in America, with the emergence of organizations such as the Land Leaguers and Home Rulers (1880).[121] However, it was in the twentieth century that the dream of a free Ireland finally started to take shape. Timothy Meagher, attempting to answer the question of who exactly the nationalists were, gives two opposing viewpoints on the question proposed by various scholars. Firstly, he mentions scholars such as Thomas Brown, who identifies the "upwardly mobile" Irish Americans, as Meagher refers to them, as those for whom Ireland under British rule was humiliating. One of the examples supporting this claim is the speech by Michael Davitt, in which he stressed the respect that successful Irish Americans deserved.[122] Secondly, Meagher quotes two historians, Eric Foner and Kerby Miller, who share the opinion that the real force behind Irish American nationalism was the working class. For those more impoverished Irish Americans, the capitalist reality of the United States was so hard to accept that they turned to the "homeland's cause." These scholars give the example of John Devoy, a nationalist who was among the Irish Americans living "their American lives in spartan simplicity, focusing myopically, relentlessly, and fanatically on Ireland's cause."[123]

Irish American nationalism helped the Irish in their integration into American society. They wanted the country of their ancestors to be built on the same principles as the United States. However, there is also an opposing viewpoint, according to which the quest for Irish freedom was an obstacle to Irish Americans, preventing them from achieving economic success in America.[124] Despite the disagreements concerning the shape of Irish American nationalism in the twentieth century, it cannot be denied that without the help of the Irish living in the New World, there would not be a free Ireland.

In 1901, the United Irish League of America was founded in the USA.[125] Strongly opposed to earlier radical movements like the Fenians, its primary goal was the restoration to Ireland of an autonomous parliament while remaining a part of the United Kingdom. The League was opposed by those in favor of complete independence. These republican organizations, active in

---

119 Meagher, *The Columbia Guide to Irish American History*, 198.
120 Padden and Sullivan, *May the Road Rise to Meet You*, 147.
121 Meagher, *The Columbia Guide to Irish American History*, 198.
122 Meagher, 199–200.
123 Meagher, 200.
124 Meagher, 201.
125 Kenny, *The American Irish*, 193.

the twentieth century, included The Ancient Order of Hibernians and Clan na Gael.[126] The former was founded in 1836 in New York, and, from the beginning of its activity, it was one of the most popular Irish Catholic fraternal organizations.[127] However, in the twentieth century, the Order had declined and Clan na Gael became the most influential Irish republican organization of the time. Under the leadership of John Devoy, the Clan propagated the idea of a fully independent Ireland.[128] Importantly, the Irish, both in America and in Ireland, supported the UILA's quest for Home Rule and not the Clan's idea of regaining the independence of Ireland through physical force.[129] This changed in 1916.

Throughout the beginning of the twentieth century, Clan na Gael maintained relations with the Irish Republican Brotherhood in Dublin. The main aim of the Clan at the time was to gain German support for the Irish cause during WWI. The quest for German support was successful, partly because of the positive relations between Irish and German minorities in the USA. On Easter Monday in 1916, armed by the Germans, republican rebels launched an uprising. Although they were counting on taking Britain by surprise, as the country was at war, the rebels knew that they did not have a strong chance against the British army. Therefore, their main aim was to earn the people's support for their cause. The Easter Rising started on April 24 and ended five days later and was followed by the rebels being executed by the British.[130] The summary execution of the leaders of the rebels drew much attention and an outcry from the public. The brutality was stressed by the American mainstream press, which up to that moment, had usually favored the British.[131] What is most important, the cruelty demonstrated by the British caused a decisive response from Irish people, who started withdrawing their support for Home Rule in favor of the option advocated by Clan na Gael.[132]

After the First World War, the Irish saw an unprecedented chance for their country to become free again. Their main aim was the recognition of Ireland as a separate country in the post-war reorganization that was taking place in Europe. In the second week of December 1918, the Friends Of Irish Freedom organized "Irish Self-Determination Week," during which "mass meetings and demonstrations were held throughout the United States in support of Irish

---

126 Kenny, 193–94.
127 Padden and Sullivan, *May the Road Rise to Meet You*, 73–74.
128 Kenny, *The American Irish*, 193–94.
129 Kenny, 194.
130 Kenny, 194.
131 Padden and Sullivan, *May the Road Rise to Meet You*, 153.
132 Kenny, *The American Irish*, 195.

freedom."[133] The events were supported by the Catholic Church, and the second Irish Race Convention (the first had been organized in 1916) was held in Philadelphia. Also, an official delegation was sent to President Woodrow Wilson, who, however, was not interested in presenting the matter during the Peace Conference. Therefore, three members of the delegation decided to take part in the Conference as the American Commission on Irish Independence. In order to do so, the Commission required formal recognition from the White House, which was flooded with petitions by the Irish from across the United States, Australia, and Argentina. Although a resolution requesting American diplomats to help the Irish in presenting their case before the Conference was adopted, President Wilson did not support the Commission. Consequently, free Ireland was not mentioned in the Treaty of Versailles.[134]

Woodrow Wilson's opposition to the undertakings made by Irish republicans probably stemmed from the fact that he was Scotch-Irish.[135] As quoted by Michael Padden and Robert Sullivan, Devoy referred to Wilson as a person who "hates the Irish with the implacable hatred of the Ulster Orangeman—the stock he comes of."[136] As stated above, there was an intense conflict between Irish Catholics and Scotch-Irish Presbyterians, sometimes turning to violence, as when Catholics attacked the parade of the Orangemen during the riots in the second half of the nineteenth century. When in 1919, Irish Republic was proclaimed in Dublin, the Presbyterians in America protested.[137] The Scotch-Irish opposed the recognition of the Irish Republic and accused the republicans of collaboration with the Germans during WWI. As a result of the Protestants' fear of Catholic retribution, once the protection of the Crown was lost, Ireland was partitioned in 1921.[138]

Irish leaders' hopes in the Treaty of Versailles were dashed but they did not abandon their dream of a free Ireland. In the aftermath of the Easter Rising, some of its leaders managed to avoid execution, usually by claiming American citizenship. Among these people was Eamon de Valera. Sometimes referred to as "the most Irish of Irishmen,"[139] de Valera was an Irish American, born in New York to a family of Irish and Spanish immigrants. In 1917, he joined Sinn Féin, a new Irish nationalist party, and soon became its leader. Having won the majority of Irish seats in the Westminster Parliament, Sinn Féin proclaimed

---

133   Kenny, 196.
134   Kenny, 196–97.
135   Kenny, 197.
136   *May the Road Rise to Meet You*, 155.
137   Kenny, *The American Irish*, 197.
138   Kenny, 197.
139   Padden and Sullivan, *May the Road Rise to Meet You*, 152.

the independent Irish Republic with its own parliament, Dáil Éireann, which, in turn, recognized the country's national forces, the Irish Republican Army, organized by Michael Collins.[140] The Irish, having proclaimed their independence, now fought to drive British troops out of their homeland. This had severe repercussions, as British Prime Minister Lloyd George, together with his government, answered with brutal force. The Royal Irish Constabulary was not enough to suppress the rebellion, so mercenaries, usually WWI veterans, were sent to Ireland to break the uprising. The atrocities committed by "Black and Tans," as they were commonly referred to, were not enough to overcome the nation that was now standing together against the occupant. It is said that even to the IRA, with their policy of using whatever force necessary, the Black and Tans were "a ruthless bunch."[141] The brutality and ruthlessness of both sides of the conflict, but of the Black and Tans especially, are portrayed in Ken Loach's *The Wind that Shakes the Barley*.

Irish American participation in the conflict was focused on opposing the Treaty of Versailles. Eamon de Valera and Joseph McGarrity founded an Irish republican organization in the USA, the American Association for the Recognition of the Irish Republic. Soon this organization gained more popularity than the Friends of Irish Freedom. However, this division in the Irish republican movement in the USA, involving, for instance, sending two separate delegations to party conventions, was an excuse for American Republican and Democratic parties to reject the Irish and their postulates.[142]

The Irish War of Independence lasted from 1919 to 1921. In 1921, the government of the UK proposed a treaty. The chief negotiator, Michael Collins, the architect of the IRA, brought to Dublin a treaty whose conditions were difficult to accept for some of the freedom fighters. The pact involved the partition of Ireland into Northern Ireland, controlled by the United Kingdom, and the Irish Free State, whose government was to swear allegiance to the King (Kenny 199). Ireland becoming a Crown dependency, similar to Canada and Australia, was a decisive step forward in the country's regaining its independence. Michael Collins himself referred to the results of the negotiations as "Freedom to achieve freedom."[143] However, the result of the treaty was still far from what the IRA was fighting for. Thus, for some of its members, the war was not over. This time, however, the outbreak of violence was aimed not at the British but at the Irish Free State. Civil war broke out in Ireland.

---

140   Padden and Sullivan, 154–56.
141   Padden and Sullivan, 154.
142   Kenny, *The American Irish*, 198.
143   Padden and Sullivan, *May the Road Rise to Meet You*, 156.

The situation of Ireland influenced the view of Irishmen in America. On the one hand, the tradition of freedom fighting must have impressed Americans. Moreover, Americans of Irish origin actively supported the country of their ancestors in its quest for freedom. However, taking into account the enormous sum of ten million dollars raised for Irish freedom fighters at the beginning of the twentieth century in America,[144] it is safe to assume that not only Americans of Irish origin supported Irish independence. Still, the refusal by both Democrats and Republicans to hear an Irish delegation seems to prove that mainstream American politicians considered the Irish too unstable to negotiate with. The politicians' reluctance stems not only from the fact that America and Britain were at that time allies, but also from the fact that the Irish were internally divided in so many aspects. Moreover, the situation in Ireland matched the traditional American view of Irishmen as people who see violence as the primary way of coping with any problem. If that was the case, then the Civil War in Ireland must have reinforced this stereotype. An excellent example of a situation in which the Irish themselves proved that violence was an essential part of their identity was the fate of Michael Collins, who should have been universally considered a national hero. In 1922, Michael Collins went to his home in Cork and was shot. The hero of the War of Independence and "the architect of the IRA" was killed because he was considered a traitor by Irishmen opposing the treaty.

6 The Second World War: The Irish Fall from Grace

During the Second World War, Ireland remained neutral. However, that does not mean that the Irish did not engage in the conflict. This participation existed on two levels. Firstly, the Irish were spread around the world, and they took part in the war as soldiers of the countries in which they lived. Thousands of Irish Americans fought in Europe and the Pacific.[145] Secondly, some Irish saw the war as a chance to stand against the Crown. The IRA led a bombing campaign in the 1930s against the British. Irish Americans opposed the campaign and started turning away from republicans.[146] The republicans even began to seek help from Adolf Hitler in their fight against the British; however, De Valera's government, embarrassed by the situation, outlawed the IRA, even interning

---

144   Kenny, *The American Irish*, 196.
145   Padden and Sullivan, *May the Road Rise to Meet You*, 162.
146   Kenny, *The American Irish*, 199.

some of its leaders and executing five of them.[147] Although Ireland remained neutral, it was the British and not the Germans who were more likely to be perceived as enemies. Thus, relations between Ireland and Britain, and between Ireland and America reached their lowest point when, in 1945, Eamon de Valera visited the German Embassy in order to sign the book of condolences after Hitler's suicide.[148] This had an enormous impact on the American perception of Ireland. In WWII, Americans fought against the Axis, and Hitler's downfall was considered a significant victory, paid for with the blood of American soldiers. De Valera's gesture was a slap in the face for the whole nation. Moreover, Hitler was associated with mindless violence and brutality. When De Valera expressed regret, even if only legalistically, it demonstrated to the Americans that the Irish were siding with such violence.

It is also important to note that at the time of the Second World War, Ireland was technically an independent state. The Constitution of Ireland, which was proclaimed in 1937, changed the name of the country from the Irish Free State to Ireland or Éire. Also, the office of the President of Ireland was established, although the country remained within the Commonwealth.

7   The Troubles

After the war, the political situation in Ireland changed dramatically. The country gained complete autonomy and freedom in 1949, with the Act of the Republic of Ireland. Thus, the fight for independence seemed to be over. Britain was no longer an aggressor, but rather a wealthy neighbor. As such, those emigrating from Ireland now predominantly chose Britain rather than the United States as their target country. Moreover, there were two other reasons why the USA ceased to be the promised land for the Irish. Firstly, Ireland became a prosperous country and, therefore, the Irish did not need to emigrate. Secondly, immigration to the USA was controlled by the state. For instance, the quotas which existed from the 1920s were raised, but there were new admission rules in effect. Only immigrants who already had families in the United States or who had skills that would be useful in the country were welcome.[149] However, the increasing prosperity in Ireland contributed to the growth of the population, which in turn was the main reason for the growing unemployment. Thus, the Irish began to emigrate again, either legally or illegally. Kenny mentions four

---

147   Kenny, 199.
148   Padden and Sullivan, *May the Road Rise to Meet You*, 163.
149   Kenny, *The American Irish*, 221–22.

groups of immigrants from Ireland in the 1980s, both legal and illegal. Firstly, the "self-consciously economic refugees" were immigrants seeking job opportunities and money in the US; secondly, there were young Irish belonging to the middle-class who stayed in the US after their tourist visas expired; thirdly, there was the brain-drain group, composed of middle or upper-middle-class professionals and university graduates; and fourthly, there were the winners of visa lotteries.[150] When it comes to legal immigrants, they were usually considered "lazy and ungrateful," or "disrespectful, irreligious and lacking in patriotism to both Ireland and the United States" by the established Irish Americans, while the new immigrants themselves saw the older generations of Irish Americans as "reactionary, puritanical and romantic in their conception of Ireland."[151] This response is inscribed in the tradition of the generation gap and cultural conflict, which could be observed also in the previous waves of immigration. As for illegal immigrants, men usually worked on building sites, especially for unlicensed contractors. Women—both legal and illegal immigrants—worked as nannies and nurses. Both men and women also worked in bars and restaurants. They were all employed predominantly by Irish Americans.[152]

The struggle for a free Ireland was over, but the northern part of the island still remained under British rule. Thus, Irish nationalism in Ireland and the US did not die but turned to a new aim—unifying the divided country. In the 1950s and 60s, the IRA led a border campaign of violence against the British.[153] At the end of the 1960s and the beginning of the 1970s, new leaders of the republican movement entered the scene, following a period of unrest in Northern Ireland, which, in turn, was the response to various acts of discrimination against the Catholic minority.[154] The new republican movement stood in opposition to the previous one. The old one was Marxist and aimed at the unification of the Republic of Ireland and Northern Ireland into one socialist state by peaceful means, while the new republicans favored violent action to reunify the Republic and Northern Ireland.[155] Thus, there occurred a split within the structures of the IRA. The old anti-treaty IRA came to be known as the Official Irish Republican Army (OIRA), or the "Stickies," while the radical members of the organization started to be referred to as the Provisional Irish Republican Army (PIRA),

---

150   Kenny, 225–26.

151   Kenny, 230–31.

152   Kenny, 230.

153   Richard English, *Armed Struggle: The History of the IRA* (London: Pan Macmillan, 2008), 73.

154   English, 179.

155   Kacper Rekawek, *Irish Republican Terrorism and Politics: A Comparative Study of the Official and the Provisional IRA* (New York: Taylor & Francis, 2011), 1.

or "Provos" with Sean McStiofain as its Chief of Staff.[156] When it comes to the unrest that caused this divide, it was later recognized as the beginning of the "Troubles," a long period of violence and terror in Northern Ireland.

During the Troubles, Irish Americans participated in the Anglo-Irish conflict in various ways. Those who rejected PIRA started funding and supporting the peace process. More radical Irish American nationalists funded the IRA. In 1968, at the very beginning of the Troubles, American rifles were sent to Northern Ireland by George Harrison, an American of Irish origin. Weapons were then being continuously smuggled from the USA to Northern Ireland under Sean Keenan's supervision. Keenan was a member of the Provisional Irish Republican Army, sent to America in 1969.[157]

In the following two decades, the Irish Northern Aid Committee (NORAID), formed in 1970, donated about 3 million dollars to the republicans in Ireland.[158] What is more, people more or less openly donated money to support the cause of freedom fighters. For instance, Mickey Rourke, a well-known Irish American actor, allegedly donated a part of his pay for *Francesco* to the IRA.[159] Money and weapons were not the only forms of help offered. Irish Americans also provided Provisionals with new identities and smuggled them into the US where they were given jobs and a place to stay. A famous example of such a case was the story of three republicans who escaped from the Maze Prison, also known as the H Blocks, in Northern Ireland and were transported to the United States where they lived from 1983 to 1992 when they were arrested by the FBI.[160]

Irish American support for the uprising and revolution in Ireland and then for the Northern Irish republican movement, showed that, at least for some of the descendants of Irish immigrants, the identity of their ancestors was meaningful. At the same time, Irish Americans were growing in prominence, actively organizing and working for the sake of American society, as they were becoming engaged in public service. Expanding American cities needed people to keep order in the streets and put out fires. Irish Americans responded to this call, mainly for economic reasons. Thus, they began working as policemen

---

156   Rekawek, 139.

157   James Patrick Byrne, Philip Coleman, and Jason Francis King, *Ireland and the Americas: Culture, Politics, and History : A Multidisciplinary Encyclopedia* (Santa Barbara: ABC-CLIO, 2008), 652.

158   Byrne, Coleman, and King, 652.

159   Amol Rajan, "Fury as Actress Tells Film Festival 'I Would Have Joined the IRA,'" *Independent*, 12 2008, Online, accessed March 2, 2016, http://www.independent.co.uk/arts-entertainment/films/news/fury-as-actress-tells-film-festival-i-would-have-joined-the-ira-927097.html.

160   Byrne, Coleman, and King, *Ireland and the Americas*, 653.

AN IRISH COLONY ACROSS THE ATLANTIC OCEAN   37

and firefighters, making these two professions their signature occupations. As has already been said, Irish American women traditionally worked as teachers, nurses, and, later, as doctors. The election of John F. Kennedy to the office of the President of the USA in 1961 is frequently cited as the primary indicator of how well the descendants of Irish immigrants were assimilated into American culture.[161]

8   The Irish in American Popular Culture

One other important aspect of the integration of the Irish into American society was their participation in American popular culture. While the pre-Famine and Famine generation of immigrants existed in popular culture only as the source of various, usually negative, stereotypes, the descendants of Famine immigrants started finding their place in society and embraced American popular culture. However, it would be wrong to assume that this influence was only one-sided, as at the same time the Irish were influencing and, together with other ethnic groups, co-creating American culture, especially as actors and athletes.

When it comes to actors, at first, Irish Americans appeared on stage and were very popular. Two such actors were Edward "Ned" Harrigan and Tony Hart; both gained popularity not only in New York where they performed but also throughout the United States in the second half of the nineteenth century. Other important Irish American vaudeville actors performing in the second half of the nineteenth century were Maggie Cline, Patrick "Pat" Rooney, and George M. Cohan.[162] With the birth of cinema, Irish American actors started appearing on the silver screen. Soon, some Irish American actors achieved international stardom. Among American actors of Irish descent are or were: Sara Allgood born in Ireland, nominated for an Oscar; Buster Keaton; John Wayne; Spencer Tracy; Errol Flynn; Bing Crosby; Joan Crawford; Anthony Quinn; Gregory Peck; Gene Kelly; Burt Lancaster; Lucille Ball, the famous eponymous character from *I Love Lucy*; Rita Hayworth; Grace Kelly; Judy Garland; Malachy McCourt; Clint Eastwood; Harrison Ford; Mickey Rourke; Bill Murray; David Caruso; Johnny Depp; John Cusack; Robert Downey Jr.; and Sean Penn. Irish Americans have thus been present in film since the beginning of its existence, and not merely as actors standing in the background, but as readily recognized stars and celebrities. This, in connection with filmmakers such as

---

161   Byrne, Coleman, and King, 650.
162   Meagher, *The Columbia Guide to Irish American History*, 105.

Leo McCarey and John Ford, allowed the descendants of the poor and rejected immigrants to become those to whom ordinary people look up.

When it comes to sports, the Irish in America were typically associated with American baseball, both as players, such as Michael J. "King" Kelly, John J. "Mugsy" McGraw, and Ned Hanlon, and also as owners and managers, for instance, Charles Comiskey (Chicago White Sox), Connie Mack (Philadelphia Athletics), and Bill Carrigan (Red Sox).[163] However, initially, their signature sport was, undeniably, boxing. Some of the Irish who came to the United States without the skills necessary to find a job turned to illegal bare-knuckle prize-fighting, which later evolved into professional boxing. The Irish dominated this new sport as early as the end of the nineteenth century. As summarized by Meagher: "there were so many Irish boxers that members of other groups took up Irish names when they entered the sport—almost as a rite of passage in order to be taken seriously."[164] Among the Irish boxers was John L. Sullivan, born in 1858 to Irish immigrants living in Boston.[165] Sullivan, also known as the "Boston Strongboy," epitomized the stereotypical idea of Irishness: "tough, loud, alternately sentimental and mean, and addicted to drink,"[166] as well as "huge, [...] ornery, inelegant, brash, proud [...]."[167] He began as an illegal prize-fighter, and it was partly thanks to his drawing power that boxing became a professional sport. He soon became a rich man and the first sports star, not only American but also international. He only lost one fight. In 1905, he fought against Jim Corbett, an Irish American, also known as "Gentleman Jim," who became the new Irish champion. Boxing also became a crucial element of the Irish stereotype.

• • •

The demographic data indicate that there are 35.6 million people in America claiming Irish ancestry, which constitutes 11.1 percent of the whole popula-tion.[168] This means that the Irish population in the USA is eight times larger than the 4.5 million-strong population of Ireland.[169] Even today, the Irish in America do not forget where their roots are. Many of them cherish the

---

163   Meagher, 105; Padden and Sullivan, *May the Road Rise to Meet You*, 220–21.
164   Meagher, *The Columbia Guide to Irish American History*, 106.
165   Padden and Sullivan, *May the Road Rise to Meet You*, 213.
166   Meagher, *The Columbia Guide to Irish American History*, 105.
167   Padden and Sullivan, *May the Road Rise to Meet You*, 213.
168   U. S. Census Bureau, "American FactFinder - Results 2013," accessed June 24, 2015.
169   Central Statistics Office of Ireland, "CSO Quicktables: Population 1901–2011," accessed June 24, 2015.

tradition of the old country and feel Irish, apart from being American. However, the American cinema has always focused not only on well-assimilated members of the Irish community but also on those who reject some aspects of American culture, stressing their Irishness.

The notion of Irishness in America has been changing since the beginning of Irish immigration to the New World. At first, the Irish were associated predominantly with Scotch-Irish Presbyterians who settled on the frontier and were perceived as violent enough to withstand the dangerous wilderness. As Protestants, they were easily assimilated into the developing colonial culture. Subsequently, with new waves of immigrants, more and more Irish Catholics settled in America. These people were also seen as "boss-controlled, violent, voting illegally, prone to alcoholism, and dependent on criminal street gangs."[170] When the rebels of the United Irishmen began settling in the US, they added the romantic idea of an Irish David fighting for independence against the British Goliath. This romantic idea undoubtedly survived in American society and is concurrent with the sentimental image of the Irish predominant in Europe. However, the stereotype of a poor and brutal Irishman-troublemaker was growing stronger, as Catholics began organizing themselves in violent gangs and mobs. Soon, as the Irish found their place in American society, and their country regained independence, new stereotypes started forming. They retained some of the old views on the Irish, but they also added new features, based on the function the Irish played in society. Despite the enormous social mobility, the Irish have achieved in America, their perception and representation are still based on positive or negative stereotypes.

For the purpose of this study, stereotypes based on occupations or social roles typical of the Irish are examined. As the main characters of the studied films are predominantly male, the focus of the analysis is on jobs or social roles stereotypically associated with the Irish. The first relevant stereotype is that of the republican fighter. The Irish, persecuted and downtrodden for most of the history of their nation, fought for their freedom. Significantly, the radical republicans were supported by some Irish Americans but rejected by the American government. Thus, the stereotype of a republican fighter might be projected from two perspectives: positively as a freedom fighter or negatively as a terrorist. Admittedly, it may also be ambiguous, especially since categorizations of the Irish fighting for freedom may not, in fact, be so clear-cut.

The second stereotype associated with the Irish in America is this of the Irishman guarding the social order, working as a police officer, or a firefighter.

---

170   Patrick O'Brien, "Irish Americans," in *The Social History of Crime and Punishment in America: An Encyclopedia*, ed. Wilbur R. Miller (Thousand Oaks: SAGE Publications, 2012), 861.

This is based on the typical occupations of the Irish, which allegedly stem from the "traditional Irish support for working people."[171] The positive stereotype of the Irishman serving as a guardian of law and order is grounded in reality. Irish American police officers and firefighters were considered "an urban cultural icon, one that was dedicated to public service, keeping the peace, enforcing the laws, and providing public safety."[172] It is even said that if it had not been for the Irish, the fire and police departments would not be as well organized and well-functioning as they are today.[173]

Furthermore, there is a very distinctive specific stereotype of Irish sportsmen, especially boxers. According to some data, at the beginning of the twentieth century, about 70 percent of New York pugilists claimed Irish origin. In comparison, 56.3 percent of boxers came from families in which both parents were Irish.[174] As boxing did not require any specialized and expensive equipment, it was accessible to the less affluent Irish, who excelled at it.

Another stereotype, inevitably associated with the Irish for the reasons mentioned above, is the Irish gangster. What started as a rivalry between tribe-like groups sharing animosities transferred from Ireland to the USA, soon changed into Irish organized crime. The person widely considered the first Irish mob boss, John Morrissey, who operated in the second half of the nineteenth century, was a stereotypical Irishman, described as "a brawler, a troublemaker, and a gangster."[175] He nevertheless had a reputation of "a tough though fair man who directed desperate immigrants to food and lodging."[176] The image of the violent man who, nonetheless, cares for his compatriots is a frequent motif in the cinematic representations of Irish gangsters. The Irish in America organized themselves in gangs which reflected the divisions and hostilities present in their homeland. This transplantation of gang culture was, on the one hand, a direct response to the hostility they encountered in WASP America[177]; on the other hand, Irish gangs soon turned against other immigrants, even Catholics, and especially against ethnic groups such as Mexican Americans and Blacks.[178] However, it is also worth remembering that Irish gangs were soon recruited

---

171   Timothy J. Paulson and Robert Asher, *Irish Immigrants* (New York: Infobase Publishing, 2009), 86.
172   O'Brien, "Irish Americans," 861.s
173   O'Brien, 861.
174   Michael T. Isenberg, *John L. Sullivan and His America* (Urbana: University of Illinois Press, 1994), 79.
175   O'Brien, "Irish Americans," 862.
176   O'Brien, 862.
177   Paulson and Asher, *Irish Immigrants*, 58.
178   James C. Howell, *Gangs in America's Communities* (Thousand Oaks: SAGE Publications, 2011), 105.

by politicians who, in exchange for laws that favored the Irish, used them to extort support from voters.[179] Therefore, the Irish, alongside Germans, Jews, and Italians, became associated with gangs in America. However, frequently, films depicting Irish gangs in America juxtapose Irish gang culture with Irish police officers, devoted to their duty of upholding the law.

Finally, a new type of character, hardly a stereotype, is that of the Irish vigilante. This character is an amalgam of the police officer, focused on protecting the innocent, the gangster, who operates outside the boundaries of the established American law, and a Catholic priest. Although this type of character is a recent development, it is based on a traditional American western hero who possesses the features of the society he defends but belongs to the outside world of villains.

These stereotypes were all created throughout the long history of the relations between Ireland and America. They survived in American society, as proved by popular culture in which they are explored as a source of plots and stories. Interestingly, both in Europe and in America, the perception of the Irish has always been a mixture of positive sentimental images rooted in perceived Celtic mysticism and a violent character stemming from the oppression the Irish were subjected to. Like the "Stage Irish" image dominant in 17th and 18th century England, the American image of the Irish was initially also predominantly negative. However, whereas Continental Europe acquired a positive view of the Irish and their struggle for independence as early as in the 19th century,[180] the American image of the Irish has always been dominated by the violent stereotype. With the birth of the cinema, this stereotype was employed in the Irish ethnotype, leading to the emergence of the prototypical cinematic Irish characters analyzed in the following chapters.

179   Paulson and Asher, *Irish Immigrants*, 58.
180   Leerssen, "Nationality: Irish."

CHAPTER 2

The Irish on the Silver Screen

As stated in the previous chapter, the Irish, at one point, dominated American entertainment, appearing as artists and athletes. It is perhaps quite natural that, when cinema emerged as a new type of entertainment, it attracted Irish performers and filmmakers who appeared in some of the earliest films produced in America and became some of the most recognizable names of the early film industry in the US. With the Irish producing films and appearing in them, the Irish began to be represented in American cinema quite early in its history.

Classical Hollywood is a period combining cinema's novelty, the steady development of cinematic technology, and well-defined, clearly established narrative and stylistic principles. The formational period of classical American cinema occurred between 1908 and 1927.[1] During that time, the American film industry moved from the East Coast to California. Laws regulating the use of film technology were established that prevented monopolies, at least for the time being, and allowed filmmakers access to tools they required. Last but not least, the transition from silent films to talkies ended cinema's infancy. During that time, studios dominated the industry, becoming centers of filmmaking for the decades to follow. In the Hollywood studio system, filmmaking was similar to factory production,[2] in which casts and crews employed on long-term contracts produced films for their studio. At the same time, the demand for new titles grew.

In the years 1908 – 1927, American cinema relocated from its cradle in the East into Hollywood, at the same time pushing the frontier of what the still new kind of entertainment could offer. In 1927, with the release of *Jazz Singer*, the first film that featured not only pre-recorded music but also some dialogue, Classical Hollywood truly began. Admittedly, the release of the experimental *Jazz Singer* did not mean that all films produced afterward were sound films. However, the year 1927 is generally considered a turning point in the history of early American cinema.

The style of classical cinema has been widely and meticulously analyzed by various researchers. Perhaps the most obvious feature of the classical style

---

1 David Bordwell and Kristin Thompson, *Film Art: An Introduction*, 8th ed (Boston: McGraw Hill, 2008), 444.
2 Bordwell and Thompson, 444.

© KONINKLIJKE BRILL NV, LEIDEN, 2021 | DOI:10.1163/9789004467972_004

is the consistency of its visual and narrative norms over a period of about fifty years.[3] However, as David Bordwell posits, the stylistic norms were not a unified and rigid system to which every film had to adhere. On the contrary, they offered filmmakers a range of artistic choices they could employ in their productions.[4] The classical style was a way of artistic expression rather than a limitation imposed on filmmakers. What limited classical American cinema was the studios' focus on the commercial aspect of filmmaking and the social context in which cinema operated. Aiming to attract diverse audiences, studios avoided controversies and tended to portray "characters and situations with some degree of ambiguity that invited audience members to reach different inferences and interpretations."[5] Such an approach led to films that were toned down, enabling studios to appeal to various social groups without the threat of their productions being rejected on ideological grounds, for example. This is an important point as it appears that the representation of the Irish in connection with violence was not considered controversial. However, violence itself was considered a delicate topic, especially in the view of the Motion Picture Production Code, commonly known as the Hays Code, after Will Hays, the president of Motion Picture Producers and Distributors of America (MPPDA).

The Code was introduced in 1930 in response to growing concerns about sex, romance, crime, and violence in film.[6] Their presence in the cinema had been debated since the end of the first decade of the 20th century[7] and throughout the 1920s,[8] which attests to the growing anxiety in America at that time about the negative influence of cinema on society. This trend continued in the 1930s, with the growing conservative tendencies in American society striving for a "return to decency."[9] Moreover, the anxiety was fueled not only by worrisome themes in films but also by scandals surrounding the industry, which sensationalist newspapers at that time were more than eager to exploit, and which contributed to the already prevalent image of Hollywood as a place plagued

---

3   David Bordwell, Janet Staiger, and Kristin Thompson, *The Classical Hollywood Cinema: Film Style & Mode of Production to 1960* (London New York: Routledge, Taylor & Francis Group, 2015), 4.

4   Bordwell, 4.

5   Paul Monaco, *A History of American Movies: A Film-by-Film Look at the Art, Craft, and Business of Cinema* (Lanham, Md: Scarecrow Press, 2010), 10.

6   Monaco, 30.

7   Gerald R. Butters, *Banned in Kansas: Motion Picture Censorship, 1915–1966* (Columbia: University of Missouri Press, 2007), 19.

8   Monaco, *A History of American Movies*, 30.

9   Richard Maltby, "The Production Code and the Mythologies of 'Pre-Code' Hollywood," in *The Classical Hollywood Reader*, ed. Stephen Neale (Abingdon, Oxon; New York: Routledge, 2012), 243.

by "promiscuity, gambling, and alcohol."[10] In these circumstances, considering self-regulation a viable alternative to government-imposed censorship, the film industry employed Hays to lead a campaign to introduce a code of production that filmmakers would adhere to.[11]

The Code, seen today primarily as the industry's self-imposed limitation on the freedom of expression, was symptomatic of the time when it was introduced. Even though it was initiated by studios, it was affected by various social organizations, "from the Boy Scouts of America to the National Council of Catholic Women," that Hays invited to act as advisors to the industry.[12] As the Catholic Church was among the outspoken supporters of censorship in cinema, Hays asked a Jesuit priest and academic teacher specializing in theater, the Reverend Daniel J. Lord, and Martin Quigley, a Catholic publisher, to write the Code.[13] Hollywood filmmakers were unwilling to accept the restrictive principles devised by Lord and Quigley, which, in 1934, led to the formation of the Production Code Administration (PCA), headed by Joseph Breen, an Irish American Catholic.[14] The main purpose of PCA was to enforce the Code, which contributed to the controversial way in which the organization has been perceived.

Thanks to the participation of dozens of organizations, the way the Code addressed the representation of sex and violence was intended to reflect general middle-class social attitudes towards these issues. In the context of the present study, the most important aspect here is the impact the Code had on the representation of violence. Even though the regulations on the depiction of violence were by no means as stringent as the norms concerning the display of issues connected with homosexuality or abortion on screen, there were a number of issues that PCA censors routinely raised objections to mainly the depictions of weapons and their use, choking, kicking and instances of sadism.[15] Its presence on the screen was not forbidden, but brutal and lethal violence was unwelcome, and if there was criminal activity present, it was supposed to be punished[16] in an attempt to produce the cumulative message that

---

10   Jennifer Mossman, ed., "Will Hays," in *Encyclopedia of World Biography* (Detroit: Gale Research, 1998), 198.

11   Mossman, 198.

12   Mossman, 198.

13   Monaco, *A History of American Movies*, 31.

14   Stephen Prince, *Classical Film Violence: Designing and Regulating Brutality in Hollywood Cinema, 1930–1968* (New Brunswick(N.B.); New Jersey; London: Rutgers University Press, 2003), 22.

15   Prince, 23–27.

16   Monaco, *A History of American Movies*, 32.

crime does not pay. Filmmakers, striving to avoid the restrictions, therefore devised new ways of representing violence on the screen. These novel methods were primarily stylistic, as PCA censors tended to focus more on the presence of violence within film narrative than on the visual style of representing violent behavior.[17] Therefore, the analysis of the role of violence in the representation of the Irish in Classical Hollywood is by no means pointless. Despite the unavoidable impact of the Code on the narrative and visual presence of violence in films produced after 1930, American filmmakers of the era found ways to represent it on the screen. However, whereas since New Hollywood, cinematic violence has been freely, openly, and often graphically represented on the screen, Classic Hollywood violence has to be analyzed more carefully, taking into account possible intricacies and symptomatic meanings connected with the cultural context in which classic American films were made.

Paul Monaco makes the interesting remark—almost a side note in a paragraph in which he summarizes the Code's treatment of violence—that "the Production Code appears to have been well ahead of the American cultural curve: intentional negative references to race and ethnicity were taboo."[18] Still, the Irish were portrayed as stereotypically violent people, sometimes to the point of absurdity. If violence is considered a negative feature, undesirable in society, then such a portrayal was arguably also negative. Obviously, it is difficult to imagine that the Irish were treated as an exception among all the ethnic groups portrayed in the cinema of the period, especially since Joseph Breen, the head of PCA, was an influential Irish American Catholic. One possible explanation is that such a portrayal was not considered negative or offensive but was somehow acknowledged: the image of the rowdy, violent Irish person was accepted as accurate. Additionally, the social sensitivity to such matters as ethnic stereotyping may have been less acute than it is now, even though, as Monaco says, the Code was ahead of its times in that matter. However, the most likely explanation may have lain in the Code's treatment of violence. Even though the Irish were presented as stereotypically violent, it was done with the use of the Code's toned-down idea of violence—not graphic enough to be considered an unacceptably negative treatment of the ethnic group.

This period marked the appearance of Irish American stars and film directors who accentuated their origins in the productions they worked on. Mary Pickford, James Cagney, and Pat O'Brien, known for their iconic roles as Irish and Irish American characters, were at the forefront of actors of Irish descent, while John Ford returned to the country of his parents numerous times,

---

17   Prince, *Classical Film Violence*, 29.
18   Monaco, *A History of American Movies*, 32.

addressing cultural differences between the Irish and Americans, and pointing to vital social and political issues connected with Ireland and the Irish in America. However, Irish characters did not just appear in films made by Irish American directors with actors of Irish descent. They were ready and available choices when the plot needed gangsters, boxers, or the working class organizing in trade unions. Such representations were based on the roles they actually played in society.

It is truly fascinating how early American films, made before the 1930s, were blatant in their representation of the Irish in America as stereotypically violent. The intertitles of some silent films analyzed below inscribe themselves in the history of the representation of the Irish, proving that the core element of the Irish ethnotype in American cinema was violence. Although the Irish stereotype evolved, together with the perception of the Irish and their position within the American society, violence remained at the heart of their representation, often accompanied by the motifs of the importance of family, devotion to duty and justice, and the ability to make sacrifices for a greater good. In this chapter, I analyze the development of the stereotype, taking into account the social roles and professions in which the Irish were represented during the classical period and showing how this representation evolved from a hetero-image of rejects and outsiders to an important part of the American auto-image.

1 Irish Film Characters of the Silent Film Era

Violence played the dominant role in the Irish ethnotype in Classical Hollywood. In fact, it appeared as one of the defining attributes of the Irish long before cinema went west. The Irish made their first appearance in American cinema in W. B. Bitzer's slapstick comedy *Levi and Cohen, Irish Comedians* from 1903.[19] This one-minute-long film shows two Irishmen beginning a performance which consists of the men fighting, mainly with the use of a rolled-up newspaper; the audience present at the performance reacts by throwing eggs and other unidentified items at the duo.[20] This short early American film is nevertheless quite telling when viewed in the context of later, not only classic, productions. The defining feature of the two rowdy characters, other than the

---

19   Lee Lourdeaux, *Italian Irish Filmmakers in America* (Philadelphia: Temple University Press, 1990), 54.

20   The film is available on the YouTube channel of The Library of Congress (https://www.youtube.com/user/LibraryOfCongress).

sign identifying them as Irish comedians, is the violence they use against each other and which they find entertaining, as evidenced not only by the fact that they must have chosen for their comedic spectacle but also by their reactions. However, the audience does not share their view and reacts negatively, perhaps showing society's lack of acceptance of violence, impatience with innate Irish violence, or simply contempt for the low quality of the spectacle. The reception of the audience's negative reaction by the viewer is emphasized by the fact that the camera presents the spectacle from the audience's perspective. The film may be seen as a foretelling of the general form of the Irish ethnotype in later productions, despite its simple premise and very rudimentary characters.

More complex Irish characters began appearing on the screen with the emergence of the first film star of Irish descent, Mary Pickford (Gladys Smith).[21] In one of her early films, a drama called *Tess of the Storm Country* (1914), directed by Edwin S. Porter, Pickford plays the role of Tessibel Skinner, a young girl whose father was wrongfully charged with murder. The film points to the main character's Irish origin "in several allusions to Irish culture," such as Tess's Irish first name and her performance in one of the initial scenes of an Irish dance.[22] Tess is presented mainly in the context of hardships she has to endure; she is poor and, together with other villagers, she is deprived of her main source of income by a wealthy individual who bans net fishing. Moreover, she has to become self-reliant when her father is arrested. Her suffering further increases when she engages in a forbidden romance with her oppressor's son and, when her beloved's sister becomes pregnant, Tess takes the baby accepting the social stigma of an unmarried single mother. Throughout, Tess accepts adversities that could easily destroy a person yet she remains strong and determined in whatever she does. This, obviously, must have made the audience sympathetic towards the young Irish American woman and corresponds well to the general representation of Irish women in American cinema, who were portrayed as strong and non-violent.

An interesting exception to this rule was an early portrayal of Irish gangs in William Beaudine's *Little Annie Rooney* from 1925. Annie (Mary Pickford), an Irish American girl living in New York, is a tomboy who looks up to her older brother, a member of an Irish gang. Her father, Timothy, is a police officer who has "Annie and Tim to raise—and the whole neighborhood to look after." The film begins in a poor dilapidated, ethnically diverse neighborhood of a large city, and a superimposed intertitle informs the viewer that Annie is in conflict with Mickey Kelly, the leader of the "Kid Kellys." Mickey and a

---

21   Lourdeaux, *Italian Irish Filmmakers in America*, 51.
22   Lourdeaux, 51.

gang of boys draw a caricature of Annie on the wall, for which Annie throws an empty bottle at them. The bottle hits the wall over their heads, sending shards of broken glass at them. Other children appear, starting a fight with the "Kid Kellys," in which the children throw empty bottles, bricks, and stones at each other. It is worth noting that, although two Irish children are in charge of the gangs, Annie's group, in particular, is ethnically diverse, with Irish, African American Jewish, and Greek children. The fight continues and is interleaved with scenes showing Annie's father and brother. The long-lasting nature of the struggle is emphasized by an intertitle which informs the viewer that "To end a fight some one must quit—but in this case, both leaders happened to be Irish." Soon, the two engage in a brutal fistfight, presented on the screen in truly pre-Code uninhibited style. For the contemporary viewer, watching the fight, lasting a few minutes, is an unusual experience, especially taking into account that Pickford was over thirty years old when she appeared in the film, while all the other gang members were played by children. Finally, the two are separated by Mickey's brother, with whom Annie becomes infatuated.

Both Mickey's and Annie's older brothers, Joe Kelly and Tim Rooney, are members of the "Big Kellys," an aspiring gang of Irish Americans. However, Tim is ostracized by some more established gangsters as he is a police officer's son. Still, Joe and Tim are friends. When Joe visits the Rooneys, Officer Rooney reproaches the leader of the "Big Kellys" for swindling Mr. Levy, a Jewish shop owner, out of ten dollars. Joe reluctantly returns the money and, when asked why he does not find an honest profession for himself, answers, "My old man drove a truck—I want a job with more dough in it." As he lives in a poor immigrant neighborhood, financial success is available to him only through crime. Officer Rooney, convinced that his son will follow in his footsteps and become a police officer, forbids his son from meeting Joe, who leaves in dismay.

Soon, at a ball for which the "Big Kellys" sell tickets, Joe enters a dispute with two armed men, Tony and Spider. He is beaten and, when Officer Rooney arrives, one of the attackers shoots and kills the policeman. In a dramatic moment, as Annie is preparing a birthday surprise for her father, a police officer arrives to inform her that her father has been murdered. Annie and Tim are left alone and in sorrow. In those difficult moments, Annie is aided by her friends and their families; she is invited to dinner by the family of Mr. Levy, where she is given a special meal, consisting of pork, which she shares with her Jewish gangmate, infuriating his father. Such fascinating intercultural details add to the portrayal of multicultural neighborhood realities in American cities in the 1920s.

Meanwhile, Tim is misled by Tony and Spider into believing that it was Joe who shot his father. He tells Annie that he is going to avenge their parent, to which Annie reacts strongly, saying that she cannot believe Joe would do such a thing. She confronts Joe, who tells her that he considered her father his best friend. As Tim begins his hunt for Joe, Annie and her gang carry out their own investigation, which brings them to the conclusion that it was Tony who shot Officer Rooney. They apprehend him and bring him to court. However, they are too late as Tim manages to shoot Joe. As Joe is taken to hospital, Annie is told by the doctor that Joe will die unless someone donates blood for him. She is the only person willing to do so. Annie misunderstands the doctor and is convinced that a blood transfusion will end her life. However, she comes to terms with that and even writes her will, knowing that she must make this sacrifice to save both Tim and Joe. The film ends with Joe starting a truck company. As he is driving through the city streets, with Annie sitting next to him and other children in the back of the truck, he lets Annie take the wheel. On their way, they meet Tim, now a police officer directing the traffic.

Annie is violent because she is deeply affected by the violence which surrounds her. However, she undergoes a transformation, changing from a tomboy fighting and pulling pranks into an Irish American woman, who strongly opposes violence, is ready to take the burden of responsibility, and even sacrifice her life to save her beloved ones. Thanks to her, both Joe and Tim are given a second chance, reject violence, and begin potentially successful honest careers. As the film provides a fairly detailed portrayal of the intercultural environment of a multiethnic immigrant neighborhood, including various languages in the intertitles, the message that it seems to project is that Irish women may be at the forefront of the transformation of violent Irish immigrants into a well-integrated and prosperous community, which, consequently, can only improve living conditions in multiethnic areas where the Irish also live.

In contrast to Irish women appearing in early American films as dramatic characters able to withstand misfortunes, male Irish characters often performed a comedic function. Such was the case of *Hold Your Horses* (1921), directed by E. Mason Hopper. The film tells the story of an Irish immigrant, Dan Canavan (Tom Moore), who works as a street sweeper. One day, he is trampled by horses pulling a carriage belonging to a rich socialite, Beatrice Newness (Naomi Childers). This leaves a horseshoe-shaped scar on his chest, granting him unbelievable luck that allows him to control reality. Dan uses his powers to become a politician, and, eventually, he begins to rule the city. He marries Beatrice but she quickly becomes disillusioned with his crudeness. Canavan uses his luck to show Beatrice that despite his coarse appearance he is worthy of her. This film is important as it uses quite a large degree of symbolism to produce the message regarding Irish immigrants in America, at the same time playing with the ironically bitter notion of "the luck of the Irish." The film is symptomatic of its times, presenting a poor and uneducated Irish immigrant as an unskilled manual worker. The horseshoe, a symbol of luck, becomes imprinted on Dan's body, granting him the power he needs to improve his life. However, gaining power is painful, and the circumstances in which he acquires luck are potentially tragic. In this context, Beatrice's last name is also meaningful, as Newness symbolizes the New World to which Dan ventured. Understood thus, Dan's story becomes a parable of the fate of Irish immigrants in the US; their first encounter with American society is painful; they are subjected to harsh treatment by the New World. This harsh treatment makes them stronger and allows them to succeed and convince their new homeland that, under superficial coarseness, they are valuable members of society.

The figure of an Irish immigrant appeared again in 1924, in Charles Hines's and Frank Griffin's *Conductor 1492*. The film is filled with stereotypes concerning the Irish in America and, therefore, worthy of closer study. Johnny Hines plays Terry O'Toole, a young Irishman working as a streetcar conductor. The film begins in Ireland with a quotation from a traditional Irish song, "A Little Bit Of Heaven":

> "They dotted it with silver,
> to make its lakes so grand.
> And when they had it finished,
> they called it Ireland."

Terry O'Toole lives in a busy Irish village in a multigenerational family and does not resemble a stereotypical Irishman forced by poverty to emigrate to the US. He does not seem to be poor; on the contrary, he is well-dressed, also in contrast to other villagers. His luggage prepared for the journey is a coffer of considerable size. When he and his father put his luggage on a donkey carriage, the animal is lifted off the ground because of the weight of Terry's belongings. Suddenly, it becomes apparent that Terry has bricks in his luggage and, as he throws them out, his comment is presented in an intertitle, saying: "If trouble there be, it's blarney I use instead of bricks." Expecting problems in America, the young Irishman is prepared either for violence or the sweet talk that might save him.

The next comedic scene exploring Irish stereotypes comes when Terry and his father, Mike, return to the "American wake" organized for Terry. When they enter the house, there is a group of people lamenting his departure to America. However, when Terry reaches for a carboy, presumably of alcohol, and shakes it, everyone suddenly loses interest in the sad occasion, instead focusing on drinking one by one from the container. When asked about his plans in America, Terry responds that he is going to become a police officer, which is one of

THE IRISH ON THE SILVER SCREEN   51

the most important stereotypically Irish professions in America. However, he is persuaded by his father to become a streetcar conductor. Terry agrees, as this means following in his father's footsteps, as he himself was a streetcar conductor in America years before. He is given a new hat and an Irish doll and is ready to embark on his journey.

In America, Terry quickly adjusts to the new environment, finds lodgings, and is employed as a streetcar driver by the Loteda Traction Company, which is run by Mr. Connelly, who controls 49% of the business. When the company owner's young son has an accident and loses consciousness on the tracks in front of a speeding streetcar, Terry climbs onto the front of the vehicle and, lifting up the child, saves his life, for which he is rewarded by the company owner. It turns out that Mr. Connelly's business partners, who are also in possession of 49% of the Traction Company, want to acquire the additional 2% in order to take control of the business and raise the ticket price, to which Connelly vehemently objects.

Later, quite unexpectedly, Terry is visited by his father, Mike, who, inexplicably, is brought to his lodgings in a police van with the police officer thanking the older Irishman for arresting a whole gang, now locked in the back of the car. It appears Mr. O'Toole managed to arrest them quite casually—as if he was predisposed for that. When the two O'Tooles meet at Terry's lodging, they do an Irish dance together with the landlady. After a series of comedic events involving the main character and his father experiencing a culture clash in the New World, it comes to light that Terry's father bought 2% of Loteda shares two years before and hid them in the doll he gave Terry as a parting gift. Hearing that the building with the doll inside is on fire, Terry's father jumps out of a rocking chair, with an intertitle saying, "I ain't missed a fire in twenty years," presenting him in the stereotypically Irish role of a firefighter. He goes into the building and finds the doll but is unable to leave because of the heavy smoke. At the last moment, Terry manages to save his father and gives the remaining two percent to Mr. Connelly.

Having gained respect and money, he returns to Ireland, introducing his bride, Mr. Connelly's daughter, to the villagers. Seeing a rich, successful Irish American family in an automobile, the villagers ask, "Terry lad—an' what did ye bring us from Americky?" upon which Terry and his wife present them with a dozen pairs of boxing gloves. As the Irish villagers cheer, Terry exclaims, "Show your nationality!" The villagers respond by starting a massive boxing match in which the whole village, old and young, men and woman, actively participate. Choosing boxing gloves as gifts is another stereotypical element used in the comical portrayal of the Irish and is symptomatic of how Americans perceived the immigrants from Ireland. With the use of character construction based on exaggerated features, especially with regard to Terry's father, the film seems to put forward the message that the Irish in America are police officers, fire-fighters, and boxers not because—being uneducated and poor, they could not find any other form of employment—but because they are nationally predisposed to these professions. Violence and the sense of danger are in their blood. However, although violence is presented here as one of the main characteristic features of the Irish, it is non-destructive and, instead, serves an entertaining or even community bonding function.

In the 1920s, Anglo-American WASP cinema audiences began to appreciate Irish characters for their "strength, courage, and often bravery."[23] Moreover, film producers portrayed the Irish in their signature professions and social roles. Gangsters aside, the Irish were presented as people who contributed to the well-being of others. Positive representations included the Irishman as a prizefighter, builder, fireman, and police officer.[24] Irish women were usually presented in the context of their families, often as widows, who were independent and concerned about their sons[25] as well as young Irish girls, referred to as colleens.[26] All these characters were usually presented as successful members of American society, with their success based on hard work and attachment to the community. Stereotypical, often exaggerated violence still appeared as the central element of the Irish ethnotype, determining character construction and paving the way for later productions to explore similar portrayals of the Irish.

The representation of the Irish in the silent film era of the American cinema concluded with two gangster films, *Underworld*, directed by Joseph von Sternberg in 1927, and Lewis Milestones's *The Racket* from 1928. *Underworld* follows the story of "Rolls Royce" Wensel (Clive Brook), an alcoholic lawyer, who is rehabilitated by a gangster called "Bull" Weed (George Bancroft), inspired by a notorious real-life Irish American gangster, Thomas "Terrible Tommy" O'Connor, an immigrant born in Limerick, Ireland.[27] The two become friends and partners in the struggle against "Buck" Mulligan, a rival gangster. The situation becomes more complicated when Wensel falls in love with Weed's girlfriend, "Feathers" McCoy (Evelyn Brent). Weed and Mulligan are ruthless and violent, brutal also towards women. In one scene, Mulligan assaults "Feathers" McCoy. The representation of the gangsters' brutality is not limited to the level of the

---

23 Lourdeaux, 55.
24 Lourdeaux, 55.
25 Lourdeaux, 57.
26 Lourdeaux, 58.
27 Jay Robert Nash, *Almanac of World Crime* (Garden City, N.Y.: Anchor Pr./Doubleday, 1981), 145–146.

THE IRISH ON THE SILVER SCREEN   53

narrative but also emphasized by visual representations and stylized acting. This is perhaps most clearly seen in an early scene taking place in the Dreamland Café, a meeting spot for local gangsters. Mulligan attacks Wensel, insulting and then beating him. The severity of the physical assault is emphasized by point-of-view shots from Wensel's perspective, allowing the viewer to see close-ups of Mulligan's face distorted with fury.

After Mulligan assaults "Feathers," he is chased and shot several times by Weed, who is soon arrested and sent to prison. Wensel and McCoy plan his escape, at the same time wondering whether or not to leave the brutal gangster to his fate and start a new life together. In the end, they decide to help Weed escape from prison but their plan fails. Convinced he has been betrayed and aware of the romance between his girlfriend and his friend, Weed kills his guard and escapes on his own. He confronts McCoy at their apartment but is surrounded by the police. During a massive shootout, Wensel sneaks into the apartment through a hidden entrance to save them. Seeing that his friend has not betrayed him, Weed helps the two escape and surrenders to the police. In the final intertitle, Weed admits that the additional hour of freedom was the most important time of his life. He says so because, after a violent life, he has learned the value of friendship. This makes him a tragic character who, despite being brutal and ruthless, is able to sacrifice himself for the greater good. Such sacrifice has become a staple element of the portrayal of Irish outlaw heroes.

If *Underworld* became the basis for representations of the somewhat tragic figure of the Irish gangster, *The Racket* focused on the figure of the incorruptible Irish police officer. Set in Chicago, the film centers on a mobster, Nick Scarsi (Louis Wolheim), whose attempt to control the whole city during the prohibition era is thwarted by Captain James McQuigg, an Irish American police officer who continuously resists bribery. Unable to convince McQuigg to cooperate, Scarsi has the captain transferred to a distant precinct. However, McQuigg arrests Scarsi's younger brother, Joe (George E. Stone), for a hit-and-run and refuses to release him, even when he is threatened by Scarsi's lawyer. Confronted by the mobster himself, he remains incorruptible, arresting the mobster and ignoring the law that prevents him from doing so without laying charges. In his vision of the law, punishment for criminals is the highest priority, more important than the letter of the law, which may be exploited by gangsters. In the end, Scarsi is shot while trying to escape from the police station.

Irish representations in the silent era of American cinema are fascinating, as they clearly serve as the basis of later representations. They prove that at the beginning of the 20th century violence was such a salient element of the Irish stereotype that filmmakers selected it as the most readily available national characteristic that the audience would recognize and acknowledge. As the construction of some of these characters is rather basic by today's standards, it is perhaps easier to identify the individual elements of their composition and, in this way, to identify the features and values that were associated with the Irish in this early period of American cinema. Violence was the key ingredient, determining the characters' actions, social roles, and outlooks, but it was accompanied by other motifs, usually related to violence or modified by it on the level of the narrative. One such motif was the importance of family and community. Annie Rooney and Terry O'Toole are willing to risk their lives in order to save their family and friends and never forget where they came from. A closely related motif is the sense of duty, most visible in the case of Officer Rooney and Captain McQuigg, for whom protecting the community is the very sense of their lives.

Apart from establishing motifs to be explored in later films, early productions of American cinema also gave Irish Americans their iconic social roles and occupations. Some of these representations were decidedly positive. *The Racket* and, to some extent, *Little Annie Rooney*, established the figure of the incorruptible police officer whose intimacy with violence makes him bold even when faced by fearsome mobsters; *Conductor 1492*, introducing Mike O'Toole, who seems attracted to fires, alludes to the figure of the Irish firefighter; the same film points to boxing as an Irish national characteristic, rather than merely a sport. However, it was the figure of the Irish gangster that seems to have dominated the Irish ethnotype in American cinema in the following years and decades. Thus, the next section will focus on the representations of the Irish in specific occupations and social roles, beginning with the figure of the Irish criminal represented in, arguably, one of the best crime dramas of the 1930s.

2   The Classical Period since 1930

As American cinema of the classical period matured, so did Irish characters represented in Hollywood films. With the addition of sound to film, an entirely new dimension opened for filmmakers, especially when it comes to character construction. An important aspect here was the actors' performance: the more expressionist style of early Hollywood productions was replaced with naturalist acting; this trend was visible already in the 1920s and continued in the 1930s.[28] During the next decades, some of the most iconic films of all time were made in Hollywood, many of which featured representations of the Irish, who

---

28   Barry Salt, *Film Style and Technology: History and Analysis*, 3. & biggest ed (London: Starword, 2009), 211.

became much more varied but continued to be portrayed in the context of social roles and professions perceived in America as traditionally and stereotypically Irish. Most importantly, however, violence still played a central role in their representation.

2.1 Violent Ways: The Irish as Gangsters

The influence of violence on the construction and portrayal of the Irish in American is clearest in the representation of the Irish gangster figure. The production that, in a number of ways, established the standards for the construction and development of the Irish gangster was William Wellman's *The Public Enemy* (1931) with James Cagney, an actor of Irish origin,[29] and Edward Woods as two Irish American gangsters, Tom Powers and Matt Doyle. Ninety years after its premiere, the film holds a critics' approval of 100% on the Rottentomatoes.com review aggregator, with most critics praising Cagney's performance and Wellman's direction.[30] It was the perfect combination of the director's and the actors' work that resulted in *The Public Enemy* setting standards for later gangster films, and what makes it a true classic is "the way [Wellman's] film presents violence and brutality, while the story arc builds expertly and the actors play off all of this with the same level of expertise."[31]

When the film begins, the two main characters are children living in Chicago in 1909. The influence of their environment on their upbringing is shown through a sequence of shots presenting beer taps from which beer is poured into glasses and small metal buckets, a brewery from which a carriage laden with barrels has just left, a bar next to the brewery, a saloon just opposite it, and another one visible just as a Salvation Army orchestra is seen marching through the street, playing music. It seems that the life of this particular neighborhood revolves around producing, selling, and consuming alcohol. The camera follows the Salvation Army and stops at saloon doors bearing a sign saying "Family Entrance." Tom and Matt, apparently in their early teens, leave the saloon through the doors with a bucket of beer, and Powers takes a sip from it, which leaves foam on his upper lip. This projects a strong and very direct message to the viewer. Both boys are shaped by the place in which they live, which may be said to be an early introduction of a redeeming feature in that their vices are not inherent but rather conditioned by their environment or social background. As beer is the essence and center of life in the neighborhood, the

---

29   Ephraim Katz, *The Film Encyclopedia 5e: The Most Comprehensive Encyclopedia of World Cinema in a Single Volume* (New York: HarperCollins, 2005), 208.

30   *The Public Enemy (1931)*, accessed January 22, 2021, https://www.rottentomatoes.com/m/1016885-public_enemy.

31   James L. Neibaur, *James Cagney Films of the 1930s* (Lanham: Rowman & Littlefield, 2015), 17.

boys are bound to be affected by its presence. Similarly, they are lured by the crime that also surrounds them.

This can be seen in the next scene, as the boys escape from a man who chases them up an escalator after they have stolen a pair of roller skates. When they reach the top, they are confronted by a police officer and they escape by sliding down the balustrade between ascending and descending escalators, laughing as they consider the whole situation a child's game. However, when Tom presents the roller skates to Matt's older sister, Molly, he is scolded by both the girl and Tom's older brother, Mike, who confronts him in the presence of Powers's father, a police officer (Purnell Pratt, uncredited[32]). This presents a portrayal of family relations similar to those shown in *Little Annie Rooney*. However, the similarity is only superficial. Whereas Tim Rooney is ready to forgo his criminal activity when influenced by his father, Tom is openly hostile and confrontational to his parent. Also, the representation of the father figure is strikingly different in the two films. Whereas Officer Timothy Rooney is a warm character, a beloved father and friend, who serves society, Tom's father is strict, violent, and aloof. When he learns his son has stolen the roller skates, he takes a belt, leads his son to the bedroom, and delivers corporal punishment, remaining silent the whole time. When confronted with the punishment, Tom once again displays his contempt for his father. He looks down on his father sitting on the bed and, holding the belt of his trousers, asks: "How do you want them this time, up or down?" The scene not only foreshadows the character's later disdain for the possibility of being punished but is also an important development of the narrative motif of Irish familiarity with violence.

Tom is no stranger to violence because of the treatment he receives from his parents. His father, while delivering corporal punishment, inoculates him against violence. Officer Powers never utters a word while punishing his son; the only message he gives Tom is through violence. At the same time, Tom's mother (Beryl Mercer) distances herself from her husband and her son and their violent ways. She is shown in the kitchen, singing cheerfully as her husband stretches the belt in preparation for what is to occur next. When she sees her son, she stops singing and looks at him silently, disappointment clear on her face. A point-of-view shot from her perspective shows the boy and his father approaching the door of the bedroom, walking away from the mother, who does not want to participate in the punishment. Violence is presented as a characteristic of men.

---

32   *The Public Enemy* (*1931*) - *IMDb*, accessed January 16, 2021, http://www.imdb.com/title/tt0022286/fullcredits.

THE IRISH ON THE SILVER SCREEN 57

Both Tom and his father are violent, which is emphasized in the early exposition of the character construction. The viewer becomes aware that Tom is a troubled child, while the father, as a police officer, serves as a protector of society against gangsters. However, unlike the father of *Little Annie Rooney*, whose service is based on opposing violence, Officer Powers is violent himself. This is an important development in the representation of the Irish police officer figure and could be seen as the first incarnation of what will be presented later as the Irish cop—a violent guardian of law and order who will stop at nothing to do his duty and whose main function is to mete out punishment to offenders. Tom, on the other hand, is violent because he does not know life without brutality and pain. The silent punishment he receives makes him stronger as he absorbs the violence, waiting for every blow of the belt with silent contempt. He continues his path towards crime: immediately afterwards, he and Matt visit a gangster called "Putty Nose" (Murray Kinnell) and sell him a set of stolen pocket watches.

As the years pass, Tom and Matt continue meeting "Putty Nose" and his gang in a bar. Judging by the gangsters' comments, they are quite low in the hierarchy but they consider themselves better and stronger, which is emphasized by Cagney's and Woods's performance. When they enter the bar their facial expressions and the gestures they make towards other men suggest confidence and self-importance. Moreover, Tom expresses deep disdain for his older brother, Mike (Donald Cook), who works and studies. In Tom's words, Mike is "learning how to be poor," as the younger Powers does not believe there is a path to success other than a life of crime. Although slightly apprehensive, Tom and Matt accept a job from "Putty Nose," who tells them to steal furs. The task is supposed to be their rite of passage to adulthood in the gang, and they receive the attributes of this new period of their lives when "Putty Nose" gives them two revolvers. However, the robbery does not go according to plan, their accomplice is shot and killed, and they barely manage to escape, chased by a police officer. Betrayed by "Putty Nose," who refuses to help them, for the time being, they resign themselves to petty theft.

Two years later, in 1917, they are both working in a transport company, stealing some of the goods they are supposed to deliver. Tom's father has already died, while Mike Powers has enlisted in U.S. Marine Corps and is ready to join the fight in Europe during WWI. The two brothers are strongly contrasted, both in appearance and character. Mike is taller, and the height difference is emphasized by the fact that the camera usually shows him standing straight, while Tom is shown next to him seated or hunched over. Mike's upright moral position and Tom's crookedness are thus stressed. Furthermore, Mike is elegant; his clothes are clean and fit well, while Tom looks disheveled, affected by the life he has chosen. As for character, Mike's sense of duty is shown by his enlisting in the army and contrasts with Tom's self-centeredness. When the older Powers tells his brother that he will now be the head of the family, Tom does not look impressed or even interested. Instead, he accuses his brother of theft; Mike reacts violently, punching his brother in the face. They may be different in their moral stance, but they are both prone to violence. The confrontation is paralleled by a later scene: Tom brings money home but Mike refuses to accept it because it comes from criminal activity. This scene also ends with Mike punching Tom, once again attesting to the moral superiority of the hardworking and morally upright Mike over his younger brother.

With prohibition in force in the USA, Tom and Matt begin smuggling and selling alcohol, which allows them to make money and gain the respect and power they have always craved. They are seen buying expensive suits, driving a car, attending lavish parties, and engaging in romances. Soon, they enter cooperation with a bootlegger, Samuel "Nails" Nathan (Leslie Fenton), and become enforcers whose task is to make speakeasy owners buy alcohol from their accomplice. Tom is presented as the more violent of the two, beating up a man who buys cheaper beer from a different source. When the man agrees to buy two barrels of beer, Tom makes him buy five instead. Violence is how money is made in Tom's world; his intimacy with violence makes him naturally predisposed to achieving power.

Meanwhile, Mike, a decorated veteran, returns home and is told by their mother that Tom has gone into politics. When informed by a police officer that his younger brother is a bootlegger and gang enforcer, he confronts Tom over dinner. He refuses to drink beer from the barrel Tom has put on the table as he considers it tainted with the blood of people his brother has murdered. Enraged, he lifts the barrel and throws it onto a coffee table, which collapses. Mike also collapses: he sits down trembling, his previously neatly combed hair in disarray and his strength faltering. Meanwhile, Tom seems unmoved and self-confident. He stands up and accuses his brother of being a murderer too since Mike must have killed people during the war. Mrs. Powers tries to reconcile the brothers but in vain: Tom leaves and moves to a hotel, unwilling to live under the same roof with Mike. At this moment, the strength which characterized Mike is gone, and it is Tom who is presented as the stronger character. He is convinced his road to success, based on self-centeredness, is superior to Mike's selfless decision. The parallel he sees between killing enemies during war and killing people for profit attests to his perception of the world as a conflict in which only the fittest survive. His violence and ruthlessness make him triumphant.

Tom lives in a hotel with his girlfriend, Kitty (Mae Clarke).[33] During a telephone conversation with "Nails" Nathan, in Kitty's presence, he tells the bootlegger that he is growing tired of the girl. What follows is the infamous "grapefruit scene." When Kitty refuses to give Tom alcohol for breakfast and suggests that he has someone else Tom pushes a grapefruit in her face, hurting the girl and leaving her crying. The brutality towards the woman who loves him and cares for him makes Tom a detestable character, for whom violence is the basic reaction. He is immature and selfish, playing with people and hurting them when he becomes bored with them. Although the film offers other instances of brutality, it is the "grapefruit scene" that directly tells the viewer that Tom is no anti-hero, but rather the full-fledged villain of the story, attesting to the title of the film. The brightly-lit hotel room in which the couple prepare for breakfast could be seen as a setting for a romance in which they would perhaps plan their future. However, for Tom, there is no life without violence. Such was the scene's impact that Mae Clark, an accomplished actress who later starred in productions such as the pre-Code version of *Waterloo Bridge* (1931), was always associated primarily with her minor role in *The Public Enemy*.[34] The relationships Tom has with women are always superficial, with the impulsive gangster becoming attracted but quickly losing interest. As Matt comments, while celebrating his own wedding, Tom is not good material for a husband. However, Tom's new girlfriend, Gwen (Jean Harlow), acknowledges that Tom is different than other men she knows, which she sees as a strength rather than weakness. This is why she considers herself a good match for Tom and suggests planning their life together.

However, in fact, neither Tom nor Matt are predisposed for family life. When Tom notices "Putty Nose" during the wedding celebration he and Matt follow him outside, leaving the bride and the guests. As the gangster pleads for his life, reminding the two young men about the song he played for them when they were children, Tom shoots him in cold blood while Matt looks in horror. Having killed "Putty Nose," Tom loses interest in the situation and says that he must call Gwen. The revenge he has exacted has no effect on him. It neither satisfies nor gives him a sense of accomplishment. It is yet another act of violence that leaves no visible mark on him. Matt, in contrast, is visibly distraught by the ruthless murder. This is also emphasized by the fact that Matt's reaction provides the only assessment device by which the viewer may gauge the degree of violence used by Tom. The camera does not show the moment

---

33   Mae Clark was uncredited in the film; see: Katz, *The Film Encyclopedia*, p.208, p. 263.

34   Katz, *The Film Encyclopedia*, 263.

of the shooting as it pans towards Matt just as Tom reaches for his revolver. The two Irish Americans have been friends for most of their lives, and Matt must have witnessed numerous instances of Tom's violence but this leaves him speechless.

Soon, "Nails" Nathan dies in a horse-riding accident and, as a newspaper headline reports, "Gangland Prepares for War." On the day of the funeral, Tom and Matt buy the horse that killed "Nails" and immediately shoot it, getting a peculiar kind of vengeance. The gang war ensues, and Tom, Matt, and their accomplices are hunted by their rivals led by "Schemer" Burns. As the two friends are walking down the street, Matt is shot and killed. On impulse, Tom goes to a gun store and steals two revolvers in order to avenge his friend. He finds "Schemer" entering a building together with his gang. Determined and, as usual, contemptuous of danger, he follows the gangsters inside. The camera shows the entrance to the building as shots are heard inside, followed by a woman screaming. Immediately afterward, Tom emerges from the building, wounded and faltering. He throws his weapons away and stumbles through the rain-soaked street, a trickle of blood coming from under his hat. Losing his strength, he says: "I ain't so tough," before falling to the ground.

The next scene shows Tom at the hospital, where he is visited by his mother, Mike, and Molly Doyle (Rita Flynn, uncredited[35]). He apologizes to his brother, but when asked what he feels sorry for, he does not specify, saying that he is "just sorry." However, he does not seem to believe that he and Mike can be reconciled. When their mother happily says her two sons are going to be friends again, Tom appears doubtful, even though he confirms his mother's words. A few days later, Tom is kidnapped from the hospital by "Schemer" Burns's men. His family is informed that Tom will be returned home. As they are preparing for his safe return, there is a knock at the door. Expectantly, Mike opens the door, but as he does so, his younger brother's lifeless body falls inside. Mike kneels down, his face contorted with anger, resembling Tom's reaction to Matt's death and suggesting that, perhaps, the chain of events presented in the film does not finish the story of violence in the family.

Tom's and Matt's rise in the world of crime and their subsequent downfall is presented as an unavoidable consequence of the life they have chosen. However, although both young men live in an area dominated by violence and the impact of their environment on their upbringing and early adulthood is undeniably strong, the film stresses the importance of personal choice. Tom's brother, raised in the same environment, chooses hard work, education, and service to his country over gangsterism, which would bring him money more

---

35   *The Public Enemy* (*1931*) *- IMDb.*

quickly and easily. As some critics observe, with such "[...] simplistic moralism, the plot of *The Public Enemy* has dated poorly."[36] However, although the overall plot is admittedly straightforward, and the "moralistic sentimentality of the script"[37] may influence the reception of the film by a contemporary audience, the construction of the two brothers is far from one-dimensional; they are by no means presented as perfectly contrasting with each other. Rather, their positions fluctuate, reflecting the choices they make. At first, the viewer may be sympathetic to Tom trying to improve his life and finding it difficult due to his harsh upbringing and the environment in which he lives. It is perhaps easier to identify with Tom than with his brother, a seemingly perfect character. However, Tom quickly reveals himself to be a misogynist and a spoilt man who exploits other people and is unable to control his innate anger and violence. It is repeatedly hinted that Mike is a thief, stealing small sums of money from his employer, which may suggest that he is not unlike his younger brother, and what separates them are the appearances that Mike is able to keep up. Instances of violence between the brothers reveal that Mike is also prone to acts of brutality but is able to control it. Moreover, his reaction to Tom's death, which parallels Tom's response to Matt's murder, suggests that he might not be able to contain his violence anymore.

The treatment of the two characters introduced an important narrative motif that would later dominate the representation of the Irish in American cinema, i.e., their inability to escape from violence. Virtually all the male Irish American characters in the film need an outlet for their innate violence, and they cannot escape its influence on their lives. Tom and Matt become gangsters, Mike enlists and becomes a soldier in WWI, and their father is a police officer, using violence as his only tool in bringing up his sons—or Tom at least. This early image of Irish American society, almost inevitably connected with violence and crime, is, on its basic level, very similar to what was presented in *Little Annie Rooney*. However, whereas the Rooneys and their friends are able to forsake violence, the Powers family is unable to do so. Tom's inevitable death is the direct result of the way of life he has chosen and is an indictment of Irish violence, which runs counter to the American moral standards. Another difference between *Little Annie Rooney* and *The Public Enemy* lies in the representation of women and their role in society. Whereas Annie is a self-reliant

---

36   Chris Whiteley, "The Public Enemy (1931)," Hollywood's Golden Age: 30 Years of Brilliance 1930–59, accessed January 17, 2021, http://www.hollywoodsgoldenage.com/movies/the_public_enemy.html.

37   Geoff Andrew, "The Public Enemy Review," TimeOut, November 4, 2012, https://web.archive.org/web/20121104223009/https://www.timeout.com/film/reviews/71552/the_public_enemy.html.

person, familiar with violence and able to carry out acts of brutality, she understands that violence inevitably leads to destruction and counteracts it, saving her family and friends in the process. Mrs. Powers and Molly Doyle are background characters. The former needs her husband to support her and, when he dies, her wellbeing depends solely on her sons. Presumably, Molly represents a similar case as, at one point, Tom remarks that Mike will be of no use to her. This degradation of the role of Irish American women from active to passive characters became a standard mode of their representation in gangster films. The characters are not explicitly referred to as Irish but are indirectly labeled as belonging to this minority through the use of surnames, stereotypes, and the settings in which they were presented.

The Public Enemy influenced the representations of the Irish in films leading to similar plot structures and development in later productions. The *Picture Snatcher* (1933) by Lloyd Bacon presents the story of Danny Kean, portrayed, again, by James Cagney, who monopolized the role of Irish American gangster in the cinema of the 1930s. Danny is an ex-gangster who, after being released from prison, decides to forsake his criminal activity and become a photographer. He resigns from the leadership in his gang, which is taken over by Jerry "The Mug" (Ralf Harolde). Soon, he falls in love with a young Irish American woman, Pat Nolan (Patricia Ellis), the daughter of a police officer, Casey Nolan (Robert O'Connor), who shot and arrested him in the past. With a mixture of luck, stubbornness, and rather poor morals, Kean manages to obtain a photograph of a firefighter who responded to an emergency call from his own house, where he found the bodies of his wife and her lover. He is also able to photograph a woman executed in Sing Sing prison with a hidden camera. When, because of his actions, Casey Nolan is demoted, he loses Pat and starts drinking. In the end, however, he manages to track down Jerry "The Mug," who is wanted for murder, and takes photos of him as he is shot by the police. Danny ascribes his actions to Nolan, who is promoted again and allows Pat and Danny to restore their relationship.

Although the film follows a completely different type of plot than *The Public Enemy*, it is based on similar narrative themes, clearly proving the existence of a consistent and already well-established stereotype of the Irish gangster. These narrative motifs include the presence of a police officer father figure, the importance of family, the character's inability to escape from violence, and his deep intimacy with it, which allows him to succeed. This intimacy, however, is well-directed as Danny uses his past to recover from adversity and fight for his future. Thus, another motif that the film employs is that of redemption, with the self-centered and immoral young man learning to care about other people. Thus, Danny's rejection of gang life allows him to become a member of American society. Similarly to *Little Annie Rooney* and *The Public Enemy*, the film provides the viewer with a clear, if not simplistic, moral that crime does not pay. However, more importantly to the context explored in this book, it portrays the Irish as stereotypically violent.

The basis for the representation of the Irish as gangsters were also real-life characters, whose stories sometimes served as sources of film plots. *Roger Touhy, Gangster* (1944), directed by Robert Florey, was based on the story of a real-life Irish American mobster, similarly to the later *Mad Dog Coll* (1961) directed by Burt Balaban, giving a fictionalized account of the life of the notorious Vincent "Mad Dog" Coll. In the context of this study, *Mad Dog Coll* is especially interesting, as the gangster is presented as a person violently abused by his father, like the fictional Tom Powers. Thus, one of the last classical gangster films featuring Irish mobsters reflected one of the first ones in the construction of the character. However, in the post-World War II era, Classical Hollywood mostly refrained from portraying the Irish as cruel gangsters. In other films, particularly in the representatives of the film-noir genre, innocent Irish Americans are likely to be accused of crimes that they have not committed. Examples of such films are *The Lady from Shanghai* (1947) by Orson Welles, and *I Wouldn't Be In Your Shoes* (1948) by William Nigh.

The gangster became one of the most typical realizations of the Irish stereotype. The trend of representing the Irish in America as unambiguously negative gangsters seems to have subsided in the 1940s, at least when it comes to representing them as main characters. In this context, both *Roger Touhy, Gangster* and *Mad Dog Coll*, both taking place in the 1930s., may be seen as reminiscences of the past. Later in the classical period of cinema Irish gangsters appeared mainly as background characters, for example in *The Undercover Man* (1949) by J. H. Lewis, or *Anatomy of a Murder* by Otto Preminger from 1959. Their presence usually served a moralistic purpose as the viewer was shown that crime brings only transient success at best, in the end leading to an inevitable downfall. They strive for power, but, in the words of Hannah Arendt, "Power and violence are opposites; where the one rules absolutely, the other is absent."[38] However, more importantly, films featuring Irish gangsters were the basis for the representation of other typecast Irish roles and occupations; the actions of characters represented in these roles were usually directed against gangsters. One such stereotypical role was that of the Irish police officer unafraid to use the innate Irish violence but in a socially acceptable way— to protect others. The second type was the Catholic priest actively opposed to

---

38   *Crises of the Republic: Lying in Politics; Civil Disobedience; On Violence; Thoughts on Politics and Revolution* (New York, NY: Harcourt Brace Jovanovich, 1972), 30, http://search. ebscohost.com/login.aspx?direct=true&scope=site&db=nlebk&db=nlabk&AN=1823732.

64   CHAPTER 2

violence represented by Irish gangsters. Whereas the figure of the Irish police officer has survived the classical period and appeared in multiple forms in New Hollywood and contemporary American cinema, the Irish priest opposing gangs has vanished almost completely.

2.2   *Against Violence: Irish American Catholic Priests*

If the function of the Irish gangster in early American cinema was to show the consequences of allowing innate violence to control one's actions, the Irish American Catholic priest was supposed to exist as the gangster's exact opposite. Such a duality of characters is clearest in Michael Curtiz's gangster film *Angels with Dirty Faces* from 1938. The film featured a truly stellar cast, consisting of, among others, James Cagney, Pat O'Brien, Humphrey Bogart, Ann Sheridan, and a popular Broadway group, the Dead End Kids. Like *The Public Enemy*, the film holds a rating of 100% on Rottentomatoes.com;[39] it is also considered one of Cagney's best films.[40]

It begins like *Little Annie Rooney* and *The Public Enemy*. The camera pans through a busy and rather rundown neighborhood, immediately pointing to the influence of the environment on the characters. However, although two Irish American friends, William "Rocky" Sullivan (Cagney) and Jerry Connolly (O'Brien), come from the same background, their lives run along two different paths. When they are still children, the two are juvenile delinquents, loitering in the neighborhood. The parallel between *The Public Enemy* and *Angels with Dirty Faces* is clearly marked by the interactions between the boys engaging in petty crimes and in conflicts with girls. The first difference between Rocky and Jerry is their approach to crime. While attempting to break into a freight wagon loaded with fountain pens, Jerry expresses doubts, saying that they steal coal because they need it to keep warm, whereas pens are of no use to them. However, Rocky answers that they might sell the pens and earn money. This serves as a foreshadowing of the further development of the characters; Jerry understands that breaking the law may be justified by a greater good, while for Rocky, it is an easy way to obtain what he needs. Rocky's charisma makes Jerry follow his friend, but they are spotted entering the wagon and are chased by the police patrolling the railway station. Jerry escapes but Rocky is arrested and taken to the Society for Juvenile Delinquents.

When Jerry visits his friend in the reformatory, Rocky seems to be in his element, casually addressing other delinquents and remarking that he is happy to

---

39   "Angels with Dirty Faces (1938)," Rotten Tomatoes, accessed January 22, 2021, https://www. rottentomatoes.com/m/angels_with_dirty_faces.

40   Neibaur, *James Cagney Films of the 1930s*, 173.

receive three meals a day. Jerry plans to appear at Rocky's trial and confess his part in the crime in the hope that this will result in a reduced sentence for his friend. However, Rocky is adamant that confessing would be a sign of weakness and an unnecessary sacrifice and decides to accept the whole responsibility. This shows the dynamics between the two characters, whose approach to crime and punishment differs, but who are ready to make sacrifices in order to save each other from punishment. However, they seem to be willing to do so for different reasons. Jerry has a deep sense of justice; he recognizes his role in the crime and knows that he also deserves punishment. Rocky, on the other hand, treats his arrest as a part of the natural course of his life, as an inevitable occurrence that he accepts.

What follows is a sequence of pages from Rocky's criminal file and newspapers, superimposed on scenes showing Sullivan's life in various penitentiaries and his criminal activity. For the petty crime he committed, he is sentenced to two years at Warrington Reform School; this is followed by a three-year sentence at State Reformatory for assault and battery; he is next sentenced to four and a half years at State Penitentiary for an alcohol-related crime during the prohibition era and later freed on a manslaughter charge, which marks his adulthood and, presumably, growing notoriety as a gangster. Scenes from his lavish life are interwoven with images of violent acts he commits and newspaper headlines reporting on his activity as his gang terrorizes the city. He is arrested and spends three additional years in prison before being finally released.

Upon his release, he visits his old neighborhood and goes to church, where Jerry is now a priest working with children. The two friends are reunited after fifteen years, their lives now completely different. They reminisce about their friendship, remembering the mischief they got up to together. Convinced by Jerry, Rocky decides to stay in the neighborhood and rents a room in a lodging house close to the church. Soon, his pocket is picked by a gang of juvenile delinquents (the Dead End Kids), whom he approaches in a building where he used to hide as a boy. When the gang learns about their victim's identity, they are apologetic and express their admiration of Rocky, who is sympathetic and decides to educate them in criminal activity. At the same time, Jerry is working with the boys, referred to as Angels, together with a social worker, Laury Martin (Sheridan), with whom Rocky was conflicted in the past and who becomes his love interest.

The introduction of the juvenile gang is a plot point indicating the beginning of a struggle between Rocky and Jerry, who represent two different approaches to violence. This is visible quite soon after the gang's first appearance in the film when the boys are playing a basketball match with Jerry as the referee. The gang is unable to play by the rules, constantly try cheating and fouling their opponents. Jerry fails to make them play fair as he is in a position of only apparent authority. The Angels understand authority in terms of physical strength and Jerry does not engage in physical confrontations; thus, he is unable to exert any influence on them. On the other hand, when Rocky becomes the referee, he slaps, punches, and elbows the boys, thus exerting the kind of influence they understand and accept. Violence seems to be the key factor in educating the boys, who, having lost the game, decide to practice in preparation for a rematch.

At the same time, Rocky is trying to recover $100,000 owed to him by his lawyer, Jim Frazier (Bogart), and reacquire his position in the criminal hierarchy, while refusing to work for another gangster, Mac Keefer (George Bancroft), with whom the lawyer collaborates. Frazier agrees to return the money to Sullivan, but he orders his men to kill him. They make an attempt on Rocky's life but he manages to trick them into murdering one of their own men. Sullivan kidnaps Frazier and receives a $100,000 ransom from Keefer. In addition to money, he also acquires information about corrupt city officials collaborating with the Irish mob. He seems fearless when dealing with the gangsters, convinced that he will succeed. When Keefer informs the police of Frasier's kidnapping, Rocky is approached in his apartment by two police officers. In his interaction with the police he maintains the same contemptuous posture, answering questions with irony and wit. At the same time, he trusts the Angels to keep his money safe in their hideout. When he is released, the boys return the money in an unopened envelope, proving that they respect their mentor; they are rewarded for their loyalty with more money, as they remark, than their parents have ever earned.

Jerry feels that he is losing his connection with the boys, who begin spending money on extravagant clothes, alcohol, and billiards. He questions them about the source of their wealth and tries to dissuade them from the path of crime. However, what he has to offer is not attractive to the boys. They say that his idea of spending time—playing basketball—offers them no prospects and that they do not believe in a reward after death. They decide to stay in a bar, surrounded by gangsters, choosing Rocky's materialism over Jerry's spirituality. One of the thugs mocks the priest for his failure to reason with the boys. The priest's reaction proves he is not unable to use violence though he is usually able to contain it. He punches the gangster, flooring him, and walks away untroubled by anyone in the pub. Thus, although raised in the same environment as his childhood friend and sharing the innate violence, Jerry is able to rise above it and subdue it, not permitting his brutal side to control him.

The previous scene acquires deeper meaning when analyzed in the context of the one that follows. The camera shows Rocky and Laury in Sullivan's apartment. Rocky is sitting on the table, towering over Laury as he explains to her the superiority of his vision of the world in which there is no place for the banality of the saying that crime does not pay. Rocky disrespects anyone who does not agree with his outlook. Although Jerry is not present, Sullivan's opinion puts him in sharp contrast to his childhood friend. Moreover, Jerry's difficulty in attracting the Angels to his peaceful and non-violent ideals is contrasted with Laury's attraction to the world of violence represented by Rocky. As he shares with her his idea of superiority over other people, she smiles while a mid-closeup on her face emphasizes her reaction, allowing the viewer to focus on her eyes, gazing at Rocky. Sullivan tempts Laury with the idea of lavishness she has already experienced in her life as a gangster's wife. She becomes attracted, just like the Angels, abandoning her social work.

Until this point, the viewer and the characters have been dominated by Rocky. Connolly, although also an important character, is pushed to the background and appears on the screen less frequently. He seems defeated, and his ideals are almost forgotten by the people who were working with him as well as by the audience. Both Irish Americans compete to dominate the neighborhood with their ideals; Jerry tries to stabilize the orbits on which the Angels venture, while Rocky is a black hole—possessing a powerful gravitational field, but ultimately only destructive in nature. As he rises in the mob hierarchy, although surrounded by people he cannot trust, he becomes even more convinced of his power and superiority. Meanwhile, rejected and resigned, Jerry spends his time in his church, where, one day, he receives money from Rocky. The money becomes an impulse for him to shift from a passive to an active character as he decides to confront his friend. The priest visits the gangster and explains that money will not be able to help him in his work with juvenile delinquents as long as the neighborhood in which they live is controlled by gangsters attracting the youth with easy access to wealth and the feeling of success in life. He accuses Rocky of teaching the boys that violence will enable them to achieve everything easily, which the gangster casually affirms, widening the chasm between them. This puts Jerry on the offensive. He warns his friend that he will use the highly publicized case of Frasier's kidnapping "as a crowbar" that will open the door to the criminal underworld and force city officials to deal with the problem of crime; he also adds that he will not hesitate to destroy Rocky if he has to. The gangster dismisses him with his usual confidence. The two shake hands, and Rocky agrees never to give money to the Angels again, while the duel between them begins.

Jerry leads a campaign against the Irish mob. He is courageous and persistent in his struggle against violence, which he leads with peaceful means— informing the public about corruption, instigating a public outcry, and forcing the politicians to take action against gangs. Even Laury, who is not a part of Sullivan's world and tries to reason with Jerry, cannot persuade him to abandon his mission. He replies that he cannot sacrifice other children for Rocky, whom he regretfully considers a lost cause. This opinion stands in direct opposition to Rocky's perception of himself as a victor. Resisting Laury's pleas and a $100,000 bribe from Keefer, Jerry goes on the radio and denounces the gangsters. Left with no choice but to silence the priest, Keefer and Frazier plan to murder both Jerry and Rocky, whom they consider a threat. Rocky overhears and confronts them, killing Keefer. The display of violence is presented in an interesting way—as Rocky shoots Keefer, the camera pans to the right, leaving Keefer in the offscreen area and focusing on Rocky's reflection in a mirror. Thus, when Rocky pulls the trigger, the viewer is presented with the reflected image of the gangster, as if he were shooting at himself. This may be interpreted as Rocky acting against himself and destroying the success and wealth he possesses. However, although his action may be considered an act of sacrifice, his success is never permanent as, collaborating with violent men and using violence himself, Rocky is part of a self-destructive group in which the eruption of such a conflict was always a matter of time. Jerry serves only as a catalyst, bringing the organization to its violent end.

In the shootout that follows, Rocky kills Frasier, some of Keefer's bodyguards, and two of the police officers who arrive at the scene. He hides in a warehouse, surrounded by the police and onlookers. Despite the police appearing in overwhelming numbers and shooting teargas in through the windows of the warehouse, Rocky does not surrender. The standoff cannot be resolved until Jerry arrives and offers the police his help. He is reminded that he is just a priest, but he refuses to let his friend die in a shootout. Jerry walks into the warehouse; the calm and peaceful way he walks up the stairs contrasts with the frantic actions of Rocky and the police officers. He moves through the clouds of teargas completely unaffected, as if he were physically detached from the world of violence into which he has stepped. Unhurriedly, he reaches Rocky, who now blames him for his failure and takes him hostage. They move out of the warehouse, and Rocky is shot in the leg and arrested while trying to escape. At the moment of his arrest, he does not show remorse; on the contrary, he maintains his contemptuous manner when addressing the police officers.

Rocky's trial is presented from the perspective of the Angels, in a sequence of scenes showing them following the stages of the trial in newspapers. Enchanted by the gangster's charisma, the boys perceive his failure as another opportunity for him to show his strength and contempt for law and order. When he is given the death penalty, the gang is impressed by his claim that he will die proud, spitting in the eye of the executioner, unbroken, and violent until the end. The boys' unchanged perception of Rocky proves that his influence on them is unwavering, and even if he dies, the momentum that he has given them will lead them into the world of crime and violence.

On death row, Rocky is taunted by a prison guard and reacts violently, instigating fierce reactions from other prisoners and proving that his pride, strength, and disrespect for the law are no mask. He confirms that he is not afraid to die when he is visited by Jerry and reveals his plan to mock the executioner. This parallels the scene from the first act when the two friends meet at the Society for Juvenile Delinquents. When arrested for the first time, Rocky considers his fate part of the natural course of life and he reacts to his imminent execution with the same acceptance. He says that in order to be afraid one must have a heart, which he was deprived of long ago. However, he genuinely cares about the Angels and asks how they are without him. Mindful of the lasting effect he has exerted on the boys and that dying with courage will cement his status as a hero to the boys, Jerry asks Rocky for an act of courage greater than he has ever shown; he wants him to resist and beg for life so that the boys would consider him a coward and would turn away from him. Despising his friend's request, Rocky refuses and punches a prison guard. During the long walk to the electric chair, Rocky maintains his composure and condescending manner, despite Jerry's begging him not to. The two friends exchange goodbyes and, as Rocky enters the execution chamber, a closeup on his face emphasizes the hatred and scorn he has towards the world. This is the last image of the character that the viewer is presented with.

However, as he is inside and the camera focuses on Jerry praying, Rocky's voice is heard from the chamber, begging for life. At the same time, the shot shifts to the image of Rocky's shadow on the wall, as he struggles with the officers tying him to the electric chair. The camera returns its focuses to Jerry and closes upon the expression of relief on his face as he listens to his friend crying and begging for life. The fact that Rocky is never shown directly begging for life and struggling signifies that, in his last moments, he fulfills his friend's request as it is not the real Rocky that shows a lack of courage. The last closeup on his face is supposed to leave the viewer with the impression that the real Rocky disappears the moment he enters the execution chamber; what he does inside is shadow theater, a performance he stages in order to spare others his fate. In his last moments, he forsakes himself and becomes selfless, destroying his image of a fearless and brutal criminal admired by young gang members. Thus, he lets go of the boys, and he joins Jerry's area of influence. Following the execution, when the prison guard who was earlier punched by Rocky comments on the convict's cowardice, the camera focuses again on Jerry, praying for his friend while being grateful for his sacrifice.

In the hideout, the Angels read a newspaper with a front-page headline reading: "Rocky Dies Yellow: Killer Coward at the End!" They cannot believe that their idol has died a coward. Jerry, who comes to visit them, confirms the information, completely shattering Rocky's image. As they are now deprived of their mentor and beacon, he invites them to pray for Rocky. The boys, one by one, leave the dark cellar of the hideout, following Jerry upstairs into a brightly-lit exterior and a hopeful future.

In the skillfully crafted plot, every scene is a component playing its part in the portrayal of the conflict between Rocky's violent world and Jerry's anti-violence ideals. The two main characters are constructed as direct oppositions in their approach to violence. They have the same background but it is their choices that shape their future. The figure of the Irish gangster is consistent with the earlier and later representations of this type of character. Rocky is a self-centered, disdainful, and immature character convinced that violence will lead him to success in life. He is presented as an energetic person, almost hectic, as if aware that he does not have much time left to live, but he is cold-blooded and calculating when necessary. Jerry, meanwhile, is his complete opposite. Mature, selfless, and caring, he is also visibly calmer, almost subdued until the end of the second act. The juxtaposition with the energetic, lively, and active gangster, engaging the audience with his antics, makes the figure of the Catholic priest arguably less interesting than that of his polar opposite. However, it serves the plot well as the viewer's reception of the Irish priest may well reflect how he is perceived by the Angels. Rocky is much more appealing to them as he uses language they understand and is not afraid to cross the boundaries the priest sets for them. However, in the end, it is the priest and his anti-violence ideals that prevail as they do not run counter to those represented by society. In this way, the priest becomes an acceptable Irish character, ultimately serving the same moralistic purpose as the Irish gangster; his function is to teach the viewer that violence leads nowhere while the success achieved by violent means is transient and leads to an inevitable downfall.

The figure of the Irish American Catholic priest serving a special role in society as a person actively opposing violence seems to have been based, like gangster figures, on real-life examples. *Boys Town*, a biographical drama directed by Norman Taurog and released in 1938, about two months before the premiere *Angels with Dirty Faces*, is based on the life and work of Father Edward J. Flanagan (Spencer Tracy), who established a community center for delinquents, "Boys Town." The film begins where the story of Jerry and Rocky has finished, on death row where Father Flanagan visits his friend, a murderer, waiting for execution. Inspired by the man's life story of hardships, the priest decides to establish a place where young people can find shelter from the world of violence and avoid the same fate as the convicted murderer. Thus, the premise of the film is remarkably similar to *Angels with Dirty Faces*, although there is no information in available sources that would suggest the latter was inspired by Father Flanagan's story. The fact that *Boys Town* offers a fictionalized account of the story of a real-life priest and the similarities in the premises of the two films may suggest the existence of a narrative pattern for the representation of Irish American Catholic priests, who might have been perceived as hope for educating young people inspired by gangsters' stories of easy success. As the Irish were stereotypically considered violent, the Irish priest, stemming from the same social and ethnic background, was an insider who knew the Irish community well and could successfully counteract their violent behavior, educating, and turning them into productive members of society. Pairing the priest with a gangster served an obvious moralistic purpose by presenting the audience with two paths, one of which was superficially attractive but led to tragic downfall, while the other, although appearing more down to earth, led to salvation in the eyes of society.

The role of Irish American Catholic priests as figures responsible for alleviating various social problems was explored by Leo McCarey in a 1944 musical comedy-drama, *Going My Way* with Bing Crosby and Barry Fitzgerald. Crosby plays the role of Father Charles "Chuck" O'Malley, an Irish American priest transferred to New York in order to take over a parish run by an older priest, Father Fitzgibbon (Fitzgerald). The two priests are contrasted mostly when it comes to their relationship with society. The younger one is more open and casual, and exists within the social structure, while the older priest seems detached from other people and locked in religious practice. This is most clearly seen in their interactions with younger parishioners, some of whom, led by Italian American Tony Scaponi (Stanley Clements), begin to have problems with the law. For Fitzgibbon, the young people's religious observance is the priority, while O'Malley actively works with them and manages to transform a gang-in-the-making into a choir. The film features numerous references to Irish culture, with Father Fitzgibbon expressing his longing for Ireland and his mother who lives there. The two priests, although initially in conflict, bond over their Irish roots, epitomized by an Irish song, "Too Ra Loo Ra Loo Rai." The sequel to *Going My Way*, *The Bells of St. Mary's*, was released the following year, with Bing Crosby reprising his role and Ingrid Bergman appearing as Sister Mary Benedict. Other representations of the figure of the Irish American Catholic priest included Father Francis P. Duffy (Pat O'Brien), based on a real-life priest, who inspires courage in soldiers of the *The Fighting 69th* (1940) in William Keighley's war film, and *The Cardinal* (1963) by Otto Preminger, in which an Irish American priest deals with issues such as racism, totalitarianism, and the choice between personal happiness and remaining faithful to the doctrine of the Catholic Church.

Regardless of the genre and plot development, the figure of the Irish American Catholic priest always actively opposed violence. However, whereas the figure of the Irish gangster, often serving as the priest's polar opposite, survived the classical period, entered New Hollywood, and regained popularity in the contemporary period, the Irish American Catholic priest in his earliest anti-violence role has disappeared completely although echoes of the figure may be detected in one of the newest incarnations of the violent Irish stereotype, i.e., the Irish vigilante featured in *The Boondock Saints*, analyzed in the section devoted to contemporary American cinema.

2.3 *Irish Police Officers*

While the Irish American Catholic priest served as the exact opposite to the Irish gangster in terms of their approach to violence, for the Irish police officer, violence was a tool used in protecting society. Irish police officers appeared in most gangster-themed films, often as background characters. As such, their function was usually restricted to participating in the final confrontation with the gangster. The prototypical Irish police officer, Captain James McQuigg from *The Racket*, is a man for whom the sense of duty is more important than the established law, which he is willing to break if necessary to arrest the gang leader. This character construction appears congruent to the apparent perception of the Irish as rebellious even when performing the social function of upholding the law. Remarkably, Irish police officers are often seen in comedies produced in the period.

East Side Kids (1940), directed by Robert F. Hill, is a comedy-drama whose main character is an unmistakably Irish policeman, Officer Pat O'Day (Leon Ames). The film was the first in a series featuring the eponymous East Side Kids, a group of young actors formed as successors to the popular Dead End Kids, from *Angels with Dirty Faces*. The film rested on a premise dictated by the appearance of the group and similar to that of Michael Curtiz's masterpiece: the main character's struggle to save a group of juvenile delinquents from lives of crime. However, this time, the character involved in saving a group of young boys is a police officer rather than a priest.

The beginning of the film is typical of other gangster-themed films of the era. After an establishing shot of New York City, the camera moves to a poor but busy neighborhood in which a group of young boys is seen loitering in the street. They start fighting over a game they have been playing, but when a passer-by accidentally bumps into one of them, they immediately unite, throwing

THE IRISH ON THE SILVER SCREEN
73

garbage at the man and spitting on him. Even though the passer-by is older and larger than they are, he decides to leave, clearly preferring not to engage in an argument with the loiterers. After he is gone, they resume the fight among themselves. The clear message to the audience is that the boys are dangerous, violence is natural for them, and they will unite if necessary.

Officer Pat O'Day is introduced in a conversation with an imprisoned gangster, Knuckles Dolan (Dave O'Brien), awaiting execution for killing a police officer. It is quickly revealed that, much like Jerry Connolly and Rocky Sullivan, the two were childhood friends. O'Day does not believe Dolan is responsible for the crime but the criminal steadfastly refuses to reveal the name of the murderer, adhering to the gangster's code of secrecy. Trying to reason with Dolan, Pat mentions the criminal's younger brother, Danny, who is likely to follow in his brother's footsteps. Danny does not know of his brother's arrest and thinks that he has gone to South America. Thinking about Danny, O'Day is preoccupied not only with the prospect of the boy becoming a criminal but also influencing other young people from his neighborhood. The introduction of the issue is rather vague, underdeveloped, and seems to be based on the premise of the third act of *Angels with Dirty Faces*; O'Day says that Danny will not believe his brother is a murderer but if Dolan dies in the electric chair he will also become a criminal. This is later slightly developed in O'Day's conversation with Dolan's sister, Molly (Joyce Bryant), in a rather simplistic way: if his brother is executed, Danny will "hate the law." In the end, the police officer decides that "This thing is [...] bigger than the law," and that he will save Knuckles in order to help his younger brother.

Like Captain James McQuigg from *The Racket*, O'Day will ignore the established law if he thinks it an obstacle to justice. The concept of justice he seems to believe in is based on clear and straightforward principles: saving a person is more important than fulfilling obligations stemming from the established law, especially if it leads to a greater good. During O'Day's conversation with Molly, the two are joined by Milton "Mileaway" Harris (Dennis Moore), with whom O'Day and Knuckles Dolan used to be in a gang. Harris's presentation is typical for gangsters of the classical period; he is elegant, affluent, and charismatic. The only person resistant to his charm is O'Day, who is not misled by the superficial appearances Harris projects.

In order to help the youth from the neighborhood, O'Day establishes a "Junior Police" sports club for them. He obtains support from local entrepreneurs and even wants to be allowed to give police badges to the boys but his request is rejected. The boys, however, are more impressed with Mileaway and his lifestyle. This creates a conflict clearly based on the opposition between Jerry and Rocky in *Angels with Dirty Faces*. The two forces try to attract the boys with the youth's future at stake. It is made clear that violence impresses the youths. They are a lot more brutal than the Dead End Kids and are shown fighting amongst each other for gang leadership. Moreover, when they taunt an entrepreneur's son, Algernon Wilkes (Jack Edwards), and it turns out that the boy is strong, easily beating three of them, they invite him to join their gang. Understanding their nature, Pat O'Day wants to create a space in which they can use their strength and energy non-destructively. It appears that he is successful, as the boys join the club and take up sports, mainly boxing and wrestling. O'Day also teaches them patriotism and defends them when they are accused of theft by a local businessman, Mr. Schmidt. When Schmidt addresses Danny, mentioning his brother, O'Day assaults Schmidt, for which he is demoted and sent to patrol streets.

Although now holding a less important position, O'Day continues running the club for the boys and trying to exonerate Knuckles. Because of his past as a gang member, he has inside knowledge, which allows him to correctly deduce that Dolan could not have murdered the police officer. He also manages to recruit Danny's friends to help him find the real culprit. When the boys receive their faux "Junior Policemen" badges they are proud. However, they are soon recruited by Mileaway's accomplice, Morrison (Robert Friske), who hires them to distribute leaflets. In reality, Mileaway, Morrison, his girlfriend May (Maxine Lesley), and Schmidt are money forgers, and the boys distribute counterfeit money with the leaflets. This is used by the gangsters to further discredit Officer O'Day, who falls from grace, his motives now questioned even by the thus-far supportive Captain Moran (Jim Farley).

The final act of the film is full of incidents. With the boys' help, Pat discovers Mileaway's counterfeiting scheme and goes after the gangsters as Captain Moran arrives to arrest him. Meanwhile, Mileaway notices Detective Joe (Alden Chase) following Danny and sets up a trap in May's apartment. The gangster shoots the police officer and takes Danny hostage. Danny learns from May that it was Mileaway who framed his brother for murder. Pat, now a wanted criminal, chases after Mileaway and his gang, whose car crashes. Mileaway returns to Schmidt and shoots his former accomplice as he suspects he has betrayed him. The criminal then escapes to a rooftop, chased by Pat O'Day and the boys. In the final confrontation, one of the boys, Fred "Dutch" Kuhn (Hal E. Chester), catches up with Mileaway, and the two fall from the roof. Dutch dies while Mileaway makes a confession that clears Knuckles and Pat of the charges. The boys return to the club, where Knuckles trains them in boxing.

The film, with its premise based almost entirely on the much better developed *Angels with Dirty Faces*, has not aged well. The function of the Irish American Catholic Priest is fulfilled here by Pat O'Day, which affects the construction of the character. However, there are some features of the character construction that had already appeared in *The Racket* and which were to be explored in New Hollywood and contemporary Hollywood. The most important feature is the character's readiness to operate outside the boundaries of the law when obeying the law would limit the character's ability to fight crime. Secondly, Pat O'Day prioritizes his duty over his private life. Throughout the film, Pat and Molly Dolan express their interest in each other. However, Pat decides to reveal his feelings for her only after he manages to help Knuckles. This subplot is underdeveloped, but nevertheless present. It would become one of the most important aspects of the Irish police officer character construction in New Hollywood and contemporary productions.

Of interest also are two police officer comedies directed by Lloyd Bacon in which the plot focuses not on crime but on family relationships. The Irish police officers resemble the father of *Little Annie Rooney* and concentrate not only on their duty of upholding the law but also, primarily, on their families' wellbeing. In *The Irish in US* (1935) the police officer is played by Pat O'Brien. In this case, the profession is used as a sign of Pat's maturity and responsibility, contrasted with his brother's lightheartedness. As the film focuses more on boxing, it is described in more detail in the next subchapter.

Bacon's *Three Cheers for the Irish* (1940), in which an aging police officer, Peter Casey (Thomas Mitchell), upholds law and order in a multiethnic neighborhood, is a better developed example of this type. He does his duty with a devotion that sometimes leads to comical situations. At the beginning of the film, in response to a woman's cry for help, he rushes to her apartment, taking out his revolver as he climbs the stairs. However, when he reaches the apartment, he realizes that the woman wants him to help her with her fussy son, who is refusing to eat his oatmeal. The humorous situation is immediately juxtaposed with a serious one as, just after leaving the building, Casey witnesses a robbery and, after being shot at, he returns fire, wounding and then arresting the robber. All this, however, is the background for his portrayal as a devoted father to his three daughters, Maureen (Priscilla Lane), Patricia (Virginia Grey), and Heloise (Irene Harvey). He has problems accepting his daughters' romantic interests and is furious when Maureen begins romancing a Scottish American police officer, Angus Ferguson (Dennis Morgan). He is asked to retire after twenty-five years of service and Ferguson becomes his replacement. Unable to cope with his retirement, Casey decides to become an alderman. Although he is a comical character, he epitomizes the positive image of the Irish police officers whose devotion to his duty does not allow him to rest.

At the same time, he is quite impulsive and is prepared to use physical violence to solve conflicts. He gets in a pub fight, for which he is arrested by

76   CHAPTER 2

Ferguson. When he is brought in front of the court, an interesting scene show-ing his devotion to justice occurs. Asked by the judge about the circumstances of the brawl, he lies, claiming that Ferguson interrupted a peaceful political dis-cussion. However, when Angus corroborates his version of events, he attacks him verbally, stating that a police officer should not lie in court, and confesses to instigating the fight. Thus, Ferguson tries to protect Casey but Casey seems to be doing everything in his power to get himself convicted because he wants justice to prevail, even at his own cost.

Angus and Maureen marry in secret and a tearful Casey tells his daughter to leave their house. He feels betrayed and cannot cope with his replacement by a Scotsman both as a neighborhood police officer and as the most important man in his daughter's life. His familial devotion and public service ethos, which are everything to him, are shattered. However, when Maureen becomes preg-nant and goes into labor, Casey is there with Ferguson, eagerly waiting for his grandchild to be born, but most of all, preoccupied with his daughter. When Maureen gives birth to twins, a boy, and a girl, Casey quarrels with Angus, demanding that the newborn should become a police officer one day, while the baby's father claims that the choice will be his son's when he grows up. Learn-ing that the marriage was not officiated by a Catholic priest, Casey rushes out of the hospital ward in search of one to make his daughter's marriage "legal."

2.4   *Destroyed by Violence: Irish Boxers*

Boxing was a popular theme in the American classical film period, even before Hollywood. One of the first short films produced by Edison Studios, *The Gordon Sisters Boxing* (1901), featured two women in a boxing match. In the classical period boxing was considered a particularly Irish sport. The stereotype of the Irish boxer in America was born before the Civil War and, as stated, 56.3 per-cent of leading New York boxers were fully Irish, while 15 percent more "had at least one Irish parent."[41] This was the result of two things; firstly, boxing is rela-tively cheap and does not require specialized equipment; therefore, it could be easily practiced by poor immigrants from Ireland. Secondly, in the nineteenth and twentieth century, the Irish, both in Ireland and in America, seemed to be obsessed with boxing.[42] With the growing popularity of Irish boxers and the strengthening of the stereotype, non-Irish pugilists, mainly of Jewish origin, started to adopt Irish last names.[43] However, as the Irish gained prominence

---

41   Isenberg, *John L. Sullivan and His America*, 79.
42   Joseph Paul Moser, *Irish Masculinity on Screen: The Pugilists and Peacemakers of John Ford, Jim Sheridan and Paul Greengrass* (Jefferson, NC; London: McFarland, 2013), 11.
43   Isenberg, *John L. Sullivan and His America*, 79.

THE IRISH ON THE SILVER SCREEN   77

within American society, they were replaced by other, more recent groups of immigrants both in low-paid jobs and in boxing. Therefore, former Irish boxers in America started working as trainers and promoters of young, usually non-Irish pugilists.[44]

Quite naturally, Hollywood quickly adopted the figure of the Irish boxer in a number of classic films. The idea of boxing as an Irish national sport, or rather pastime, was addressed in the "Show your nationality!" scene from *Conductor 1492* analyzed earlier. Boxers in American films were often, although not exclusively, Irish Americans. The variety of genres of films featuring Irish boxers resulted in the employment of numerous narrative developments and patterns. The figure of an Irish boxer had multiple incarnations, with violence playing the most important role in the boxers' portrayal. Moreover, their representations usually did not focus so much on the discipline as on the presence of violence in the life of the characters outside the boxing ring. An interesting version of the character, which, like the priest and police officer, seems to have evolved from the gangster film, appeared in *The Life of Jimmy Dolan*, directed by Archie Mayo, which premiered in 1933. In many ways, the film seems to have set the standard for the representation of the Irish boxer figure in American cinema, especially when it comes to the effect of violence connected with boxing on the main character.

The film begins with a boxer, Jimmy Dolan (Douglas Fairbanks, Jr.,) knocking out his opponent in the ring and winning a Light-Heavyweight Championship. He is cheered by the audience and gives an interview on the radio in which he addresses his mother, saying that now he has the money he will use it to buy a house for her. He is offered a celebratory drink but refuses, saying that he lives clean. The bout he has just won does not seem to have left a mark on him, which may suggest that the fight was not very demanding, and he has won quite easily. This establishes the main character as a perfect embodiment of sporting values. He is undeniably a talented pugilist and, despite his celebrity status, he appears humble and stresses the importance of family values. When he is invited to a party, he refuses, saying that he must first visit his mother. This image seems too good to be true, and, in fact, the next scene shows Jimmy in his apartment accompanied by Goldie West (Shirley Grey), both of them drunk and listening to Jimmy being praised on the radio. Jimmy pushes Goldie violently when he becomes annoyed with her. Soon, they are joined by Goldie's friend, Budgie (Fifi D'Orsay), accompanied by two men, one of whom

---

44   Patrick R. Redmond, *The Irish and the Making of American Sport, 1835–1920* (Jefferson, NC; London: McFarland, 2014), 269.

78 CHAPTER 2

is Charles Magee (George Meeker), a reporter, and the other his manager, Doc Woods (Lyle Talbot).

During the party that ensues, Jimmy does not resemble the cheerful champion from the beginning of the film. He is somber, sarcastic, and disillusioned with people who exploit his success, particularly with his manager, whom he considers "a friend for fifty percent." Bitterly, he says he does not believe in idealism and friendship and refers to people who disinterestedly help others as "suckers." He also admits that he does not have a mother and that family values are a part of his public image. When Magee announces that he is going to write about Jimmy's true nature in a newspaper, the boxer attempts to bribe him and, when this fails, he punches the reporter, who smashes his head on the fireplace and dies. This goes unnoticed by Jimmy, who is too drunk to realize what he has done. Woods punches Budgie, who falls into an armchair, unconscious. Woods and Goldie transport Jimmy out of the apartment.

They drive to Jimmy Dolan's training quarters, where they leave the boxer since they cannot trust him. Knowing what he is really like, they know that he will do everything he can to protect himself. Woods steals Jimmy's expensive watch and drives away with Goldie. They are spotted speeding by two police officers and, during a high-speed chase, crash their car and die on the spot. The car burns, and Woods, wearing Jimmy's watch, is identified as the pugilist. When Jimmy wakes up the next day he learns from a newspaper that he is now considered dead. He visits his attorney to whom he expresses no remorse for the death of Woods and Goldie, saying only that his girlfriend "was all right." This lack of attachment to people distances the viewer from Jimmy. Like Irish screen gangsters, he is self-centered and despises other people. Although his violence is channeled into boxing rather than crime, the character construction resembles that of Tom Powers from *The Public Enemy*. Jimmy fights throughout his life, and violence is, for him, the only way to achieve success. His disregard for others is conveyed by his dismissive attitude to the murder he committed earlier. His only concern is his own wellbeing. Advised by the attorney to "stay dead," he assumes a different name, Jack Daugherty, alters his appearance, and goes into hiding. However, the most important change that occurs to him is that he begins to be afraid. He is no longer in control of his life, and he cannot resort to violence as his characteristic southpaw, i.e., left-hand, style may betray him. Meanwhile, Detective Phlaxer (Guy Kibbee), an awkward, discredited police officer whose actions led to the conviction and execution of an innocent man, suspects it was not Jimmy who died in the car accident and begins an investigation.

On the run, an exhausted Jimmy ends up on a farm owned by Peggy (Loretta Young) and her Aunt (Aline MacMahon), who look after children with

THE IRISH ON THE SILVER SCREEN   79

disabilities. At first, he decides to leave the moment he regains his strength but he is convinced by "Auntie" to stay and start working on the farm, which appeals to his sense of pride. However, he seems completely unadjusted to living and working on a farm, has difficulty waking up early to start work, and has to be taught by children how to milk cows. This does not deprive him of his sense of superiority as he deems it necessary to explain the meaning of some vocabulary he uses to Peggy. As time goes by, he seems to adjust to life on the farm and falls in love with Peggy. He also participates in preparations for a charity boxing match to raise the $2,000 required for the farm's mortgage; however, he still seems to be doing everything for his own benefit and does not understand Molly's selfless idealism in helping the children. It is only when she explains to him the idea of unconditional love that he starts to realize he is able to move beyond his selfish nature. He, therefore, volunteers to participate in another boxing match against King Cobra (Sammy Stein), planning to employ violence to good use. At first, he is deemed "too small" to fight the notorious boxer but he proves his strength by punching the boxing promoter, who, impressed, allows him to fight. As Jimmy prepares for the match, his old selfish nature competes with idealist notions he has acquired from Peggy. Jimmy's new self is tested when Detective Phlaxer discovers a photograph of him taken on the occasion of the charity boxing match and arrives to apprehend him the day before the fight with King Cobra. He makes plans to escape but when Peggy, Auntie, and the children prepare a surprise party for him and present him with a boxing robe, trunks, and a horseshoe for good luck, he is genuinely touched. During a moment of silence, he takes a look at the women and children, all admiring him not because of his success and wealth but because of his apparent selflessness. When Peggy kisses him passionately and asks him to stay on the farm for good, he decides not to escape. To fool Phlaxer, he abandons his trademark southpaw style and joins the match.

Before the boxing match, he and other volunteer pugilists are approached by King Cobra, who taunts them, boasting about his strength and brutality. A change in Jimmy's attitude is visible when he disinterestedly helps a nervous young boxer, Smithers (John Wayne), terrified of the unstoppable King Cobra. When it is Jimmy's turn to take on King Cobra, with Phlaxer in the first row of the audience, the pugilist cannot use his usual and effective left-handed style. King Cobra easily overpowers Jimmy, and the umpire begins to count him out. He manages to stand up but after a short exchange, he starts losing again and barely survives the first round. Meanwhile, Peggy and the children listen to the commentary broadcast on the radio. As the next round ends, Jimmy looks beaten, bleeding from his nose, while King Cobra looks unscratched and ready for the fight. As Dolan is sitting in the corner, he sees Auntie on his right and

Detective Phlaxer on his left. He realizes that the time has come for him to make a final decision; he can revert to his old style and possibly win the money while revealing his identity and getting arrested, or lose and remain free. Choosing the latter, he survives one more round but is now severely beaten. As he is sent to the floor again, Phlaxer tells him that he has recognized him and is going to denounce him. On hearing that, Jimmy decides to sacrifice his freedom and, finally using his own technique, he starts winning. However, the injuries he has sustained take their toll, and he is knocked out by King Cobra.

As Jimmy is recovering after the fight in the locker room, Phlaxer comes to arrest him. The scene parallels the beginning of the film. This time, Jimmy is beaten, bruised, and broken, not only because of the brutal fight, but most of all because he has lost everything. At the beginning of the film, he is shown wearing the mask of the perfect sportsman, who prioritizes his family, lives a "clean life," and epitomizes socially accepted ideas that his fans and audience can identify with. Then, during the course of the film, he assumes the mask of Jake Daugherty. Both masks serve to hide Jimmy's true nature as a selfish, violent man, who disregards other people. He loses his first disguise because of a violent act he committed; his second mask is smashed in a brutal fight which he took part in to help the people he loves and cares for. However, the man under the disguise does not resemble the selfish and brutal person he used to be. When Peggy, Auntie, and the children visit him, he still lies to them, but only because he is ashamed of whom he really is.

Beaten and broken, Jimmy is taken by Phlaxer to the train station. He does not resist arrest, ready to take responsibility for his past deeds. When the detective hears why Jimmy was participating in the fight, he tells him he is a "softie" and a "terrible sucker" for trying to help Peggy and the children, to which Dolan answers that he "would do that all again." Realizing that Dolan has changed, Phlaxer remarks that, perhaps, he has mistaken the pugilist for someone else and, as he boards the train alone, adds, "So long, Daugherty." As the detective disappears, Jimmy answers, "So long ... sucker," the last word no longer sounding taunting. It is said with affection, as if it were a term of endearment. Jimmy realizes that his old self is gone and that he is now the kind of person he once despised. Now, however, he embraces his new identity and begins a new life.

Like other films analyzed in this section, *The Life of Jimmy Dolan* has a strong moralistic undertone visible in the development of the main character, whose construction is based on a gangster figure. As a professional boxer, Jimmy is a violent person; therefore, to make his intimacy with violence socially acceptable, he constructs a disguise that endears him to the public. This allows him to achieve success. He projects an image of a simple and humble young man, willing to spend his money on his beloved mother's needs. In reality, like gangster

THE IRISH ON THE SILVER SCREEN   81

figures, he leads a double life; he spends money on his whims, lives a presumably lavish life, and feels superior to other people. However, as in the case of the Irish gangster, Jimmy Dolan's success is transient; like the gangsters—ultimately destroyed by the violence they use—Jimmy's life is shattered when he kills Magee.

Thus, the film consistently presents violence as an ultimately destructive force, capable of taking over a person's life. When Jimmy tries to redeem himself he fails, once again losing everything. His second failure may surprise viewers expecting a happy ending in which he defeats the brutal and monstrous King Cobra, wins the money, and helps the children. But this would contradict the overall anti-violence message. Jimmy cannot triumph through violence; he must reject it and humble himself in front of the police officer for whom his arrest would be a personal success and who represents society demanding condemnation for his crime; in this way, the pugilist-turned-fugitive may become a person he once called a "sucker"—someone who lives in harmony with other people, helping disinterestedly when necessary. As the film ends, he realizes that his greatest triumph was becoming such a person.

A more lighthearted, although also quite violent, look at boxing is presented in the 1935 Lloyd Bacon comedy mentioned above, *The Irish in US*, which relies on various elements of the Irish stereotype in portraying the life of the Irish American O'Hara family, consisting of three brothers—Pat, a police officer, Mike (Frank McHugh), a firefighter, and Danny (James Cagney), an aspiring boxing promoter—and their mother (Mary Gordon). The men are devoted to Ma O'Hara, but she favors Danny, turning a blind eye to his various antics, allowing him to sleep late, and scolding Pat when he tries to convince his younger brother to join the police force.

The conflict between the brothers becomes more pronounced when Danny falls in love with Pat's girlfriend, Lucille (Olivia de Havilland). Danny invites his protégé, Car-Barn Hammerschlog (Allen Jenkins), to a family dinner, to which Lucille has also been invited. Hammerschlog is conditioned to falling into a fighting rage whenever he hears a bell ring. During the dinner, the doorbell rings, and the boxer begins attacking the family members, knocking out Pat and Mike. Unable to see Lucille home, Pat trusts his brother to accompany his girlfriend. While driving her home, Danny learns that, contrary to what Pat claims, Lucille is not planning to marry him. In turn, she seems infatuated with the young boxing promoter. Their relationship develops, putting more and more strain on the brotherly love. Despite his light-spirited nature, Danny loves his brother and does not want any conflict between them. He holds his older brother in high regard and, when Pat is called a crook in his presence, he punches the slanderer, knocking him down.

Danny prepares Car-Barn for a fight, but just before the event, Hammer-schlog is knocked out by his opponent in the locker room. Left with no other choice, Danny enters the ring himself but appears no match for the champion. Encouraged by Lucille, who professes her love to Danny, Pat rushes in to help his brother, giving Danny a motivational speech and coaching him. Empow-ered by both his brothers, Danny knocks his opponent out, becoming cham-pion and proving the Irish have boxing talent in their blood.

A different look at boxing is offered by the 1936 screwball comedy, *The Milky Way*, directed by Leo McCarey. It tells the story of an Irish American milkman, Burleigh Sullivan (Harold Lloyd), who becomes the boxing world champion by accident. When Sullivan sees his sister, Mae (Helen Mack), being assaulted by the world boxing middleweight champion, Speed McFarland (William Gar-gan), and his bodyguard, Spider Schultz (Lionel Stander), he rushes to help her. In the fracas, he ducks as McFarland is knocked out by Schultz. However, as everyone believes that it was Sullivan who defeated the champion with a sin-gle punch, he becomes a boxer promoted by Gabby Sloan (Adolphe Menjou). Sullivan begins a successful boxing career, but he is unaware that the matches have been fixed, and Sloan's plan is to make him famous only to let him lose in a fight against McFarland. He becomes self-absorbed, obnoxious, and, like Jimmy Dolan, revels in his popularity.

In a development typical of a screwball comedy, before the final fight, McFarland is first kicked in the face by a colt and then hit in the head with a door. This leaves him concussed and, during the confrontation with Sullivan, he is knocked out. The comical aspect of the character construction is based on the fact that although Sullivan is an Irish American he has no talent for boxing. He is obviously less athletic than other boxers, enters the boxing arena wearing glasses, and repeatedly escapes from it before his first fight. Given the ubiquity of Irish boxers, this must have been viewed as extremely humor-ous by the audience in 1936. Although Sullivan appears somewhat clumsy, he becomes popular, and the public believes that he may be a successful boxer. This may be explained by his Irish origin, which predisposes him to become a boxer. Moreover, his boxing career changes him, and his initial amiable nature is replaced by self-centeredness. He is contrasted with McFarland, a true Irish boxer, who begins as a rowdy character who solves problems with violence and evolves into a sympathetic figure, winning Mae's affection.

A more sinister look at the career of an Irish American boxer is presented in Mark Robson's *Champion*, a drama/noir sports film telling the story of Michael "Midge" Kelly (Kirk Douglas). As the film begins, Kelly is a boxing champion entering the ring, cheered by his fans and a commentator who stresses his pop-ularity, pointing out that the audience is cheering not only their hero but also

THE IRISH ON THE SILVER SCREEN 83

his story of rising from "the depths of poverty to become the champion of the world." The film becomes retrospective, showing Midge and his brother, Connie (Arthur Kennedy), traveling through the night on a cargo train on their way to California, where they have invested in a restaurant. They are beaten and robbed by a group of thugs and thrown out of the moving boxcar. They are picked up from the road by Johnny Dune (John Danheim as John Day), a boxer, and his girlfriend, Grace (Marilyn Maxwell), who is visibly disgusted by the two brothers. Midge, in turn, considers her a stiff-upper-lip type of person. Immediately after arriving in Kansas City, they get into trouble while looking for work. Midge shows his violent nature when he assaults a business owner who calls Connie, who walks with a cane, a gimp. This prompts a boxing promoter to offer Midge $35 for a fight. Confident in his fighting prowess, Midge agrees but is quickly beaten by his opponent. Despite earning only $10, Midge is noticed by a boxing trainer, Tommy Haley (Paul Stewart), who invites him to his gym in Los Angeles. Haley sees potential in Midge, tells him he "has guts" but lacks proper technique. Midge responds with his typical contempt and dismisses the trainer as he walks away with Connie. Even after losing his first match, with his face bruised after the fight, he is overconfident.

The brothers reach California only to learn that the investment they have made was a fraud, and now, far away from home, they have nothing. Instead of owning a restaurant, they must work as waiters and dishwashers. Both of them become romantically interested in Emma (Ruth Roman), the restaurant owner's daughter, and Midge is forced into marrying her once her father learns about their romance. However, he is not interested in his bride and instead begins training with Haley, who reshapes the young man from a brawler into a pugilist. After years of struggling, Midge begins to feel that he is able to achieve success. This motivates him to push forward, training hard with Haley, winning boxing matches against local opponents, and, eventually, becoming a title contender. In the boxing ring he is fast and brutal, always focused on his opponents, his face emotionless. As Midge's social status changes, he assumes, like Jimmy Dolan, the mask of the perfect sportsman, who cares about other people and can be treated as a role model for those who want to improve their lives through hard work. When he is approached by mobsters who want him to throw a fight against Johnny Dunne, he first agrees but then decides to fight the best he can. He defeats the more experienced boxer in one round.

However, under the disguise of a sportsman, Midge is an opportunist, relentlessly exploiting the people around him. This is clearest in his relationships with women. After he defeats Dunne, he is approached by Grace, who, at one point, casually remarks that she is "expensive" and likes "pretty things." She does not hide her motives and is clearly attracted to the winner whom she may herself exploit. The woman seems to be in control at first, convincing Midge to fire his manager and friend, Haley, and instead allow Jerome Harris (Luis van Rooten), a man with ties to the mob, to lead him to the championship. However, Midge agrees not because he wants Grace to stay with him but because Harris makes it possible for him to become a champion. The pugilist's decision alienates Connie, who travels back to his mother to Chicago with Emma, whom Midge is no longer interested in. Meanwhile, his relationship with Grace becomes strained when he casually declares that he cannot marry her because he is, in fact, legally married and his wife lives in Chicago. During an emotional scene, as Grace seems distraught by the news, professing her true love for Midge, he prepares to leave and, when asked about his plans, announces that he has a date with a woman who is sophisticated, unlike Grace, who is only interested in wealth and comfort. Knowing Midge's secrets, Grace threatens to "make the biggest stink that's ever smelled in this town," but Midge grabs her arm, hurting her, and, smiling, tells her to be "a good little girl" or, otherwise, he will put her in hospital. He ends their relationship violently and considers it fair since they were exploiting each other throughout their short relationship. He does not need Grace anymore as he is now romantically involved with Palmer (Lola Albright), Jerome Harris's wife. Palmer is an artist, a sculptor, and, unlike Grace, she is sensitive and genuinely loves Midge. She convinces Midge to ask Jerome to give her a divorce. Kelly agrees to talk to his manager, who, instead, offers him a large sum of money in return for ending his relationship with Palmer. The woman is shocked when Midge agrees and leaves her, ruining their plans and proving that he never really loved her.

His career continues to develop, and, finally, he is confronted again with Johnny Dunne, who is now determined to defeat Kelly. Midge starts training for the fight, just like he did in the past. For a moment, it seems that he is determined to improve his life; he turns to Haley for help and hires him as his manager and he tries to repair his relationship with his estranged brother and Emma. However, the viewer quickly learns that Midge will never change for the better. Connie and Emma are now a couple and are planning to get married; Midge refuses to grant Emma a divorce and rapes her. This despicable use of violence against Emma completes Midge's downfall. The first time he uses violence in the film is to defend his brother; now, he uses it to hurt people he does not need anymore and destroy their lives. The flashbacks catch up with the beginning of the film and we see Midge entering the ring, cheered by the audience, with the exception of the people he has hurt and who know that, under the mask of the perfect sportsman and the embodiment of the American Dream, there is a calculating, self-absorbed man, who only understands violence.

THE IRISH ON THE SILVER SCREEN 85

Confident in his strength and abilities, Midge manages to knock his opponent down in the first round, as he did in their first fight. However, this time, Dunne gets back up, and, in the ensuing brutal exchange, he begins winning. Severely beaten, bruised, and bleeding, Midge refuses to throw in the towel; in the final round, he channels his aggression and rage into a powerful blow, knocking out Dunne and winning the fight. However, his victory is only momentary as he dies of a cerebral hemorrhage. Connie and Emma, now free from his toxic and violent influence, can begin a new life as they disappear in the darkness.

Like *The Life of Jimmy Dolan*, *The Champion* is a story of the violence that transpires outside the boxing arena and severely affects the boxer's life. However, unlike Jimmy Dolan, Midge Kelly can never escape its destructive influence. It is rooted too deeply in him, becoming the main factor determining his personality. From the very first flashback to the last scene in the film, the viewer is constantly reminded of how violent Kelly is. Seen from the perspective of the whole film, the scenes in which he defends his brother may seem like excuses to engage in brawls, which is perhaps most clearly seen in his reaction to his first boxing match in which he loses but seems fulfilled. If Jimmy Dolan is a character who must have lost his way sometime before the film begins and deserves redemption because of his later selfless actions, Midge Kelly is never portrayed as a person the viewer would like to identify with. He is the personification of destructive violence and his boxing career, portrayed with the emphasis on cold, calculated brutality and criminal connections, happens in addition to his other acts of violence.

A special variation of the Irish boxer figure was the ex-boxer, a character unable to escape from violence and its destructive nature. In *The Champ* (1931), ex-boxer Andy "Champ" Purcell (Wallace Beery) struggles with alcoholism and gambling, which cost him his career and strain his relationship with his eight-year-old son, Dink (Jackie Cooper). The film focuses on the father-son relationship, whose dynamic is guarded by the son's expectations and belief in the father, who constantly fails as a parent. The last straw comes when Purcell loses Dink's pony, Little Champ, while gambling. Realizing he will never be a good father, he decides to send the boy away to Dink's mother, Linda (Irene Rich). However, the boy runs back to his father and, with his support, Purcell begins training again with the intention of winning enough money to buy Little Champ back. He decides to take part in a boxing match against a Mexican boxer, a heavyweight champion, younger and stronger than he is. Seriously injured, Purcell refuses to surrender and, seeing his son and remembering all the times he has failed him, finds the strength to knock his opponent out. Having won the money, he is able to give the pony back to his son but succumbs to his injuries and dies, leaving Dink in pain. Although it may seem that the film presents Andy Purcell as a moral victor, he is, in fact, a person who has lost in the end. He has failed his son so many times that he loses the wider perspective of what the boy really needs; Dink does not need Little Champ; he needs Champ, his father. The joy the boy feels when he is reunited with his pony is transient and disappears when his father collapses and is taken to the locker room, where he dies. Thus, the destructive nature of violence shatters the life of not only a boxer but also his son.

A considerably more positive portrayal of an ex-boxer appears in one of the most famous American films featuring Irish characters, John Ford's *The Quiet Man* (1952). Sean Thornton (John Wayne) is an Irish immigrant who, having become a successful boxer, travels back to Ireland to reclaim a farm that belonged to his family. The film is interesting for the study of the Irish ethnotype in American cinema, as it takes place in Ireland and is filled with Irish themes and picturesque landscapes but its plot is constructed around the motif of violence. Ford, an Irish American director, born John Feeney, planned to film Maurice Walsh's short story "The Quiet Man" during the period of his more personal, Irish-themed films in the 1930s; however, it was not until the 1950s that he was able to secure funding.[45] As Joseph McBride notes, the problems with the funding may have stemmed from the fact that the main character in Walsh's 1933 short story, Shawn Kelvin, later renamed Paddy Bawn Enright, is an Irish American boxer who takes part in the Irish War of Independence as a member of IRA and the general mood of the story is less optimistic than Ford's nostalgic but mostly lighthearted film.[46]

The film thrives on characteristic aspects of the Irish stereotype. The first scene at the train station where Sean arrives and asks for directions to Innisfree presents the Irish as open and helpful, but also quarrelsome: a group of them argue, rather than simply showing Thornton the way. The Irish American does not seem to understand the mentality of the people, is ignorant of their customs, and is driven only by nostalgia induced in him by his mother's stories. Based on her recollections, he manages to find the old cottage where he was born, hidden in the picturesque landscape near the foot of a hill. He plans to buy the cottage and live a peaceful quiet life. When he arrives at Innisfree, he meets Mary Kate Danaher (Maureen O'Hara), with whom he falls in love. However, Mary Kate's brother "Red" Will Danaher (Victor McLaglen) also intends to buy the cottage. Sean and Will have their first confrontation in a pub; Will accuses Sean of taking "liberties that he shouldn't have" with his

---

45 Joseph McBride, *Searching for John Ford* (Jackson: University Press of Mississippi, 2011), 214.
46 228.

sister (in fact, Sean only greeted Mary Kate). He calls Danaher a liar, at which point the diegetic music played in the background abruptly stops, and the bartender reacts by stepping back in anticipation of a fight. Danaher attacks, but Sean refuses to fight, instead ducking and escaping. When the local priests arrive and order Will to calm down and shake hands with the American guest, he reluctantly does so, but as they are shaking hands, both men attempt to squeeze each other's hand, both of them squirming in pain.

When Thornton arrives at the cottage on a cold, windy evening he finds Mary Kate, now his neighbor, cleaning the place and preparing it for him. He kisses her, and she reacts violently, slapping him. However, as she leaves, she kisses him back before running away to her brother's house. As their relationship develops and they plan marriage, Sean's ignorance of Irish customs becomes visible again when he announces that he does not care for Mary Kate's dowry, consisting of furniture, jewelry, and money. The woman insists that the dowry be accepted as her contribution to the marriage and the representation of her value. Then, when Will refuses to agree to their marriage, Sean does not consider it a serious obstacle, considering Mary Kate's will more important than her brother's. Eventually, Will is tricked into allowing Sean to marry his sister but after the wedding, he learns of the deception and decides not to release Mary Kate's dowry. Thornton reacts with indifference and, as he attempts to leave with his wife, who is protesting against her brother's decision and her husband's lack of understanding, he is punched in the face by Danaher and knocked out.

As he lies on the floor, a flashback shows how he accidentally killed an opponent during a boxing match, explaining his aversion to violence. The retrospective scene is different in its style from the rest of the film. It begins with Sean approaching the camera, his face expressing the horror of what has just happened. In a counter-shot, his opponent's lifeless body lies in the ring. Another reverse-shot presents the referee pushing away the terrified Sean, who is taken to his corner by his trainer and his assistant. A doctor and police officers appear in the ring, and Sean's worst fears are confirmed when they put a white towel on the dead man's face. As photographers illuminate the scene with their camera flashes, a series of closeups of the faces of Sean and his entourage, the former terrified, the latter rather indifferent, emphasizes the deeply personal dimension of the portrayed event, which ends Sean's boxing career. The meaning of the scene corresponds to the representations of violence in other boxing films of the era. Violence is a destructive force and using it in sport is playing with fire. However, in the Irish context, represented by the townsfolk, it is a natural part of the world and appears to be tamed and controllable. Thus, Mary Kate cannot understand her husband's decision not to fight for her dowry. Back in the cottage, they discuss the matter, Mary Kate expressing grief over the loss of her possessions. During their conversation, Mary Kate stands inside of the cottage while Sean remains outside. They are separated by the Dutch door (or half door), with its lower part closed and the upper one open. The door symbolizes the cultural barrier between them; Sean, as an Irish American, is only able to perceive and understand a portion of his Irish heritage, and he is unwilling to even attempt to understand it all. He loves Mary Kate just as he loves Ireland: superficially and without trying to accept her customs and traditions. His inability is the result of his rejection of violence. It is only when he agrees to reclaim the dowry that she lets him into the cottage.

However, once they are both inside the cottage, the distance between them continues to grow. Mary Kate tells her husband that she is going to take care of their cottage and "wear his ring," but she will refrain from any sexual relationship as, without the dowry, she does not consider their marriage valid. Having said that, she locks herself in the bedroom, putting another door between them. This time, Sean kicks the door open and violently assaults his wife, pulling her hair and kissing her. He then lifts her up and throws her on their bed, which collapses; Mary Kate starts crying when her husband slams the door behind him. The contemporary viewer finds it difficult to accept the main character's violent treatment of his wife. Sean unleashes his violence against a person who loves him and only wants him to understand the importance of Irish traditions. This proves that, although the manslaughter he has committed gave him a degree of self-control, he is a violent man after all. What is more, Mary Kate's reaction to the event is also quite surprising, as, when she is assaulted, she returns the kiss and only starts crying when Sean has disappeared behind the door. This may be interpreted in the context of the symbolic role of the door visible in the whole sequence of scenes. When Sean violently destroys the door, he seems to have embraced the importance of the tradition; when he slams it again, she knows that he still does not understand it. The whole sequence reveals a great tension between the characters, displayed in their attitude to the violence that is also present in their relationship.

Sean's refusal to fight is further explored in the next several scenes. In the morning, the townspeople bring to the cottage Mary Kate's furniture, the only part of the dowry that Will has agreed to release. Mary Kate is overjoyed until she learns that her brother has decided to keep the money. She commands Sean to take action but he refuses, dismissing the whole issue and saying he did not marry her for the fortune she inherited. Later, they travel to the town, where they meet Will. Mary Kate pushes Sean into demanding the return of the money and, when he professes his unconditional love for her, she calls him a coward. He reacts angrily but his anger is directed against his wife, not his brother-in-law, which prompts Mary Kate to ride away in their carriage, leaving him in the town. Sean confronts Will in a pub but is unwilling to fight him. He leaves, mocked by Danaher, who promises to fight with only one hand if that would make Thornton more comfortable. Sean visits a Protestant Minister, Reverend Cyril Playfair (Arthur Shields), an ex-boxer himself, and confides in him about the reasons for his refusal to fight. Playfair, whose hobby is collecting information concerning sports, knows about Sean's past and understands his decision, stressing that it was an accident and not Sean's fault.

However, Thornton reveals that the boxer he killed, Tony Gardello, was an honest man, a husband, and a father, who always fought clean; yet, he admits, "I didn't go in there to outbox him. I went there to beat his brains out. To drive him into the canvas, to murder him. That's what I did." Obviously, he does not confess to murdering with malice aforethought but rather reveals what kind of a person he used to be: a man obsessed with violence, for whom boxing was not so much a sport as a vent for expressing his violent nature. Thus, the film expresses a similar view on violence connected with Irish boxers as earlier boxing films presented in this chapter: it is a corrupting and destructive force capable of taking control over a person. Killing Gardello in the ring made Sean re-evaluate his priorities in life, and he sees money as too unimportant to fight for; however, Playfair helps him realize that he must fight for his wife and there is no other way for him but to respect the Irish traditions and accept Danaher's challenge, urging Thornton to start training.

The next day, Mary Kate plans to escape to Dublin in an attempt to provoke Sean's reaction. As Thornton arrives at the train station, two railway workers are preparing for a fistfight after one of them has called the other one a liar, a background event reminding the viewer of the importance of violence in the Irish tradition. However, as the two men are raising their fists and are about to begin, other people around them react calmly, proving that Irish violence in Ireland is natural and acceptable. This stereotypical image of the fighting Irishman is reminiscent of the previously mentioned mass fistfight scene from *Conductor 1492*. Now understanding what he has to do, Sean rushes Mary Kate out of the train and leads her to Danaher's on foot, followed by railway workers, bystanders, and local people who join them on their way, eager to witness a fight for which they have been waiting for a long time. On their way, Sean violently pulls, jerks, and drags his wife on the grass. When she tries to punch him he ducks and kicks her. Thornton's violence towards his wife is unacceptable, but the onlookers seem to respect it and enjoy the situation, with one of the women approaching Sean with a stick and saying: "Mr. Sean! Here's a good stick to beat the lovely lady." The comment makes the whole experience even more uncomfortable for the viewer and serves as an exaggeration of the stereotypical role of violence in the life of the Irish. The crowd cheers as Sean seems to have finally embraced his violent Irish nature. Such a representation of the Irish, cheering and even exacerbating Sean's brutal behavior towards Mary Kate, must be one of the most uncomfortable and offensive displays of the violent Irish stereotype in American cinema.

When they arrive at Danaher's farm, Mary Kate can barely walk and is dragged by Sean, the two of them now followed by a large crowd of people. Sean addresses Danaher, demanding £350 of the dowry, and when Will refuses, he pushes Mary Kate, and she falls on the grass next to her brother. Angrily, Sean declares, "You can take your sister back. It's your custom, not mine." As the crowd begins laughing, Will pays Sean the money, which Thornton promptly burns. This enrages Danaher, who attempts to punch Sean. However, the ex-boxer avoids the blow and knocks his brother-in-law to the ground. Mary Kate, now sure that her husband is not a coward, but a true man who is able to use violence, declares she will go home and prepare supper and confidently walks away, to the accompaniment of cheerful non-diegetic music. This turn of events comes as a surprise to the viewer, as she ignores the violence she has just been subjected to; Sean is probably similarly confused as he is left speechless. The woman's reaction after being dragged, pushed, and kicked is also an element of the display of the stereotype. Being Irish, Mary Kate understands violence and feels more attached to Sean's violent nature than to his previous romantic behavior. Her comment indicates that, for her, things are back to normal, and she takes on what she perceives to be the wife's duty. As an Irish American, Sean does not wholly comprehend the situation but sees that, through violence towards her and towards her brother, he has saved his marriage.

However, the violent spectacle is not over, and the onlookers eagerly await the main fight of the day. Danaher stands up and punches the unsuspecting Sean, knocking him to the ground. The two men fight and a chaotic brawl breaks out among the spectators too, only to be interrupted when the town's matchmaker, Michaeleen "Óge" Flynn (Barry Fitzgerald), announces that "this is a private fight" they cannot participate in. However, Sean and Will are eager to continue and keep on exchanging blows, moving around the field and then the road to the town while doing so. The fight draws the attention of numerous other people. The Widow Sarah Tillane (Mildred Natwick), once resentful towards Will, on seeing him fighting, becomes attracted to him. Police officers seeing the two men fighting surrounded by a crowd of spectators now approaching the town appear to call for reinforcements but in fact, take a bet from their inspector. An older man receiving last rites on his deathbed, hearing the commotion, gets up and joins the crowd. An interesting comment is made by Father Lonergan

(Ward Bond), who states that it is his duty to stop the fight, but he seems so interested in it that he decides to ignore this responsibility. Finally, the two combatants are invited to a pub, as residents of a neighboring town—"thousands of them"—are expected to arrive. Inside the pub, they profess a liking for each other. However, the fight is not over as Will refuses to accept porter from Sean and splashes a glass of beer in Sean's face. In response, Sean knocks Will out, sending him through the pub, shattering the door, and into the street. Later, at night, Mary Kate waits for Sean and her brother, who come to the cottage together, both drunk and singing, sit at the table and start celebrating.

The sequence of scenes presents violence as a powerful bonding force. In America, Irish violence may be destructive, leading to downfall and suffering. However, Irish people are accustomed to it, and brutality is such an integral part of their culture that they thrive on it. Back home in Pittsburgh, violence destroyed Sean's life and led him to a serious crisis. In Ireland, it helps him repair his marriage and establish a relationship with his brother-in-law. Being intimate with Irish violence requires training in customs, traditions, and ways of taming brutality and changing it from a destructive to a creative and socially-accepted force. Sean may have considered himself a violent man who wanted peace and quiet, but it is only in his parents' homeland that he learns how to control violence. Although the fight between the two brothers-in-law is long, fierce, and brutal, they do not seem to be seriously injured, proving the non-destructive representation of Irish violence.

The film's heavy reliance on the association of the Irish with violence projects an interesting view of the differences between Irish Americans and the inhabitants of Ireland within the context of the Irish stereotype. The Irish in America are unable to fully express their culture, in which violence plays an important if not defining role. Thus, their violent character is not completely formed; it lacks social guidance, which in turn leads to the perpetuation of violence and its control over their lives. In contrast, the Irish in their own country have tamed violence, which has lost its destructive character, is restrained and fully controlled by its users, and has a bonding function.

The Quiet Man abounds in scenes that seem designed to make the viewer feel uncomfortable. In doing so, they address the affective level of the viewer's identification with Sean, who also considers the customs and traditions of the country wild and difficult to understand. What he experiences and has to do in Ireland stands in sharp contrast to the fairy-tale land of his mother's stories reflecting "the anguished, sometimes neurotic longings of the Irish diaspora."[47]

---

47   McBride, 510.

Ford's use of the stereotype is remarkable in his acknowledgment of the American view of not only his own ethnic group but also of the land of his ancestors. It is important that, while taking the viewer on a nostalgic journey to Ireland, the director addressed the most salient element of the Irish stereotype, i.e., violence. The "stage Irish" background characters may be considered offensive, while Sean's violence against his wife, although pictured as a charade serving in his struggle against the traditional perception of marriage in Ireland, is surely uncomfortable and unacceptable for the contemporary viewer. Nonetheless, the film remains John Ford's most personal film, and Sean Thornton, in many ways, may be considered the director's alter ego. This makes *The Quiet Man* a truly unique view of the violent Irish stereotype and a fascinating look at the prevalence if not ubiquity of the Irish stereotype in classical American cinema.

The popularity of the Irish boxer figure is reflected by the large number of classical films involving this character, especially when compared to the Irish police officer figure. Interestingly, three of the films analyzed or mentioned in this section were later remade. A refreshed version of *The Life of Jimmy Dolan* appeared in 1939 as *They Made Me a Criminal*; *The Milky Way* was remade in 1946 as *The Kid from Brooklyn*; and a remake of *The Champ* was released during the New Hollywood era in 1979. Despite various changes to the plots of the remakes, their main characters remained Irish. Finally, similarly to gangster figures, real-life boxers also served as inspiration for classical films; in 1942, Raoul Walsh directed *Gentleman Jim*, James Corbett's biopic with Errol Flynn in the title role. Finally, the boxing past was used as a background element in the main character construction in *Great Guy* (1936), with James Cagney as an ex-boxer engaged in an uncompromising struggle against gangsters.

2.5   *IRA Films*

The Irish War of Independence, the subsequent Civil War, and the depiction of the IRA was a sensitive subject for most filmmakers and Hollywood studios during the classical period. Nevertheless, the figure of the Irish freedom fighter appears in three Hollywood films of the era. In 1935, John Ford's *The Informer* became the first American film focusing on the IRA. Ford's film was quite personal, as his cousin, Martin Feeney was a member of IRA during The War of Independence, and the director "[...] felt a powerful allegiance to the cause of Irish nationhood."[48] Due to the controversial subject matter and downbeat mood, the film was rejected by five major studios before being accepted by RKO.[49]

---

48   McBride, 215.
49   McBride, 215.

THE IRISH ON THE SILVER SCREEN   93

The film, based on Liam O'Flaherty's novel of the same name, takes place in Dublin, Ireland, in 1920. The exposition begins with a quotation from the Bible referring to Judas's doubts after betraying Jesus, which is followed immediately by Gypo Nolan (Victor McLaglen), reading a wanted poster announcing a hunt for his former comrade, Frankie McPhillip (Wallace Ford). Gypo stares at the advertised reward of £20 before tearing the poster down and destroying it angrily. As he continues his walk through the dark and foggy streets of Dublin, he is accompanied by a diegetic patriotic song sung by a young man. When he stops, the poster, carried by the wind, smacks his leg, indicating the main premise of the film and establishing the conflict between national duty and personal gain which Nolan will have to face. Moreover, the beginning of the film establishes Gypo as a violent man. During his walk, he encounters his girlfriend, Katie Madden (Margot Grahame), a prostitute who has just been approached by one of her clients. In a fit of rage, Gypo lifts the man in the air and violently throws him to the street. Katie remarks sadly that she needs money and, as they quarrel, we see an advertisement in the window above them for £10 tickets to America.

Meanwhile, Frankie McPhillip manages to avoid a patrol of Black and Tans and meets Gypo in an eating house. When Gypo sees his comrade, low-key lighting focuses the viewer's attention on his eyes, as he is considering betraying Frankie; as the camera moves to McPhillip's well-lit face, a fragment of the wanted poster, advertising the £20 reward, is superimposed onto the character. As they discuss their present situation, Gypo reveals that he was discharged from the IRA for his refusal to execute a Black and Tan. He stresses the fact that he is now considered a traitor both by the British and the Irish. When Frankie leaves, Gypo continues to consider betrayal. He ventures again to the streets and returns to the ticket advertisement. As he gazes at the advertisement, the scene is illuminated by the light from the window, stressing Gypo's difficult situation and emphasizing the hope he sees in America. At the same time, backlit with low-key lighting, Gypo is a shadowy silhouette which he remains as he goes to the Black and Tans to betray Frankie. When McPhillip visits his mother (Una O'Connor) and sister, Mary (Heather Angel), a large group of Black and Tans arrive to arrest him. However, the IRA fighter refuses to surrender. In a shootout, he kills several Black and Tans before being killed by gunfire in front of his mother and sister.

Back at the station, Gypo reluctantly accepts his reward and leaves, his guilty feelings emphasized by shadows and the images of the wanted poster appearing in front of his eyes. Grieving over his deed, he tries to rationalize his betrayal, convincing himself that everything he did was for Katie. Repeatedly, he encounters a blind man who seems to be an oblivious witness to Gypo's betrayal as he was the only person present when the informer left the station. While participating in a wake for his friend, he drops coins, a clear allusion to Judas, and leaves hurriedly, convinced that everyone now suspects him of the betrayal. Subsequently, two IRA men approach him, and he is taken to Commandant Dan Gallagher (Preston Foster), who offers to reinstate him in the IRA if he discovers who betrayed Frankie. Gypo eagerly accepts and promptly informs Gallagher that McPhillip was sold by a tailor, Mulligan (Donald Meek), who, apparently, had a grudge against Frankie. The simple-minded and slow-witted Gypo is contrasted with the calm and cold IRA fighters, who are reluctant to believe in his hectic and chaotic claims. The only person willing to believe him is Gallagher, who orders one of his men to follow Nolan.

Getting drunk after his apparent success in convincing the IRA of his innocence, Gypo assaults a prosperous-looking man for staring at him and then a police officer who reacts to the assault. The crowd witnessing the scene reacts cheerfully, welcoming the return of "the good old Gypo." The celebration of violence is a typical element of the Irish stereotype projected in American cinema. Gypo savors the moment, proud of the attention and admiration he is receiving from the crowd. Deemed "King Gypo" for his strength, patriotic values, and violent behavior, he invites the crowd to the Fish and Chips and, craving for more veneration, he spends a considerable portion of his reward on buying everyone a meal. He then begins searching for Katie, and, lured by his friend, Terry (J. M. Kerrigan), he ends up at a high-class party, where he spends most of his reward. With Gypo present, the party becomes loud and the host worries they will attract the attention of the police. In response, Gypo threatens the remaining guests that he will "crack their skulls open" if they call the police. When one of the men accuses Gypo of lack of respect for women and punches him, Gypo seems unaffected; he casually and dismissively pushes the man, who falls into an armchair and collapses onto the floor.

Meanwhile, Dan Gallagher visits his lover, Mary McPhillip. When Mary reveals to the Commandant that Gypo was the last person Frankie met before returning to his house Nolan is put on trial before the IRA. On his way to the IRA headquarters, he fights with one of Gallagher's men and is thrown down the stairs. However, this does not seem to affect him as he playfully claims that he would take on all of the IRA men in a fight. He then makes a false statement regarding Mulligan's involvement in Frankie's death but despite his efforts, Mulligan is exonerated and let free. Confronted by Dan, Gypo tearfully confesses to betraying Frankie and is sentenced to death. However, before the sentence can be carried out, he escapes by beating up an IRA fighter. Others present declare him a monster, not a man.

THE IRISH ON THE SILVER SCREEN   95

He rushes to Katie, to whom he reveals everything he has done. Katie meets Dan and Mary and pleads for Gypo's life, but Gallagher is relentless and informs her that Gypo is a threat to the whole organization and to Ireland. He is assaulted in Katie's apartment and, after a violent struggle, he manages to beat three IRA men. However, as he is about to run free, he is shot several times by another IRA fighter waiting outside. Dying, he finds the strength to stagger into the church where Frankie's mother is praying. He confesses the betrayal to her and asks for forgiveness. As she absolves him, he approaches the altar, and, raising his hands, he joyfully exclaims, "Frankie, your mother forgives me!" before falling to the floor.

The first American representation of an IRA fighter is quite unusual in its approach to the subject matter, especially in comparison to contemporary Hollywood films about Irish republicans. Gypo is a slow-witted character and has difficulty comprehending the gravity of his situation. Unable to predict the consequences of his actions, he becomes trapped in a sense of guilt. In fact, his participation in the IRA is only a background element as he never expresses his attachment to patriotic values. The viewer is left to wonder if Gypo joined the IRA only because of his violent nature, although is expelled from the organization for refusing to execute a Black and Tan. Throughout the film, he descends into despair, driven by his sense of guilt. He is drunk for most of the runtime, and his behavior is chaotic. Easily coerced by Terry, he uncontrollably spends the money that offers him and Katie the chance to start a new life in America. As such, he is not a character the viewer might identify with. However, as noted by Daniel Moran, the press kit for *The Informer* referred to Nolan as an "'Irish giant' who, ultimately, is true to himself as well as to 'the traditions of his race,'"[50] in an attempt to win the audience's sympathy for the rather unattractive hero.

In contrast, Dan Gallagher, a secondary character, resembles IRA characters in contemporary American cinema. He is a romantic hero, torn between his personal views on Gypo and his actions and his duty towards his organization and the country. Gallagher is ruthless but he does not believe in violence for its own sake; instead, as he explains to Katie and Mary, he tries to help Gypo but chooses obedience to the decision of the IRA court. When he learns Gypo's whereabouts he immediately orders his men to kill the fugitive but he never expresses satisfaction or triumph; on the contrary, the decision weighs heavily on him. Another secondary character whose construction resembles

---

50   Daniel Moran, "Printing the Legend of John Ford's 'The Informer,'" *New Hibernia Review /
      Iris Éireannach Nua* 15, no. 4 (2011): 133.

more recent representations of IRA fighters is Frankie McPhillip, who decides to fight until the end against numerically superior British forces and dies a tragic death.

Another element introduced in the film and present in later representations of IRA is the anti-violence stance of Irish women. When Gypo is sentenced to death, Mary McPhillip objects, asking Dan Gallagher why Irish people must kill each other. She and Katie later plead unsuccessfully for Gypo's life. In Dan's view, women do not understand the nature of Irishmen's patriotic duty. They are unable to understand the gravity of the situation. However, in the end, it is Frankie's mother who holds power over the wild and brutish Gypo. When he approaches her in the church he is dying but his wounds are less important to him than the forgiveness only Mrs. McPhillip can grant. In forgiving Gypo, Frankie's mother does not contradict patriotic duty but expresses a more important anti-violent, unifying attitude that the Irish must accept in order to survive as a nation. She understands the tragedy of the man kneeling in front of her and, in her rejection of violence, a destructive force that instigated the catastrophic turn of events, she brings a conclusion to Gypo's struggles. This is something that the violent Irish men cannot do.

A year after the release of *The Informer*, H.C. Potter's drama *Beloved Enemy* premiered. The film is a retelling of the classic story of love between representatives of two conflicting sides. Denis Riordan (Brian Aherne), leader of a group of Irish freedom fighters during the War of Independence in 1921, falls in love with an English aristocrat, Helen Drummond (Merle Oberon). With the violent struggle in the background, the plot focuses on the difficult love between the characters and, despite the obvious and serious obstacles, the Romeo-and-Juliet-like story has a happy ending.

The final film that should be mentioned here is a British-American co-production, *A Terrible Beauty*, directed by an American director, Tay Garnett, which premiered in 1960. It is set in Northern Ireland during the Second World War and follows a number of narrative elements established by *The Informer*. Firstly, the main character, Dermot O'Neill, joins the IRA over his mother's objections. He is encouraged to join by his father, presenting viewers with a contrast between women's anti-violence stance and men's sense of duty. In this context, Dermot's girlfriend's strong reaction to the news of his joining the IRA is significant; Neeve Donnelly (Anne Heywood) decides to end their relationship, convinced that he will become a murderer.

Moreover, Dermot is a character who faces an impossible choice between personal convictions and his sense of duty towards the organization and his country. Obedient to his sense of patriotic duty, he must face a number of personal losses. He has to choose between the love of his girlfriend and the love

THE IRISH ON THE SILVER SCREEN   97

of his country. Then, as he takes part in IRA operations against the British, he loses his best friend, Sean (Richard Harris), who is arrested and sentenced to ten years of prison. Finally, learning that his commandant, Don McGinnis (Dan O'Herlihy), has decided to retaliate by attacking a police barracks where police officers' wives and children live, he leaves the IRA, for which he is severely beaten. Rescued by the police, he becomes an informer and has to stand trial.

Lastly, the film presents violence as a destructive force that, once released, inevitably leads to tragedy. Bella (Marianne Benet), Dermot's sister, who is in love with McGinnis, frees her brother, allowing him to be reunited with Neeve, but pays the ultimate price for her deed. As she returns home, wearing her brother's coat, she is accidentally shot by McGinnis, who has set a trap for Dermot. The film concludes with the IRA commandant's painful realization that his quest for vengeance has resulted in the murder of the woman he loved.

The representation of the IRA in the film is decidedly negative. Its members are shown as opportunists willing to collaborate with the Nazis in coordinating their attack on a British power plant. When the attack is thwarted by the police, they are ready to abandon their own comrades who are captured. Instead, they attempt to murder the police officers' families. The collaboration with Nazi Germany, the lack of unity, and the willingness to harm the innocent when unable to win a fight all hamper viewer identification with the organization's superficially patriotic ideals. Such a negative portrayal of the IRA is uncommon in American cinema and contrasts with what we see in *The Informer*, *Beloved Enemy*, and in contemporary cinema (below). It probably results from the fact that the film was a British-American co-production.

2.6   *The Irish and Union Violence*

The representation of the Irish in connection with union violence was another element of the Irish stereotype explored in classical Hollywood. However, compared to the overall representation of other types of Irish figures, in all three eras of Hollywood history, the portrayal of Irish people's role in trade unions was rather marginal. Nevertheless, two films exploring this theme are unquestionably among the best Classical Hollywood films featuring the Irish ever made.

The first is *The Valley of Decision* (1945), directed by Tay Garnett and starring Greer Garson as Mary Rafferty, a young Irish American maid, and Gregory Peck as Paul Scott, her employers' son. A sharp contrast between the social classes of the two ethnic groups is established immediately in the exposition, narrated by Paul and Mary. As the camera presents an elegant upper-class neighborhood, Paul introduces the place as the hill in Pittsburgh where his family lived in 1873. The view of the clean and peaceful neighborhood is replaced with that of a steel mill owned by Paul's father, William Scott (Donald Crisp). Industrial buildings are submerged in smoke from the mill's chimneys as Paul stresses the importance of steel for the future of America. As the camera pedestals down and pans right, it shows the roofs of a poor working-class district located just outside of the mill. Mary takes over the narration, introducing the workers: "Hundreds of families from the farms of Ireland, who had found a new home in the city of steel." The view of the poor Irish neighborhood contrasts with the sophisticated upper-class district, while the mill constitutes a point of contact between the two areas and their inhabitants. Moreover, Mary's narration stresses the out-of-place character of the Irish, who moved from Irish farms—symbolizing closeness to nature—to "the city of steel" and the civilizational progress it represents.

Mary crosses the boundary between the two worlds when she becomes a maid in the Scotts' mansion. Her new job causes problems at home: Mary's father, Pat (Lionel Barrymore) resents the Scotts for a job-related accident at the mill in which he lost the use of his legs. Mary, however, is happy to have a job. She quickly becomes fascinated with the upper-class milieu of the Scotts' mansion. Initially, some of the family members mock her Irish origins but she quickly finds her place in the house and befriends the family.

Paul performs a special role, as, like Mary, he also traverses the boundary between the two communities. He stresses the importance of the mill workers, is eager to help Mary during her first day at work, and visits Jim Brennan (Preston Foster) at the Irishman's home where they work together on the design of a new furnace for the mill. As his family are also immigrants, he understands the role of diligence and hard work in achieving success. Mary and Paul become romantically involved in each other; their relationship develops slowly but steadily over the years and is accepted by the Scotts. Interestingly, it is Mary's father who steadfastly rejects any possibility of his daughter marrying Paul.

The film is mostly about their romance but in the context of the present study, it is the social situation of the Irish and the violence they use to fight that is of interest. Although the Scotts seem to ignore the social distance between Paul and Mary, the family belongs to the favored WASP category of immigrants while the Irish are underprivileged and effectively unable to achieve rapid success in the USA. Jim Brennan organizes a strike in the mill, crippling the business, and plans to use violence. Will Scott Jr. (Dan Duryea), Paul's brother, prepares to bring in strike-breakers from Detroit. While Paul tries to persuade his father, William (Donald Crisp), that the problems can be solved by negotiation, protesters appear outside the window and throw a rock that hits Paul in the head. Paul remains adamant in his view that negotiations will help prevent further violence, blaming not the union but a group of hoodlums for attacking him.

THE IRISH ON THE SILVER SCREEN   99

Paul and his father meet the workers on the bridge at the mill, in a place established as the middle ground between the two classes and ethnic groups. The negotiations are at first successful, with William affirming the importance of the Irish workers and agreeing to all their demands. With the tense situation almost defused, Will Jr. arrives with a group of strike-breakers, causing the Irish to retaliate, incited by Pat Rafferty, who shoots William Scott and is subsequently killed by an armed guard. In the ensuing chaotic fight, Jim Brennan is also shot and killed. As a result, the two communities become separated and Mary, for whom "the blood on the bridge would never wash off," decides to end her relationship with Paul. Their separation symbolizes the realization of the incompatibility of the two worlds. Thus, the violence instigated by the Irish as an immediate reaction to the appearance of the strike-breakers is a destructive and divisive force that shatters any chance of cooperation between the Irish workers and the WASP steel mill owners.

After many years, the two communities are bridged again thanks to Paul's mother, Clarissa (Gladys Cooper), who regularly visits Mary, now a successful dressmaker. During one visit, she declares that she will bequeath her one-fifth share in the mill to Mary. Moments later, she suffers an attack of pain and collapses. Mary takes her to the Scotts' mansion, where she meets Paul, now unhappily married to Louise (Jessica Tandy), with whom he has a son. Mary decides to stay with the Scotts to help them look after Clarissa. When Mrs. Scott dies, the family gathers to discuss the future of the mill. The majority of them want to sell it with only Paul and Mary opposing the idea. Outvoted, Mary pleads with Paul's sister, Connie (Marsha Hunt), reminding her of her grandfather, an immigrant who came to the US with nothing and built a successful industry. When Mary adds that she will allow Connie to take the income from her share, as she owns "a lovely little business" and does not need more wealth, Connie decides against selling the mill, although she rejects Mary's offer. Paul ends his marriage, sending Louise away and keeping their son. He leaves with Mary.

The film contains the motifs of violence and love as two opposing forces. The tragedy flowing from an act of brutality separates the two communities, destroying any chance of coexistence, symbolized by Paul's and Mary's relationship. Significantly, the Irish are presented as more likely to oppose coexistence than the rich Scott family. This produces an interesting message about the Irish community. It is not so much that they are rejected as that they refuse to be integrated. However, this is true only of the older Irish workers. The younger ones are more willing to integrate with established American society. As a result, the image of the Irish in the film is not uniformly negative. Having tasted the upper-class milieu and using the social skills she has acquired,

Mary establishes a business, which elevates her social status. She becomes a middle-class business owner and then advances to the upper-class because of Clarissa's inheritance. While doing so, she manages to transfer her values and use them to modify the upper-class perception of the world, showing some of the Scotts that money is less important than remembering the hardships their immigrant ancestors had to survive in order to achieve success in America. While doing so, the Irish woman transforms the world around her and is able to reunite with Paul, effectively linking the two estranged social and ethnic groups.

The 1950s saw the return of the motif of union violence associated with the Irish in America. In the famous *On the Waterfront*, directed in 1954 by Elia Kazan, Terry Malloy (Marlon Brando) is an Irish American longshoreman working on the waterfront in Hoboken, New Jersey. He feels allegiance to the violent world of Irish Americans working on the Waterfront, whose leader is the union boss Johnny Friendly (Lee J. Cobb). The film brilliantly explores the reality of the Irish waterfront, which "covered a broad expanse of political and spiritual geography on both sides of the North River, the portion of the Hudson lying between the West Side of Manhattan and Hudson County, New Jersey."[51] The Irish were attracted to the area for economic reasons.[52] The community of the longshoremen and their families did not resemble the nineteenth-century ghettos where the famine generation of the Irish struggled with poverty. However, the Irish waterfront was not free from violence. According to James T. Fisher, the principle serving as the foundation of the community was a peculiar Irish ethos composed of their acceptance of and intimacy with violence, alcoholism, rejection of all authority and outsiders, and, above all, the code of silence.[53] Such are the circumstances behind Malloy's dilemma of whether or not to testify against Friendly when the latter murders another longshoreman, Joey Doyle, in order to prevent him from testifying.

Alongside the motif of violence explicitly serving as one of the identifying characteristics of the Irish, *On the Waterfront* presents a variety of themes usually associated with physical violence in the context of Irish Americans. Firstly, Terry Malloy is an ex-boxer who was compelled by his brother Charley (Rod Steiger) and Johnny Friendly to lose a fight. Secondly, the most important secondary characters include a Catholic priest, Father Barry (Karl Malden), who

---

51 James T. Fisher, *On the Irish Waterfront: The Crusader, the Movie, and the Soul of the Port of New York* (Ithaca: Cornell University Press, 2011), xi.

52 Fisher, 5.

53 Fisher, 6.

THE IRISH ON THE SILVER SCREEN   101

is based on a real-life Irish Jesuit, Father John M. Corridan.[54] Father Barry, typically of Hollywood depictions of Irish priests, performs the traditional role of
an Irishman opposing violence among his compatriots. However, he also knows
the Irish understand violence and uses it himself, punching Malloy in the face
in order to convince him not to kill Friendly. Thus, he is one of the "tough, courageous Irish priests" to which the viewers were accustomed.[55] The attachment to
family is also explored, as Charley, Friendly's right-hand man, betrays the union
boss, telling Terry to escape, and is murdered as a result. Malloy wants to avenge
his brother violently, but Father Barry, knowing that the spiral of violence leads
to the demise of everyone who uses it, convinces Malloy to exact his revenge by
testifying against Friendly. When Malloy does so, he is rejected by the community and faces unemployment as nobody on the docks wants to hire him. Terry
confronts Friendly, and their confrontation comes to blows. The former boxer
Malloy gains the upper hand but he is soon overpowered by Friendly's thugs
and severely beaten. This event marks the end of Friendly's control over the
docks, as having witnessed Friendly's defeat and his inability to defend himself without help, the longshoremen decide to follow Malloy, who manages to
stand up triumphantly despite being wounded. The scene reinforces the image
of the Irish longshoremen presented in the film as a tribe of warriors, with the
strongest man elected leader of the tribe. This is further emphasized by the fact
that women seemingly do not play a significant role in this tribal community.
However, one woman, Edie (Eva Marie Saint), starts the chain of events leading
to the overthrow of the union leader, as she is the one who, with Father Barry,
convinces Malloy to testify. Thus, Edie serves both as an example of an anti-violence Irish woman and a link between contemporary society, based on law and
order, and the violent tribal community of longshoremen.

2.7   *Irish American Combatants*

Quite early in the 1930s, the Irish started appearing on the screen as soldiers.
These representations were unambiguously positive and focused not only on
the importance of patriotic duty and personal sacrifice but also on the abil-
ity of Irish Americans to function well within the units they belonged to. The
Irish American Spud McGurke (Roscoe Karns) is among the soldiers sent to a
Philippine jungle to save a group of children during a violent coup in Henry
Hathaway's *Come On Marines!* (1934). However, the film focuses less on combat

---

54   Kenneth R. Hey, "Ambivalence as a Theme in *On the Waterfront*," in *Hollywood as Histo-
      rian: American Film in a Cultural Context*, ed. Peter C. Rollins (Lexington: University Press
      of Kentucky, n.d.), 173.

55   Fisher, *On the Irish Waterfront*, ix.

102   CHAPTER 2

and more on the soldiers' realization that the "children" they were supposed to rescue are, in fact, attractive young women. *Submarine D-1* (1937), directed by Lloyd Bacon, features two Irish American sailors, Butch Rogers (Pat O'Brien) and Sock McGillis (Wayne Morris), showing the conflict between the men over Ann Sawyer (Doris Weston), whom they meet ashore, while stressing their cooperation, camaraderie, and friendship when they are onboard their submarine. During exercises, the craft suffers a serious failure and is disabled while submerged. The two friends have to work together to save the lives of their fellow crew members as they must abandon the crippled vessel. Contrasting the behavior of the two men while on shore and on board the submarine, the film projected an important message about the Irish, who, privately, may have been rowdy and brutish, but at the same time were devoted to their duty, valiant, and cooperative when in the line of service. The message was reinforced by a very high degree of realism: the script was written by Frank Wead, a former Navy officer and there was input from Cmdr. G.W.D. Dashielle, the director's technical adviser.[56] Chief Terry A. Gardner (US Navy Retired) called the film the most realistic submarine movie ever made.[57]

In the 1940s, the Irish started appearing as combatants in various conflicts, including the World Wars. One such film is the 1940's *The Fighting 69th* (above) by William Keighley with James Cagney as Jerry Plunkett. America had not yet joined the Second World War and the film is set during the First World War. It depicts a real-life regiment with a fictionalized main character. The regiment is composed mostly of Irish American New Yorkers who distinguish themselves with patriotic bravery. The main character, however, is a cocky thug who has no respect for the tradition of his regiment or the lives of his comrades. As a result, he is guilty of the death of some of his fellow soldiers but redeems himself by sacrificing his life. At one point, one of the soldiers claims that Plunkett is "his own worst enemy" because of his unruly behavior and rejection of authority. If the unit is seen as a symbol of society, most soldiers represent well-integrated Irish Americans, who use their innate familiarity with violence, bravery, and sense of duty for the common good; Plunkett symbolizes a person who is not yet integrated and has to adjust but change is possible and even such an ill-adjusted Irishman can become a valuable member of society. Such a reading of the film may be symptomatic of the change in the perception of the Irish: no

---

56   Hal Erickson, "Submarine D-1 (1937) Synopsis," AllMovie, accessed February 6, 2021, https://www.allmovie.com/movie/submarine-d-1-v112135.

57   "What Is the Most Realistic Submarine Movie Ever Made?," U.S. Naval Institute, October 1, 2019, https://www.usni.org/magazines/proceedings/2019/october/what-most-realistic-submarine-movie-ever-made.

longer do they self-destruct because of their opposition to the governing ideas of the society in which they find themselves; instead they embrace the patriotic values which they defend with their lives.

Irish heroism at war, integration with the rest of society, and the ability to use innate devotion to duty in leading others were presented in Howard Hawks's *Air Force* (1943), telling the story of the crew of a USAF B-17D bomber christened *Mary-Ann*. The crew is led by Capt. Michael "Irish" Quincannon (John Ridgely), who commands them in spite of a personal conflict with his new aerial gunner, Sgt. Joe Winocki (John Garfield), who was expelled from flight school after an inquiry by Quincannon found him guilty of causing an accident. Quincannon is an experienced pilot who has served as an instructor; he is devoted to his crew, finding time to meet the young Private Chester's (Ray Montgomery) mother and console her when her son leaves for Honolulu with the rest of the crew. He is also a devoted husband and father, keeping a gift from his son in the cockpit as a good-luck charm. En route from San Francisco to Honolulu, he approaches Winocki and stresses the importance of every member of the crew, but the Polish American is unable to understand the message.

The unarmed bomber is diverted from Honolulu to Maui, because of the Japanese attack on Pearl Harbor on December 7, 1941. While repairing their bomber after an emergency landing they are attacked and have to escape. From the air, they witness the destruction in Pearl Harbor and Quincannon comments, "Take a good look at Pearl Harbor. Maybe this is something you'll want to remember." Thus, the Irish American voices the patriotic duty of remembering the attack on the American base. After landing in Hawaii, they head to Wake Island. While airborne, they listen to President Roosevelt addressing Congress to declare war on Japan. Quincannon locks his gaze on the gift from his son, knowing that he will need good luck in addition to his skill to return to his family. Finally, the crew heads to the Philippines, where they join the fight in their first combat assignment. When they land in Clark Field, Quincannon must inform one of the crewmembers, Sgt. Robert White (Harry Carrey), of the death of White's son, a pilot, who was killed before getting airborne.

Suddenly, the sound of the alarm forces the crew to take off and fight Japanese fighter planes who enjoy overwhelming numerical superiority. The crew fights valiantly, but the *Mary-Ann* is hit numerous times and loses her engines. Quincannon is wounded and he orders his crew to abandon the plane, planning to stay on board himself. Realizing the Captain is unable to fly the plane, Winocki disobeys the order, stays inside the plane, and does an emergency belly landing as he cannot lower the landing gear. In the field hospital, Quincannon slowly succumbs to his wounds. As he is dying, he congratulates

Winocki on his landing, asks about the plane, and, in his last moments, losing consciousness and with eyes closed, issues orders to his crew, reliving the most important thing in his life, i.e., piloting a bomber. Left without their commanding officer but inspired by his sacrifice, the crew steal parts from other damaged B-17s and repair their plane. Most importantly, the experience changes Winocki, who begins to understand the sense of sacrifice and the importance of duty over his personal issues. Later, they manage to successfully lead an assault on a Japanese fleet heading to Australia, and some *Mary-Ann* crewmembers are visible among pilots preparing for the bombardment of Tokyo.

Cpt. Quincannon, identified as an Irish American not only because of his Irish-sounding last name but also his moniker, "Irish," represents an Irishman well integrated into American society. With his bravery and devotion to duty, he leads his men and inspires them even in his death. As the film itself was clearly designed to be war propaganda, the function of the Irish American Quincannon is ideologically vital. War required a united nation and the well-integrated Irish in America may have been considered an example to other minorities, such as Polish Americans represented by Sgt. Winocki. The film was successful in delivering its message at the time of its release. Although some contemporary critics consider it "a borderline cringeworthy drama,"[58] in 1943, it was "a continuously fascinating, frequently thrilling and occasionally exalting show which leaves you limp and triumphant at the end of its two-hour ordeal."[59]

The same ideological function was performed by the dramatization of the story of the five Irish American Sullivan brothers, who served together on a light cruiser, *USS Juneau*, in the Pacific. *The Fighting Sullivans* premiered in 1944, two years after the *USS* Juneau was destroyed. The film introduces the brothers when they are baptized and returns to them at intervals of several years. As the story progresses, the viewer becomes familiar with Al (Edward Ryan), Frank (John Campbell), George (James Cardwell), Matt (John Alvin), and Joe (George Offerman), seeing them grow up, raised by their father, a railroad conductor, and their mother. They fight, climb a water tower to wave their father goodbye as he leaves for work, and promise their mother never to get in a boat again after an accident with a boat. The viewer is with the brothers when Al marries Katherine Mary (Anne Baxter), when the two have a

---

58   Christopher Lloyd, "Air Force (1943)," *The Film Yap* (blog), January 16, 2012, https://www.thefilmyap.com/movies/air-force-1943/.

59   Bosley Crowther, "' Air Force,' South Sea Thriller, Arrives at the Hollywood -- 'Immortal Sergeant' Is Newcomer at the Roxy," *The New York Times*, February 4, 1943, sec. Archives, https://www.nytimes.com/1943/02/04/archives/air-force-south-sea-thriller-arrives-at-the-hollywood-immortal.html.

baby, and when they hear about the Japanese attack on Pearl Harbor, in which their friend, Bill Bascom, serving on the USS *Arizona* is killed. The brothers enlist in the Navy, planning to avenge Bill. Eventually, they are allowed to serve together on the *USS Juneau*. During the Battle of Guadalcanal, their ship is hit and begins sinking. Al, Frank, Matt, and Joe manage to find each other in the chaos, but George is trapped below decks, in the sickbay. He tells them to leave him behind but they cannot leave one of their own. The scene is interrupted by an explosion, after which a fade to black leaves the viewer unsure about the brothers' fate—suddenly and violently detached from the characters they have accompanied for almost the entire film so far.

A Navy officer arrives at the Sullivans' house to inform the family that all five brothers have been killed. Going to work, their father stops at the water tower from which his sons would cheer him as children and salutes, commemorating his children. Having become almost a part of the family, the viewer can feel the grief of the father, who recognizes and accepts his sons' role in the war. To memorialize their death and their parents' loss, a U.S. Navy destroyer, the *USS The Sullivans*, was named after them in 1943.[60]

The film does not show the war in gory detail, nor does it excessively glorify war. Its function is to tell the American viewer about an Irish American family who made an enormous sacrifice to defend the country at a time when Ireland remained neutral and unwilling to participate in the conflict. Thus, the intimate portrayal of the family, although with the focus on their Irishness visible from the very first scenes of Catholic baptism, is not presented in terms of a hetero-image but projects American rather than Irish values as they were perceived at the time.

An ideologically similar function was performed by Lt. J. G. "Rusty" Ryan (John Wayne) in John Ford's 1945 war film, *They Were Expendable*, which was also based on real events from World War II. Ryan is the executive officer in a US Navy PT boat squadron. He is eager to fight and wants to prove himself in combat. As the command is unconvinced of the PT boats' usefulness in combat, the squadron is given only non-combat assignments. This frustrates the squadron members and Ryan writes a transfer request. Soon, the boats and their crews prove their capabilities when they destroy a Japanese cruiser and are given more demanding assignments, such as evacuating General Douglas MacArthur and his family from Corregidor. Finally, Ryan and his friend and commanding officer, Lt. John Brickley (Robert Montgomery), become trainers for a new squadron of PT boats.

---

60   Lawrence H. Suid, *Sailing on the Silver Screen: Hollywood and the U.S. Navy* (Annapolis, Md: Naval Institute Press, 1996), 72.

106   CHAPTER 2

Following World War II, Irish Americans were still pictured in the context of their bravery during the conflict. Some films were inspired by real events, such as W. A. Wellman's *Island in the Sky* (1953), in which John Wayne plays Captain Dooley, a military pilot who struggles to keep his crew alive when their transport plane crashes in the Canadian wilderness. Other films were biographical productions devoted to real-life Irish American soldiers. John Ford's *The Long Gray Line*, in which Tyrone Power portrays Martin Maher, an Irish immigrant, who works at West Point as a civilian employee and enlists to improve his financial position. He becomes an instructor and teaches his students tradition, but also boxing. Eventually, his cadets include, among many others, George Patton and Dwight D. Eisenhower. Maher earns their respect and plays a role in their formation as officers. The film ends with a parade organized in his honor at West Point as he is retiring. Hearing unmistakably Irish music accompanying the parade, the viewer acknowledges not only the role of a single Irish immigrant in the development of national heroes but also recognizes the Irish effort in building American society.

The most famous example of a post-war film featuring a real-life Irish American combatant is undoubtedly *To Hell and Back* (1955), directed by Jesse Hibbs, and starring Audie Murphy—considered the most famous American soldier[61]—as himself in the story of his struggle during World War II. The film might be considered an extreme case of a biographical production because it presented Murphy's own exploits as a soldier during the war and was based on his own memoir. Initially, the actor strongly opposed the idea of filming his autobiography because he did not wish to relive the trauma and he knew the film would not represent it properly.[62] During the war, Hollywood war films served an obvious propaganda purpose; after the war, they still tended to glorify the conflict, omitting atrocities experienced by soldiers daily, toning down violence, and adhering to the Production Code, even though there were no direct guidelines in it regarding the portrayal of violence.[63] For a veteran, aware of the ideological issues involved in the way Hollywood tended to portray the war, the prospect of allowing such a film to be produced was unacceptable. When Murphy finally agreed, he made it a condition that the film would

---

61   Joanne Mattern, *Audie Murphy* (Hockessin, Del: Mitchell Lane Publishers, Inc., 2015), 25.
62   Bob Larkins and Boyd Magers, *The Films of Audie Murphy* (Jefferson, N.C.; London: McFarland, 2009), 89.
63   Jeanine Basinger, "Translating War: The Combat Film Genre and Saving Private Ryan," *Perspectives on History*, October 1, 1998, n. pag., https://www.historians.org/publications-and-directories/perspectives-on-history/october-1998/translating-war-the-combat-film-genre-and-saving-private-ryan.

present him, not at the center of attention, but rather as a member of a team of soldiers.[64] He also initially objected to the idea of starring as himself, recommending Tony Curtis, but finally agreed and, apart from appearing in the film, was also an adviser to the director.[65]

The conditions Murphy set before agreeing to film his autobiography could be seen as an extension of the way he perceived himself: not as a hero by himself, but as a member of a group of heroic men. This emphasized the purpose of the representations of Irish American combatants as valuable members of society—people who understood their place within its structures and were willing to defend it. The film itself focused on the relationship between the soldiers, showing Murphy in the context of the unit, not the other way round. Murphy's Irish bravery and intimacy with violence are emphasized in the climactic scene portraying his famous feat of courage. When his company is forced to retreat, Murphy stays behind as an artillery spotter. Then, as the Germans advance, threatening his company, he jumps on a damaged tank, mans the vehicle's machine gun, and directs fire at the enemy, disregarding the fact that the burning tank may explode. He is wounded, but this does not stop him from thwarting the German. From the point of view of the viewer, Murphy's action proves not only his incredible courage but a readiness to sacrifice his life for his men.

Rather than diminish Murphy's earlier accomplishments, the feat—portrayed almost at the end of the film—appears as a logical result of his previous actions and his most important feature of character: he never gives up. He is the eldest son among nine children born in a poor family of Texas sharecroppers and raised by a single mother. Obliged to help his mother, he starts working while still very young, and, following the Japanese attack on Pearl Harbor, he sees enlisting as the means of supporting himself. Rejected by the US Marine Corps, the Navy, and the newly formed paratroopers, he joins the regular infantry and is sent to North Africa. He is soon promoted to corporal, and then, when he displays his leadership skills, he becomes a sergeant, and, finally, he receives an officer's commission, becoming a second lieutenant.

Murphy's climb through the ranks, from a recruit rejected by the more prestigious units, through an enlisted infantryman to an officer takes place in the context of a multiethnic company, including representatives of the old privileged WASPs, another Irish American, a Native American, an Italian American and a Polish immigrant. Therefore, his military progress reflects the changes in the position of the Irish within multicultural American society. The Irish, once

---

64   Larkins and Magers, *The Films of Audie Murphy*, 89.
65   Larkins and Magers, 89.

108   CHAPTER 2

rejected, become recognized and valuable members of society and surpass other ethnic groups in social mobility. Their rise in society does not deprive them of their Irish closeness to violence, which non-Irish Americans might well consider madness. However, in times of turmoil, the line between such madness and heroism is blurred.

•••

The Irish entered American cinema as violent brawlers engaged in senseless fighting and, therefore, rejected by the audience. With the development of the cinema, they were presented in more developed roles, but violence remained a constant feature of their representation. With the examples of such early films as *Little Annie Rooney* and *Conductor 1492* in mind, it would be unfair to say that all their early representations were negative. Admittedly, the characters portrayed in these films had problems but they were able to overcome them and become valuable members of society. Those early stories may be seen as a foreshadowing of what would become of the Irish in America and how they would be represented in the cinema. As violence was a stereotypical constant, the characters were often presented in the context of their attitude to aggression. When these types of characters are seen as a continuum, a steady progression from ruthless gangster to a heroic soldier can be drawn.

The presence of Irish gangsters in early American films was a reflection of how Irish men were perceived. The Irish gangster in America was ruthless, selfish, and extremely brutal, also towards women. Such a man used violence to satisfy his personal needs and considered honest work unrewarding. However, gangsters were not the only Irish characters present on the screen. They were opposed by Irish police officers and priests, who understood the significance of community and their role in building American society. It is significant that police officers were rarely main characters, and thus it was the Irish priest who was more likely to successfully oppose an Irish gangster. This was because the Irish gangster, because of his violent tendencies, was beyond saving, so the priest's work focused on improving the prospects of youth. An Irish police officer in America, despite his sense of duty, was only able to stop the individual gangster, not prevent violence. An exception here would be Officer Pat O'Day in *East Side Kids*, but as already noted, the construction of this character was based on Father Jerry Connolly from *Angels With Dirty Faces*. Regardless of their function in the plot, most Irish characters, although essentially Irish American, exist outside mainstream society; the gangsters are obviously social rejects but the priests and the police officers, concentrating on work within their multiethnic neighborhoods, also do not seem to fully belong to American society and, therefore, should be perceived in terms of a hetero-image, as outsiders, rather than as a part of the rich and complex auto-image of the American society.

The representation of the Irish in the context of boxing, a signature Irish discipline in the early 20th century, was initially similar to the representation of gangsters. The Irish boxer was, at first, selfish, self-centered, and quick to use violence as a way to satisfy his desire for success. This selfish Irish violence was, again, destructive and led to the downfall of the character. However, unlike gangsters, boxers were able to redeem themselves and become valuable members of society. Following World War II, in which Irish Americans proved themselves as some of the most important national heroes, Sean Thornton in *The Quiet Man* was no longer an outsider, but rather, despite his violent past, a full-fledged Irish American, whose attachment to Irish culture was only superficial and based on stories he heard from his parents as a child. This is contrasted with the hetero-image of the Irish in Ireland, including Irish republicans from the early days of Irish freedom and the conflict in Northern Ireland: still relying on violence as the immediate and readily available reaction to everyday situations.

Finally, films portraying Irish Americans as combatants, especially in World War II, directly or indirectly, featured them as valuable members of society. This trend was also visible in non-violent genres made during the war, in which the Irish were portrayed as heroes Americans needed. In 1942, James Cagney, whose earlier roles included Irish gangsters, starred as George Michael Cohan in the Oscar-winning biopic *Yankee Doodle Dandy*. The Irish hero of American popular culture was played by the actor who had lent his appearance to some of the most notorious cinematic gangsters of the era. In both violent war films and non-violent genres, the Irish sense of duty, their devotion, and their ability to sacrifice themselves for the greater good were features that made them not only accepted by society but also allowed them to rise above other ethnic groups as leaders. However, this does not mean that the Irish were no longer presented in the context of violence. On the contrary, their violence became a feature society needed as a self-defense mechanism. In this form, it entered New Hollywood.

CHAPTER 3

The Irish in New Hollywood

The sixties were a time of a profound cultural transformation in America. Ethnic minorities began to cherish the liberty which, up to that moment, had been limited for them. The proponents of the sexual revolution challenged Americans' attitudes towards issues such as sexual expression, the sexuality of women, and homosexuality. For the Irish in America, the most profound occurrence was the election of John F. Kennedy, a Roman Catholic Irish American, to the office of President of the U.S. Perhaps for the first time in the history of the United States, the world of culture, with all its opportunities, seemed to belong to the young: the post-war Baby Boomers. These changes also affected American cinema, which, led by a younger generation of filmmakers, entered the era now referred to as the New Hollywood.

In *Easy Riders, Raging Bulls*, a book on this shift in Hollywood, Peter Biskind describes the American counterculture of the sixties and the people who epitomized it in terms of an earthquake that shattered the existing order. According to Biskind, this earthquake changed the paradigm of American cinema. Red-Scare-induced themes were replaced and filmmakers searched for new formal ways of expression.[1] This does not mean that Classical Hollywood was deprived of creativity. On the contrary, filmmakers such as John Ford, David Lean, and Robert Wise, created masterpieces long before the dramatic shift described by Biskind. However, when it comes to film production, an exciting change occurred. During the Golden Age of Hollywood, also known as the classical film era, which began in the 1920s, film production was dominated by large studios, with only a small portion of the industry left for independent filmmakers. The decline of the studio system left a massive void which was quickly filled by young, ambitious, and independent directors and actors. Thus, as Paul Monaco puts it, the trend was reversed, and independent filmmakers contributed to two-thirds of the films produced in 1960.[2]

Although the shift from the classical cinema to the period of greater individuality was noted as early as the end of the 1950s, it is 1967 that is generally accepted as the beginning of New Hollywood. The premiere of *Bonnie and Clyde* in that year is regarded as the onset of the new era, with *Time* announcing

---

1 Peter Biskind, *Easy Riders Raging Bulls: How the Sex-Drugs-And Rock 'N Roll Generation Saved Hollywood* (New York: Simon and Schuster, 2011), 14.
2 Paul Monaco, *The Sixties, 1960–1969* (New York: University of California Press, 2003), 24.

© KONINKLIJKE BRILL NV, LEIDEN, 2021 | DOI:10.1163/9789004467972_005

the "New Cinema: Violence... Sex... Art" and calling the film an indication of an ongoing Hollywood renaissance.[3] For the critics cited here, the film's most important strength was the performance of Faye Dunaway and Warren Beatty. It was acknowledged that their superb acting was possible because of director Arthur Penn's "ability to extract inspired performances from actors."[4] Directors were seen as the driving force behind the production of films.

Whereas the directors of classical cinema frequently saw themselves as "nothing more than hired help (over-) paid to manufacture entertainment, storytellers who shunned self-conscious style lest it interfere with the business at hand,"[5] New Hollywood directors, such as Stanley Kubrick and Woody Allen, led the changes. They considered themselves and were regarded as artists and auteurs who shaped their films from the beginning until the closing credits. Moreover, the filmmakers working on a given motion picture were no longer all employed by a studio on a full-time basis. They were independent artists hired by the studio on the basis of negotiated contracts. The independence from studios gave some filmmakers, but mostly directors, the possibility to express their views and ideas on the cinema screen. However, this certainly does not mean that the classics should be considered less free in their creative expression and, therefore, inferior to the New Hollywood directors. Arguably, some Classical Hollywood directors are still the best American cinema has to offer.

The fact that the filmmakers were independent meant it was nearly impossible to point to any standard narrative features in New Hollywood productions. However, in his *Hollywood Incoherent: Narration in Seventies Cinema*, Todd Berliner attempts to formulate the characteristic features of narration in New Hollywood. Firstly, as Berliner says: "Seventies films show a perverse tendency to integrate, in incidental ways, narrative and stylistic devices counterproductive to the films' overt and essential narrative purposes."[6] By this, he means the inclusion in films of incidental situations disrupting the chain of events presented in the narration. For instance, in Don Siegel's *Dirty Harry*, the main character suddenly starts spying on a naked woman when he is supposed to be on the lookout for a dangerous criminal. Together with the main character, the camera focuses on the woman, forgetting about the main plot.

---

3 Peter Krämer, *The New Hollywood: From Bonnie And Clyde To Star Wars* (London: Wallflower Press, 2005), 1.

4 Ephraim Katz, *The Film Encyclopedia* (New York: HarperCollins, 2005), 1072.

5 Biskind, *Easy Riders Raging Bulls*, 15.

6 Todd Berliner, *Hollywood Incoherent: Narration in Seventies Cinema* (Austin: University of Texas Press, 2010), 51.

112   CHAPTER 3

This is not to be confused with lack of causality: according to David Bordwell, it is through the principles of causality that the plots retain their coherence.[7] Thus, if the plot is coherent overall, and the viewer can comprehend it, the causality is not disturbed by chance events. Secondly, Berliner writes, New Hollywood was situated between classical American films and the art cinema of Europe and Asia in terms of filmmaking. The cinema of the 1970s, he continues, retained the narrative structure of classical films while employing some of the narrative devices characteristic of art cinema.[8] Another feature of the New Hollywood cinema, particularly of the 1970s, lies in its choice of characters. Starting with the first New Hollywood film, i.e., *Bonnie and Clyde*, the directors constructed sometimes morally ambiguous or even overtly negative characters. In this way, such films induced "spectator responses more uncertain and discomforting than those of more typical Hollywood cinema."[9] What is more, New Hollywood was focused on, as Berliner puts it, irresolution.[10] It was common to leave loose ends in the plot, and in some cases even the main plot remained unresolved. When it comes to the films studied here, the best example of an unresolved plot is the final scene of *The French Connection*, discussed below. Finally, the cinema of the 1970s preferred the use of digressions over the moments of excitement or suspense.[11]

Of the features enumerated by Berliner, the most relevant for this study is the presence of morally ambiguous characters. It was now possible to have violent Irish characters appear as positive heroes, acceptable because they actively protected society. What is more, they were often contrasted with non-violent secondary characters whose passivity was an obstacle in the main character's struggle against a violent villain.

The end of New Hollywood was marked by the appearance of two blockbusters, Steven Spielberg's *Jaws* (1975) and George Lucas's *Star Wars* (1977), which started a shift of Hollywood's interest from the art of auteurism to box office success. This was combined with the extravagant demands of some directors for total control over film production and the budget, which in some cases led to spectacular disasters. The most famous example is Michael Cimino, director of the famous *Deer Hunter* (1978), who went so far over budget on *Heaven's Gate* that the film flopped, leading to the sale of United Artists Studio.[12] *Heaven's*

---

7   David Bordwell, *The Way Hollywood Tells It: Story And Style in Modern Movies* (Berkeley: University of California Press, 2006), 100.

8   *Hollywood Incoherent*, 51.

9   Berliner, 51.

10   Berliner, 52.

11   Berliner, 52.

12   Gordon Gray, *Cinema: A Visual Anthropology* (Oxford; New York: Berg, 2010), 28.

THE IRISH IN NEW HOLLYWOOD   113

Gate and Francis Ford Coppola's *One from the Heart* (1982), also a similar financial disaster, are regarded as marking the end of the New Hollywood era.

1   Don Siegel's Dan Madigan and Harry Callahan

In 1968, Don Siegel directed *Madigan*, a thriller in which Richard Widmark
portrays the eponymous detective Daniel Madigan, working for the New York
Police Department. Siegel, recognized as one of the real American *auteurs*
"with a consistent style and point of view,"[13] was a director known mainly for
thrillers, such as *Invasion of the Body Snatchers* (1956), widely considered an
allegory of the Cold War with the alien-controlled "pod-people" epitomizing
Americans lured by communism.[14] In *Madigan*, Siegel presented the story of
an Irish American police officer.

Madigan and his Italian partner, Rocco Bonaro (Harry Guardino) get into
trouble trying to arrest Barney Benesch (Steve Ihnat): they are distracted by
Benesch's naked girlfriend, allowing the criminal to take their guns. Because
Benesch is wanted for murder, their superior (Henry Fonda) gives them seven-
ty-two hours to catch him. Despite facing severe consequences, Madigan does
not concentrate only on his assignment, instead trying to reconcile his work
with his private life. He spends some time with his wife Julia (Inger Stevens),
who is frustrated because of his dangerous job, and with his mistress Jonesy
(Sheree North). In the end, Madigan and Bonaro track down Benesch, but not
before the criminal kills two police officers with Madigan's gun. The two detectives manage to corner Benesch in Spanish Harlem, where Madigan is mortally
wounded before Bonaro kills Benesch.

Within the context of this study, *Madigan* may be seen as an exploration of
the motif of the impossible choice between one's family and duty. This motif
became very common in the representation of Irish Americans in New Hollywood films. Madigan is unable to focus on his duty even under the pressing
circumstances. There is no way to live simultaneously in a world of violence
and the world of social order represented by family. Madigan's wife is frustrated; thus, his family suffers but when he tries to be by her side, he neglects
his duty. The impossibility of living in two opposing realities leads inevitably
to his death.

The role of women in the film is limited to distractions for the main character. Madigan's gun is stolen because he is looking at Benesch's girlfriend. He

---

13   Katz, *The Film Encyclopedia*, 1257.
14   Katz, 1257.

neglects his duty because of his wife. Finally, the fact that he has a mistress only adds to the distance between Madigan and his wife and his duty as a police officer. This is only the first example of the further limitation of the representation of Irish American women that had already started in the classical period.

Madigan may be seen as Siegel's first attempt to explore the figure of the Irish cop, as he reused some of the central motifs from the film in *Dirty Harry* (1971). Apart from being a commercial success, the movie set the standards for the genre. Clint Eastwood's portrayal of the eponymous character, created by Harry Julian Fink and Rita M. Fink,[15] is a milestone in crime thrillers and had an enormous impact on popular culture in general.

Although *Dirty Harry* has been studied from various perspectives as the embodiment of an American hero, its main character has never been analyzed in the context of his ethnicity. This is mainly because the film does not focus on Callahan's biography, showing only traces of the character's personal life before the film takes place. However, he is almost universally considered an Irish American, despite only vague references to his national identity in the film. In *Dirty Harry*, it is said that he comes from Potrero Hill, an area in San Francisco known for its large Irish American population.[16] Moreover, Callahan's surname indicates that he must be, at least partly, of Irish origin. The fact that Callahan never refers to himself as being Irish American stems from the characteristics of the period in which the film was produced and the function which he performs. The surname Callahan is an anglicized variant[17] of the Irish surname Ó *Ceallacháin*, which comes from the Irish word *caellach*, meaning "strife."[18] From this perspective, it is curious that the creators of the character did not take an interest in his ethnic identity, but instead used the stereotype of an Irish American police officer and attributed violent behavior to him. This being so, the Irish surname serves as a label, i.e., Irish American, with which violence is readily associated. Such is the automatic activation of a stereotype. Unfortunately, there is no information concerning the circumstances in which the character of Harry Callahan was created. However, his surname suggests that while envisaging a harsh, brutal cop whose intimacy with violence is unquestionable, his creators automatically associated the intimacy with violence with the Irish nationality, using the well-established Irish

---

15   Marc Eliot, *American Rebel: The Life of Clint Eastwood* (New York: Crown/Archetype, 2009), 353.

16   Potrero Hill Archives Project. and Peter Linenthal, *San Francisco's Potrero Hill* (Charleston SC: Arcadia, 2005).

17   Other variants include "Callaghan" and "O'Callaghan."

18   E. Seary and William Kirwin, *Family Names of the Island of Newfoundland* (St. John's, Nfld: McGill-Queen's Press - MQUP, 1998), 78.

THE IRISH IN NEW HOLLYWOOD   115

ethnotype. Thus, the character's development throughout the first film and its sequels, which were not directed by Siegel, provides a fascinating insight into the evolution of the perception of violence associated with the Irish in America. Within the broader context of the whole theme of the violent Irish police officer, it also lays the foundations for the development of such characters in future films.

While Dan Madigan was harsh and sturdy, his brutality was limited to certain occasions. For Harry Callahan, the use of violence seems to be natural, as he considers brutality the only useful tool in his profession. This difference in Don Siegel's view of violence appears to be associated with the characteristics of the decade in which *Dirty Harry* was made. The 1970s are often considered "the era of the beginning of the crime boom in America,"[19] which may be attributed to several internal factors, such as the Watergate crisis which led to serious public distrust in the government,[20] combined with externals ones, such as the peak of the Cold War with the Soviet Union and the 1970s recession. In these circumstances, Americans felt a need for protection; before the 1970s, the police in the U.S. were rather unpopular because police officers were seen as too brutal.[21] However, *Dirty Harry* was released "in the wake of some of the most tumultuous events in U.S. history," [22] when people started turning to the police again.

In this difficult period, audiences responded to an old type of hero: an uncompromising enforcer of the law who fought crime. Callahan's similarity to the old Wild West gunslingers was palpable and, therefore, he is sometimes described as an urban Western hero.[23] America may not have needed a hero of Irish origin, but it was logical, as it was a direct continuation of the general perception of the Irish in America. Who could defend Americans from increasingly violent criminals better than an Irish American, for whom violence was a well-established part of his ethos, cultivated in American cinema since its early days?

The film begins with a reference to the apparent atmosphere of insecurity characteristic of the period. The viewer is presented with a shot of a wall on

---

19   Shahid M. Shahidullah, *Crime Policy in America: Laws, Institutions, and Programs* (Laham: University Press of America, 2008), 12.

20   Julian Zelizer, "Opinion: How Nixon's Scandal Still Hurts America - CNN.Com," *CNN.Com*, July 7, 2014, http://edition.cnn.com/2014/07/07/opinion/zelizer-watergate-politics/.

21   Nicole Rafter, *Shots in the Mirror: Crime Films and Society* (Oxford; New York: Oxford University Press, USA, 2000), 75.

22   Rafter, 75.

23   Brian Baker, *Masculinity in Fiction and Film: Representing Men in Popular Genres, 1945–2000* (London: Continuum International Publishing Group, 2006), 99.

which are inscribed the names of San Francisco police officers with dates next to their names and a dedication: "In tribute to the Police Officers of San Francisco who gave their lives in the line of duty." The surnames suggest the police officers belonged to various national minorities in the USA, which emphasizes the universal need to uphold law and order in the city. What is more, this first shot establishes the main character as one of those who risk their lives for the safety of other citizens in the violent city of San Francisco. The next scene shows, through crosshairs, a young woman swimming in a rooftop pool. Were it not for crosshairs, the woman would seem idyllically detached from the violent world in the city streets below. However, her safety is illusory, as the sniper whose point of view we share destroys this illusion and the equilibrium with one shot. The murderer, referring to himself as Scorpio, threatens to kill again, unless the city pays him a ransom. This is where the main character, Inspector Callahan, appears.

Callahan is presented from the first as a loner who does not need other people's company. His utterances are short, precise; he does not feel the need to engage in small talk. His nickname "Dirty Harry" is also meaningful. Throughout the film, various explanations are advanced for his name. The most obvious one is that "dirty" somehow relates to "violent." Throughout the film, Harry is criticized for being excessively brutal. Another explanation is that Harry hates everybody, with the suggestion that "everybody" refers to minorities. This projects a powerfully negative image of Harry, who is despised by his fellow officers because of this hatred, understood as a stigma, or dirt that cannot be tolerated. The final explanation is given by Harry himself: he takes "every dirty job that comes along." Curiously, all these explanations fit some of the stereotypes associated with the Irish in America. Firstly, they were considered violent and brutal. Secondly, they were thought to be opposed to other national minorities. Finally, they were treated as a cheap workforce and given the worst jobs possible. By means of his nickname and his surname, Harry is established as a stereotypical Irish American who, nevertheless, performs a vital role in 1970s America.

Another motif explored in *Dirty Harry*, almost ubiquitous when it comes to the portrayal of Irish characters in American cinema, is the main character's rejection of authority. Callahan is shown in sharp opposition to people representing authority over the city, such as the Mayor, the Chief of Police, and Harry's lieutenant. When asked about the investigation's progress, Callahan replies: "Well, for the past three-quarters of an hour, I've been sitting on my ass in your outer office waiting on you." Callahan evidently has no patience with bureaucracy and believes the Mayor is wasting time he could spend pursuing Scorpio. Nevertheless, his comment is calm, and he does not use any

THE IRISH IN NEW HOLLYWOOD 117

unnecessary gestures. He seems to ignore the conversation and speaks only when provoked to comment on something the others present in the office have said. Harry is then criticized for the violent behavior he exhibited in one of his previous assignments.

> The Mayor: "Callahan... I don't want any more trouble like you had last year in the Fillmore district. You understand? That's my policy."
> Harry Callahan: "Yeah, well, when an adult male is chasing a female with intent to commit rape, I shoot the bastard that's my policy."
> The Mayor: "Intent? How'd you establish that?"
> Harry Callahan: "When a naked man is chasing a woman through a dark alley with a butcher knife and a hard-on, I figure he isn't out collecting for the Red Cross."

The conversation, once again, establishes Harry Callahan as a violent police officer. However, it also provides an insight into the way he understands the law—as a means to legitimize brutality in order to protect the innocent against those who use unacceptable, illegitimate violence. What is more, for Callahan, the mere intention to commit a crime is sufficient reason for a person to be punished. This uncompromising view of the law—as not only violent retribution but also as violent crime prevention—seems to be a drastic response to the extreme violence and injustice of the period.

The following scene is among the most famous in American cinema. Harry enters a diner and orders a hot-dog. Sitting at the bar, he notices a car parked in front of the bank. Sensing immediately that a bank robbery is in progress, he asks the owner of the diner to call the police. When he starts to eat, he hears a bank alarm going off, followed by a shot. He casually takes his gun—a Magnum .44 revolver—and walks out of the diner shooting and wounding one of the robbers. Next, he shoots and kills the driver of the robbers' getaway car, and finally, he kills the third robber, ignoring the fact that he is wounded. He approaches the robber he has wounded and, seeing the man reaching for his shotgun, Callahan delivers one of his famous monologues:

"I know what you're thinking. "Did he fire six shots or only five?" Well, to tell you the truth, in all this excitement I kind of lost track myself. But being as this is a .44 Magnum, the most powerful handgun in the world, and would blow your head clean off, you've got to ask yourself one question: Do I feel lucky? Well, do ya, punk?"

The robber leaves the shotgun be and asks Callahan to tell him if he had any shots left. Callahan aims at him and pulls the trigger—the chamber is empty. He walks away, laughing, leaving the terrified criminal lying on the pavement.

This scene can be interpreted in various ways. It may show Callahan is a gambler if one assumes that he did not know if there was a shot left or not. On the other hand, it may present him as a professional who knows exactly how many bullets he has fired and remains calm though he knows he is effectively unarmed while the criminal has a shotgun within reach. His weapon is a symbol of his strength while also reminiscent of the wild west hero's revolver. Also, the repetition of the monologue by Harry at the end of the film may suggest that it is not the first time he has ever said it.

Harry seems not to care at all about any injuries he sustains. He is more concerned with the fact that the doctor wants to cut his trousers to treat the wound on his thigh. It may indicate that Callahan accepts violence even when he is its victim. Another scene supporting this view takes place when Harry is mistaken for a pervert and beaten by a group of angry residents of a building in which he was looking for the suspect. When Harry's partner arrives to save him and threatens to arrest the angry crowd, Harry defends them. He understands the situation and accepts violence as a way of reducing the danger to society. If he is perceived as a threat, in his opinion, the residents are entitled to resort to violence.

The scenes described above are parts of the secondary plot, which shows Harry Callahan as a police officer who is always on duty. These involve, for instance, cooperating with firefighters in rescuing a man threatening suicide by jumping from the roof of a building. Harry is taken to the roof, where he first frightens and then knocks out the man who wants to jump. Once again, he uses violence for a greater good.

Another crucial aspect of the film is the story of Harry's partners. At the beginning of the film, Harry mentions some of them—Fanducci, who was killed, Dietrich, who was wounded, and DiGiorgio, who is in hospital. He is then assigned another partner, a rookie police officer Chico Gonzalez, who is also an educated man with teaching credentials. The fact that all these partners bear surnames which denote their ethnic background as Italian, German, and Hispanic Americans, is crucial for the following reason: all these partners are either killed or wounded in the line of duty. Harry cannot find a partner who is his equal: he is the only one able to survive in the city's violent environment. The Irish American is presented as if violence has always been his natural environment. The motif of Harry's partners recurs in all the sequels.

The main plot of the film follows Harry in his pursuit of Scorpio. The murderer informs the police that unless his demands are met, he will choose an African American (referred to with a racial slur in the film) or a Catholic priest. Either way, in this move, Scorpio targets minorities. The choice of a Catholic priest may be significant because of Callahan's Irish origin, though he does not

THE IRISH IN NEW HOLLYWOOD   119

seem to be a religious person. When Callahan and Gonzalez thwart the killer's attempt to shoot a priest who volunteers to be bait, Scorpio kidnaps a fourteen-year-old girl whom he then rapes and buries alive. These despicable acts represent the extremes to which crime and a criminal may go, and establish Scorpio as the most depraved character in the film. He destroys the innocence of the fourteen-year-old and condemns her to even more suffering. It also puts him in control of the course of events, as the Mayor and the Chief of Police decide to meet Scorpio's demands and send Harry with the ransom. Harry is supposed to go alone, so he decides to take a balisong (a butterfly knife, commonly associated with criminals) with him. His lieutenant makes clear his disgust that a police officer knows how to use such a weapon. This, again, places Callahan somewhere in-between what is accepted (the law and order, tradition, American values) and what is not (violence, progress, minority-related problems). However, Harry decides to use his partner as a backup when he is instructed to run from one public phone to another, as he has to answer each phone at a given time and follow Scorpio's instructions.

Finally, determined to save the kidnapped girl, Callahan arrives at the park where Scorpio awaits. The scene is symbolic, as Harry has to surrender his gun while standing under a giant sculpture of a cross. This makes him vulnerable, and the killer gains the upper hand as he beats Callahan, who falls under the cross. The murderer tells him that he is going to let the girl suffocate to death, even though he has been given the ransom. Callahan fails as a savior and, as he is about to become Scorpio's next victim, Gonzalez arrives and saves his partner, sacrificing himself for Harry. Scorpio escapes, wounded. Although severely beaten, Callahan goes back to work and tracks Scorpio down. The killer escapes but Callahan corners him on a football field. There, Harry tortures him by stepping on his wounded leg. The killer screams in pain and finally tells Callahan where the kidnapped girl is buried. This infamous scene divided audiences and critics alike. In his *Masculinity in Fiction and Film: Representing Men in Popular Genres, 1945–2000*, Brian Baker points to the scene's ability to compel the viewer to "validate the act of compulsion by a further act of witness."[24] Viewers may justify Harry's action may because the life of the abducted girl is his priority. It is too late to save her as she is already dead. Harry's torture of Scorpio emphasizes the fact that in Callahan's world, which reflects Siegel's vision of America in the 1970s, only violence is the answer to criminals' brutality. It is further underlined by the fact that Scorpio is released from prison because he was arrested without a proper warrant.

---

24   Baker, 94.

120   CHAPTER 3

Harry is deeply shaken because of the killer's release. The viewer has to admit that the law, in its traditional, civilized form does not function properly. It is Callahan's brutality that is the proper form of retribution for crimes. Harry says that "the law is crazy," which places him in opposition to characters who believe that it is Callahan who is insane. The viewer must side with him, as he seems to be the only one who understands the mechanisms of the world in which he lives. However, he seems oblivious to the fact his interrogation methods rendered Scorpio's release inevitable.[25]

Meanwhile, Chico Gonzalez quits his job to go into teaching. He wants to distance himself from the violent world and his wife supports his decision. Harry expresses his understanding of his partner's decisions. At the same time, when asked why he does not quit, he answers, "I don't know. I really don't know." This pertains to the motif of the inability to escape from violence, characteristic of the portrayal of the Irish.

Harry pursues Scorpio on his own. He follows the killer, preventing him from murdering again. In one of the earlier scenes, Harry and his partner drive through the city with its streets full of decadence, of which Harry is critical. Although violent and not necessarily accepted by society, Harry is still a part of the more traditional and conservative approach to life. Scorpio, on the other hand, represents the more liberal viewpoint. He is a part of the new world, which becomes evident when he visits a strip club, while still being observed by Callahan.

The pursued murderer pays a black man to beat him and frames Callahan for it. Harry is suspended, and Scorpio can kill one more time. He murders a shop owner and then kidnaps a school bus with children still on board. This act is symbolic of crime threatening the foundations of American society in the 1970s. The children, who symbolize innocence and hope for the future, are threatened by the murderer. Helpless, the Mayor gives Scorpio his word of honor that the killer will not be harmed in any way, and he will be given a plane as a means of escaping from the country. However, Callahan does not care whether the Mayor retains his honor or not. As the children are ordered to sing a song for the kidnapper, Harry jumps on the bus from a bridge. In his efforts to dislodge Callahan Scorpio almost crashes the bus. He takes one of the children hostage and the showdown takes place by the water's edge. Although Scorpio is holding the boy right in front of him, Harry shoots and wounds him. The monologue is repeated but this time the injured criminal reaches for his gun and Callahan shoots him. The force of the bullet propels Scorpio into the

---

25   Baker, 95.

THE IRISH IN NEW HOLLYWOOD

water. Harry looks at the body of the killer and throws his police badge into the water, rejecting the law, which almost made innocent children die and the killer escape. Apart from Harry's western-like actions when it comes to dealing with criminals, the scene seems to further establish him as a direct descendant of a western hero. It is similar to the final scene of Fred Zimmerman's *High Noon* (1952) in which Will Kane (Gary Cooper) throws away the marshal's star before he leaves, filled with contempt for the town he has just saved.

One final observation about *Dirty Harry* concerns the role of women. As in *Madigan*, they are reduced to elements of the background, and when they appear, they create confusion. In one scene, when Harry is in pursuit of a suspect, he notices a naked woman in a window. He begins staring at her and is mistaken for a voyeur. When he and his partner are observing the church where Scorpio is supposedly going to strike again, Harry's attention is distracted by a woman undressing in front of her window. She then invites a couple to her flat, while still naked. This almost causes a tragedy: while Callahan is distracted the killer attacks. Thus, the film is exceptionally chauvinistic, as is its main character. Women represent the new liberal world, filled with crime and depravity. In this respect, the girl raped and murdered by Scorpio becomes a symbol of the lost innocence of 1970s America. The other symbol is Harry's late wife, who is only mentioned in passing. She symbolizes the family values which are lost for the main character and the world that surrounds him. This is why he supports Chico Gonzales's decision to quit his job as a police officer and become a teacher.

Giving the main character an Irish surname and, therefore, an Irish identity is symptomatic of the existence of a deeply rooted stereotype that Irish Americans are violent. This sets Callahan in opposition to what Tamás Vraukó refers to as the White Anglo-Saxon Protestant, or WASP hero. Typically, a WASP hero was the main character and the protagonist of British and American fiction.[26] Therefore, the narrative discourse compelled the viewer to share such a character's outlook. However, as Vraukó observes, "recently the supremacy of the WASP hero has been challenged. Not one of the other stereotypical figures of those who have always been present in Anglo-Saxon fiction and movies has grown more powerful, but the role of the character has changed, and new stereotypes appeared."[27] This new position adopted by, or rather for WASP heroes, is that of often abusive authority. Examples of this are authority figures in *Dirty Harry*.

---

26   Vraukó, "Changing Stereotypes – The Altering Role of the WASP Hero" (PAAS Conference, Katowice: University of Silesia, 1999), n. pag.

27   Vraukó, n. pag.

122   CHAPTER 3

Thus, if the role of a WASP character in a film is to represent abusive and incapable authority, to be rejected by the viewer, the point-of-view character should be a person who is a contradiction of the WASP figure. If this is the case, then labeling a character Irish American Catholic is, arguably, the best choice, especially if the stereotypes associated with the Irish in America are taken into account. As Vraukó puts it:

> Another challenger of the WASP hero is the rugged Irish cop (detective, private eye, etc.) Many of the movies in which Bruce Willis and Clint Eastwood are starring, also place the white, Anglo-Saxon characters on the wrong side. They are the bureaucratic, narrow-minded superiors – police chiefs, lieutenants, ignorant White House officials etc. – who prevent the Irish cops from performing their duty.[28]

The author refers here to Clint Eastwood in *Dirty Harry* and Bruce Willis in *Die Hard*. As explained below, *Die Hard* takes over elements of the cinematic Irish cop ethos created by Don Siegel in *Dirty Harry*.

However, even though the WASP authority is abusive, it still represents the established law and order, which makes the point-of-view character who opposes WASP authority an outlaw. Harry Callahan is an outlaw hero in the sense proposed by Robert Ray, which is especially evident in the way he perceives the law, but also in his everyday behavior. When Ray proposes as the outlaw hero's motto, "I don't know what the law says, but I do know what's right and wrong,"[29] it is easy to believe that this could be one of Callahan's lines from *Dirty Harry*. Another characteristic that makes Callahan an outlaw hero is his skepticism about civilization, expressed in his perceptible detachment from society.

Another difference between the WASP hero police officer and Siegel's Irish cop is the way they understand the concept of law and order. Whereas for the former, the law is based on bureaucracy and formalities, the latter's perception of the concept verges on what Chad Lavin describes as "criminal justice," i.e., vigilante justice. As Lavin puts it: "the figure of the vigilante confidently equates revenge with justice. Embodying the liberal tension between heroism and institutionalism, the vigilante has played a prominent role in the American consciousness, from early American lynch mobs through 'Dirty'

---

28   Vraukó, n. pag.
29   Ray, *A Certain Tendency of the Hollywood Cinema, 1930–1980*, 62.

THE IRISH IN NEW HOLLYWOOD   123

Harry Callahan."[30] Thus, although Callahan represents the established law and order, he also appears to be a vigilante, i.e., he rejects authority while being its tool.[31]

As a tool of the legal system, Callahan represents the extreme of one aspect of justice. Philosopher Jan Edward Garrett, quoted by Wanda Teays in *Seeing the Light: Exploring Ethics Through Movies*, identifies three aspects of justice. The first is distributive justice based on providing "rewards and burdens." The role of retributive justice is to punish those who break the law. Finally, compensatory justice "looks at restitution for suffering a harm."[32] Harry Callahan represents the extreme of retributive justice, going even further than "an eye for an eye:" for him threatening someone's life is punishable by death.

In its portrayal of the hero, the film is very traditional in its use of binary oppositions between society with its desire for a peaceful life and rejection of violence on the one hand and Scorpio on the other. The liberal Scorpio opposes conservative society and symbolizes the dangers associated with the cultural revolution of the 1970s. The hero's bridging of two opposing sides is also very traditional. Harry Callahan is both a conservative upholder of society's law and a violent instrument of extreme retribution, which is characteristic of Scorpio. This means he is rejected by society but he is the only one able to oppose the killer.

His vision of the law is based on different principles than those of society's establishment and therefore can be accepted only temporarily. This too makes him similar to the traditional western heroes. Callahan's view of the law is based on vengeance (his main aim is to avenge the girl Scorpio rapes and buries alive), retribution (the punishment for killing is death), and the use of violence (he tortures Scorpio). This vision of the law matches later portrayals of the law advocated by Irish outlaw characters, especially Irish newcomers in the USA.

Irish Americans, as represented by Harry Callahan, are conservative supporters of traditional society. Callahan is violent, and, as an outlaw hero, he understands the law differently, but he still opposes the liberal world of decadence and depravity represented by Scorpio. This representation of the main character seems to compel the viewer to accept the previously rejected Irish

---

30   Chad Lavin, *The Politics of Responsibility* (Urbana: University of Illinois Press, 2008), 124.

31   This is later addressed in *Magnum Force*, in which Callahan is confronted with a group of vigilantes to show that his methods are, in fact, not exactly vigilantism.

32   Wanda Teays, *Seeing the Light: Exploring Ethics Through Movies* (New York: John Wiley & Sons, 2012), 190.

124   CHAPTER 3

violence as a lesser evil than the emerging liberalism. The condemnation of the cultural revolution was so strong that, as Peter Biskind puts it his article "Any Which Way He Can," "In the highly polarized political climate of 1971, many people felt that *Dirty Harry* said it was okay for cops to trample civil liberties in the pursuit of crooks. Plus, the Scorpio Killer wears a peace sign, as if Siegel and Eastwood were turning a whole generation of kids into a bunch of Charles Mansons."[33] The motif of violent Irish cops, clearly referenced in *Dirty Harry*, has been present in American cinema ever since, as evidenced by the further sections of the monograph. However, Harry Callahan himself has undergone various modifications in the sequels to the first film, becoming increasingly liberal.

While in *Madigan*, Don Siegel only used an almost generic, rather incompetent Irish cop, in *Dirty Harry*, he developed it into a character who is competent because of his familiarity with violence, but at the same time acceptable to the viewer. This acceptability stems from the tradition to which the construction of the main character refers and the hero's uncompromising attitude to the naturalistically presented violent world. By choosing an Irish American identity for his character, Siegel once again explored the stereotype of the Irish cop, thus referring to something familiar to the viewer, but he legitimized Irish violence as the only force able to protect society from crime.

2   Ted Post's *Magnum Force* and James Fargo's *The Enforcer*

The popularity and commercial success of the original *Dirty Harry* led to the production of four more films with Clint Eastwood reprising his role. However, only two were produced during the New Hollywood era, with the remaining two aimed solely at commercial success and with the main character becoming less violent, more tamed, and more of a generic police officer.

Ted Post's *Magnum Force* (1973) was the first step in taming Siegel's Irish cop. Many critics had pointed to the fascist overtones in *Dirty Harry*. Pauline Kael referred to it as "fascist fantasy," claiming that the fascist potential of the action genre "surfaces in this movie."[34] The next film about Callahan could either follow the pattern or alter it slightly. Kael's comment allegedly led Eastwood to

---

33   Peter Biskind, "Any Which Way He Can," in *Clint Eastwood: Interviews, Revised and Updated*, ed. Robert E. Kapsis and Kathie Coblentz (Jackson: University Press of Mississippi, 2012), 149.

34   Pauline Kael, *5001 Nights at the Movies* (New York: Henry Holt and Company, 1991), 148.

THE IRISH IN NEW HOLLYWOOD   125

persuade Post to adopt a story in which Harry Callahan would voice his opposition to vigilantism. As David Sterritt puts it,

> When someone says vigilante justice is validated by the principle of ret-
> ribution, Harry replies, "When the police start becoming their own exe-
> cutioners, where's it gonna end?" The official criminal-justice system is
> woefully poor, he adds, "but until someone comes along with changes
> that make sense, I'll stick with it."

However, despite the apparent shift in its orientation towards vigilantism, the
film did not reduce brutality. Indeed, it is known as "the most violent 'Dirty
Harry' movie, with many bloody killings and a fair amount of nudity."[35]

The beginning of *Magnum Force* returns to the theme of the law's inadequacy familiar to viewers of the first film. When the court releases a well-
known mobster, an unidentified police officer on a motorcycle stops the car
in which the criminal drives away from the court. Furious, the mobster says, "I
want him out of this job," indicating that he is in control of the established law
enforcement authorities. The police officer shoots everyone in the car. From
this point on Harry Callahan faces a supposed dilemma: to affirm his place in
the police force or to allow vigilantism to emerge.

The film uses motifs from Don Siegel's film. Firstly, Harry's superior, Lt.
Briggs (Hal Holbrook), is against Callahan's methods, which he deems excessively violent. This, once more, establishes Harry as an outcast, opposed to the
WASP authorities. Secondly, Callahan's partner—Earlington Smith—is a representative of an ethnic minority (African American). There are also subplots in
which Harry always shows up in the right place at the right time to fight various crimes. For instance, early in the film, Harry thwarts an attempt to hijack a
plane when, dressed as a pilot, he enters the cockpit to take off the runway and
kills all the hijackers. On another occasion Callahan thwarts robbery in a shop,
killing or wounding each of the robbers and freeing the hostages.

However, the main plot of the film puts the conservative Harry in a position
where he must defend the decadent and liberal part of society. After his first
victim, the killer cop targets a group of people partying in a pool, who are later
revealed to be mobsters. The vigilante, again wearing a traffic officer's uniform,
attacks them with a machine gun and an explosive device, killing everyone.
Next, a pimp is killed after brutally murdering a prostitute. Just before being
shot by the vigilante, the pimp tries to bribe the traffic officer and says, "You

---

35   Howard Hughes, *Aim for the Heart the Films of Clint Eastwood* (London; New York; New
      York: Palgrave Macmillan, 2009), 56.

know who I am?" again showing the corruption within the structures of the established law enforcement authorities. The next victim is a mobster during a sexual encounter with a woman and a man. The motif of a sexual relationship between three people appears for the second time in the series, and, again, it symbolizes society's departure from family values. However, this time, the mobster is the victim of violence. He is killed while naked, which contrasts with the killer's full police uniform, including a helmet. This symbolizes the mobster's helplessness and complete exposure in front of not only the vigilante but also the viewer.

To further soften the image of Harry, his interactions with women, elevated from victims and background figures to active characters, are shown. When Harry suspects his old friend, McCoy, of being the killer cop, he visits McCoy's estranged wife to investigate and confirm or disconfirm his suspicions. However, Carol McCoy starts seducing Harry, who does not seem to be indifferent to her attempts. Another woman who is interested in Harry is his Asian hippie neighbor, Sunny. During their first meeting, she asks him, "What does a girl have to do to go to bed with you?" to which Harry replies that she should try knocking at his door. We see Callahan in his apartment looking at a photograph of his late wife. This indicates his transition from the world of traditional family values to the more liberal world symbolized in the series by women. Harry embraces, quite literally, this new reality, but at the same time, he does not reject the conservative world, as evidenced by the subsequent events.

When McCoy is murdered, it becomes apparent to Harry that it is one of the newly met traffic officers that is the vigilante. After a shooting tournament, he gains evidence that supports his suspicion. He shares his discovery with Lt. Briggs, who is skeptical and says a mobster, Frank Palancio, is the main suspect. Harry is ordered to arrest Palancio, and he chooses the four rookies as his backup. However, someone warns the mobster and his men that "people dressed as cops" are going to "hit them." When they see Harry approaching the building in which they are hiding, they make an interesting observation. According to them, the "big guy," as they refer to Callahan, does not look like a police officer, and the kind of gun he uses "is not a cop's gun." They are more willing to accept that Harry is one of them than that he is, in fact, a police officer. Thus, even his appearance sets him apart from his fellow police officers. During the arrest, one of the rookies is killed, along with Palancio and all his men.

The rookies are revealed to be a vigilante death-squad. They visit Harry at the parking lot and ask him to join their ranks. They tell him that with the current state of the world in which they live, there is no question of whether or not to use violence, and he, of all people, should agree with their point of view. Harry

THE IRISH IN NEW HOLLYWOOD   127

objects strenuously, affirming his attachment to the police force. He opposes vigilantism, although he does not oppose the use of violence. This puts him in between the world of legal justice and the world of the criminal justice of vigilantism. However, Harry's intimacy with violence stems from the fact that he is an Irish American, and this differentiates him from the killer cops.

The vigilantes ride away on their motorcycles, leaving Callahan in the parking lot. The next day, however, they leave a bomb in his mailbox. Sunny nearly triggers the explosion while trying to open the mailbox but Callahan violently pushes her away and she falls to the floor. A neighbor, who evidently does not know Callahan, appears and tells him to stop tampering with the box, or he will call the police. When the neighbor learns that there is a bomb in the building, he starts panicking. Harry tells him that if he had paid attention to the neighbors' threats and remarks, they would all be dead. The neighbor says nervously, "No, I don't want to get involved!" and vanishes, an indication that it is society itself that obstructs law enforcement by rejecting violence and setting the standards of behavior for law enforcers; however, when it comes to taking action, people "do not want to get involved."

Harry tries to contact his partner, Earl, but the black police officer dies when the bomb hidden in his mailbox explodes. Another Callahan partner from a minority dies, reinforcing the idea that only Callahan can withstand violence, since rather than rejecting it he embraces it.

Callahan calls Lt. Briggs for help and when he arrives, they drive away with the defused bomb to the police station. On the journey, it is revealed that Briggs is the leader of the vigilante death squad. He tells Harry he should have joined when he had the chance and Briggs points to the similarities between Callahan and the killer cops. Harry remains firm in his attachment to his values and beats the lieutenant. The three remaining members of the death squad arrive and Harry kills all of them.

Briggs pulls a gun on Callahan but rather than kill him he plans to frame him for the massacre of the mobsters, confident that Callahan's word will mean nothing when confronted with his testimony. Unknown to him, however, Callahan has turned on the bomb's timer mechanism and as Briggs drives away the bomb explodes. The scene contradicts the way the film has addressed vigilantism up to this moment. Harry goes far beyond the limits of the established law and order and into the area of illegal vigilantism. He commits murder, suggesting that, perhaps, he does accept vigilantism to some extent.

Magnum Force presents Callahan as an outcast, too violent for other police officers. He is described as a "killer" and "maniac" by Lt. Briggs—the mastermind behind the death squad of vigilantes. Even criminals see him as not necessarily matching the image of a police officer. At the same time, he stands firmly against vigilantism, which, to his mind, is also a departure from the law. Consequently, the film emphasizes the differences between Harry and the gang of vigilantes on various levels. Firstly, there is a contrast between Callahan's "usual cheap jacket and slacks" and "his usual beaten-up car" and the gang's "shiny metal uniforms" and "gleaming motorcycles."[36] Therefore, the most easily discernible difference is provided on the visual level. Secondly, Harry's rejection of vigilantism appears in the form of verbal confrontations between him and the gang.[37] Therefore, although he belongs to the world of violence, he remains a part of established law enforcement. As in the first film, he does not believe in the law which allows criminals to walk free without any punishment but he does not place himself above the law.

His relationship with Sunny symbolizes his attraction to the liberal world, which she represents both as an emancipated woman and as a member of an ethnic minority. She is symbolic of Harry's chance for a healthier life. When she first visits Callahan, she asks him if he always lives in the dark. This may refer to Harry's apartment, but also to the world in which he lives. In this context, her name might symbolize his chance for stepping out into the light. However, she may also be a moment's distraction, as Harry is unable to abandon the dark world of violence, which is evidenced by his inability to quit his job.

The four rookies and Lt. Briggs are symptoms of the dissatisfaction of society with corrupt police. At first, the viewer might sympathize with them, as the violence they use appears almost justifiable. Their victims, criminals living in a decadent world, symbolize the liberal world with which the conservative America of the 1970s was confronted. However, when they kill a police officer, their violent behavior becomes unacceptable, and so neither Harry nor the viewer can side with them.

The rather basic binary oppositions from the first film remain in place, though this time the liberal world is represented not by Scorpio but by the mobsters targeted by the vigilantes. The killer cops represent vigilantism, which is in opposition to the values cherished by society. However, they are similar to society in their conservatism. In this respect, they might be seen as society's reaction to violence coming from the liberal world. This reaction is unacceptable because vigilantism opposes the established law and order. Vigilantism is undoubtedly similar to Harry Callahan's view of the law as violent retribution; however, in the view of the system of values represented by the central character, it is an exaggeration. Callahan may use excessive force, but he only uses it if someone's life is in direct danger. He does not agree with

---

36   Paul Smith, *Clint Eastwood: A Cultural Production* (Minneapolis: University of Minnesota Press, 1993), 102.

37   Smith, 102.

THE IRISH IN NEW HOLLYWOOD 129

everything in the world he lives in but he does not place himself above it, trying to change it. Although he is an outcast, he works within society and for society. As he puts it, he works "for the city."

Harry Callahan is consistent with earlier representations of Irish Americans in the USA but shows a later stage of Irish integration into American culture. Although Irish Americans retain some characteristic stereotypical features of their ancestors, and—like their ancestors—are seen by society as outcasts, they are willing to defend the values cherished by this society. In this respect, they are conservative rather than liberal. This well-established feature of the Irish minority is connected with the cultural background from which they stem. Harry Callahan is also presented as a rebel who opposes his superiors and never shows any kind of respect towards them. This too is a stereotypical image of the Irish. Irish Americans, as represented by Callahan, are contrasted sharply with other ethnic minorities, which, although also willing to join the police, are unable to withstand the level of violence plaguing America of the 1970s.

These observations are supported by the third film in the series, *The Enforcer*, which follows the pattern established by *Dirty Harry* and modified by *Magnum Force*. This time Callahan is dealing not only with the cultural revolution of the 1970s but also with the threat of communism, represented by a terrorist group called the People's Revolutionary Strike Group, his main enemy in the film.

As in the first two films, Harry is shown doing his police duty in a series of background events. He and his partner, Frank DiGeorgio (John Mitchum) are called to the scene of an armed robbery. The robbers are holding several people hostage inside a liquor store, and they demand a police vehicle with a radio as a getaway car. Harry drives his car through the window of the shop and then kills or wounds all of the robbers, one of whom is castrated with a bullet from Callahan's Magnum .44.

Again, Harry is at odds with his commanding officer, Captain McKay (Bradford Dillman), who accuses him of excessive use of force. He also adds that the minorities have had enough of this kind of behavior. This is an apparent reference to one of the dominant motifs in the portrayal of Harry in the first film, as the main character opposes or even despises minorities. For McKay, minorities are "American citizens as well." Harry seems ambivalent.

Interestingly, although belonging to a minority himself, Callahan sees himself as an American, reflecting the views represented by some of the Irish of the second and third post-Famine generations who strove to become "perfect Americans." McKay's surname suggests Scottish or Scotch-Irish origins[38] and he is more open to change than Callahan. He regards Callahan's *modus operandi*

---

38   Seary and Kirwin, *Family Names of the Island of Newfoundland*, 332.

130 CHAPTER 3

as a "Wild West show" reflecting the view of Harry as a lonely western hero, not accepted by society but nevertheless needed when society is in danger.

Harry is transferred to the Personnel Department. His opinion that "personnel is for assholes" proves that it is action and the violence connected with it that he needs. Nevertheless, he obeys, and one of his first assignments is to test new police inspectors, some of whom are women, as a result of Affirmative Action in the 1970s. Callahan voices his disapproval of women working as police officers. He considers the female candidates weak and suitable only for less dangerous assignments. For his views, he is called a "Neanderthal" by other members of the commission. However, one of the candidates, Kate Moore (Tyne Daly), impresses Callahan with her knowledge of the law. After Callahan is transferred back to the Homicide Department, Moore becomes his new partner.

After the cold-blooded psychopath Scorpio and the morally ambiguous killer cops, Harry's opponents in *The Enforcer* do not seem that interesting. The People's Revolutionary Strike Force (PRSF), led by Bobby Maxwell (DeVeren Bookwalter), discharged from the army due to mental problems, seems more comical than dangerous. With a group of followers, he steals weapons, including anti-tank LAW rockets, from a warehouse, killing DiGiorgio. Their brutality is best seen when Maxwell kills one of his followers—a young woman wounded in the raid. However, as Howard Hughes puts it:

> For all their brutality there is a comedic ineptitude to their brand of terrorism. Operating from their conspicuous van with flames on the side and kidnapping the mayor using a 25,000-volt paralysing Teaser gun, they're kind of outfit who might write a return address on a letter bomb.[39]

The poor construction of Harry's opponents and their shallowness mean the viewer loses interest in their confrontation with Harry Callahan. Although it is supposed to form the main plot and the climax of the film, it appears only as an addition to the character's other actions. A much more impressive figure is "Big" Ed Mustapha (Albert Popwell), the leader of a black militant group, initially suspected of being responsible for the attacks carried out by the PRSF. When it turns out that Mustapha is innocent and he promises to help Callahan, his whole group is arrested by McKay. Callahan and Moore are due to receive a commendation from the Mayor for the arrest but Harry publicly and angrily rejects it and as a result, is suspended. When the mayor is kidnapped by the terrorists and Mustapha is released, Callahan meets "Big" Ed, who tells him

---

39   Hughes, *Aim for the Heart the Films of Clint Eastwood*, 59.

THE IRISH IN NEW HOLLYWOOD   131

there is an ethnic conflict in progress and that Callahan is on the wrong side. Mustapha appears to acknowledge Harry's ethnic roots and wants to show him that he should side with the minorities. Callahan's American self is dominant as, although he is suspended, he continues to pursue the terrorists who killed DiGiorgio.

Callahan, a declared chauvinist, obviously does not want to work with his new partner but has to obey. Kate Moore is portrayed as being unsuitable for police, sometimes comically so. In the morgue, she has to leave the room in which DiGeorgio's body is examined. In a chase scene, she is no match for the suspect as she is wearing a skirt and heels. She can only watch as Harry chases the suspect, even jumping after him from the roof of one building onto the roof of another one. The background music underlines the comical aspect of the scene. Also, she is presented as being somewhat obsessed with sex, as she makes allusions to Harry's choice of weapon. The purpose of all these devices is to reflect Harry's extremely conservative perspective on women: they should not become police officers as it is a job for men.

Nevertheless, she proves herself a valuable partner and assists Harry in pursuing the criminals to Alcatraz Island, where they are holding the Mayor. They free him but Moore is shot in the process. Harry kills Maxwell with a LAW rocket. The Mayor thanks him and promises a reward but Harry does not want anything from him. The final scene shows the helicopter that brought the ransom for the Mayor, and Harry looking at the dead body of Kate Moore.

Harry Callahan's character evolves slightly during the first three films but the central motifs in the construction of this character remain the same: excessive violence, inability to escape from violence, rejection of authority, vengeance, conflict with (other) ethnic minorities, conservatism, and violent law enforcement. These motifs can be found in other films studied here, in which the characters belong to ethnic minorities. One motif that changes is chauvinism, as Harry accepts a woman not only in terms of a sexual relationship but as a partner—the most important person in his life. Women are attracted to Harry but he does not have time for romantic relationships as his police duties always come first. Religious themes, such as the motif of Harry as savior, seem to show that the violence he uses will not save society from criminals. It is, however, a way of punishing them.

3   Jimmy "Popeye" Doyle: *The French Connection*

The figure of the brutal Irish American police officer is also explored in *The French Connection* (1971), directed by William Friedkin, and its sequel (1975),

132   CHAPTER 3

directed by John Frankenheimer. Both films were commercially successful, but it was Friedkin's that received critical acclaim, receiving Academy Awards for the best director, best picture, actor, and editing.[40]

Jimmy "Popeye" Doyle (Gene Hackman) is a police officer working for the Narcotics Department of New York Police Department. Early in the film, we see him and his Italian American partner Buddy "Cloudy" Russo (Roy Scheider) chasing a black man through the streets of New York. The man picks up a knife and wounds Cloudy's arm. When they catch him they beat him until he gives them the information they are seeking. They view torture as a tool in police work.

Two other motifs characteristic of the Irish are used in the portrayal of Doyle. Firstly, he laughs at his wounded partner and tells him, "Never trust a nigger," to which Russo answers: "He could have been white." Doyle corrects himself: "Never trust anyone." Thus he displays the conflict between the Irish and other ethnic minorities in America. The juxtaposition of Irish Americans and Italian Americans, even when presented as partners, is similar to that in the Dirty Harry films, in which Frank DiGiorgio is Harry Callahan's partner. Secondly, Doyle invites Russo to go out for a drink. Drinking, although absent from the Dirty Harry series, is a quintessential motif in the representation of the Irish.

Popeye's instincts for crime are similar to that of Callahan's. While drinking, he notices a man and a woman who spend time with mobsters. He does not know them and he suggests that he and Russo follow them "just for fun." Following the couple, Popeye and his partner stumble upon a drug trafficking operation in which the man and the woman from the bar, Sal and Angie, are intermediaries between a group of Americans and a French criminal, Alain Charnier (Fernando Rey), who is also the main antagonist in both films.

Doyle is well-known to criminals. When he and his partner go to a bar in which black drug dealers meet, he enters shouting: "Popeye's here! Hands up!" Upon hearing this, the dealers drop all their drugs on the floor. Popeye threatens some of them, asking one of them if he knows his name, to which the dealer responds with "Doyle." Popeye asks him again, and this time he is satisfied with the answer, as the criminal responds with "Mr. Doyle." He arrests two random dealers, locking them in phone booths, but his real aim is to talk to his informer. He pretends to beat the man he is looking for and locks himself into a separate room with him so they can talk. However, he has to hit him for real so as not to blow his cover in front of the dealers. Doyle uses violence with no second thoughts. He seems accustomed to it and never hesitates.

---

40   Katz, *The Film Encyclopedia*, 497.

Doyle's rejection of authority is also characteristic of the representation of the Irish in America. He is at war with his superior, Walt Simonson, who tells Popeye he does not believe in his "hunches," as one of them "backfired in the past." Next, he also accuses the two police officers of only arresting petty criminals, albeit in large numbers—"over a hundred arrests." The conflict between Popeye and Simonson may not be as visible as is the case of Callahan and his supervisors, but it is present. When Doyle and Russo have to work with the FBI agent, Bill Mulderig (Bill Hickman), overseeing the operation against the drug traffickers, Doyle's conflict with authority reemerges. Mulderig laughs at Popeye's appearance and his habit of keeping his gun strapped to his ankle. He also blames Doyle for the death of a police officer sometime in the past.

Like Harry Callahan, Popeye finds it easy to attract women. In one scene, he is driving his car when he sees an attractive young woman on a bicycle. He slows down to stare at her. In the next scene, Russo has to break into Doyle's apartment when he visits his friend. Inside, he finds a bicycle and women's clothing lying all around. Popeye himself is cuffed to his bed by his feet and cannot get up. While looking for the key to free his friend, Russo finds the woman Popeye was staring at in the previous scene. Naked, she covers herself and hides in the bathroom. While waiting for Doyle to dress, Russo looks at his friend's scrapbook and comments on it, saying: "The scrapbook is like you: messed."

The New York of this film is not as decadent and spoilt as San Francisco in the Dirty Harry series but it is nevertheless a dangerous place to live in. This is because the most dangerous criminals seem to live beyond the reach of the law. In one scene, Charnier is shown eating in a cozy expensive restaurant while Doyle is observing him from outside, trembling from the cold as he eats a sandwich and drinks a cup of coffee. Doyle cannot go into the restaurant to sit and wait for the criminal to finish his meal because he cannot afford it. Another scene shows Sal visiting Joel Weinstock, the man who is going to buy drugs from Charnier. Weinstock's office is located at "the top of Empire State Building," which symbolizes the fact that he is out of reach of the law.

In American cinema, the Irish are frequently shown to be the source of violence or mishaps, even if indirectly. *The French Connection* also explores this stereotype. A sniper trying to kill Doyle misses and kills a woman pushing a stroller, leaving the baby alone on the pavement with strangers. Doyle pursues the sniper, who eludes him and hides on a train. Doyle confiscates a car from a random driver and begins chasing the murderer. Knowing the police officer is right after him, the killer hijacks the train, killing two men in the process. The train driver seemingly dies of a heart attack and the train crashes. The injured murderer tries to escape, but Doyle kills him, shooting him in the back.

Doyle's instinct is shown once again when he finds the drugs Charnier intends to sell hidden in a car brought to the USA by a French actor, Deveraux, hired by Charnier. Doyle and Russo allow the actor to take the car to Charnier so that they can follow him and arrest all those involved in the operation. In the ensuing gunfight a police officer is killed and Doyle, pursuing Charnier, shoots at a silhouette in a doorway killing Mulderig. Russo is horrified but Popeye seems not to care at all. He reloads the gun and continues the chase. His mission is to fight criminals and if this involves collateral damage, then so be it. The final images of the film show title cards informing the viewer that all those involved in the trafficking scheme avoided severe punishment, as if confirming the futility of the Irish cop's action in the White Anglo-Saxon Protestant world.

The sequel, entitled *The French Connection II*, follows from the events of the first film. Doyle arrives in France in order to arrest Charnier, who is living peacefully in Marseille. Once again, Doyle's reputation precedes him and he is an unwelcome guest. Inspector Henri Barthélémy (Bernard Fresson) tells Popeye he is worried by his unpredictability and his reputation as someone who does not "go by the book." He gives Doyle a desk next to a toilet, which Doyle takes as an insult, and asks Popeye how many people he has killed, answering the question himself: five. The suggestion is that the French policeman balks at violence and considers killing the last resort. Perhaps he has never killed before.

Initially, Doyle is a burden for the French police. He has problems not only with the language but also with the way the police in Marseille operate. After a police raid on drug dealers, in a scene reminiscent of the first film in the series, Doyle chases and catches a black suspect. However, when French police officers arrive, they restrain Popeye rather than the suspect. It is revealed that he is not a criminal but a police officer infiltrating the dealers. His colleagues let him go, but he is murdered a moment later by the criminals who witnessed the scene.

Doyle spends time in a bar, trying to talk to French women and managing to befriend a bartender with whom he drinks. It is also in this scene that Doyle acknowledges his Irish origin. When the girls reject his advances, he says: "How would you like to kiss my Irish ass?" Unlike Callahan, Doyle flaunts his Irish roots, which is made plain in this scene to the viewer.

It is revealed that French and American police are using Doyle as bait in order to find Charnier. They know that Popeye is visible in the streets of Marseille, as he simply stands out from the rest of the passers-by. Therefore, two French policemen follow Doyle all the time. He shakes them off and is immediately kidnapped by Charnier's people, who imprison him and subject him to violence. They inject him with heroin, turning him into an addict who welcomes the injections, over the course of a few days.

Doyle divides his time between the room in which he is given the drug and the toilet to which one of Charnier's men takes him. On one occasion, an interesting meeting between him and an old lady takes place. The lady enters Doyle's room and starts speaking English. She tells him she is an Englishwoman who has lived in Marseilles for forty-two years. At first, it appears that she sympathizes with him; however, a close-up reveals that she is, in fact, stealing Doyle's watch. Her arm has needle tracks on it. It is curious that in a film about an imprisoned Irishman, an English woman is one of the people who guard him in his prison. This becomes even more significant when it is borne in mind that she does not reappear in the film. It is almost as if Doyle's trip to Europe has put him in a situation similar to his ancestors in Ireland.

When Doyle finally reveals to Charnier that he does not know anything about his current operations, the drug lord orders his men to kill him. He is injected with a heavy dose of heroin and then thrown out of a car right next to the police station. Henri orders the unconscious Doyle taken to the police cells, where he is resuscitated and treated for an overdose. All this is kept off the record by Henri, who does not want to tarnish Doyle's reputation. Finally, Popeye wakes up, his first words being: "What are you looking at, asshole?" He is given the "cold turkey" treatment and suffers from withdrawal symptoms, symbolizing his struggle with powerlessness in the face of crime. Doyle survives and emerges much more durable than before. In this sense, his ordeal is a rite of passage he needed to take in order to be able to function in the foreign land. Later in the film, he is seen throwing away a packet of heroin, indicating that the treatment was successful, and he is free from his weaknesses. The drug, used on the streets of the increasingly liberal American cities, symbolizes the changing world which Doyle has successfully rejected.

Having regained his strength, Doyle arrives at the hotel in which he was imprisoned and sets it on fire. He tortures one of the thugs who kidnapped him and learns Charnier's whereabouts. With Henri and his men he first thwarts one of Charnier's operations and then raids the warehouse. After a long chase, he loses Charnier, who gets into a motorboat. As he is sailing away, Doyle calls his name and shoots him twice.

There are numerous similarities between Callahan and Doyle, the most important being that both of them use excessive violence as a means of upholding the law. This seems to be an Irish feature, as it is rejected by other police officers, except for Russo, although even Russo cannot accept Doyle's accidental killing of the FBI agent Mulderig. The binary oppositions used to juxtapose Doyle and society are also similar, except for the conservative-liberal opposition present in the Dirty Harry series of films. Doyle seems more open and liberal and the world in which he lives therefore does not appear as gloomy and decadent as Callahan's San Francisco.

136   CHAPTER 3

4   Union Violence

The familiar motifs of violence and betrayal appear also in Martin Ritt's *The Molly Maguires* (1970). Ritt, whose career as an actor and director was disrupted in the 1950s because of his communist sympathies, presents mine workers fighting with their capitalist employers in an ambiguous way, allowing the viewer to decide whether they are the heroes or villains of the story.[41] The Molly Maguires were a secret society of coal workers whose aim was to secure higher wages and better working conditions from the oppressive capitalist mine owners. The history of the Mollies dates back to Ireland, where the members of the organization "were a loosely organized group of vigilantes who executed their own system of retributive justice."[42] The idea of retributive justice in the hands of the people must have been popular in a country such as Ireland, which was under British control. Moreover, as already stated, the Irish had become accustomed to the fact that the only way to fight the oppressors was with violence. Together with the steady influx of Irish immigrants to the USA, the stories of the Mollies traveled across the Atlantic Ocean and reached Irish communities. As the author of the article quoted above puts it: "In the popular imagination of the time, the Molly Maguires were fevered immigrant-terrorists bent on destroying capital and property."[43]

The suspected leader of the secret society of miners, John Kehoe, played in the film by Sean Connery, was also a real-life person. Interestingly, there is some doubt whether the real Kehoe was the leader of the Mollies or even if the society really existed in America. According to some theories, the Mollies and their activity in America were fabricated by mine owners who wanted to use the violent reputation of the Irish to squash the labor union movement after the Long Strike in Pennsylvania in 1875.[44]

Nevertheless, although John Kehoe and also James McParland (Richard Harris), a private detective working for the Pinkerton National Detective Agency, are both based on real people involved in the Molly Maguires episode, the events presented in the film are fictionalized. The historical account in which the reputation of the Irish as violent and brutal people was used against them was fictionalized and shown as real events. This fictionalization must

---

41   Alexander Rocca, "The History Page: Down the Mines. A 19th-century union, a charismatic businessman and an alleged conspiracy" in *The Daily*, April 10, 2012. <http://www.thedaily.com/page/2012/04/10/041012-opinions-history-maguires-rocca-1-3/>

42   Rocca, n. pag.

43   Rocca, n. pag.

44   Joseph G. Rayback, *History of American Labor* (New York: Simon and Schuster, 2008), 133.

THE IRISH IN NEW HOLLYWOOD

have also involved transforming the story with the use of stereotypes. The film is riddled with stereotypical representations.

To begin with, Irish violence is ubiquitous and inescapable. Firstly, the Irish miners are presented as excessively violent terrorists. In one of the first scenes, John Kehoe and two other Molly Maguires are seen planting explosives in a mine they work in. They also organize assassination attempts and other terrorist acts. Secondly, the Irish American detective McParland, using the name McKenna, must start a fight when he first arrives in town in order to gain the miners' respect. Next, an interesting conversation between McParland and the local police captain takes place in which the policeman, a Welsh immigrant, says that the Irish respect only "a blow and a hard head" and adds that "that gang is crazy" to which McParland replies: "That's not crazy, it's only Irish." As an Irishman, McParland understands violence and is, therefore, the only one able to infiltrate the Mollies.

The violence is also a form of entertainment: during a rugby match, the townsmen are shown beating their opponents in a quite literal sense of the word while the women cheer. The only person in the community who opposes violence is a Catholic priest who considers it a sin. However, he only opposes union violence, as he cheers along with the rest of the town during the game of rugby.

The Irish in the film are opposed to any kind of authority. The whole idea of the Molly Maguires is to force the owner of the mine to raise the wages. However, in the initiation scene, when McParland/McKenna is accepted into the Ancient Order of Hibernians, one of the passwords is "Will tenant-right in Ireland flourish?" to which the proper response is: "If the people unite and the landlords subdue." Also, when McParland's love interest Mary (Samantha Eggar) tells him that the owner of the mines is an Irishman like him, the detective replies that the rich man is a Protestant, and therefore, not like him. The Protestants are associated with the ruling class, which is to be opposed.

Finally, there is an opposition between the Irish and another minority, in this case, the Welsh. It is with the Welsh that the Irish play the game of rugby and win. The match symbolizes their conflict. Also, the Welsh police captain is the main antagonist of the film. On a few occasions, he uses any excuse to beat McParland, and it is on his orders that one of the Mollies is shot along with his wife while asleep. The animosity is presented as long-lasting and rooted in the history of the stormy relationship between the Irish and Britain, which the Welsh represent. As such, they are the old authority the Irish oppose in almost a natural way but here, in the US, they represent a new form of oppression. Thus, the presence of the Welsh as the opponents of the Irish and representatives of the oppressive state stresses the connection between the old world

138   CHAPTER 3

and the new world in which the Irish live and the continuity of their persecution. As such, the violence that they use seems to be understandable and
acceptable.

One additional theme used in the representation of the Irish in *The Molly
Maguires* is the motif of the betrayal of one's own people. McParland denounces
Kehoe and is promptly rejected by the Irish: Mary, who was ready to leave the
town with him, changes her mind, leaving McParland with the realization that
he will have to live with the guilt and the sense of loss for the rest of his life.
Although McParland is constructed with the same narrative motifs as the rest
of the Irish community, he remains faithful to the established law and order
and does not follow the retributive justice of his people. He is rewarded by
American society with a better-paid post. Thus, American society uses McParland and his innate violence and rewards him when, having completed the
assignment, he rejects violence. Harry Callahan and Jimmy Doyle are outcasts
because, although they perform service to society, they do not reject brutality
after the work is done.

5   Gangsters and Boxers: Old and Tired

The New Hollywood era brought a new look at the well-established motifs of
Irish gangsters and union violence as well as to Irish policemen. In classical
films, Irish gangsters were usually presented as young people for whom violence was a tool with which they could quickly achieve success in life. However, this success was transient as violence was ultimately destructive and led
to their downfall. Those parable-like stories may have fulfilled educational
purposes, showing society that social work is necessary in order to reshape the
lives of those less fortunate. The New Hollywood version of the Irish gangster
provides a different perspective on such a character, as it seems to show the
result of criminality at a later stage in life. At the same time, it forms a continuity with the characters of the past as it presents the inevitable downfall of an
aging man who has not rejected violence.

An Irish gangster appears in Peter Yates's *The Friends of Eddie Coyle* (1973).
Yates was a British director who was especially good at choreographing action
scenes.[45] The film paints an unsentimental picture of an aging gangster who
has run out of options and is facing his demise. Eddie Coyle (Robert Mitchum),
despite his age and criminal experience, is a small-time gangster working as

---

45   Katz, *The Film Encyclopedia*, 1489.

an intermediary between gun dealers and bank robbers. To avoid a prison sentence he becomes an informer for Dave Foley (Richard Jordan), an agent of the Bureau of Alcohol, Tobacco, Firearms, and Explosives (ATF). Coyle is also a patron of a pub owned by his friend and business partner, Dillon (Peter Boyle).

Violence in *The Friends of Eddie Coyle* plays a background role and may at first seem more genre-dependent than associated exclusively with the Irish. However, it is present in Eddie's stories and appears as a constant threat and a source of fear. Eddie's situation is the result of his violent life. Although Coyle is never seen doing anything violent, when he threatens a younger gunrunner, Jackie Brown (Steven Keats), the man is clearly afraid of the older gangster. Eddie is a violent person but prefers to use verbal violence as a form of intimidation. In one of the first scenes, Eddie talks to Jackie Brown about the time he failed to fulfill a contract he had with some gangsters. As a punishment, Eddie had his fingers broken. In talking about it, he gives the impression he understands the punishment was necessary. He understands violence and its necessity: the punishment made him an honorable and dependable man. However, it also led him to a situation in which there is no escape from punishment. What is more, the fact that the plot centers on Irish Americans implies a continuous presence of the connection between the ethnic group and problems with the law.

The motif of violence as a threat to the family is also explored in the film. Family is the main driving force behind the character's actions. Eddie wants to avoid prison because he does not want to be separated from his family. The violent world in which he lives threatens to separate him from his nearest and dearest. When a group of gangsters want to rob a bank, they first kidnap the family of the bank owner and threaten to kill them if their demands are not met. Each bank owner obeys and gives the robbers the money they demand. Violence threatens the very existence of the family and, by extension, society. This motif was used in previous decades, and it would appear in later films too.

The motif of betrayal, usually dictated by the characters' need to escape violence, frequently plays a significant role in the representation of the Irish on screen. Coyle betrays his people—in this case, his partners in crime—and rejects violence. However, betrayal cannot go unpunished either. Violence and betrayal intertwine, trapping Eddie in a complicated web. He cannot escape the mob without betraying them but betrayal leads to his violent end. The viewer is constantly aware that Eddie Coyle is old, tired, and alone in a violent world. Replaced by younger gangsters, he wishes only to spend the rest of his life with his family. At the same time, he is himself a violent man who has existed in the mob structures all his life. He, therefore, understands the consequences of betrayal, and his inability to escape from violence. His attempt

140   CHAPTER 3

to begin a normal life is, from the very beginning, futile. It comes as no surprise that "The Man," the elusive boss of the Irish mob orders Dillon to murder Coyle. Eddie meets Dillon at a hockey match where he gets drunk; intoxicated and unconscious, he is driven to a secluded place where Dillon executes him.

The Irish gangster in the 1970s is only a shadow of his 1930s incarnation. Tom Powers and Rocky Sullivan were young and energetic. The plot perfectly reflected their nature, as their actions were shown as rather hectic, spontaneous, and performed as quick responses to various things. They controlled the situation, remaining active almost until their demise, which was also dramatic and resulted from the violent struggle. By contrast, Eddie Coyle is slow and worn-out; he struggles and is easily manipulated by both the gangsters and Foley. Rather than an agent, he is an instrument. His demise is similarly bland and anticlimactic—he is too drunk to even realize he is about to die. His intoxicated helpless state is a perfect extension of the character development. The old Irish gangster is a threat to no one but himself.

A similar treatment of the old established Irish character is visible in boxing films. The arrival of *Rocky* (1976) signaled the end of the Irish dominance as boxers. However, even before Sylvester Stallone's film, the twilight of Irish boxers was announced by John Huston's *Fat City* (1972), an adaptation of Leonard Gardner's novel, starring Stacy Keach as Bill Tully, an aging small-time boxer well past his prime and living in Stockton, California. The town is presented in disarray and disintegration and, as the camera moves through the streets, it focuses on elderly people and the homeless visible everywhere. This is not a place that is on the up, where young people seek new opportunities. It is a reflection of the state of the main character, who is introduced lying on the bed and staring blankly at the ceiling. He appears to have no reason to get out of bed other than to find a cigarette lighter. A half-empty bottle of liquor completes the depressing image.

Tully finds a purpose in life when he meets Ernie Munger (Jeff Bridges), a talented young boxer, in a gym. The two spar but Bill quickly tires and cannot keep up with the much younger man. Later, at a bar, he keeps thinking about Ernie and tells his friends—among them Earl (Curtis Cokes)—how impressed he is by Ernie. This gives him some perspective on his own life. Once a promising boxer, Tully married a woman who "destroyed his peace of mind," and left him when he started losing fights. As a result, he started drinking and now works picking fruit and vegetables, a job commonly associated with immigrants, whom he accompanies. Thus, his social standing is reduced to the status of his immigrant ancestors. Unhappy in his love life, he lives with the alcoholic Oma (Susan Tyrell), who cheats on him with her ex-boyfriend, Earl. He decides to return to boxing and reclaim the life and position he once had.

THE IRISH IN NEW HOLLYWOOD

Meanwhile, Munger visits a boxing promoter, Ruben (Nicholas Colasanto). In Ruben's gym, the other young boxers training are African American and Latino, in contrast to classical Hollywood's representations of almost exclusively Caucasian boxers. We see how boxing has changed from when it was a typically Irish sport. Later, at night, Ruben tells his wife how special it was to have a "white kid" in the gym who could attract audiences as much with his talent as with his ethnicity, now uncommon in the boxing world. During his first fight, against a young Latino boxer, Ernie is introduced as "Irish Ernie Munger." When he protests that he is not an Irishman Ruben explains to him that Irish means "white" in the boxing world. Thus, although the character is not of Irish origin, the stereotype of the Irish boxer is attached to him as a reference to the past. Despite his unquestionable potential and skill in the ring, he loses his debut. He is even less successful in his second fight, as an African American boxer knocks him out immediately after the first round begins. He must re-evaluate his priorities when his girlfriend, Faye (Candy Clark), becomes pregnant. In need of money, he, like Tully, starts picking fruit and vegetables, thus following the same path in life as the older boxer.

Bill returns to Ruben with Ernie. He pays his old debts and begins training. However, his personal life interferes with his resolve to return to boxing and he continues drinking heavily. In his first fight, he faces an aging Mexican boxer, Antonio Lucero (Sixto Rodriguez), who is clearly in bad shape and is asked whether he has consulted a doctor before the match. In the first round, both Tully and Lucero quickly tire and the initially dynamic fight quickly turns into an almost lethargic exchange of punches. Eventually, Tully wins by a technical knock-out but he is in such bad shape that he is only vaguely aware of his victory. Despite the cheering he gets from Ruben, he quickly becomes disillusioned with his plan to return to boxing as a way of becoming successful when he is paid only $100 for his victory. He visits Oma in her apartment but finds out from Earl that she does not want to see him again. Some time later, wandering the streets drunk and disheveled, he meets Ernie. He invites him to a drink, but Munger refuses, saying that he must return to his wife and son. They eventually go to have a cup of coffee together. While being served by an elderly man, Billy comments on the man's age, clearly unhappy with his life. As he turns to look at other people present, the camera closes in on his eyes and, as it switches to a point of view shot presenting the people around them, the action freezes and the sound fades out before returning to the close-up on Billy's face. This symbolizes Tully's state as he understands that he will remain in this still world where nothing is ever going to change for him. Trying to hold on to the only person who reminds him of who he used to be, he emotionally asks Ernie to stay a while with him. As they sit in silence, drinking coffee, the film ends.

In the classical cinema, Irish gangsters and boxers were similar: they used violence as a quick route to personal success. This success never lasted long because of the destructive character of violence. New Hollywood Irish gangsters and boxers are also alike: old and worn-out has-beens. *Fat City* is an extremely pessimistic view of Irish boxing. Not only is Bill Tully's story one of failure but Ernie Munger is stereotyped as Irish—and in the 1970s Irish boxers are curiosities, somewhat nostalgic relics of the time gone by. Tully's attempt to restart his career is doomed to failure. He will never be a champion and his personal life is a downward spiral of alcoholism. Ernie may have potential but must accept that he will never be a first-class boxer. If he continues to follow in Bill's footsteps, he will end up just like him. His refusal to drink with Tully is a sign of his departure from Tully's path.

The fading world of Irish boxers made the 1970s perfect for a remake of *The Champ* (1931), mentioned in the previous chapter. The story of an aging champion fitted perfectly with New Hollywood's pessimistic vision of Irish boxing and was remade in 1979 by Franco Zeffirelli with Jon Voight as Billy Flynn. Like Andy Purcell from the 1931 film, Flynn is an ex-boxer, an alcoholic, and a gambler, raising his son, T.J. (Ricky Schroder), for whom he is a hero and a role model. Despite some differences in plot, the film's main premise is unchanged. Flynn attempts to box his way to success and become the parent his son deserves despite his age and poor health—the result of injuries in the ring and heavy drinking. In the end, Flynn faces a much stronger opponent and although, like Purcell, he wins the fight he succumbs to his injuries, leaving T.J. hysterical at the loss of his father and champion. Thus, the film conforms to the pessimistic vision of Irish boxers dominant in New Hollywood.

6   Other Representations of the Irish in New Hollywood

Another old role played by the Irish in cinema—the main characters of musicals—did not disappear completely. However, even in a musical from the 1970s, the Irish had to be portrayed as violent people. In Martin Scorsese's *New York, New York* (1977), Jimmy Doyle (Robert De Niro) is a brawling saxophone player. He is also violent at home, and, as a result, he loses Francine (Liza Minelli), his wife, and the mother of his son. Again, violence is a threat to family values, and the leading Irish character has to choose between a violent life alone and a peaceful life at home.

The period also saw the appearance of the figure of the Irish American firefighter. One of the stereotypical jobs of Irish Americans was portrayed in the famous *The Towering Inferno*, in which firefighters led by Michael O'Hallorhan

(Steve McQueen) fight a fire that breaks out on the eighty-first floor of the fictional tallest building in the world—the Glass Tower in San Francisco. The Irishman is unequivocally positive and focuses on the positive aspects of the Irish stereotype. From the moment he appears on the screen, it is evident to the viewer that O'Hallorhan is a professional. However, similarly to other representations of the Irish he is quite harsh, duty-bound, and unapproachable, which is, arguably, best reflected in the following dialogue inside an elevator shaft:

O'Hallorhan:	"We'll go down by rope. We're gonna rappel down to 65, get on top of that elevator, use it as an exit."
A young fireman:	"I can't make it. I'll fall. I know I'll fall."
O'Hallorhan:	"Okay. Then you better go first. That way, when you fall, you won't take any of us with you."

O'Hallorhan's reaction is quick and sharp. He appreciates the difficult and dangerous situation and knows survival depends on fast, decisive action. There is no room for doubt and if he allows himself to express compassion towards the young inexperienced fireman all of them will be put in danger. This behavior, pertaining to the idea of the survival of the fittest, corresponds to a very traditional vision of masculinity. In such a view, compassion may be seen as a feminine characteristic and, therefore, cannot be expressed by the leader of a group of men.

Significantly in the context of cinematic representations of Irish American firefighters, *The Towering Inferno* only shows the professional side of the firefighter's life. O'Hallorhan appears on the screen when the fire starts, and we learn virtually nothing about his personal life. Admittedly, this may be because the film focuses on just one fire; contemporary films stress the conflict between firefighters' personal and professional lives, making the characters much more complex.

•••

New Hollywood began with *Bonnie and Clyde*, a film that romanticized violence, turning unacceptable characters into pop-cultural icons. Irish violence in Hollywood remained unsentimental but began to be considered useful as a deterrent to crime. This was made possible because of the characteristics of the time when the films featuring Irish characters were produced and how their characters were constructed. The latter is visible through the characters' traits, which, in turn, are displayed through their actions in the analyzed films. The plot, which forms the surface structure of the film, is built of narrative motifs constituting the deep structure of a narrative. Therefore, it is possible to study a character through the study of narrative motifs used in their portrayal.

The most prominent narrative motif appearing in the films analyzed here is violence. Violence is always the central concept in the variety of narrative themes around which the plots are constructed. The plot compels the characters to show their attitude towards various kinds of violence and from there other motifs appear. For instance, characters might want to reject violence but rejection means betraying their community and endangering their family. This involves the narrative motifs of the inability to escape from violence, of betrayal, and of the choice between family and violence. In New Hollywood films, the central motif of violence is used in the construction of Irish characters irrespective of their occupation or social role. Thus, the motif of the Irish cop and its variant the Irish detective, Irish priest, Irish gangster, and other motifs involving occupations, as well as the Irish husband/wife and father/mother, attributed to a given character identify this figure based on his or her attitude towards violence.

The Irish cop in New Hollywood films is a brutal male who uses excessive violence against criminals. He is a largely one-dimensional figure whose only function is to fight crime. Characters of other ethnic origins are portrayed as inept or obstructive. The Irish cop's understanding of the law is based on an extreme form of the old Irish idea of retributive justice, in which crime is punishable with death. The stereotype here is, however, to no small extent, positive as an Irish cop never deliberately hurts innocent people. This character is in a difficult situation because he comes from a violent world but protects the world of the law and a social order based on the rejection of violence; therefore, the Irish cop belongs to neither world. He is an outcast, resembling the traditional western hero and, therefore, becoming a new incarnation of this hero.

As a period seen as a departure from classical cinema, New Hollywood re-evaluated and transformed traditional Irish film characters. The New Hollywood image of an Irish cop seems to be an evolution of the classical version of the uncompromising character present in *The Racket*. In early classical films, starting with *Little Annie Rooney*, such characters usually stood out from their Irish compatriots. They were respected as they constituted a barrier between American society and the violent Irish community. A similar function was performed in classical films by Irish priests, who always stood firmly against violence. In New Hollywood, this character is presented as someone who protects the community but rather than rejecting violence or opposing it, he embraces brutality, which he sees as the only viable tool in a very personal crusade against crime.

THE IRISH IN NEW HOLLYWOOD   145

The figure of the Irish gangster also evolved: from a real threat to society to someone whose time has passed and who can only wait for the inevitable end. On the one hand, the New Hollywood representation of the Irish mobster seemed to be an appropriate conclusion to the story of the classical version of such a character. Choosing the path of crime leads to illusory success but the bitter end comes sooner or later for those who act against society and its rules. On the other hand, the depressing vision of the end of the Irish mobster stems from the fact that such a character was no longer considered a serious threat. In the 1970s, America was plagued by much more severe problems than Irish mob violence, which was the central theme of films in the 1920s or 1930s. The external threat caused by the heightened tension between the USA and the Soviet Union during the Vietnam war and the perceived internal uncertainty caused by the destabilization of a formerly rigid social order as a result of deindustrialization and the cultural revolution proved more serious than the old threats. By that time the Irish had also become respected members of society, proving themselves as valiant soldiers and skillful politicians.

Irish boxers met a similar fate. Their fading world is presented extremely pessimistically as they struggle to regain their status as champions. However, they have been replaced by younger and stronger representatives of other ethnic groups and they have no place in the boxing world, serving only as somewhat nostalgic reminders of the past. The violence, to which they turn in order to reclaim their position, is not a reliable tool as, even though they may win a fight, they cannot win back their lives.

What remained unchanged in the stereotype from classical to New Hollywood, was the inevitability of violence, the motif of betrayal, and the need to choose between duty and family. Violence is still inescapable, directing the characters' lives and denying them success. When asked why he is a police officer, Harry Callahan says he does not know. The Irish familiarity with violence, impossible to explain based on the plots of the analyzed films, is easily explained by the existence of the stereotype of the violent Irishman. In a violent life, there is no place for family. The private lives of the characters in the films discussed are a mess, not because they do not want a harmonious life, but because they have no choice. Harry's wife is dead, his romance with Sunny ends between *Magnum Force* and *The Enforcer*, and Kate Moore, who might have become Harry's romantic interest, is shot in the line of duty. "Popeye" Doyle is single and prefers casual sex to long-term relationships. James McParland's happiness ends when he chooses duty over the love of a woman.

Moreover, McParland is punished for betraying the Irish community he infiltrated. Likewise, punishment reaches Eddie Coyle when he tries to become an informer. As in the classical *On The Waterfront* and *The Informer*, this motif makes the Irish community resemble a tribal group to which one owes complete loyalty if one does not want to be rejected or even killed.

Finally, the films studied here focus on depictions of Irish masculinity. As shown in New Hollywood, it is primitive and based on the old Darwinian and Neo-Darwinian notion of survival of the fittest. What is more, violence is identified with action since only violent characters are active, while non-violent ones represent passivity in the face of social disorder and problems in life. Thus, social stability can be achieved only by reacting violently to brutality, as in the Irish idea of justice based on violent retribution. At the same time, violence is not a viable response to personal problems.

In conclusion, Irish characters in New Hollywood are even more troubled and violent than their classical predecessors. They also seem to represent two trends in the evolution of the Irish stereotype in American cinema which continue in the contemporary period. Firstly, extremely violent Irish cops appear and break with the traditional role of non-violent protectors of the neighborhood and family life that had been dominant in the portrayal of Irish police officers in the classical period. In their case, violence is accentuated unprecedentedly and serves as a line of defense against crime and social disorder. Secondly, the gangsters, boxers, and, to a lesser extent, trade union members, are New Hollywood's comments on their earlier incarnations and their changing place in the world. Nevertheless, the Irish in New Hollywood continue to be presented as primarily violent, despite their improving social status in the US, which attests to the fact that Irish violence, like the brutality associated with the outsider hero of the western, is useful to society.

CHAPTER 4

Contemporary Hollywood: The Irish as Outlaw Heroes

The appearance of blockbusters and the financial failure of New Hollywood's auteurs' experimentation gave rise to a new era in the history of Hollywood. At first glance, this new period seems to contrast sharply with New Hollywood. Whereas the cinema of the nineteen-sixties and the first half of the nineteen-seventies offered the viewer films that were their directors' artistic expressions, contemporary American cinema focuses on profit. However, this is an oversimplification as neither independent cinema nor auteurs have disappeared entirely from Hollywood. Contemporary Hollywood forms a heterogeneous landscape that offers researchers and critics a variety of possibilities when it comes to approaching film. Thus, in order to give a broad perspective of the role of violence in the representation of Irish stereotypes in contemporary American cinema, this section focuses on a variety of productions, including blockbusters, mid-range pictures, and independent films.

The filmmaking industry quite quickly realized that genre films were ultimately more successful than those that followed the patterns of personal cinema rooted in Europe.[1] Blockbusters seek enormous financial success. David Bordwell describes them as "must-see movies," "launched in the summer or the Christmas season, playing off a best-selling book or a pop-culture fad like disco."[2] Ticket sales are not the most important source of income but are instead a preliminary stage of profiting. Blockbusters are followed by profitable franchises—music, toys, and, more importantly, by sequels—based on the same premise, frequently following a similar pattern but still appreciated by audiences. Many of the films analyzed in the following chapters have sequels, sometimes very similar to the original productions. They are analyzed only if they contribute to or differ from the construction of the main characters.

Bordwell argues that storytelling in contemporary films is coherent.[3] These new films frequently refer to one another and also to classic Hollywood productions. Bordwell draws a parallel between contemporary filmmakers and mannerists who sought new ways to be innovative, while still aware of the old

---

1   Bordwell, *The Way Hollywood Tells It*, 3.

2   Bordwell, 3–4.

3   Bordwell, 6–7.

© KONINKLIJKE BRILL NV, LEIDEN, 2021 | DOI: 10.1163/9789004467972_006

Renaissance masters, such as Michelangelo and Leonardo da Vinci.[4] Contemporary Hollywood should not be considered an epoch completely detached from classical cinema and New Hollywood but rather their descendant. Contemporary Hollywood generally uses the same patterns and stereotypes in representing particular themes but uses new creative ways to do so.

Unlike New Hollywood, contemporary American cinema is filled with various representations of the Irish and Irish Americans. These representations often involve the professions typically associated with the Irish, such as police officer and firefighter but they also include references to gangs and Irish freedom fighting. In order to study various types of characters over a period of approximately thirty years, the characters in this section are analyzed according to their profession or the social role they represent, rather than chronologically.

The films studied here, especially those made in contemporary Hollywood, seem to present a dichotomy of Irish characters based on their adherence to or rejection of American law, thus creating a contrast between lawful and unlawful heroes. This has been noted and analyzed by Robert Ray, who calls it the opposition between the official hero and the outlaw hero.[5] Ray traces it back to the traditionally American opposition between society, epitomized by the civilized man, and the individual, or the natural man.[6] This is seen in westerns, for example, in which towns and their community are centers of civilization in the otherwise wild world of the American frontier, populated by Native Americans and outlaws. In westerns, society needs an outsider to protect it from villains, who usually belong to the world of nature. The outsider hero in westerns possesses the features of the villain and bridges the gap between society and the outside world.[7] This construction changed as the western genre developed.[8]

Ray presents numerous differences between the official and the outlaw hero. Firstly, the outlaw hero is immature, unlike the official hero.[9] The former is prone to "whims, tantrums and emotional decisions,"[10] while the latter is characterized by "sound reasoning, judgment, wisdom, and sympathy based

---

4   Bordwell, 16.

5   Ray, *A Certain Tendency of the Hollywood Cinema, 1930–1980*, 58–63.

6   Ray, 58.

7   Will Wright, *Six Guns and Society: A Structural Study of the Western* (Berkeley: University of California Press, 1975), 142–43.

8   John Storey, *Cultural Theory and Popular Culture: An Introduction* (London, New York: Routledge, 2015), 120–123.

9   Ray, *A Certain Tendency of the Hollywood Cinema, 1930–1980*, 59–60.

10   Ray, 59.

THE IRISH AS OUTLAW HEROES   149

on experience."[11] Secondly, the outlaw hero rejects society, which is usually shown in his[12] relationships with women: he is either a loner or unsuccessful with women.[13] Conversely, the official hero embraces society, accepts its values, and is able to live in it.[14] Finally, the most important difference between the outlaw and the official hero is their approach to the law. The outlaw hero sees law as a constraint, as it is "the sum of society's standards" and "a collective impersonal ideology imposed on the individual from without."[15] The official hero embraces the law as a part of the social order in which he lives.

As well as the western incarnation of official and outlaw heroes, there were numerous other versions based on a similar set of differences. According to Ray, the most typical examples of outlaw heroes include "the adventurer, explorer, gunfighter, wanderer, and loner," while official heroes included the "teacher, lawyer, politician, farmer or family man."[16] President Abraham Lincoln has been analyzed in the context of the dichotomy.[17] James Malanowski claims that while Lincoln is an official American hero,[18] his defiance of American society's standards makes him an outlaw hero, contributing to his greatness.[19] In the present monograph outlaw heroes include a Northern Irish republican, a gangster, and a vigilante, while police officers, firefighters, and boxers represent official heroes.

Outlaw heroes are not necessarily negative characters and should not be treated on a par with villains. On the contrary, stories of outlaw heroes frequently oscillate between their traditionally positive image in folklore and the negative aspects of their lives, as in the case of Billy the Kid, a traditional American outlaw hero.[20] The individualism attributed to the outlaw hero is not always useless to society. As Christopher Garbowski notes, while excessive individualism may hinder the development of civil society, it is a fact that "civil society is to no small extent the product of modern individualism."[21]

---

11   Ray, 60.
12   While analyzing the two types of heroes, Ray takes into account only male characters.
13   Ray, *A Certain Tendency of the Hollywood Cinema, 1930–1980*, 60.
14   Ray, 61.
15   Ray, 62.
16   Ray, 59.
17   James Malanowski, "Abraham Lincoln: The President as Outlaw," in *Lincoln: A President for the Ages*, ed. Karl Weber (New York: PublicAffairs, 2012), 147–161.
18   Malanowski, 148.
19   Malanowski, 161.
20   Graham Seal, *The Outlaw Legend: A Cultural Tradition in Britain, America and Australia* (Cambridge, UK; New York: Cambridge University Press, 1996), 106.
21   Christopher Garbowski, *Pursuits of Happiness: The American Dream, Civil Society, Religion and Popular Culture* (Lublin: Maria Curie-Sklodowska University Press, 2008), 10–11.

150   CHAPTER 4

Outlaw heroes, as defined by Robert Ray, are individualists who reject society and especially its laws for being an obstacle to their freedom. Unlike more selfish villains, outlaw heroes can do things that serve a higher purpose. Therefore, such characters will include Northern Irish republicans, vigilantes, and some gangsters. However, as this and the following chapter will prove, in the case of the Irish, the categories are not always clear-cut, allowing for the presence of some less than prototypical examples of both official and outlaw heroes. Consequently, to differentiate the Irish police officers who follow the ideals of the American law and those who seem to reject it, another category is proposed: the Irish cop will serve as a label for Irish police officers presented as outlaw heroes.

1   Irish Cops: Labeled as Irish

If New Hollywood was when the stereotypical violent cop was born, it is in contemporary Hollywood that he has matured, appearing in various incarnations. Sometimes he is overtly Irish—his nationality is stated explicitly—and sometimes only an Irish surname identifies him, making it possible to combine generic and Irish violence in the character. Characters based on stereotypical Irish police officers are inspired not only by Dirty Harry and his unforgiving approach to crime but also by earlier instances of such characters from classical cinema. In this case, they serve as guardians of law and order but not necessarily judges and executioners. However, the following films present characters who are outlaw heroes even though their function in society is that of police officers.

1.1   *The Twilight of Dirty Harry*
The original and most famous Irish outlaw hero—Dirty Harry—did not survive his transition to the blockbuster era very well. Whereas *Sudden Impact* (1983), directed by Clint Eastwood, might be seen as an interesting stage in the evolution of the main character and his disillusionment with the law he has sworn to protect, the final film in the series—*The Dead Pool* (1988) by Buddy Van Horn—is merely a play on the formula created by the previous parts. In both films, a noticeably older Callahan is still troubled by his outlook on retributive justice, which he understands as "an eye for an eye." This places him on the boundary between law and crime and turns him into society's violent defensive measure against violence. Thus, the basic formulaic premises of the series are employed but it is the details that matter as they present Harry's changing attitudes to various situations.

THE IRISH AS OUTLAW HEROES   151

Eastwood's *Sudden Impact* is an example of a rape-revenge film. In these movies, a rape victim uses lethal force to exact revenge on the rapists.[22] Applying such a formula to a Dirty Harry film creates an unusual situation for the main character when he becomes personally involved with the rape victim—Jennifer Spencer (Sondra Locke). Spencer and her younger sister are gang-raped by a group led by Mick (Peter Drake), leaving the younger girl catatonic, which is similar to another rape-revenge film, *Death Wish* (1974). As pointed out in the previous section, although Harry's methods make him similar to a vigilante, he still works within the boundaries of the law. *Sudden Impact* presents "the often-hazy distinctions between justice and vigilantism,"[23] which is one of the main features of rape-revenge films. Jennifer Spencer is a vigilante as she follows her vision of retributive justice outside the boundaries of the law. Initially, Callahan's intentions towards her are ambiguous; ultimately, however, he decides to help her. Callahan's siding with a vigilante proves that he has changed. It is perhaps his growing disillusionment with the law that makes him help Jennifer. As Allison Young notes, Harry is a police officer "suffering under the requirements of the legal process" and is "thus 'victimized' by law."[24] On the other hand, as Young puts it, he is juxtaposed with a woman who is a vigilante, i.e., she goes beyond the limits of the law as she is similarly disillusioned with it.[25] Thus, in helping her Callahan seems to have reached the point at which he can no longer remain utterly faithful to the ideals he has sworn to protect. Led by Spencer, he goes beyond the limits of the legal system, embracing completely his vision of the law based on extreme retribution.

Although the film was commercially successful, not all the reviews were favorable. Kevin Thomas focused on its exploitative characteristics, Vincent Canby criticized the screenplay and primitive direction, and Gary Arnold referred to the obviousness of the plot and the poor impression made by the main character and Eastwood himself.[26] Eastwood had not wanted to return to Dirty Harry and the film was initially meant for Sandra Locke alone.[27] In his *When Movies Mattered: Reviews From A Transformative Decade*, Dave Kehr even goes as far as to state that Eastwood was not "comfortable with Harry Callahan." He compares the character's bravado in the three previous films,

---

22   Young, *The Scene of Violence*, 45.

23   Alexandra Heller-Nicholas, *Rape-Revenge Films: A Critical Study* (Jefferson: McFarland, 2011), 56.

24   Young, *The Scene of Violence*, 47.

25   Young, 47.

26   Heller-Nicholas, *Rape-Revenge Films*, 57.

27   Heller-Nicholas, 57.

152 CHAPTER 4

especially in the first one, with his withdrawal in the fourth film.[28] Kehr does, however, praise the skillful presentation of the contrast between Callahan and Spencer.

The contrast consists of binary oppositions that develop and become increasingly complicated as the film progresses. The film presents two stories which at some point intersect.[29] Harry's story is at its core comical. He is visibly and comically surprised at the sight of Threlkis suffering a heart attack during the wedding scene. Comic relief is also provided by his dog, Meathead. Spencer's part, on the other hand, is tragic and gloomy. The tragedy she suffered in the past is impossible to forget. Her quest for vengeance is intended to bring her solace. Both two stories present violence as the dominant element of the world they portray. In Spencer's case, it is the generic violence of a rape-revenge film. Callahan represents both the generic brutality of the crime thriller and the Irish violence ascribed to the film by virtue of his surname.

The comical perspective on—since it is represented by Callahan—stereotypically Irish violence differs from the serious New Hollywood perspective on the subject. However, it is by no means new and nor is it unique in contemporary Hollywood cinema.[30] Moreover, Eastwood refers directly to previous Dirty Harry films. The viewer is treated to scenes in which Harry shows disrespect towards his superiors and scenes in which other law enforcers show a lack of understanding for him. In accordance with tradition, Harry's minority partner, this time the African American Horace King (Albert Popwell), is killed by the gang when he visits Callahan. These predictable elements are in sharp contrast to Spencer's story.

At the intersection of Spencer's and Callahan's stories, Harry is drawn from the comical perspective into the serious one. His attention is again focused on matters regarding his perception of the law, as he shares it with Spencer. The role of women is more fully developed than in the previous films. Jennifer Spencer is no background figure, nor is she used to show women's inability to cope with the "man's world" of law enforcement. She is quite successful in what she does, i.e., killing criminals, and she is, therefore, Harry's equal: some critics dubbed her "Dirty Harriet."[31] The appearance of Harry means she does not complete her quest herself, altering the formula of the rape-revenge film.[32] If it

---

28 Dave Kehr, *When Movies Mattered: Reviews from a Transformative Decade* (Chicago: University of Chicago Press, 2011), 79.

29 Heller-Nicholas, *Rape-Revenge Films*, 56.

30 See the sections devoted to vigilantism and uncategorized characters.

31 Heller-Nicholas, *Rape-Revenge Films*, 57.

32 Young, *The Scene of Violence*, 48.

THE IRISH AS OUTLAW HEROES   153

were not for Callahan, Spencer would have been murdered by Mick; however, the fact that she needs his help does not diminish her role as a vigilante. This is evidenced by the scene in which Mick and his gang almost kill Harry. Beaten and thrown into the sea, he loses his Magnum revolver, i.e., the attribute of his superiority over criminals. After this he is firmly a part of Spencer's world: he now pursues the rapists instead of the vigilante. The appropriateness of his choice is emphasized by the fact that he survives, emerges from the water, and retrieves an even more powerful version of his gun—a Magnum AutoMag. In this case, accepting vigilantism as a way of enforcing justice coincides with Harry's vision of the law.

The major problem of *The Dead Pool*, the last film in the series, lies in its repetitiveness. As put by Marc Eliot, "the film did not have much going for it."[33] However, there were also positive opinions, e.g., for Howard Hughes, although "by no means the best of the series, *The Dead Pool* is a notable improvement on its predecessor."[34] Hughes praises the film for its ironic approach to the figure of Callahan and also called it an intentional comic book.[35] The film continues the more comical approach to violence in *Sudden Impact*. It is set in the world of filmmakers and critics, giving the film self-referential irony. Harry and his partner investigate a series of murders whose victims are connected with film director Peter Swan (Liam Neeson). Swan and his friends play "dead pool"—a game in which they try to predict the death of film industry people and other celebrities.

The film's comical approach to violence is its most important feature. However, violence in *The Dead Pool* is more generic than Irish, as the film is a nonspecific crime thriller. Nevertheless, it contains an important comment about on-screen violence, voiced by Peter Swan, who tells Harry: "Death and violence—that's why my films make money ... they're an escape."[36] The film, therefore, plays both with the conventions of the previous Dirty Harry films and comments on violence on the screen in general. As such, despite its shortcomings and repetitiveness, it may be considered an appropriate conclusion to the *Dirty Harry* film series.

1.2   *The Dawn (and Twilight) of John McClane*

John McClane (Bruce Willis), the main character in the *Die Hard* series, is another American cop with an Irish surname. Like Callahan, McClane appears

---

33   Marc Eliot, *American Rebel: The Life of Clint Eastwood* (New York: Harmony Books, 2009), 242.

34   Hughes, *Aim for the Heart the Films of Clint Eastwood*, 75.

35   Hughes, 191.

36   Hughes, 77.

154 CHAPTER 4

in five films. Just as the *Dirty Harry* series may be studied in terms of the main character's transformation during the shift from New Hollywood to the blockbuster era, so too may John McClane's transformation be studied in terms of the development of contemporary cinema: the films cover virtually the whole period. Twenty-five years passed between the premiere of the first film and the last film in the series. *Die Hard* by John McTiernan was released in 1988 and was tremendously successful. It was referred to as a "high-tech, high-voltage thriller"[37] and "the film that changed the face of action-adventure films for years to come."[38] The warm reception from critics and audiences led to a follow-up, *Die Hard 2* (Renny Harlin) in 1990; the second sequel, *Die Hard With A Vengeance* was released in 1995 and directed once again by McTiernan. The lasting popularity of the main character led to the production of a fourth film, *Die Hard 4.0*, or *Live Free or Die Hard* (by Len Wiseman), as it is known in the USA, in 2007. Finally, the last film so far premiered in 2013 and was entitled *A Good Day to Die Hard* (by John Moore).

One of the chief similarities between *Dirty Harry* and *Die Hard* is the main characters' disrespect for established legal procedures and their vision of the law, according to which the most dangerous criminals deserve to die. Both have Irish surnames. This is the only clue to Harry Callahan's ethnic origin but John McClane's identity as an Irish American seems to be explicit, especially in the films directed by McTiernan.

Although all the films in the series, unlike *Dirty Harry* and its sequels, acknowledge the plots of the previous films, *Die Hard* and *Die Hard With A Vengeance* are the two most closely related parts. In the first, McClane is a New York Police Department detective visiting his wife, Holly McClane née Gennaro (Bonnie Bedelia), a senior employee in the Japanese Nakatomi corporation in Los Angeles, at Christmas. He arrives at Nakatomi Plaza, the high-rise building owned by the corporation, in a limousine driven by an African American driver, Argyle (De'voreaux White), during the office Christmas party. While McClane is alone in Holly's office, the party is interrupted by a group of terrorists commanded by Hans Gruber (Alan Rickman). McClane eludes the terrorists, who capture all the Nakatomi employees, including Holly. Armed only with his gun and running barefoot, the detective faces twelve well-armed and well-trained criminals who pretend to be terrorists but, in reality, want to rob a safe located in the building. McClane starts killing them one by one and manages to establish contact with an LAPD police officer, Al Powell (Reginald

---

37   Phil Hardy, *The BFI Companion to Crime* (New York: Continuum, 1997), 106.
38   John Kreng, *Fight Choreography: The Art of Non-Verbal Dialogue* (Boston: Thomson Course Technology, 2008), 32.

THE IRISH AS OUTLAW HEROES 155

VelJohnson). He is repeatedly wounded, beaten, and humiliated. In the end, he kills Gruber by throwing him out of a window.

Die Hard With A Vengeance, the third film in the series, begins with an explosion in the middle of New York. The bomber—a man calling himself Simon (Jeremy Irons)—demands that John McClane go to Harlem wearing a sandwich board saying, "I hate niggers." McClane obeys and is almost immediately approached by a gang of African Americans. He is saved by Zeus Carver (Samuel L. Jackson), a Harlem shopkeeper. Simon, revealed to be Hans Gruber's brother, orders McClane and Carver to do a series of tasks across the city. However, the whole scheme is only a distraction as Simon and the criminals he leads intend to rob the Federal Reserve Bank of New York. With Zeus's help, McClane manages to thwart Simon's plan, killing the members of the group and, eventually, Simon himself.

Although there is a direct link between the two *Die Hard* films made by John McTiernan, there is an interesting difference in their representation of McClane's ethnic identity. In the first film, McClane is a typical American lone hero. Like western heroes, he is an outsider defending a community to which he does not belong. In this reading, the building symbolizes a western town whose inhabitants are unable to defend themselves and which is overrun by criminals. McClane's status as a western hero is emphasized by the apparent randomness of his presence in the building.

However, unlike classic western heroes, he does not kill the criminals in a series of duels or a climactic shootout. Instead, he uses all possible measures to eradicate them. When he kills one of the criminals, Tony, he puts a Santa Claus hat on the dead man's head and sends him down in an elevator with a note saying: "Now I have a machine gun. Ho, ho, ho." This is no doubt intended to throw the other criminals, especially Tony's brother, off-balance but is nevertheless cruel and largely unnecessary. On the one hand, McClane is on his own and needs to resort to extreme actions not only to save his wife and the other hostages but also to survive. For example, he throws the body of another dead criminal onto Al Powell's car in order to get Powell's attention. However, he also shoots at Powell's car, almost killing the police officer, and he seems to enjoy shooting.

Finally, in the confrontation with the most dangerous criminal, Karl (Alexander Godunov), whose brother John killed at the beginning of his struggle with the gang, McClane's murderous side is on display. The cop and the criminal decide to fight hand-to-hand as they "are both professionals." The contrast between them is striking. Karl appears more powerful and dominating. Moreover, he is fully clothed while McClane remains barefoot and is disheveled after the struggle he has endured so far. Although there is undeniable savage

156   CHAPTER 4

imagery in the way Karl is presented, Eric Lichtenfeld points to McClane's savagery, emphasized by his appearance.[39] Karl quickly turns out to be stronger
but McClane seems more violent. He shouts, "You motherfucker, I'm gonna kill
you! I'm gonna fucking cook you, and I'm gonna fucking eat you!" while beating
Karl violently. He then strangles him with a chain.

At the end of the fight, McClane is severely wounded, limping, and left with
only two bullets. Nevertheless, in a standoff resembling *High Noon*, he uses
his apparent weakness to deceive the remaining criminals, kill one of them,
and shoot Gruber, propelling him out of the building through a window. Gruber grabs Holly and it looks like he will drag her down with him but McClane
frees her, killing Gruber. When McClane emerges from the building with Holly
by his side he does not resemble a western hero or Harry Callahan who, having defeated the criminals, calmly leaves the scene of the crime. McClane's
wounds show the severity of his struggle. What is more, Karl suddenly appears
and goes to shoot McClane but is killed by Powell. This also runs counter to the
established formula of a western hero, since Karl, as one of the main antagonists in the story, should be defeated by McClane.

However, in a more metaphorical sense, McClane contributes to Karl's death
not only because of their earlier hand-to-hand fight. The characters in the film
represent and are defined by two approaches to violence. Most are victims of
violence. They include the Nakatomi employees, but also Los Angeles police
officers and FBI agents wounded and killed by Gruber's gang. Al Powell is a
victim of violence because he once shot a boy carrying a toy gun and he has
had to live with the guilt. Other characters use violence for various reasons.
They include the gang, for whom violence is how they can acquire money, and
McClane, who uses brutal methods in order to free his wife and the other hostages. The fact that the hero uses violence for moral reasons makes it acceptable to the viewer. It becomes a positive force counteracting Gruber and his
gang's brutality. However, whereas Gruber's violence is planned and carefully
executed, almost to the point where it can be described as elegant, McClane's
violent actions are spontaneous, instinctual, and rough. This difference is
emphasized by Gruber's and McClane's appearance: Gruber is in a clean suit,
McClane is barefoot and disheveled.

What is more, McClane is, to some extent, a source of violence. He destroys
Al Powell's equilibrium and entangles him in a fight. Powell had sworn never to
use a gun again but he is forced to break his promise because of McClane. This
motif of a hero being a source of violence as well as the only way to cope with
it is common to the representation of the violent Irish stereotype.

---

39   Eric Lichtenfeld, *Action Speaks Louder: Violence, Spectacle, and the American Action Movie*
      (Middletown: Wesleyan University Press, 2007), 164.

THE IRISH AS OUTLAW HEROES   157

However, in the first film, as in the *Dirty Harry* series, McClane is identifi-able as Irish, or possibly Scotch-Irish, only because of his surname. His image as a western hero appears repeatedly throughout the film. It is projected indirectly by transferring formulaic devices, such as motifs used in westerns, into the world of *Die Hard*. The connection is expressed directly too: Gruber refers to McClane as a "cowboy." Since the cowboy is a classical American hero, McClane's American identity is emphasized, only his surname hinting at Irish origins. He is, therefore, an American hero whose construction includes some elements of the Irish stereotype. However, as Lichtenfeld notes, McClane's "sig-nature one-liner" which he uses when killing the main antagonist, "Yippie-kay-yay, motherfucker," combines the classic ethos of the western hero's bravery with modern profanity.[40] It is, therefore, possible to assume that McClane is a character in whom the classic ethos is mixed with savage and instinctual Irish violence.

In the third film, his Irish origins are more pronounced. The construction of the main character in *Die Hard With A Vengeance* shares many similarities with the first film. McClane's disheveled appearance is first contrasted with that of the other police officers. On his first appearance, McClane is hungover and it is revealed that his wife has left him. His fellow detectives look down on him, doubting whether their suspended colleague is ready to return to duty. This degradation of the main character, who appeared as a strong hero in two previous films, is further emphasized by the first task given to him by Simon; i.e., by wearing the sandwich board with the racial slur written on it in public. One of the first people to witness McClane's Harlem walk is an elderly woman who stops in disbelief. McClane is plainly distressed by the knowledge that he is offending an innocent person.

In the course of action, McClane and Zeus Carver are seen running around the city, solving Simon's puzzles. Although Zeus seems a match for McClane's verbal abuse, he is frequently terrified by the detective's actions. McClane kills without qualms, which has been established in the series by that point, but he also endangers innocent people's lives when he drives a taxi through a crowded Central Park. It is clear McClane will stop at nothing to thwart Simon. His brutality is not as extreme as in the first film but it is also, to a large extent, spontaneous.

At one point in *Die Hard With A Vengeance*, when Simon's real aim has already been revealed, the gangster admits that avenging Hans was only an addition to his real plan, as he did not like his sibling. "There's a difference, you know," he says, "between not liking one's brother and not caring when some

---

40   Lichtenfeld, *Action Speaks Louder: Violence, Spectacle, and the American Action Movie*, 164.

158   CHAPTER 4

dumb Irish flatfoot drops him out of a window." A significant claim—if the focus of *Die Hard* is on McClane's American identity and the focus of *Die Hard With A Vengeance* is on his Irish roots, then the question arises whether the way he is presented corresponds to an Irish or American stereotype.

The answer to this becomes apparent when McClane's characteristics, set out above, are studied in connection with his ethnic origin. The concept of the law as extreme retribution is Irish, stemming from Ireland's cultural and historical background. The McClane of the first film is more like Harry Callahan with the emphasis on his being a cowboy—the classic American hero. However, like Callahan, his familiarity with violence, characteristic of the Irish, is clear. McClane's surname is a label that explains his violence. Although almost nothing is known about McClane's life before the events in *Die Hard*, it is safe to assume his violence did not suddenly appear as a result of his meeting Gruber's gang. Additionally, McClane's version of the violent Irish stereotype goes beyond earlier films. He is fiercer, more savage, less precise. Harry Callahan is a marksman; McClane disposes of criminals in whatever way he can, including hand-to-hand combat. He is also more brutal and on numerous occasions derives pleasure from injuring and inflicting pain on his enemies. His savagery and disrespect for the rule of law, combined with his inability to form a successful relationship with his wife, clearly indicate that, like Callahan, McClane is an outlaw hero.

The three remaining films, *Die Hard 2*, *Live Free or Die Hard* and *A Good Day to Die Hard* are not so closely linked as the productions described above but they do contain references to earlier films. McClane's doings in the previous films are acknowledged but the only thing linking them is the main character. *Die Hard 2: Die Harder* is set apart from the other films by the fact that McClane's opponents are actual terrorists, rather than thieves. McClane does not hesitate to use their methods: he takes hostage General Esperanza, the "spiritual leader" of the terrorists, in order to exchange him for his wife's safety. McClane's competency and skill as a police officer are acknowledged by his opponents, who seem to respect him as a worthy adversary. Although McClane and the terrorists fight for different reasons, they are similar in their disillusionment with America. The terrorists have been recruited from special forces, the country's best of the best, who, however, follow a South American dictator. McClane is disillusioned with a bureaucracy that enables terrorists to infiltrate even those parts of society's structure that should be particularly well protected. Thus, the film's view of America is cynical and violence is seen as a tool to alter the state of the country.[41]

---

41   Robert Cettl, *Terrorism in American Cinema: An Analytical Filmography, 1960–2008* (Jefferson: McFarland, 2009), 108.

THE IRISH AS OUTLAW HEROES   159

The two latest films are typical examples of blockbusters built on the formula of a successful earlier production. They do not introduce anything new and are repetitive, although they are admittedly good action films that appeal to John McClane fans. In both the fourth and fifth films McClane has to save his children. In *Live Free or Die Hard*, terrorists kidnap John's daughter, Lucy (Mary Elizabeth Winstead), and in *A Good Day to Die Hard*, the detective travels to Russia to save his son, Jake (Jai Courtney), who turns out to be a CIA operative. Both films fit the continuum of the series but do not add anything new to this study.

The central motifs in the construction of the Irish American detective John McClane are similar to those in previous productions. The family man willing to risk his life to save his family is a universal motif, not specifically connected with the Irish. However, the fact that McClane's family life suffers because of his violent life is a motif typically seen in connection with Irish characters. In the third film, in which the main antagonist addresses John's Irish origin, the detective's family does not appear, and it is only mentioned that Holly has left him. Moreover, when McClane calls her, he immediately has to end the conversation in order to pursue Simon. Another recurring motif in representations of the Irish stereotype is the inability to escape violence. In each film, McClane finds himself accidentally in the center of a major gang or terrorist operation and has to fight to survive. However, all the motifs used in the *Die Hard* films discussed here originate in the character's intimacy with violence, which becomes the dominant narrative motif in the series. McClane can cope with all the situations he encounters because of his ability to use violence. In order to explain this intimacy, the detective is given an Irish surname, which justifies his otherwise unexplained violent character in terms of the Irish stereotype.

1.3   *The Irish Killing Machine:* RoboCop

The violent Irish stereotype was also used in a now-classic science-fiction thriller, *RoboCop*, which like virtually all successful blockbusters was followed by two sequels. There was also a remake. The original film was directed in 1987 by Paul Verhoeven. It was inspired by several science-fiction productions, including Ridley Scott's *Blade Runner* (1982) and James Cameron's *The Terminator* (1984), as well as a Japanese cartoon *8 Man*.[42] *Dirty Harry* was also a source: it is difficult to overlook the similarities between RoboCop and Dirty Harry's law enforcement methods, dedication to justice, and cold and indifferent stance when undertaking violent actions.

---

42   M. Keith Booker, *Alternate Americas: Science Fiction Film and American Culture* (Westport, Conn: Greenwood Publishing Group, 2006), 215.

160   CHAPTER 4

RoboCop presents a vision of the future in which the explosion of crime in Detroit has led to the degeneration of its society, illustrated in news broadcasts with grotesque commercial breaks. Gangs control the streets and the government's importance seems diminished. A major corporation, Omni Consumer Products (OCP), controls virtually every significant aspect of Detroit citizens' life, including hospitals, prisons, police, and governance, or as Susan Jeffords puts it, "OCP controls all of the services citizens in the 1980s have come to expect the government to provide."[43] This all-encompassing conglomerate focuses solely on profit and not on peoples' needs.

OCP plans to demolish the dystopian Detroit and establish a new city in its place—a utopia in which mechanical law enforcers guarantee the citizens' safety. Preliminary tests are not encouraging. A malfunction causes one of the guardian robots to kill an OCP executive. The corporation leaders decide, therefore, on a different project—a robotic police officer with a human brain. The corporation is soon given a chance to put the plan into action when a police officer, Alex Murphy (Peter Weller), newly transferred to North Detroit, is severely wounded during his first patrol. Despite the doctors' efforts to save him, he is pronounced dead, and, under the terms of an agreement between OCP and the police, his body is used to build RoboCop. He is activated initially with no memory of his life as Alex Murphy; however, he is recognized by his former partner Ann Lewis (Nancy Allen) and begins to regain memories of his wife and son. Nevertheless, he follows his programming and begins his quest to eradicate crime from the streets of Detroit. He is hugely successful and becomes a hero to other police officers.

RoboCop begins to suffer from the memories of his death as Alex Murphy. He recognizes the criminals who killed him and begins hunting and killing them. It is revealed that the leader of the gang that murdered Murphy, Clarence Boddicker (Kurtwood Smith), works with the OCP president, Richard Jones (Ronny Cox). However, RoboCop cannot arrest Jones due to the "Fourth Directive," a part of his programming that forbids him to hurt any OCP executive. Because of this, RoboCop is what Daniel Dinello describes as "a violent, yet submissive, quasi-human robot."[44] With the help of Ann Lewis RoboCop faces and kills Boddicker and his gang. Finally, he is also able to shoot Jones when the latter is fired by his superior. When asked his name, RoboCop replies "Murphy," which shows "the triumph of human individualism over

---

43   Susan Jeffords, *Hard Bodies: Hollywood Masculinity in the Reagan Era* (New Brunswick, N.J.: Rutgers University Press, 1994), 108.

44   Daniel Dinello, *Technophobia!: Science Fiction Visions of Posthuman Technology* (Austin: University of Texas Press, 2005), 135.

THE IRISH AS OUTLAW HEROES   161

technologized replication"[45] and the prevalence of Murphy's identity as a person over the imposed function of a corporate tool.

RoboCop 2 (1990), directed by Irvin Kershner with a screenplay by famous comic book artist Frank Miller, was made because of the excitement surrounding the first film. Although frequently described as "lackluster," it follows the story of the original *RoboCop* quite successfully.[46] It is the continuing story of RoboCop who now refers to himself as Alex Murphy. A police strike exacerbates the already poor conditions in Detroit. The deterioration of the city is best seen in a grotesque sequence at the beginning of the film. A homeless old woman is almost killed by a car and is then robbed by a man. The man, in turn, is mugged by two young women who are subsequently nearly killed in an explosion. Murphy is not on strike. He pursues Cain (Tom Noonan), a man who distributes a powerfully addictive designer drug called "Nuke," and Cain's accomplices, including his girlfriend and a violent young boy, Hob.

RoboCop manages to track Cain down but he is lured into a trap and nearly destroyed when his body is cut into pieces by the gang. Barely functioning, Murphy is left by the gang outside a police station. His fate remains uncertain due to OCP's unwillingness to repair him. When he is finally repaired, an OCP psychologist, Dr. Juliette Faxx (Belinda Bauer), introduces into his system several hundred directives that prevent RoboCop from using violence. He, therefore, becomes ineffective in fighting crime in Detroit, preferring to harangue criminals than fight them. When he learns that the only way to delete the directives from his system is to use a potentially lethal high-voltage charge, RoboCop takes the risk and erases the directives. Now completely free from programming, he arrests Cain, injuring him in the process.

A significant theme appearing throughout the first half of the film is OCP's inability to create another RoboCop. All attempts to do so fail, as other cyborgs commit suicide soon after activation. Juliette Faxx's solution to the problem is to use Cain's brain in *RoboCop* 2. She hopes to control him through his addiction to "Nuke." Cain is at first successful, wiping out his old gang but his homicidal urges resurface when, during the presentation of the new cyborg, he sees a portion of "Nuke" and starts shooting at everyone. He is stopped by Murphy and other strike-breaking police officers. Murphy manages to destroy Cain's brain, tearing it out of the machine and killing the criminal, while the OCP executives plan to blame Faxx for Cain's carnage.

RoboCop 3, directed by Fred Dekker in 1993 and starring Robert John Burke as Murphy, was widely criticized by critics and fans alike. Kevin Thomas of *Los*

---

45   Jeffords, *Hard Bodies*, 112.
46   Booker, *Alternate Americas*, 216.

162 CHAPTER 4

Angeles Times described it as a series of car chases and brutal battles "occasionally interrupted by melodramatic exchanges in which the cast punches out its dialogue rather than speaks it."[47] Unlike its predecessors, it was rated PG13, meaning the main character's violence was tamed and reduced. An interesting shift took place in *RoboCop*, a 2014 remake directed by José Padilha with Joel Kinnaman as Alex Murphy. This time, Alex survives an assassination attempt and the cybernetic transformation saves his life. With his abilities enhanced, he exerts revenge on criminals who destroyed his life. Although he is equipped in non-lethal weapons, such as a taser, he does not refrain from killing lawbreakers, including a corrupt police officer.

The first two films concentrate on the main character and are therefore pertinent to the study. Like *Dirty Harry*, *The French Connection* and *Die Hard*, the first film in the *RoboCop* series uses labeling, giving an Irish surname to a police officer. The difference is that Alex Murphy is not shown as a violent policeman before he is transformed into RoboCop. After the transformation, he becomes like Harry Callahan with his methodical and precise actions. Despite the machine's armored and bulky structure, suggesting a certain clumsiness, RoboCop deals with criminals with a precision that allows him to be effective. Like Callahan and McClane, he is a cowboy figure, which is illustrated by the way he twirls his gun before holstering it, Wild West gunslinger style. In *RoboCop 2*, it is stated that Murphy is an Irish Catholic. As in *The French Connection II* and *Die Hard With A Vengeance*, the character's ethnic origin—up to this moment only signalized by his surname—is made explicit.

By the end of the first film Murphy has managed to uncover fragments of his personality, which is both fortunate and tragic. Murphy's status as RoboCop is that of a machine, not a person. He is property of OCP, a corporation "identified with an unquestioning, strongly materialistic position."[48] This symbolizes the enslavement and objectification of people by corporations. On regaining his identity as a man, he is no longer a mindless machine but his status within the corporation does not change. Thus, he becomes a man aware that he will never be anything more than a machine, property. This tragic vision of the main character is emphasized by Murphy's inability to change his status in any way. After each police operation he returns to police headquarters where he is examined by technicians. The place where he rests resembles a cage, another

---

47   Kevin Thomas, "Movie Review : Mechanical 'RoboCop 3' in Need of Policing," *Los Angeles Times*, November 5, 1993, http://articles.latimes.com/1993-11-05/entertainment/ca-53331_1_original-robocop.

48   Jessica R. Johnston, *The American Body in Context: An Anthology* (New York: Rowman & Littlefield, 2001), 13.

THE IRISH AS OUTLAW HEROES   163

symbol of his enslavement by the corporation. A critical moment comes when he removes the helmet that leaves only his lips visible. Regaining his face, Murphy becomes fully aware not only of his past but also of his present predicament. This awareness is emphasized by the unnatural appearance of his face. Thomas Foster observes that the face resembles a mask "stretched over a mechanical armature," which, according to the author, was a deliberate decision by Paul Verhoeven in order to stress Murphy's condition.[49]

The theme of Murphy's struggle to sustain his regained identity is further developed in the second film. Still experiencing visions of his son and wife, he stalks them, observing them from a police car parked outside their home. Severely disturbed, Alex's wife, Ellen (Angie Bolling), hires a lawyer and plans to sue OCP. She also plans to meet RoboCop in person as she believes that he is her husband. Before the meeting, RoboCop is repeatedly asked his name and enrages an OCP official by saying it is Alex Murphy. The official begins ridiculing RoboCop for trying to maintain his human identity, pointing out that he is only a machine and can never be a husband again. During the meeting, RoboCop is without his helmet so his wife recognizes him as Alex Murphy. However, realizing that the OCP official is right, RoboCop tells Ellen to touch his face and when she remarks on its coldness, he lies that he was given the face in order to honor Alex Murphy. The woman leaves crying. Even though Murphy acknowledges his identity as a machine in front of Ellen, the scene shows that in reality he is very human. He understands he can never return to his family and sacrifices his most crucial link to his life as Alex Murphy.

A key scene in the development of the theme of Murphy's identity comes when he is rebuilt after sustaining heavy damage by Cain's gang. The large number of directives he is given symbolizes the rules imposed on law enforcement by bureaucracy. The directives are intended to make RoboCop more successful in fighting crime but they hinder him and are incongruent with the reality of Detroit. The directives regulate each and every aspect of his behavior, in sharp contrast to the directives from the first film, "1. Serve the public trust, 2. Protect the innocent, and 3. Uphold the law," which represents the American vision of the law. RoboCop risks his life to delete the new directives and as a result is left only with Murphy's common sense and his innate Irish violence. There is now no externally imposed guidance. This is clearly a feature of an outlaw hero, who sees the established law as an obstacle and chooses "natural law" instead.[50] What is more, as Jessica Johnston points out, the fact that Murphy risks his life

---

49   Thomas Foster, *The Souls of Cyberfolk: Posthumanism as Vernacular Theory* (Minneapolis: University of Minnesota Press, 2005), 193.

50   Ray, *A Certain Tendency of the Hollywood Cinema, 1930–1980*, 62.

to delete the directives the effectively block his personality demonstrates "an 'inner' desire to break free from his programming, although that very programming has rendered him unable to *articulate* such feelings."[51]

As stated above, OCP tries to develop a new RoboCop. It becomes apparent that Murphy is the only suitable candidate. The explanation given by Juliet Faxx is that Murphy was "top of his class, a devout Irish Catholic, a family man," leading her to conclude that all of this proved that he had a strong sense of duty, which allowed him to survive being trapped in the machine. Thus, being Irish is an indication of being dutiful and conscientious, at least in police officers. This view of the Irish stereotype, although admittedly positive, carries a more indirect implication. When Murphy is deprived of his family, faith, even of his own body, his profession remains the only element of his previous identity. However, his sense of duty seems to overshadow the previous building blocks of his personality as he does not commit suicide like the other RoboCop candidates. Instead he continues to do his duty even though his life has been taken away from him. In this respect, Murphy's sense of duty connected with the role of a police officer seems to be the decisive element in the construction of his identity.

The central motifs used in the construction of RoboCop are similar to those used in the creation of other main characters described so far in this chapter. As RoboCop, Murphy is an Irish American police officer who uses excessive violence against criminals. He cannot escape his fate, as his Irish origins condition his intimacy with violence. This, in turn, prevents him from having a family, another motif associated with the stereotypical representation of Irish American police officers.

The film explores one more typically Irish theme. As stated, the Irish in America were frequently associated with trade unions and labor violence. This touches upon a broader motif of the Irish rejection of authority, rooted in the nation's history. Murphy is an Irish American oppressed by the corporation, which deprives him of all vital aspects of life, except for his devotion to duty as a police officer. In an act described by Johnston as recycling, the corporation takes his body and turns him into a tool, depriving him of his identity;[52] he becomes property, a slave whose existence depends only on who is in power in the corporation and on OCP's finances. When he is severely damaged in *RoboCop 2*, some corporation officials debate whether repairing him might be too expensive. As seen, he regains his identity, rebels against the corporation by wiping out his directives, and destroys the new RoboCop.

---

51   Johnston, *The American Body in Context*, 13.

52   Johnston, 13.

THE IRISH AS OUTLAW HEROES   165

Nevertheless, when the two elements of the construction of his identity—his sense of duty as a stereotypical Irish cop and his rejection of authority—are combined, Murphy chooses the former over the latter. This is seen when the Detroit police go on strike against OCP: RoboCop does not stop carrying out his duties. Quite understandably, his colleagues begin to reproach him for breaking the strike. The sense of responsibility is, however, the main driving force behind Murphy's actions; moreover, it seems to be an innate feature because even when he deletes his directives he encourages other officers to go back to work. This is similar to Richard Harris's portrayal of James McParland in *The Molly Maguires*. McParland starts identifying with his fellow Irishmen in their opposition to the mine owners but his sense of duty as a Pinkerton detective proves stronger than his attachment to the Irish mining community. Similarly, Murphy cannot give up his responsibilities as a police officer and does not take part in the strike because being a police officer is the only aim that is left in his life.

The *RoboCop* series is known for its graphic presentation of violence, the main driving force for the characters' actions. The scene of Murphy's death is extremely brutal, with the police officer's body massacred with shotgun shells. This is, however, only the beginning: his transformation into RoboCop, although it happens offscreen, is also a brutal process, as doctors and technicians dismember Murphy's body. RoboCop's creation is, therefore, possible thanks to violence and in response to violence in the streets. As RoboCop, Murphy is violent and he kills with precision and great accuracy, seen at its clearest when he saves a woman from being raped by two men. One of them uses the woman as a human shield between himself and RoboCop; Murphy shoots through the woman's skirt and between her legs so that she remains unhurt and the assailant is castrated by the bullet. Most important, however, is the fact that Murphy's intimacy with violence gives him a sense of purpose as his first goal when he regains his memories is to kill those who destroyed his former life.

Moreover, the world in which RoboCop lives is corrupt and violent. It is run by corporations who control crime and law enforcement and support one or the other to gain profit. The brutality is emphasized by the aforementioned fake commercials which include, for instance, a family of four shouting at each other while playing a tabletop game called "Nukem," or a car anti-theft system which electrocutes anyone attempting to steal a vehicle, advertised as "MagnaVolt: Lethal Response." RoboCop, similarly to Harry Callahan and John McClane, is also such a lethal response to the problem of crime.

•••

Representations of the Irish in American films that revolve around one of the professions stereotypically associated with the Irish draw on several sources and therefore come in several variations. One of these patterns is based on the New Hollywood version of *Dirty Harry*. Its two primary elements are the motif of a western hero—a solitary gunslinger protecting society from crime—and the stereotype of the violent Irishman. These two combine in a construction in which the generic violence of the western hero is supplemented and explained with the stereotypical violence historically associated with the Irish. The generic violence seems to be one of the characteristics of the world in which a given film is set, while the Irish violence allows the main character to survive in this brutal world.

Several narrative motifs connected with violence are used in constructing the main characters. Firstly, the Irish cop is intimate with violence; he knows how to use it effectively and with precision so that even when his actions put innocent people's lives in danger, only criminals are hurt. This implies the character has control over violence. Secondly, the Irish cop rejects authority, usually personified by WASP police officers and officials who reject violence as a feature of criminals. However, the Irish cop is ultimately victorious: violence turns out to be the only appropriate response to criminal brutality. The third motif used in the construction of the characters is the fact that they cannot escape violence. The Irish cop is always in the center of events that instigate his violent reaction and his only escape is more violence. Finally, his sense of duty is illustrated by forcing him to choose between his profession and family life: he chooses professional duty.

The contemporary films in the *Dirty Harry* series and productions inspired by Harry Callahan differ from their New Hollywood counterparts in the way they represent women. In New Hollywood films about violent police officers, women are usually background characters who need protection or serve as sexual objects. Even if they try to be equal to the main character, as seen in *The Enforcer*, they are ultimately doomed to failure. In the films discussed above in this chapter, women are still secondary to the main male characters but they are no longer helpless. In *Sudden Impact* and *Dead Pool*, there are two strong female characters who cooperate with the main character and are not just his romantic interests. John McClane's wife needs to be rescued in the two first films of the *Die Hard* series but she is by no means a passive observer. She shows her violent side when she punches a TV reporter who has recklessly put her children's lives at risk in the first film and then endangered the flight she was on in the second. In *RoboCop*, Ann Lewis is seen as a brutal and competent police officer in her very first scene when she subdues a male criminal. Thomas Foster points to the sexual role reversal, which the scene depicts on

THE IRISH AS OUTLAW HEROES   167

a deeper level. The author also stresses the fact that the main male character's initial vulnerability is contrasted with Lewis's resilience.[53] What is more, among the antagonists there are also women, whose function reflects the role of the positive characters. They support the main antagonist and are brutal and dangerous but they nevertheless remain secondary to the male opponents of the main character.

2   Northern Irish Republicanism

The nineteen-eighties and nineties saw IRA increased activity. Hollywood responded with several productions in which the IRA or similar organizations play a significant role. The present analysis concentrates on one such film, *The Devil's Own*, with a number of similar films presented for comparison. Importantly, American films devoted to Northern Irish republicanism always feature Irish American police officers and the agents of other American law enforcement agencies. Although these law enforcers are always official heroes, they are nevertheless presented and analyzed in this section to study the contrast between them and the republicans.

Widely regarded as a pro-IRA film, *The Devil's Own* (1997), directed by Alan J. Pakula, presents a contrast between the main characters similar to that in the two films presented above but differs in its approach to Northern Irish republicans. The premiere of the film was met with controversy because of its biased view of the conflict in Northern Ireland.[54] It gained much publicity when Diana, Princess of Wales, took the fifteen-year-old Prince William and twelve-year-old Prince Harry to see it in the Kensington Odeon. Not only did she persuade the cinema staff to allow a twelve-year-old to see a PG-15 film but it also happened six days after two Royal Ulster Constabulary officers were killed by the Provisional Irish Republican Army (PIRA).[55] The film was rumored to have been plagued by script revisions caused by arguments between the main actors and the director. Finally, even Brad Pitt, who played one of the main characters, referred to it as "the most irresponsible filmmaking—if you can call it filmmaking—that I've ever seen."[56] It is worth remembering that Alan

---

53   Foster, *The Souls of Cyberfolk*, 197–98.

54   Cettl, *Terrorism in American Cinema*, 105–6.

55   Michael Streeter, "Princess Tries to Defuse Row over Trip to IRA Film," The Independent, accessed August 13, 2013, http://www.independent.co.uk/news/princess-tries-to-defuse-row-over-trip-to-ira-film-1257620.html. *The Independent.*

56   Cettl, *Terrorism in American Cinema*, 106.

168   CHAPTER 4

J. Pakula was one of the most respected directors of Hollywood, who gained fame after the box-office success of *All the President's Men* (1976).[57]

Despite the film's poor reviews and ratings, it is very interesting for this study, as it is riddled with stereotypical representations. The first scenes of the film show a simple working-class family's life in Northern Ireland. Their seemingly peaceful existence is destroyed by the assassination of the father of the family. This is a decisive turning point for Frankie McGuire, who, having witnessed his father's death, joins the ranks of the republicans. He is next seen as an adult (Brad Pitt) in command of the Falls Road Active Service Unit of the PIRA in a skirmish against British troops on the streets of Belfast.

Defeated by the troops, Frankie and the remnants of his unit move into hideouts. Frankie is then given a new identity and, as Rory Devaney, moves to New York City, aided by an Irish American judge, which reflects the activities of NORAID. He is given shelter in John O'Meara's (Harrison Ford) house. O'Meara is a police officer, unaware of his guest's true identity. The two even become close friends, as O'Meara cherishes the traditions of his Irish forebears.

Frankie/Rory begins working on a building site but his real aim is to buy stinger missiles and smuggle them to Northern Ireland with his friend from the PIRA, Sean. They contact an arms dealer, Billy Burke (Treat Williams). While waiting for delivery of the weapons, Frankie lives peacefully in America, becoming increasingly attached to his hosts, and falling in love with Megan Doherty (Natascha McElhone)—a girl who also escaped from Northern Ireland and works as a nanny. Meanwhile, Tom O'Meara's partner and friend shoots an unarmed man. Tom is torn between friendship and responsibility because he must decide whether or not to protect his partner or by committing perjury on his behalf.

The carefully planned transaction with the arms dealer encounters difficulties and must be postponed, enraging Burke, who assaults O'Meara and his wife and then kidnaps Sean. Working on a hunch, O'Meara finds the money allocated for the transaction and confronts Frankie/Rory, who admits he is in the IRA. Tom and his partner arrest Frankie and take him to the police station. On their way, the young Irishman escapes, killing O'Meara's partner. He does so without any second thoughts, although he knows the man very well.

Frankie learns that Sean was brutally murdered. He avenges him, single-handedly killing all Burke's men, and then executing the arms dealer himself. Meanwhile, O'Meara realizes his guest ranks high in the PIRA. A British Intelligence agent pursuing Frankie tells O'Meara he is also suspected of being connected with the republicans in Northern Ireland, simply because he is of Irish

---

57   Katz, *The Film Encyclopedia 4e*, 1055.

origin. However, O'Meara remains faithful to his American role as a police officer and rather than letting Frankie escape, he tracks him down. The two shoot each other simultaneously but it is Frankie who dies.

While in the USA, Frankie McGuire is shown as calm and somewhat shy but he is, in reality, violent and brutal. The scene in which he fights the British troops is mirrored by the shootout between Frankie and Burke's men. Also, at one point, when Frankie visits Burke, he shoots one of his men in the knee in order to show his determination. On the other hand, he cares about his hosts, treating them as a substitute for his real family, which he lost when his father was murdered. However, although he is given a chance to abandon his obligations and try to live a peaceful life with Megan, Rory is unable to forget his duty. The patriotic ideals he believes in are stronger than anything else. Similarly to Liam McGivney (below), who created a new non-violent personality, Frankie creates Rory. Moreover, like McGivney, Rory cannot escape death and violence, which are his elements, inextricably inscribed in his life.

O'Meara's devotion to family and duty is similar to McGuire's. His wife and daughters are central to his life. He is also shown to be a devoted Catholic. He has to make a choice when his Irish self is confronted with his American identity: he has to decide whether to help Rory (by leaving him to complete his mission) or to follow his moral code and try to arrest the dangerous PIRA member. Even though he understands Rory's motives, he cannot help him. At one point, he states: "I understand why he's doing what he's doing. If I had to endure what he's endured, if I was eight years old and saw my father gunned down in front of my family, I'd be carrying a gun too, and I wouldn't be wearing a badge." As a police officer, he is very different from Harry Callahan and characters based on him. Although his Irish origin is clearly stated, he renounces violence and does not accept it in anyone else. However, when Burke's men appear in his house, O'Meara cannot mount a defense without the violent Frankie's help. At the end of the film, O'Meara becomes focused on stopping Frankie. He wants to arrest him but McGuire leaves him no choice. Thus, Tom needs to resort to violent action.

Moreover, although in his work as a police officer O'Meara encounters violence, it is McGuire who brings violence into his world, which threatens Tom's family. O'Meara understands that Frankie is the source of violence. He sees the young Irishman as a person caught in a vicious circle of violence. At one point, the following conversation between the two takes place:

Tom: "What's the money for? I was thinkin' guns. I was thinkin' IRA."
Frankie: "I need that money, Tom!"

| Tom: | "Why? So other eight-year-olds can watch their fathers gunned down in front of 'em? If this money leaves here, more people will die. Can you tell me that won't happen?" |

O'Meara seems to believe Frankie can renounce the path of violence he has followed so far. He holds on to this conviction even on learning that Harry Sloan of British intelligence wants to shoot Frankie. Tom sees arresting the young Irishman as a way of saving him, as he would be protected by American law. However, Frankie does not see that as an option. When O'Meara confronts him and says "the killing must stop" he answers: "Then you'll have to kill to stop it. Gets a bit complicated, doesn't it?" He sees himself as a part of the world of violence and for him the only escape from it is death.

On some level, O'Meara is a father figure for McGuire. Frankie lost his father when still a child and seems to miss the simple life, as shown on social occasions such as the welcoming dinner at O'Meara's house and the confirmation of his daughter. Frankie tries to get through to O'Meara by describing the situation in Northern Ireland and referring to his Irish identity. Tom, for his part, sees Frankie as the son he never had. When the young Irishman arrives at his house, he tells him that he is happy to have another man about the place. Both, however, put their ideals above personal feelings and their confrontation, therefore, seems unavoidable. The film's last line is spoken by Tom: "We never had a choice… You and me."

The image of Irishmen projected by the film is quite telling. Irishmen from the North are portrayed as violent but brave people fighting against oppressive invaders. Frankie McGuire is not a mindless terrorist who kills for no reason; the British took his father away from him, destroying his life. His whole life is marked by the quest for vengeance and not violence for the sake of violence. What is more, this seems to be universal for PIRA fighters, as "Frankie" in Irish slang is a way of referring to a person from Belfast.[58] During the sequence of scenes showing the British army assaulting the PIRA, Northern Irish republicans are shown as fearless defenders in the face of overwhelming force. Even mortally wounded, the republicans do not lose the will to fight against their enemies.

Thus, one of the defining characteristics of the Irish from Northern Ireland is their opposition to the British, who seem cold and distant, as evidenced by Sloan, who kills prisoners. He is also distrustful of the Irish and suspects Tom O'Meara is involved with the PIRA because of his Irish surname. The British

---

58 "Frankie," Dictionary of Irish Slang, Slang.ie, accessed August 11, 2013, http://www.slang.ie/index.php?county=all&entry=Frankie&letter=F.

THE IRISH AS OUTLAW HEROES   171

are presented as a unified force, most of them in suits or uniforms. When discussing the conflict in Northern Ireland, Frankie and his compatriots point to the injustices the Irish experience under British occupation. At one point, in the first fifteen minutes of the film, Frankie comments on the peace process in Northern Ireland, saying: "They say the word peace, but at the end of the day, all they want is surrender." The viewer's image of the situation in Northern Ireland is from the point of view of the main character, a member of the PIRA. In another scene, when McGuire tells Tom about his father, the police officer asks, "Did they catch the fuckers?", to which Frankie answers, "They were the fuckers." This, again, puts the British in the role of the oppressive regime.

The representation of Irish Americans is different from that of their Northern Irish compatriots. Some descendants of the Irish assimilated into American culture have a distorted perception of their country, which is caused by American stereotypes regarding Irish culture. Although O'Meara and his family seem to cherish the traditions of their ancestors, their image of Ireland is not entirely accurate. They greet Frankie with what they think is a traditional Irish dish and are surprised when he admits he has never eaten it before. What is more, although the Irish Americans are seen celebrating with Irish music and dancing, the Northern Irish are rather too focused on everyday dangers to be seen partying. Finally, the traditional conflict between the Irish and the Italians in America is addressed when Tom and Frankie play a game of billiards against two Italians in a pub.

The image of Northern Ireland presented in the film emphasizes the tragedy of the country. At first, the viewer is shown a peaceful village but the serenity of the scene, underscored by Irish music, is illusionary, as this is where Frankie's father is killed. The music then changes to *God Be With You Ireland* by Dolores O'Riordan, who, in one line, sings, "They tried to take my pride, but they only took my father from me." This vision of the British as a nameless "them" emphasizes the dominance of Frankie's point of view throughout the film. The next image of Northern Ireland in the film is a shot of Belfast with pro-IRA murals and graffiti.

As in *Patriot Games* (below), boys play football in the street, which is then reflected by Frankie and Sean playing football with an empty can on a New York street. When the British forces attack, people seek shelter wherever they can. One shot shows a soldier aiming an assault rifle at the PIRA with a woman and a child standing right behind him. These images are then contrasted with the view of America, especially O'Meara's house.

The dynamic of the conflict in *The Devil's Own* is constructed on the basis of the contrast between an Irish republican newcomer and an Irish American representative of well-assimilated immigrants. Other films also use a similar opposition in their depiction of Irish republicans. However, whereas Frankie McGuire/Rory Devaney is a character whose actions are, at least to some extent, justified by the plot, this is not always true for other such films.

The Patriot Games, directed by Philip Noyce, is the story of an American, Jack Ryan (Harrison Ford), who visits London with his wife Cathy (Anne Archer) and their daughter. Meanwhile, a group of Northern Irish republicans (a PIRA splinter group) are preparing to assassinate a member of the royal family—Lord William Holmes. Ryan witnesses the attack and intervenes, shooting one of the terrorists, a young man named Paddy. His elder brother, Sean Miller (Sean Bean), while being arrested by the police, swears he will take revenge. Soon, he escapes from a prison transport and follows Ryan to the USA.

The film presents a contrast between Jack Ryan, an Irish American who seems to consider himself more American than Irish, and Sean Miller, a Northern Irish republican. The two characters are constructed using similar narrative motifs. Both cherish family life and are ready to kill and die for their next of kin. They are also patriots willing to risk their lives for their country. Family values and patriotism are the main building blocks in the characters' construction and the difference between the two men's approach to the values these motifs represent causes the conflict between them. What also differentiates them is their approach to violence and, it follows, the idea of the law to which they adhere.

Miller is a violent man, and his idea of the law is based on extreme retribution. He believes the British are invaders and therefore he has a right to kill them. When Ryan shoots his brother, Miller's life is consumed by his quest for vengeance, which involves killing the CIA agent and his family. Ryan, on the other hand, adheres to the American vision of the law in which the innocent must be protected, and violence is acceptable only as a means of achieving this. Thus, when Lord Holmes and Ryan's family are in danger, the Irish American does not hesitate to kill. When Miller and his group injure Ryan's daughter, the CIA operative does all he can to hunt down the criminal in a quest for vengeance. Thus, he embraces his Irish identity and the violence it entails because the only way he can fight his enemy is by becoming like him.

A similar construction of the main characters is to be seen in another IRA film, released two years after *Patriot Games*. *Blown Away*, directed by Stephen Hopkins, is set in Boston. Jimmy Dove (Jeff Bridges) is a heroic police officer—an explosives expert working for the Boston police bomb squad. Meanwhile, another explosives expert, Northern Irish republican Ryan Gaerity (Tommy Lee Jones), escapes from the Castle Gleigh prison in Northern Ireland and flees to Boston, where he spots Dove on TV. It emerges that Dove, then known as Liam McGivney, used to be Gaerity's comrade in arms.

THE IRISH AS OUTLAW HEROES 173

Unlike Tom O'Meara and Jack Ryan, the main character played by Jeff Bridges represents two separate identities, which may function as binary opposites. One of these identities—Liam McGivney—belongs to a Northern Irish freedom fighter and a bomber; the other—Jimmy Dove—is an Irish American police officer who disarms bombs to save innocent lives. This dualism is critical in the context of his national identity. Jack Ryan from the *Patriot Games* is wholly assimilated into American culture but McGivney could not assimilate so he created and assumed the identity of Dove—an American of Irish origin. In this way, he moved up in the world and took a position which, theoretically, would be assumed by his descendants. The categories important in the construction of this character resemble those describing Ryan, as he values his family above all other things. He is also willing to risk his life to protect the innocent, which corresponds to the American ideal of the law traditionally presented in action films.

Gaerity is presented as a maniac obsessed with explosions, making him more similar to Sean Miller than to Frankie McGuire. He wants to see himself as an artist in constructing elaborate bombs but from Dove's American point of view he is a savage from a violent land. Dove tells his wife Gaerity was "too crazy" for the IRA, warning the viewer that his brutality goes beyond the expected. Gaerity plans to hurt Dove by targeting everything his former accomplice loves, i.e., his friends and family. By depriving him of the building blocks of his new identity, Gaerity wants Dove to revert to his former identity and kill Liam McGivney. It is especially important that Gaerity blames Dove for the death of his sister. Thus, his motivation is similar to McGuire's and Miller's.

The films juxtaposing the violent Irish newcomers with assimilated Irish Americans, who are peaceful and ready to serve society but capable of violence when necessary, project two very different visions of Irishness. Although *Patriot Games* does not refer to Ryan's Irish roots, only suggesting such origins, the book on which the film is based is explicit on this matter in several places. One is when the queen visits Jack in hospital and wonders why an Irish American would save a member of the royal family. Ryan's answer contains examples of "prototypical professions" of the Irish in America. He mentions Irish American police officers, firefighters, and FBI agents, summing up with the observation that in America, the Irish are the law enforcers, protecting order in society.[59] As an Irish American, in both the novel and the film, Jack Ryan follows a strict moral code; he defends the innocent, without heed for his own safety. Like Tom O'Meara, he is devoted to his family and when his wife and

---

59   Tom Hayden, *Irish on the Inside: In Search of the Soul of Irish America* (London; New York: Verso, 2003), 308.

174   CHAPTER 4

daughter are in danger he is willing to defend them at all costs. He does not
shrink from violence but only when there is no other way to fight brutal enemies threatening the innocent.

The Irish are portrayed ambiguously. Miller and the members of the IRA
splinter group he belongs to are incredibly violent. Even the Provisional Irish
Republican Army distance themselves from the splinter group, considering
their methods too brutal. Northern Ireland is shown to be under British government control, with military checkpoints separating areas of Belfast and the
police taking brutal action against insurgents. Belfast itself appears impoverished and dirty, with pro-republican graffiti painted all over the walls and
fences; in the background, children are playing football. The stereotypical presentation of the Irish is illustrated by Ryan meeting a member of Sinn Féin,
Paddy O'Neill (Richard Harris), in a pub with Irish music by Clannad playing
in the background when the splinter group murders their compatriots from
the PIRA.

Because the PIRA oppose the splinter group, the image of the PIRA projected by the film is not entirely negative. Clancy's novel, on which the film
is based, emphasizes the ambiguity of the PIRA even further, as the splinter
group, referred to as the Ulster Liberation Army (ULA) is described as "Maoist."[60]
Thus, in the book published in 1987, Jack Ryan is fighting against a group that is
not only violent but also communist. The film, which premiered in 1992, makes
no reference to communism, focusing on the Irish aspect of the story instead.
However, it should be noted that it does not seem to condemn the IRA directly.
Instead, it projects an ambiguous image of the PIRA, as in *The Devil's Own*.
This corresponds to the aforementioned mixture of positive and negative perceptions of the Irish in Europe and in the US, which undoubtedly affect the
ethnotype present in the studied films.

Additionally, as in *The Devil's Own*, the Irish are also juxtaposed with the
British, who appear in various positions of power. Apart from Lord Holmes,
the Secretary of State for Northern Ireland, other British characters include
officials, judges, and lawyers, police officers, and soldiers. Thus, regardless of
the function they perform, they symbolize control, even oppression, if perceived from the perspective of the Irish. Nevertheless, they also represent an
orderly society. For an Irish person to become one of the British is considered
an unspeakable crime in the eyes of their compatriots. When Miller escapes
from prison he executes a Northern Irish police inspector as a traitor.

The image of Northern Ireland and its inhabitants in *Blown Away* is shown
through the character of Gaerity and is similar to the one presented in *Patriot*

---

60   Tom Clancy, *Patriot Games* (New York: Penguin Books Group US, 1988), 17.

Games. The beginning of the film shows Castle Gleigh Prison—a gloomy place whose inmates speak Irish. There is no solidarity among the prisoners and Gaerity murders one of them in order to escape. In the first half of the film, a short black-and-white retrospection shows Northern Ireland through images of British soldiers and armored vehicles in the streets. It ends with Gaerity's sister shouting, followed by a bomb exploding. To emphasize the gloomy atmosphere of Northern Ireland and the effect it had on Jimmy's life, the next scene shows Jimmy vomiting at the thought of his past in the old country. However, despite all the terror and gloom associated with Gaerity's actions in Northern Ireland, the film states directly that Gaerity was rejected by the IRA because his methods were too brutal. This makes the IRA an ambiguous organization, similar to its image in *The Devil's Own* and *Patriot Games.*

Blown Away also presents the Irish in America stereotypically. Jimmy and Kate's wedding is celebrated with traditional Irish music and dancing. In another scene, Dove's uncle, Max, is seen drinking Guinness in a pub. On meeting Gaerity he says he has lived in America since he was twelve and the only thing he does not like about his new homeland is the way people speak, as their accent "lacks the music." Subsequently, they raise their glasses with the traditional Irish language toast "Sláinte!" Moreover, the bartender, wearing a Guinness T-shirt, seems more interested in a boxing match on TV than in his customers and he comments loudly on the fight. Finally, in numerous scenes, Gaerity is seen listening to U2, an unmistakably Irish band. All these images add to the stereotypical representation of the Irish on screen.

The pattern in the three films above is broken in another IRA film, 1997's *The Jackal.* Directed by Michael Caton-Jones, it stars Bruce Willis as a terrorist hired by the Russian mob to kill the Director of the FBI, and Richard Gere as Declan Mulqueen, an ex-PIRA sniper serving a prison sentence for gunrunning in the USA. The film was widely criticized, mainly for its implausible plot. In one review Roger Ebert called it "a glum, curiously flat thriller about a man who goes to a great deal of trouble in order to create a crime that anyone in the audience could commit more quickly and efficiently."[61] However, arguably the best evaluation of the film's quality was Robert Cettl's verdict: "a depersonalized but efficient Hollywood blockbuster."[62]

Mulqueen claims he was not a bomber during his time with the PIRA but he is a trained sniper and gunrunner, and a violent man. However, he is not

---

61   Roger Ebert, "The Jackal Movie Review & Film Summary (1997) | Roger Ebert," accessed August 13, 2013, http://www.rogerebert.com/reviews/the-jackal-1997. <www.rogerebert. com>

62   Cettl, *Terrorism in American Cinema,* 163.

a negative character because, as Cettl notes, his participation in the conflict in Northern Ireland stemmed from "ideological conviction," which differentiates him from the cold professional killer played by Willis.[63] Trapped in prison, he cannot return to Ireland. Thus, his chosen path of violence has cost him everything he cared for. He treats the opportunity to help the FBI as a chance to regain his freedom. It is not directly stated whether he wants to return to Northern Ireland to continue the fight or if he simply misses his homeland. The Jackal (Willis), who seems to be a violent force of nature rather than an actual person, represents the violent world in which Declan Mulqueen used to live. The ex-PIRA fighter's mission against the terrorist may be seen as a final rejection of violence. Thus, he is able to do the only thing that seems impossible for the Irish newcomers in *The Devil's Own*, *Patriot Games*, and *Blown Away*: break with violence and, to some extent, accept what America has to offer, and survive.

The second pattern for representing Irish Americans working in American law enforcement is to juxtapose them with a Northern Irish freedom fighter. The portrayal of such characters varies according to how much they have assimilated into American culture. The three Irish American characters appearing in *Patriot Games*, *Blown Away*, and *The Devil's Own* represent various stages of Irish assimilation into American culture and multiple levels of law enforcement. Jack Ryan does not stress his Irish roots, Jimmy Dove hides his true identity, and Tom O'Meara considers himself Irish, though his knowledge of ancestors' country is rather superficial. The three characters' upholding of the law shows they have rejected the violent Irish past and that the American part of their identity is dominant. It is possible, then, to conclude that for an Irishman who wants to become an American, it is vital to reject the violent Irish idea of the law and accept the American one.

The members of PIRA and other terrorist groups appearing in the studied films represent the Irish idea of the law, based on extreme retribution. The Irish freedom fighters represent a spectrum of characters. Liam McGivney has quit his violent life; Frankie McGuire is a romantic hero whose sense of duty does not let him start a new life when he is given a chance to do so; Sean Miller is a violent murderer motivated by revenge, similarly to Ryan Gaerity; finally, Declan Mulqueen is ambiguous as it is not known whether he will forsake the fight for freedom. Importantly, the characters who reject violence and, even if only temporarily, accept the American vision of the law are given a chance to start anew in America, like Jimmy Dove, or return to Ireland, like Declan

---

63   Cettl, 163.

THE IRISH AS OUTLAW HEROES   177

Mulqueen. However, the freedom fighters who cannot swear off violence have to die, as their vision of the law and justice does not correspond to the American one.

Significantly, the freedom fighter characters' actions are guided by three narrative motifs: the loss of a significant other, revenge, and the importance of the father figure. Each of the characters studied here is motivated by the loss of a significant person and feels the need or is given a chance to avenge them. Such a person may be a family member—a father (Frankie McGuire), sibling (Sean Miller, Ryan Gaerity), or even an unborn child (Declan Mulqueen)—or a significant other partner (Declan Mulqueen and Liam McGivney). The loss drives them to seek revenge. In Mulqueen's case, retaliation is direct, i.e., aimed at the person responsible for the loss; McGuire blames his loss on the oppressive British regime and in his case revenge is indirect, not aimed at any person in particular. This, in turn, is emphasized by the fact that the people who killed his father were wearing masks, making them anonymous. Gaerity and Miller target not only the people directly responsible for the death of their close ones but also their families.

The Irish characters in the films analyzed here seem to be focused on the father figure, a feature also of the gangster films analyzed below. Frankie McGuire (*The Devil's Own*) witnesses his father's death and became a republican fighter for the PIRA; he then finds a father figure in John O'Meara. It is also the role of the father to protect the family. Therefore, Jack Ryan is an influential father figure, for whom family is of the utmost importance. Finally, Liam McGivney's uncle serves as his father figure. At the same time, his alter ego, Jimmy Dove, is a father figure for his foster daughter, whom he protects from harm. Mothers, if present at all, are either reduced to background characters or portrayed as people in need of their husbands' protection. This too is a feature of other films analyzed later in this chapter and might, therefore, be considered an essential trait in the construction of the Irish stereotype.

The character's loss is the result of three levels of violence, as defined by Johan Galtung. According to Galtung, violence against a given social group such as a minority becomes culturally acceptable and is sanctioned by the group in power. This causes the downtrodden group to rebel violently, which is met by violence from the group in control.[64] Three levels of violence—cultural, structural, and direct—are present in all the films studied here which deal with the representation of Irish freedom fighters. What is more, since the group controlling the legal system of a given society is the source of structural

---

64   Galtung, *Peace by Peaceful Means*, 200.

violence, this kind of brutality is, according to Merrill Singer, "legal or at least overlooked and tolerated and hence usually unpunished."[65] Direct violence used in response to structural violence may take the form of terrorism but the subordinate group may approve of it, seeing it as freedom fighting. This has allowed various directors to assume different points of view when representing Irish freedom fighters.

The fact that none of the films present the PIRA in an entirely negative light is meaningful in the context of the interaction between structural and direct violence. In *The Devil's Own*, the PIRA is presented most positively, as an army of brave romantic fighters willing to sacrifice their lives for the freedom of their homeland. In *Blown Away* and *Patriot Games*, the PIRA is seen in an ambivalent way. The films do not present the organization in a decisively positive or negative way; additionally, it is clearly stated that the main antagonists are too violent, or even too insane to be members of the "Provisionals." This makes the PIRA an organization that is implicitly less brutal and more civilized than the main antagonists who, in both cases, are willing to kill a mother and a child for the sake of revenge. In *The Jackal*, the PIRA is only briefly mentioned. However, the main character, effectively a PIRA assassin, is seen as a heroic man, finally rewarded with freedom by another heroic character—an American federal agent.

The main reason for this ambivalent to positive view of the PIRA seems to stem from one more aspect of the interaction between structural and direct violence and themes common to the history of the USA and Ireland. In her book on violence as a response to globalism, Cornelia Beyer defines imperialism as "a combination of structural violence (especially in terms of inequality and inequity) and hard policies." These policies rely on interventionism and control, usually with military power, but also within the spheres of politics and economy.[66] The fact that the USA used to be a part of the British colonial empire and fought for independence may have contributed to the more positive view of the PIRA in the eyes of the filmmakers whose work is discussed here, despite the organization being recognized as a terrorist one. The fact that the main characters are presented as brave romantic heroes if their connection to the PIRA is stated directly, or as murderous psychopaths too violent to belong to the "Provos," may serve as a compromise between the negative view of the PIRA as a terrorist organization and its positive perception as freedom

---

65   Merrill Singer, *Introduction to Syndemics: A Critical Systems Approach to Public and Community Health* (New York: John Wiley & Sons, 2009).

66   Cornelia Beyer, *Violent Globalisms: Conflict in Response to Empire* (Farnham: Ashgate Publishing, Ltd., 2013), 55–56.

fighters—between attachment to law and order and the tradition of fighting for freedom.

Moreover, terrorism understood as a response to structural violence explains one more aspect of two of the analyzed films: *The Devil's Own* and *Patriot Games*. The definition of terrorism coined by Beyer and stemming from Galtung's notion of structural violence identifies it as a violent action taken against "a commonly acknowledged elite."[67] The British in the abovementioned films are perceived as such an elite, which explains why they are represented as being in power. This perception is shared by both Americans and Irish. The difference between the two films is that *Patriot Games* acknowledges the British right to Northern Ireland, which is illustrated by the main Irish American character accepting a knighthood. The protagonist of *The Devil's Own* rejects it, which is again based on the primary Irish American's character reaction to a British official.

Finally, this peculiar ambiguous-to-positive view of the IRA seems to be present in all the films studied, irrespective of when they were made. However, a very subtle pattern can be seen if the representations of the IRA freedom fighters are studied chronologically. The least enthusiastic—though not negative—image of the Provisional Irish Republican Army is seen in *Patriot Games* (1992). *Blown Away* (1994) only mentions the IRA as an organization that does not accept violent criminals. *The Jackal* and *The Devil's Own* (both films premiered in 1997) present IRA as romantic, real freedom fighters willing to sacrifice their lives for their country.

What is more, in the first two films, the main antagonists are Northern Irish terrorists who are not in the IRA. The latter two films present IRA freedom fighters as protagonists, with the antagonists being Americans (in both *The Jackal* and *The Devil's Own*) and the British (*The Devil's Own*). Thus, more recent films present the violent Irish as increasingly positive characters. This can be seen not only in IRA films but also in various productions analyzed below.

There is an evident opposition between the Irish and Irish American characters in terms of the categories they belong to: official or outlaw hero. With their adherence to the ideals of American law and order, the Irish American law enforcers in the films analyzed here are official heroes. Their presentation as mature and experienced men who are, in most cases, successful husbands and fathers, further emphasizes this view. By contrast, the Northern Irish republicans reject American law and are unable or unwilling to form relationships; they do not have a place where they belong and are individualists, even

---

67   Beyer, 56.

if they belong to a republican organization. At the same time, their motives may be presented in a way that allows the viewer to identify with them, as in the case of Frankie McGuire[68] of *The Devil's Own*. Even if the main antagonists of *Patriot Games* and *Blown Away* are outlaws, not outlaw heroes, Frankie McGuire and Declan Mulqueen of *The Jackal* are Irish outlaw heroes.

Moreover, although Irish women are, one might say, traditionally underrepresented in the studied films, they also perform a particular function in the plots. In all of them, female characters represent traditional family values in opposition to violence. In *Patriot Games*, *Blown Away*, and *The Devil's Own*, Cathy Ryan (Anne Archer), who is never explicitly said to be of Irish origin, and Kate Dove (Suzy Amis), and Sheila O'Meara (Margaret Colin) represent families the male characters must protect. Thus, they are the reasons why Jack Ryan, Jimmy Dove, and Tom O'Meara resort to violence. However, in this case, violence serves a greater good and is, therefore, acceptable. Additionally, Megan Doherty, Frankie McGuire's love interest, although connected to the PIRA, represents an opportunity for the ordinary life that Frankie cannot have due to his sense of duty. As such, although also a patriot, she stands for another type of Northern Irish patriotism; she supports republican fighters but is not violent herself. Thus, while Irish men are represented as outwardly violent, or intimate with violence and able to resort to it for the greater good, Irish women are mothers and supporters, who see alternatives to violence. This is emphasized by some of their professions: Cathy Ryan is a doctor, Megan Doherty a nanny; thus, both are in the caring profession.

3   Irish Gangs: The Great Return

The well-established figure of the Irish American gangster has also found its way into contemporary Hollywood in almost unaltered form, though there is one major difference: some of them are now women. A panoply of Irish gangsters in American cinema is present in several contemporary films, focusing on the representations of both historical and fictional characters, gangs, and events connected with them. Currently, the Irish "male, criminal sensibility," is one of the main themes explored by filmmakers employing the Irish stereotype in their productions.[69]

---

68   Admittedly, the fact that a popular actor plays the character is also crucial in the process of identification.

69   Roderick Flynn and Patrick Brereton, *Historical Dictionary of Irish Cinema* (Lanham, Md.: Scarecrow Press, 2007), 9.

THE IRISH AS OUTLAW HEROES 181

In *Bad Boys* (1983) by Rick Rosenthal, the main character, Mick O'Brien (Sean Penn), a small-time juvenile delinquent living in Chicago, is sent to the Rainford Juvenile Correctional Facility when he accidentally kills an eight-year-old boy, younger brother of Paco Moreno (Esai Morales), Mick's Mexican American rival. The primary conflict in the film is between O'Brien and Moreno, representatives of two ethnic minorities. The conflict is resolved through violence, as the two characters engage in a brutal fight. However, its outcome is affected by the actions of Ramon Herrera, a former Latino gang member who tries to divert Mick from the path of violence. It is thanks to him that, at the last moment, Mick decides not to kill Moreno. Therefore, the film focuses on various facets of co-existence between the Irish and other ethnic minorities and seems to point out that violence is not the means of achieving success. Whereas New Hollywood showed American cities as scenes of the struggle between various minorities in which extreme violence is the ultimate response to brutality, *Bad Boys* represent a different approach. Herrera might be a member of an ethnic minority hostile to Irish Americans, but he can nevertheless see through the existing divisions and help O'Brien. Although he cannot wholly eradicate Mick's violent behavior, he is nevertheless able to curb it. Therefore, even though the film explores the stereotype of Irish violence, it points to cooperation between various conflicting minorities as a way to control it.

Mick's violence puts him on the path to self-destruction. Even though the film, described by some critics as "an underrated masterpiece,"[70] is quite direct when it comes to displaying the repulsive and immoral world of juvenile crime in Chicago of the 1980s, Mick is hugely attracted to it. Deprived of the romanticism connected with the world of crime that was sometimes present in New Hollywood, the film focuses on mindless brutality, which, once set in motion, is almost impossible to stop. Mick O'Brien aspires to this world. He is tempted by the power he associates with being a gangster but there is nothing romantic about being a criminal, and Mick soon learns this when his girlfriend, J.C. (Ally Sheedy) is raped by Paco Moreno. Mick is indirectly affected by J.C.'s tragedy, and this marks the beginning of his transformation from aspiring criminal to a person for whom there is still hope, as he decides not to kill Moreno. Even though O'Brien finally resorts to violence as a primary response to Moreno's actions, his brutality seems to be properly directed and tamed enough for him to achieve victory in both the physical and moral struggle against Paco. However, this comes at a price: the violent showdown leaves him emotionally shaken rather than cathartic.

---

70   Felix Vasquez Jr., "Bad Boys (1983)," *Cinema Crazed* (blog), June 12, 2012, http://cinema-crazed.com/blog/2012/12/06/bad-boys-1983/.

182   CHAPTER 4

Mick's transformation corresponds to the apparent change in the perception of the Irish that took place in American cinema. After New Hollywood's heavy emphasis on racial conflict,[71] the possibility of cooperation between characters of different cultural and national backgrounds began to be considered. This resulted in films with social commentaries. The Irish are now presented as people intimate with violence but still with a chance of leaving the path to self-destruction. This, it is suggested, can be achieved through non-violent cooperation with other ethnic minorities

Irish and Italian gangsters are contrasted in Joel and Ethan Coens' critically acclaimed *Miller's Crossing* (1990). The film focuses on Tom Reagan (Gabriel Byrne), an Irish American working for an Irish mob boss, Leo O'Bannon (Albert Finney), who controls the criminal underworld in an unnamed city during the prohibition era. The first scene, which seems to be an homage to *Godfather*, presents an Italian gangster, Caspar (Jon Polito), asking an unseen boss permission to kill a Jewish bookmaker, Bernie Bernbaum (John Turturro). At this point, the viewer might expect the boss to be a stereotypical Italian mobster; however, when the camera switches to the person Caspar is talking to, the man turns out to be an elegant Irish American, whose ethnicity is unmistakable, as Caspar refers to him as Irish. The conflict between Caspar and O'Bannon puts the story in motion and serves as the background for Tom Reagan's misadventures in the world of gangsters.

Tom Reagan of *Miller's Crossing*, a man of reason, or, as he is sometimes referred to in analyses, a "thinker,"[72] avoids using violence directly, even though he works for the criminal underworld boss. The film associates violence with active behavior, while the rejection of violence is identified with passivity. Whereas boss O'Bannon is a violent man, Tom is peaceful, even to the point of accepting violence used against him, as he is frequently beaten. In her book on the films of Ethan and Joel Coen, Erica Rowell refers to Reagan as "a punching bag" and writes that his "ability to take such abuse says something about his manhood."[73] Whenever there is a need for physical confrontation, Tom appears fragile and unable to abandon his passive stance. At the same time, however, Tom seems to understand the need for violence and its ubiquity in the world of crime, albeit he does not see himself as a person who could resort

---

71   Philip Jenkins, *Decade of Nightmares : The End of the Sixties and the Making of Eighties America: The End of the Sixties and the Making of Eighties America* (New York: Oxford University Press, USA, 2006), 46.

72   Bradley L. Herling, "Ethics, Heart and Violence in Miller's Crossing," in *The Philosophy of the Coen Brothers*, ed. Mark T. Conard (Lexington: University Press of Kentucky, 2009), 143.

73   Erica Rowell, *The Brothers Grim: The Films of Ethan and Joel Coen* (New York: Rowman & Littlefield, 2007), 74.

THE IRISH AS OUTLAW HEROES   183

to using violence directly. When he is beaten by gangsters working for Lazarre, a man to whom he owes money, Tom does not consider this unjust. On the contrary, he accepts the beating, understanding that it is a part of the gangster code, which he has violated. The perpetrators also appear sympathetic to Tom and even admit they have been instructed by Lazarre not to break his bones. Reagan asks them to send Lazarre his regards. When he starts collaborating with Italians and is ordered to kill Bernie Bernbaum, he is unable to do it. With Tom's gun pointed at him, Bernie says: "Look into your heart." Tom tells him to run and hide, proving that violence is not in his nature. However, as the film reaches its climax, there is another confrontation between Tom and Bernie. Again, Reagan points a gun at Bernbaum's head and the bookmaker repeats the words that saved his life during their first meeting: "Look into your heart." Tom's answer, however, is different this time. "What heart?" he asks, before shooting Bernie in the head.

Killing Bernie marks the end of Tom's transformation from a man of words to a man of deeds. His initial refusal to commit violent acts himself does not seem to prevent him from being able to cope with the reality in which he lives. His intimacy with violence not only makes him a valued adviser to the crime lords but also allows him to operate skillfully in the world of gangsters. This same understanding of the violent world's mechanisms also enables him to accept that he sometimes must be subjected to violence himself.

Irish gangsters recur in Martin Scorsese's works. His 1990 crime film *Goodfellas*, based on Nicolas Pileggi's non-fiction book, *Wiseguy: Life in a Mafia Family*, is loosely based on the story of Henry Hill, a real-life mobster.[74] Hill was a member of the Lucchese family, "the smallest of the big five crime families"[75] active in New York. The story in the film is narrated by Hill (Ray Liotta), who recounts the most important events in his life, starting from his childhood. He is an interesting character, as he is of mixed Irish-Italian descent; Henry's father is Irish, and his mother comes from Sicily. Hill works for the Italian Mafia. Like the majority of contemporary Hollywood films analyzed in this study, *Goodfellas* emphasizes the characters' ethnic origin.

The construction of Hill's identity seems to be a mixture of features Hollywood usually employs in cinematic representations of Irish and Italian gangsters. This is especially noticeable here, as Hill's two closest friends are an

---

74   Margalit Fox, "Henry Hill, Mobster of 'Goodfellas,' Dies at 69," *The New York Times*, June 13, 2012, sec. N.Y. / Region, http://www.nytimes.com/2012/06/14/nyregion/henry-hill-mobster-of-goodfellas-dies-at-69.html.

75   James Mannion, *The Everything Mafia Book: True Life Accounts of Legendary Figures, Infamous Crime Families, and Chilling Events* (Avon, MA.: Everything Books, 2003), 124.

Italian and an Irishman. In one scene, a Mafioso sitting in a bar points to Henry and Jimmy "The Gent" Conway (Robert De Niro), one of Henry's friends, and tells the bartender to give "those Irish hoodlums" something to drink. When Jimmy responds that he is the only Irishman there, Henry does not correct him. This may suggest that, living mainly among Italians, Henry is more likely to embrace his mother's Sicilian origin as his own because he associates all the attractive aspects of being a gangster with Italians. He seems to associate his Irish roots with his violent but ultimately weak father, who never achieved anything.

However, when Tommy DeVito (Joe Pesci) is preparing to become a "made-man," i.e., a Mafia member, Henry says that he and Jimmy could never be accepted into the Mafia as they are both Irish. Thus, he acknowledges his Irish identity, emphasizing its dominance over his Italian identity, since the fact that his mother is Sicilian does not matter to the Mafia. This, in turn, is interesting in the historical context, as Irish gang members usually opposed other minorities and Italians are usually presented in the film as an ethnic group in opposition to the Irish.

Similarly to Mick O'Brien from *Bad Boys*, Henry Hill of *Goodfellas* sees the world of crime as something attractive—a different reality he has always aspired to in order to escape from the harsh life. Although he is somewhat reluctant to use violence directly, he understands that it is necessary in the world in which he lives. This understanding of violence stems from the fact that his Irish father would frequently beat him when Henry was a child. For Hill, violence is such a regular part of life that, recounting this aspect of his childhood, he says: "Everybody takes a beating sometimes." Ultimately, he breaks away from the world of violence but not of his own free will. Rather, it is because he wants to save himself from people who are threatening him and his family.

A very dark vision of the consequences of choosing violence and another look at the idea of retributive justice is presented in *Sleepers* (1996) by Barry Levinson. The film is about four childhood friends, two Irish, Michael Sullivan (Brad Renfro) and John Riley (Geoffrey Wigdor), and two Italian, Tommy Marcano (Jonathan Tucker) and Lorenzo Cacaaterra (Joe Perrino). The boys are represented as typical hoodlums, whose future has not been decided yet. They are influenced by an Italian American Catholic priest, Father Bobby (Robert De Niro) and a local gangster, King Benny (Vittorio Gassman), a well-established set-up familiar from *Angels with Dirty Faces* and later, similar films. After nearly killing a man while robbing a fast-food seller, they are sentenced to a correctional facility where they are sexually assaulted by the guards. Choosing the path represented by King Benny leads to personal tragedy, which affects the rest of their lives. When they become adults, they exact revenge on the

THE IRISH AS OUTLAW HEROES   185

people who hurt them. Tommy (Billy Crudup), and John (Ron Eldard), now criminals, shoot a particularly brutal guard, Sean Nokes (Kevin Bacon). Michael (Brad Pitt), who is an Assistant District Attorney, and Lorenzo (Jason Patric), a newspaper reporter, decide to help them and obtain the conviction of the remaining molesters. Lorenzo also convinces Father Bobby to give the former wards a false alibi in court. However, their victory over their tormentors does not mean their past is erased. After helping clear Tommy and John, Michael resigns from his office and moves to England, where he lives alone, working as a carpenter; Tommy is murdered, and John becomes an alcoholic and drinks himself to death. Only Lorenzo, who originally received a shorter sentence, achieves some measure of success. Thus, the film presents the consequences of young people choosing violence, as represented by a gangster, over peace, as represented by a priest. It employs a well-known narrative pattern, also focusing on the mutual experience of the Irish and Italians as representatives of persecuted communities.

Martin Scorsese focuses on the historical conflict between Irish immigrants and WASP American "Natives" in *Gangs of New York* (2002), set in nineteenth-century New York and based on Herbert Asbury's book, *Gangs of New York: An Informal History of the Underworld* (1927). The film begins with what appears to be the culmination of a rivalry between two gangs: the Natives, composed, as the name suggests of gangsters born in America, and the Dead Rabbits, an Irish gang. Bill "the Butcher" Cutting (Daniel Day-Lewis), the leader of the Natives, kills "Priest" Vallon (Liam Neeson), leader of the Dead Rabbits. Vallon's son, Amsterdam (Leonardo DiCaprio), witnesses his father's death. He takes the knife his father was killed with and buries it together with a medal he was given by his father immediately before the fight. He grows up in an orphanage, knowing he will one day avenge his father. Sixteen years later, he returns to Five Points, the area of Manhattan where his father died, in order to kill Cutting just as he is about to celebrate another anniversary of his victory over the Dead Rabbits.

The film shows the very beginnings of the Irish rise to importance. Initially, they are outsiders, despised by New Yorkers born in America. However, what gives them strength is the vast number of new Irish immigrants arriving in New York. Amsterdam tells the Irishmen gathered around him: "You know there's more of us coming off those boats every day? Some say 15,000 Irish a week! Get all of us together, and we ain't got a gang, we got an army!" Only a spark is needed, he says, for the Irish to use the power that stems from their numbers. This line suggests an interesting connection to another film by Scorsese, *The Departed*, in which the Irish are shown in control of the streets of another large American city, Boston.

186   CHAPTER 4

In *Gangs of New York*, violence is ubiquitous but does not seem to be a distinctively Irish feature. As in the films discussed above, violence is associated with control; this is explained by Cutting, who tells Amsterdam:

> Cutting: "I'm forty-seven. Forty-seven years old. You know how I stayed alive this long? All these years? Fear. The spectacle of fearsome acts. Somebody steals from me, I cut off his hands. He offends me, I cut out his tongue. He rises against me, I cut off his head, stick it on a pike, raise it high up so all on the streets can see. That's what preserves the order of things. Fear."

Cutting's environment and peers are brutal, and even entertainment, such as throwing knives, is best appreciated when it involves violence. When Cutting beats Amsterdam during the anniversary ceremony, the spectators ardently encourage Cutting to hurt him, advising how to slice him up. Treating Amsterdam as an animal to be butchered by Bill they lose their humanity and become a mindless mass directed by mob mentality into violence. As a result, the viewer cannot sympathize with Cutting. The violence associated with the Irish, on the other hand, is acceptable as it is used in self-defense. While the Natives use knives and hatchets—hence Cutting's nickname—the Irish use the *shillelagh*, an Irish club traditionally used for fighting.[76] The crudeness of this unsophisticated weapon contributes to the stereotypical image of the Irish as uncivilized and brutal but at the same time proves their valiance and ability to endure against their better armed enemies.

The final confrontation between the Irish and the "Natives" coincides with the eruption of the New York City draft riots. The streets of New York are the scene of chaotic bloodshed in which angry mob targets and murders African Americans, the wealthy, and children from an orphanage. Soon, the army arrives and begins shooting at the mob. As Dead Rabbits and Natives are ready to fight, they are shelled by American navy artillery. In the ensuing chaos, Cutting manages to attack Amsterdam and cut him with his knife but another explosion throws both of them to the ground. Cutting is wounded and the two men see how the appearance of the army has united their men, who assist each other in escaping from a fire. As Cutting utters his final words, "Thank God, I die a true American," Amsterdam stabs him and holds his hand as he finally dies. He is buried next to Priest Vallon. The film ends with a shot of the graves with New York seen in the background. A montage of images shows

---

76   John W. Hurley, *Shillelagh: The Irish Fighting Stick* (Pipersville, PA: Caravat Press, 2007), 345.

THE IRISH AS OUTLAW HEROES 187

how the city has changed and developed until the World Trade Center appears on the skyline and the graves disappear entirely. Thus, the film shows how the "Natives" and the Irish are ultimately united as they live in the same country and experience the same problems. The final montage seems to suggest that the city has developed thanks to the struggles and cooperation between the ethnic groups that inhabit it.

The motif of the inability to escape from inherent Irish violence is seen in David Cronenberg's *A History of Violence* (2005), in which Viggo Mortensen plays Tom Stall, the owner of a diner in a small town in Indiana. Tom leads a peaceful life with his wife Edie and their two children, Jack and Sarah. The equilibrium of their life is destroyed when two men try to rob the diner. Protecting a waitress, Tom swiftly kills the robbers, which makes him a hero and draws the attention of an Irish gangster, Carl Fogarty, who is convinced that Tom is actually Joey Cusack, a henchman of the Irish Mob in Philadelphia. When Tom scolds his son for using excessive violence in a confrontation with a high-school bully, Jack runs away and is kidnapped by Fogarty and his men, who want Tom to return to Philadelphia. Tom has his son released but refuses to return to his violent past in the mob. He manages to defeat Fogarty's men but the gangster wounds him. However, before the Irish mobster can kill Tom, he is shot and killed by Jack. In hospital, Tom admits to Edie that he is really Joey Cusack in an emotional conversation. Although Edie is repulsed by her husband's past, she later lies to the town's sheriff, protecting Tom's identity. The events awaken Tom's inherent brutality and he becomes violent towards his wife. Tom/Joey travels to Philadelphia to make peace with his older brother, Richie, a mob boss. Once there, Richie reminisces about how he wanted to strangle Joey when they were small children and how he still wants him to die. They fight and Tom kills Richie. The film ends with Tom and his family sitting together at their table in silence, tense and shocked. The viewer is left to wonder whether they will ever be able to return to their peaceful lives.

The 2006 drama, *The Departed* by Martin Scorsese, is another look at the world of Irish gangs in America, after his *Goodfellas* (1990) and *Gangs of New York* (2002). Although based on a 2002 Hong Kong film, *Infernal Affairs*,[77] Scorsese loaded *The Departed* with Irish themes. It is arguably the most Irish-orientated production in Scorsese's oeuvre, making it a fascinating subject for analysis.

It is the story of two Irish American police officers in Boston. The ambitious and hardworking Colin Sullivan (Matt Damon), on finishing the Police

---

77   Laremy Lagel, "Infernal Affairs vs. the Remake, The Departed," Film.com, October 5, 2006, http://www.film.com/movies/infernal-affairs-vs-the-remake-the-departed.

Academy, joins the Special Investigations Unit in the Massachusetts State Police, whose main task is to investigate a criminal organization controlled by an Irish American mobster, Frank Costello (Jack Nicholson). However, unknown to most people, Colin is, in fact, Costello's protégé, and he has become a police officer in order to infiltrate the police and serve as Costello's inside man. The second police officer, Billy Costigan (Leonardo DiCaprio) is a trainee at the Academy when he is also recruited by the Special Investigations Unit. Because of his family ties with South Boston organized crime, he is given the job of infiltrating Costello's mob. Although he formally becomes a police officer, he is removed from the academy and goes to prison on a false charge in order to create a cover story acceptable to the mob.

The infiltrators begin working in their respective organizations: while Costigan supplies information about Costello to Captain Queenan (Martin Sheen) and Staff Sergeant Dignam (Mark Wahlberg), Sullivan keeps Costello informed about the Unit's every move. Both young Irish Americans are connected on a different level as they fall in love with the same woman, Madolyn Madden (Vera Farmiga), a psychiatrist working for the State Police. While Colin's relationship with her is overt, with the two planning to get married, Costigan first visits her as a patient and soon becomes her lover. Meanwhile, when the police attempt to arrest Costello and he escapes, both Costigan and Sullivan realize that their respective organizations have been infiltrated and begin hunting for each other. At one point, Costigan nearly succeeds in arresting Sullivan after he meets with Costello, who gives his double agent an envelope containing information about his men. Sullivan, however, escapes and the two Irish Americans remain unaware of each other's identity. Sullivan makes a difficult decision when he informs Costello's men about Captain Queenan and the still-unidentified "rat" on the roof of an abandoned building. Costigan escapes but Queenan is thrown off the roof and hits the ground, dead, right in front of Billy.

Soon after Queenan's death, Sullivan learns that Costello is an FBI informant, which makes him reconsider his allegiance to the gang, as he worries Costello will reveal his role. Meanwhile, acting on information supplied by Costigan, the police apprehend Costello and his men during a cocaine deal. In the ensuing gunfight, nearly all the mobsters are killed. Costello himself is shot by Sullivan, who becomes the hero of the unit. With Costello dead and the assignment completed, Costigan appears at Sullivan's office in order to have his identity restored and to receive money for his work. While there, he sees Costello's envelope on Sullivan's desk and flees. Realizing his double identity has been discovered, Colin deletes Billy's file from the computer, destroying all the information regarding Costigan's work for the police.

THE IRISH AS OUTLAW HEROES   189

However, it turns out that Costello had been recording all his conversations with Colin. He leaves the recordings to Costigan, who sends a copy to Sullivan and his fiancée; Madolyn listens to it and realizes her prospective husband is, in reality, a mobster. Sullivan agrees to meet Costigan on the roof of the building where Queenan was murdered in order to persuade Billy not to reveal the recordings. When two police officers arrive, Costigan takes Sullivan hostage and leads him to an elevator. As they reach the ground floor, Trooper Barrigan (James Badge Dale), another member of the Special Investigations Unit, appears and shoots Billy in the head. When another police officer arrives, Barrigan kills him too and reveals to Sullivan that he was also a member of Costello's organization. Sullivan, however, does not feel secure knowing that somebody else is aware of his double identity, so he shoots Barrigan and identifies him as Costello's man. He also recommends Costigan be posthumously awarded the Medal of Merit. After Costigan's funeral, Sullivan returns home disillusioned about his future, as his pregnant fiancée has decided to leave him. As he enters his apartment, he is shot in the head by Staff Sergeant Dignam in revenge for the death of Queenan and Costigan.

The Departed is rich in references to the Irish, and all three main characters stress their Irish origin. Jack Nicholson's character is partly based on Whitey Bulger, an Irish American gangster who gained notoriety among Bostonians.[78] The film begins with a prologue in which Frank Costello refers to the history of the Irish in America, focusing on their rise to prominence. He says, "Twenty years after an Irishman couldn't get a fucking job, we had the president. May he rest in peace," and then juxtaposes the success of the Irish with African Americans who, he claims, do not realize that taking what one needs is the only way to achieve something. He also owns an Irish pub, which serves as the headquarters for his men. While drinking, Costello's men raise toasts with the Irish word "Sláinte." At one point, seeing a man sitting at the bar, Costello exclaims, "Who let this IRA motherfucker in my bar?" before laughing and allowing the man to stay. On another occasion, he sings part of "Mother Machree," an Irish song whose title was adopted by John Ford for his 1928 silent film about the problems Irish immigrants faced at the beginning of the twentieth century. Finally, in the scene in which he is killed, Costello is wearing a T-shirt with "Irish" written on its front. Sullivan does not stress his Irish descent as strongly as Costello but he does, for example, tell his psychiatrist fiancée that "Freud said that the Irish are the only people who are impervious to psychoanalysis." Also, when, during a crisis, he tells her to leave him, he adds: "I'm fucking Irish, I'll deal with

---

78   Vincent LoBrutto, *Martin Scorsese: A Biography* (Westport, Conn.: Greenwood Publishing Group, 2008), 384.

190   CHAPTER 4

something being wrong for the rest of my life." Costigan is acknowledged as Irish by Queenan and Dignam. Although he does not emphasize his descent, in one scene, he brutally beats two Italian mobsters when they insult the Irish.

All these references to Irishness emphasize the uniqueness of Irish culture and identity but they also portray them as outsiders in American society. The Irish remember their past, cherishing their culture and traditions expressed in language and chanting, even if their knowledge of their ancestors' culture is only superficial. This creates an almost tribal culture with its own rites, codes, and secrecy. They are presented as non-conformists, which, it is suggested, stems from their culture: at the beginning of the film, Costello says to young Colin: "A man makes his own way. No one gives it to you. You have to take it. *Non serviam*" ("I will not serve"). Colin immediately recognizes the phrase, responding: "James Joyce."

The connection between the Irish and violence is truly inextricable. Costello presents Colin Sullivan with two options for his future life: "When I was your age, they would say we can become cops or criminals. Today, what I'm saying to you is this: when you're facing a loaded gun, what's the difference?" Thus, the future of an Irish person, in the world constructed in *The Departed*, must be connected with violence and depends on a person's attitude to it. Interestingly, such a view of South Boston Irishmen has been confirmed by Mark Wahlberg, who comes from the area.[79] Other career opportunities exist but the community ostracizes people who choose different professions. This happens to Billy Costigan's father, an airport baggage handler, although he comes from a family with ties to organized crime. The ubiquity of violence in the Boston Irish community blurs the distinction between its acceptable and unacceptable expressions. Violence is the fundamental response for criminals but also for police officers, which is understandable in a world in which these two social groups permeate each other. Also, unacceptable instances of violence are acceptable for the Irish. This is best seen when the mother of a murdered robber believes her son was killed because "he did something wrong," against his people, i.e., something other than a robbery. Finally, a book entitled *Violence* can be seen on Madolyn's shelf as she listens to Billy talking about hiding his true identity in the presence of Costello, whom he refers to as a mass murderer. Even in a place that is supposed to be a safe haven, Costigan cannot escape violence.

A similar theme is present in Ben Affleck's critically acclaimed *The Town* (2010). Doug MacRay (Affleck) and "Jem" Coughlin (Jeremy Renner) live in Charlestown. The neighborhood is introduced as a "[...] blue-collar Boston

---

79   Annette Wernblad, *The Passion of Martin Scorsese: A Critical Study of the Films* (Jefferson, N.C.: McFarland, 2010), 204.

THE IRISH AS OUTLAW HEROES 191

neighborhood [which] has produced more bank robbers and armored car thieves than anywhere in the world." In addition, "Bank robbery became like a trade in Charlestown, passed down father to son." Doug, who works at Boston Sand and Gravel, and Jem are members of a gang targeting banks and armored cars transporting money. They usually work for a local Irish mob boss and flower store owner, Fergus "Fergie The Florist" Colm (Pete Postlethwaite).

Born in Charlestown, Doug loses his mother when he is twelve. His father, a bank robber, goes to jail and Doug is taken care of by Jem's family. He is a talented hockey player but has to give it up because of his violence towards other team members. With no chance for social advancement, his only option in life is to follow in his father's footsteps.

During a heist, Jem takes a bank manager, Claire Keesey (Rebecca Hall) hostage. They quickly release her but Jem is preoccupied with the fact that Claire lives in the same neighborhood and might recognize them. Doug follows her to make sure she is not cooperating with the police. He makes contact with her and they eventually develop a relationship. Doug confides in her and, although he only tells her about his official profession, he resolves to change his life for her. However, love does not conquer the violence in him and when local hoodlums vandalize Claire's car he and Jem assault the perpetrators with blunt weapons and firearms.

FBI Special Agent Adam Frawley (Jon Hamm) begins to suspect that Doug, Jem, and two of their friends are responsible for a series of robberies. He approaches Claire, suspecting her of collaborating with the gang and she is devastated to learn of her boyfriend's double life. Doug, determined to give up crime, approaches Fergie the Florist, who demands that he take part in one last robbery, threatens to hurt Claire should Doug refuse, and reveals that he led Doug's mother to suicide. Reluctantly, Doug agrees but the robbery does not go as planned. Jem and two other gang members are shot and killed by the FBI and police. Doug escapes and, in order to protect Claire, murders Fergie and his henchman, Rusty (Dennis McLaughlin) in cold blood. He flees, leaving Claire a substantial amount of money, which she spends on renovating a local sports hall for children. As Claire reads a message Doug left her, the camera shows him standing by a cabin, somewhere in Florida, looking into the distance.

Similarly to *The Departed*, the film makes numerous references to the main characters' national identity, which is emphatically Irish, rather than Irish American. Firstly, there are visual references, consisting of Irish symbols. Jem wears a Celtic cross and has a tattoo on his neck which Claire refers to as "One of those fighting Irish tattoos." Another Irish tattoo is to be seen on Rusty's forearm. It shows the outline of Massachusetts with the Charlestown zip code and is a genuine tattoo: McLaughlin is a Charleston native and first-time actor to whom Affleck gave the role.[80] This proves the director's attention to detail and desire to represent the Irish American community of Charlestown realistically. Other visual references to Irishness include shamrocks on the main characters' sweatshirts and one painted on the building where they prepare for a robbery. Their Irish identity is made clear by other characters' comments on their actions. One of more interesting lines is delivered by Frawley, who—while interrogating Doug—criticizes his refusal to cooperate, saying that he will break him "Despite [his] pitiable, misguided, Irish omerta." This provides an interesting link between the Irish code of silence and the Italian term used to describe secrecy in the Mafia. Another interesting reference to Irishness is the non-diegetic Irish tune playing when Doug visits his father in prison. This may be seen as a symbol of the main character returning to his roots. However, the main function of all the references to the characters' Irish origin is to put them in the context of the hetero-image of the Irish, who—as gangsters—exist outside of society.

The Irish gangster entangled in union violence can be found in Scorsese's crime epic *The Irishman* (2019), based on the novel *I Heard You Paint Houses* by Charles Brandt, and distributed by Netflix. Both the film and the novel recount the life of a real-life Irish American gangster involved in trade unions, Frank Sheeran (Robert De Niro). Similarly to *Goodfellas* but unlike *The Departed*, the film presents the life of an Irish gangster working as a henchman for the Italian Mafia. Scorsese's absolute mastery in storytelling allows various stages of Frank's life to unfold in a Chinese box narration. The main story begins after the war with Frank working as a truck driver delivering meat. He begins selling beef illegally to a gangster, Skinny Razor (Bobby Canavale), and is accused of theft. He is defended by a trade union lawyer, Bill Bufalino (Ray Romano), a cousin of Russell Bufalino (Joe Pesci), the head of a Pennsylvania crime family. This opens the doors to the two worlds in which Frank is going to live from now on: the Italian controlled world of crime and the Irish world of trade unions.

Frank befriends Russell Bufalino and, from a small-time thief, he advances to the position of Mafia hitman. Thanks to his connections with organized crime he meets Jimmy Hoffa (Al Pacino) and rises within the trade union, becoming Hoffa's bodyguard and close friend. From now on, he exists in two intertwined realities, inextricably linked by a network of reciprocal relationships between their participants. Scorsese presents the Mafia and trade unions as elements

---

80   Gayle Fee and Raposa, "Tough Guy's Tattoo Is Talk of 'The Town,'" *Massachusetts Film Office* (blog), accessed February 17, 2021, https://mafilm.org/2010/09/19/tough-guy%e2%80%99s-tattoo-is-talk-of-%e2%80%98the-town%e2%80%99/.

THE IRISH AS OUTLAW HEROES 193

of the same system, affecting America even to the extent of influencing John F. Kennedy's presidential election, according to Sheeran. Their unity is clearest when Frank wins the Teamsters' Man of the Year award: at the lavish celebration, trade unionists mix with gangsters in the presence of the Mayor of Philadelphia.

Like *Goodfellas*, the film focuses strongly on the Irish gangster's position in the Mafia. Despite his friendship with Bufalino, as an Irishman, Frank's status in the organization is, by default, lower than that of Italian mobsters. For his Italian bosses, he is a tool, useful and respected, but ultimately as disposable as the guns he throws into the water every time he shoots someone. On the other hand, the trade unions are dominated by the Irish and Jimmy Hoffa's organization rivals Italian-controlled unions, which Hoffa considers inferior. Ironically, he reaches the highest positions available to him in the two organizations at the same time. During the celebration when he is awarded the Teamsters' Man of the Year title, he receives a gold watch from Hoffa and a gold ring from Bufalino. Both gifts are symbols of not only friendship, but also Frank's status within the organizations: Bufalino says: "Only three people in the world have one of these, and only one of them is Irish." From now on, Frank wears both symbols of his position, indicating his ability to exist in the two worlds.

However, he has to choose between Bufalino's Mafia and Hoffa's trade union when Hoffa, on his release from prison, decides to break with the Mafia. Despite being Hoffa's friend, he plans and carries out his assassination, proving his loyalty to the Italian Mafia and severing his ties with the Irish trade union. This is reflected in his personal life. The attitude of one of his four daughters, Peggy, may be seen as a measure of Frank's descent into the life of crime. As a child (Lucy Gallina), she is afraid of Bufalino and does not accept him, despite the expensive gifts he gives her. She is also afraid of her father being a part of the violent world Bufalino represents for her. By contrast, she trusts Hoffa and treats him as a beloved family member. She is also proud of his union activities, which she sees as selfless support for workers. For her, Frank's participation in Hoffa's trade union is ultimately positive and acceptable. When Frank shoots Hoffa, Peggy, now an adult woman (Anna Paquin), suspecting her father's involvement, breaks with him completely. Frank is unsuccessful in his attempts to regain her trust.

As an Irishman, Frank is portrayed as violent and ruthless. Although he says his army experience in World War II is the source of his intimacy with violence, it is implied that he is naturally predisposed to violence. When a shop owner shoves young Peggy, Frank beats him violently in the street outside his shop, kicking him in the face and breaking his hand in front of Peggy. His violence

194   CHAPTER 4

scares her. Thus, the war seems to awaken his innate violence and teach him how to use it rather than creating it. During the war, he learns what it means to be violent, disregarding any consequences of his actions. When reminiscing about how he executed two German prisoners of war, he does not think of it as a war crime, but wonders why the soldiers were so meticulous in digging their own grave. Scorsese draws a parallel between understanding violence and understanding a foreign language. During one of Frank's first conversations with Russell he reveals his knowledge of Italian, which he says he learned during the war. Bufalino is impressed with his proficiency but the language is only one aspect of the two men's ability to communicate. Both of them also understand violence as a means of communication, sending messages to rival mobsters, and voicing allegiances. It is Frank's proficiency in violence that ultimately allows him to become a Mafia hitman. When he executes mobsters, he describes his actions in a voiceover, showing how skillful and meticulous he is in killing people.

As one of the most recent films analyzed in this book, *The Irishman* alludes to well-established elements of the Irish stereotype, reimagining some of them, and presenting a decidedly pessimistic vision of the Irish gangster. Sheeran fights for his country in the war, like numerous other Irish Americans. However, after the war, he is not a hero and works a low-paid blue-collar job. He turns to crime for the money to support his family. Violence is the only characteristic that he can use to quickly become rich. But the life of crime changes him, destroying his family. He divorces his wife, estranges his daughters, and murders his friend, Jimmy Hoffa. Thus, as in other representations of Irish gangsters in American cinema, violence in *The Irishman* is ultimately destructive, granting only transient success. The gangsters, one by one, succumb to violence or are arrested. Frank, reaching old age, is by no means a victor, as he is abandoned by everyone and lives his final days in a nursing home, planning his own funeral. As the viewer leaves Frank in his room, the old mobster is all alone with his thoughts and memories.

As well as the violence motif, nearly all the films analyzed in this subchapter have a father figure motif. In *Bad Boys*, the role of the father figure is played by Herrera, who guides O'Brien in an attempt to help him avoid ruining his life. Herrera's influence, however, is weak, as the main character follows a pattern of initial rebellion and then slow acceptance of the father figure's values. A more interesting realization of the motif is to be found in *Goodfellas*, as it is closely related to the contrast between the representation of the Irish and Italians in American cinema. For Italian gangsters, the role of the father is usually played and embodied by the Mafia boss, which is especially clear in Francis Ford Coppola's *Godfather*. It is this father figure who sees to it that the organization

THE IRISH AS OUTLAW HEROES   195

follows *la via vecchia* or "the old ways,"[81] whose most important aspect is loyalty, both to the leader and to the Mafia, considered and referred to as "family."

Representing a mixture of Irish and Italian stereotypes, Henry Hill has a strong, albeit violent, Irish father and a loving Italian mother. The mother, though aware her son works for gangsters, is happy because the family Henry works for comes from the same region in Sicily as she does. She is ready to protect her son from her husband's anger and seems indifferent when Henry misses a month at school. This seems to correspond to an essential Italian stereotype, the *mamma italiana* who supports her son, unable to reject him, and her only criticism of his actions is based on her fear for his safety. [82] The father, on the other hand, seems to determine Henry's life, as he seems to be the one who teaches him that violence is, in fact, an integral part of life. Moreover, it is the Irish heritage of Henry's father that prevents him from becoming a made-man. Within the context of the Italian stereotype, the fact that Henry cannot be accepted as a member of the Mafia emphasizes the adherence to *la via vecchia*. In the context of the Irish stereotype, the dominant, although involuntary, role of the father in this matter—outweighing the mother's Sicilian heritage—corresponds to the father's central position as the most important figure in the stereotypical Irishman's life.

Sleepers presents a well-established dualism between two father figures. Father Bobby is much like Jerry Connolly of *Angels with Dirty Faces* or Chuck O'Malley of *Going My Way*. King Benny is the equivalent of Rocky Sullivan. Both try to attract the boys to their particular view of violence. This time the gangster option wins, leading to violence and life-changing tragedy. The fact that the two father figures are Italian rather than Irish makes a direct connection between the two ethnic groups, stressing the similarity of their experience in America, which is illustrated by the fate of the boys; an Irish American and Italian American become gangsters, while the other two, also representing the two ethnicities, are in lawful professions.

The most straightforward realization of the father figure motif is in *Gangs of New York*, where it is intertwined with the motif of revenge that gives Amsterdam Vallon direction when he witnesses his father's death. He considers his father a hero and his world is shattered. As is typical in portrayals of the Irish, the mother is absent from his life. The young Vallon devotes his life to

---

81   Peter E. Bondanella, *Hollywood Italians: Dagos, Palookas, Romeos, Wise Guys, and Sopranos* (London: A&C Black, 2004), 178.

82   "La Mamma Italiana: Interrogating a National Stereotype | Research Network Funded by the Arts and Humanities Research Council," accessed November 22, 2014, http://lamammaitaliana.wordpress.com/.

avenging his father and, in doing so, he becomes a member of Cutting's inner circle. The older Native considers Amsterdam his son, but the familial feeling is not reciprocated. However, Cutting seems unable to kill Amsterdam and he only brands him with the "mark of shame" as a traitor. True, he does not see in the young man a worthy adversary but paternal feelings must play some role in his restraint. When he beats Amsterdam into unconsciousness, he does so because he was rejected as a father, and he uses the only kind of expression he knows, i.e., violence. Finally, when Amsterdam kills Cutting, he is able to start his own life, without the burden of revenge.

The father figure motif is especially well developed in *The Departed*. Firstly, and most importantly, Frank Costello is a father figure to both Colin Sullivan and Billy Costigan. Costello's version of the Irish American father is dark and destructive. Costello begins shaping the identity of Colin when the latter is approximately twelve.[83] Coming from a rather low-income family, the boy is easily impressed by Costello's strength and wealth and becomes his apprentice, devoting his entire life to serving Frank as an inside man in the police. Colin even calls Frank "Dad" when he calls him with information on police activity. However, at the end of the film, Colin realizes that Costello was using him and that the mobster's authority is the source of his problems. In their final confrontation Costello tries to tell Sullivan he has always considered him a son but Colin interrupts and questions his motives: "A son? To you? Is that what it was about? All the murdering and fucking and no sons?" Thus, he attempts to reconstruct his own identity and become a true police officer. However, Billy Costigan's involvement makes this reconstruction impossible and Colin remains an opportunist who will do anything to gain respect and prestige.

Although Costello is sometimes analyzed as a father figure for Billy Costigan, Captain Queenan seems the better candidate. Firstly, it is Queenan who creates Billy's identity as an infiltrator, or even as a criminal, effectively deciding his further personal and professional life. Costigan trusts Queenan as the keeper of his original identity and one of his few links to his real life. When Costello's men assault Queenan in the abandoned building, they ask him where his "boy" is. They mean Costigan but Queenan's answer suggests he thinks they mean his son. This serves a similar purpose to Sullivan referring to Costello as "Dad" during phone calls. Finally, as a true Irish father, whose role is to be a hero for his son, Queenan sacrifices his life to save Billy. As mentioned, when he is thrown from the roof his body hits the pavement right in front of Costigan and his blood splatters Billy. The scene can be interpreted as a blood

---

83   Wernblad, *The Passion of Martin Scorsese*, 204.

THE IRISH AS OUTLAW HEROES 197

sacrifice but also as another expression of the father-son relationship—a relationship based on blood—between the two men.

The similarity of the function of Costigan and Sullivan in their respective organizations, as well as their appearance, can also be interpreted in terms of their relationship with father figures. Their physical appearance—seen especially in the scene in which Billy follows Colin—emphasizes their shared ethnic background and function, as well as their difficulties in achieving the goals set by their "fathers." The main difference between the two characters, however, is that Billy's father figure is ready to help him even if it means sacrificing his own life. Colin, meanwhile, has to accept being controlled by a toxic father figure who is slowly destroying his life. Finally, the similarities between the two are emphasized by their love for the same woman. It is not known which one of them is the father of the child she carries.

The scenes involving father-son relations mirror each other. Firstly, Costello and Queenan both send their "sons" to infiltrate their enemies. Secondly, the "fathers" constantly remind them that their missions must be completed. Finally, both infiltrators eventually lose their "fathers," which has a profound impact on their lives, affecting their identity. When Sullivan shoots Costello, he has difficulty accepting his new identity as a hero of the police unit.

Nevertheless, he quickly comes to terms with the fact that he is free from the toxic father figure's influence and seems ready to reconstruct his identity. Billy's world, on the other hand, is shattered by Queenan's death because he is now left alone against the mobsters: the captain's death means Sullivan can delete Billy's files, effectively depriving him of his true identity.

An interesting reference to family values seems to be made with the presence of two secondary characters, Trooper Barrigan and Staff Sergeant Dignam. If Costello and Queenan are seen as fathers to Sullivan and Costigan respectively, then Barrigan and Dignam are their brothers. Dignam, obviously Queenan's protégé, constantly taunts Costigan. However, in the end, it is he who avenges Billy and the captain, which reveals that he cared for the two men on a very personal level. Trooper Barrigan's identity as a Costello's man is not revealed until the end of the film, and it is he who shoots Costigan. Thus, in both cases, the brother figures kill the main characters.

In *A History of Violence*, Tom strives to save his son from violence. As a henchman of the Irish mob, Tom is tainted with violence and carries it with him, no matter where he goes or what identity he assumes. Jack has grown up in a peaceful Indiana town but seems equally predisposed to violence as his father. He is outraged when Tom reproaches him for using violence against a bully. When Tom tells him, "In this family, we do not solve our problems by hitting people!" Jack answers, "No, in this family, we shoot them!" In response,

Tom slaps his son in the face, proving that he has not escaped violence. Jack does not hesitate to shoot Fogarty in the back to protect his father. Tom stands up, his face covered in Fogarty's blood, and looks at his son as if overcome with conflicting emotions of pride and terror.

In *The Town*, the father figure motif is marked early in the exposition with the reference to bank robbery as a profession passing from father to son. This recurs when Doug says he had to follow in his father's footsteps when he was expelled from the hockey team. Also, during the final heist, as the four young gangsters are preparing for the robbery, the elderly Fergie tells them he can see their fathers' faces when looking at them: it is not only Doug who is continuing a family tradition. However, although fathers are important as questionable role models for the gangsters, it is the lost mother who is the most important person in Doug's life before Claire's appearance. Doug is convinced his mother left him when he was very young and recollects how he spent a long time looking for her and preparing posters that would help him find her. He plans to move to Florida as he suspects his mother is there. Thus, when he kills Fergie, it is as much because of his need to protect Claire, as his desire for revenge.

Finally, *The Irishman* portrays a father who fails to give support to his daughters. As Irish American women, Frank's daughters do not inherit their father's innate violence and do not understand it. When Frank beats the shop owner in front of Peggy, he understands it to be his responsibility as a father but the girl is deeply shaken and begins distancing herself from him. By shifting his identity from Irish to Italian, Frank chooses Russell as a father figure: Bufalino tells him, "You know how strong I made you? You know how strong? You're my kid. Nobody... Nobody can fuck with you. Nobody." The Mafioso creates Frank's new identity, reshaping him and giving him purpose and protection.

As well as exploring motifs related to family, *The Departed* also devotes attention to Irish masculinity, especially in Sullivan and Costello. When he is first introduced as an adult, Colin Sullivan is seen playing American football with his colleagues from the academy against a team of firefighters. After the match, he calls the firefighters "homos," revealing himself as a bigot. Later, when he becomes a police officer, he whistles at a woman working in the same office, which presents him as sexist. Represented in this way, Irish masculinity stands in opposition to homosexuality and dominates femininity. It is visible also in Costello and Captain George Ellerby (Alec Baldwin), Sullivan's superior in the unit. The former emphasizes his masculinity in his relationship with his wife, Gwen (Kristen Dalton), who taunts him, suggesting his relations with other mobsters have sexual undertones. Ellerby discusses the importance of marriage with Colin. According to Ellerby, marriage is essential to one's career

THE IRISH AS OUTLAW HEROES   199

because everyone can see that a married man is not a homosexual and that he is stable; additionally, marriage proves a man's sexual prowess. However, although Colin tries hard to meet the standards imposed by his environment, he is revealed to be impotent in a conversation with Madolyn. Furthermore, due to his actions, he is rejected by the woman. The woman in gangster films is thus heavily objectified. A relationship with a woman is a necessary component in the male character's public image, but not much more than that.

Although the dominant position of Irish men over women has been one of the most salient features in the construction of Irish gangsters since at least the notorious "grapefruit scene," the 2019 American crime drama *The Kitchen* challenges this well-established stereotype. The film is an adaptation of a comic series by the Vertigo imprint of DC Comics and was directed by Andrea Berloff. Although not well-received by critics—it only holds a score of 24% on Rottentomtoes.com—Berloff's production is an interesting reinvention of the classical Irish gangster story. In 1978, three Irish mobsters are arrested in Hell's Kitchen in New York. Although the new leader of the mob, Little Jackie Quinn (Myk Watford), promises to support their wives, Kathy Brennan (Melissa McCarthy), Claire Walsh (Elisabeth Moss), and Ruby O'Carroll (Tiffany Haddish), he does not keep his word and they resort to crime.

The film begins with James Brown's "It's a Man's, Man's, Man's World," an obvious choice for such a story. A sequence of scenes quickly establishes the division of social roles assigned to men and women and the nature of the relationships between the main characters and their husbands. Jimmy Brennan (Brian d'Arcy James) kisses Kathy goodbye as she stays home with their children. Claire, cowering in fear, puts a cold compress on her swollen cheek as Rob Walsh (Jeremy Bobb) taunts her and throws the ice away. Ruby serves Kevin O'Carroll (James Badge Dale) beer, which he rejects because it is not the kind he likes best, and accuses his wife of being lazy. His mother, Helen (Margo Martindale), is present and clearly supports her son's opinion. While the women stay home, the three mobsters rob a store. They are apprehended by two FBI agents but they beat them violently and are about to escape when NYPD arrives to arrest them.

After the trial, the wives meet with the mob in a pub. They sit separately, clearly existing outside of the organization, and it seems that African American Ruby, especially, is unwelcome. Meanwhile, Helen, Kevin's mother, sits with the mobsters, who respect or fear her. This is a departure from the usual portrayal of Irish gangsters, whose mothers are background characters or entirely absent. Helen resembles a *mama italiana* more than a stereotypical Irish mother. She is not only aware of her son's role in the mob but also seems to be an influential figure in the criminal organization who does not have to worry about her well-being after her son is arrested. The three wives, on the other hand, begin searching for jobs, but, as they admit, they have no skills or education. Devoted to their husbands, they have become subjugated and lost their own place in the world but they do not lack the resourcefulness and strength that allow them to take matters into their own hands. They start their own gang. However, unlike men, they have virtually no other option, which they know from experience.

They begin by collecting protection money from local businesses. Soon they recruit two Irish mobsters as their enforcers but they encroach on Little Jackie's operations. Threatened by the mobster, they ask Helen for help but since she is part of the male-controlled world the only advice she offers them is to run. Soon, Claire is attacked by Little Jackie but is saved by Gabriel O'Malley (Domnhall Gleeson), a Vietnam veteran and ex-hitman. After Gabriel shoots Jimmy, Claire kicks the dead body, unleashing her frustration after years of abuse. Later, when O'Malley teaches the women how to dispose of the body, only Claire has the stomach to stay in the bathroom during the macabre lesson. With Gabriel now working as their enforcer, they quickly expand their influence, filling the void left after Little Jimmy's demise and taking over the mob. They force Jewish businessmen to hire Irish unions for construction work and negotiate splitting their area of influence with the Mafia in exchange for allowing Italians to participate in the deal with the Jewish community. They surpass their husbands in expanding the organization and, when the three of them are about to be released from prison, the women know that they are more successful on their own.

As the plot develops, Claire and Ruby become increasingly violent, adopting the characteristic so far reserved for male Irish gangsters. Claire in particular, who develops a romantic relationship with Gabriel, seems prone to violence. She does not want Gabriel to carry out executions, as she prefers to do them herself. When Rob, released from prison, learns of his wife's romance, he furiously assaults her but she stands up to him for the first time in her life and shoots him in the chest. Ruby becomes self-absorbed and opposes Kathy's willingness to support the local Irish community. As an outsider, she has always felt rejected; now, it is she who rejects everyone else. When Helen tells her that Kevin will come back and throw her out into the street, she pushes her down the stairs and breaks her neck. With Kevin released, Ruby cannot return to her previous life and pays the Mafia to kill her husband and his closest associates. When Kevin is murdered while in bed with his mistress, Ruby kisses him on his forehead before asking the assassins to clean up the bodies. It is also revealed that she was responsible for the three mobsters' arrest as she was planning to take over from the start.

The only person who seems to reject violence to a larger extent is Kathy. She is a caring mother and, although she is now in charge of the Irish mob, she does not engage in violent actions herself. She cares about the neighborhood and is loved by the local community. When Ruby pays the Mafia to murder her husband and his men, she begs them to spare a young mobster and her husband. However, in the reality in which she lives now, there is no place for compassion; as a result of her actions, Claire is killed by the mobster she asked to spare. Moreover, although her relationship with Jimmy seems to be based on reciprocal love and mutual respect, Jimmy betrays her and tries to take over the mob. She leaves her husband to the Mafia, who kill him. Now insulated against betrayal, she meets Ruby and Gabriel, who intend to kill her. However, she brings members of the local Irish community with her, clearly showing Ruby who the real leader is. Gabriel decides to leave and Ruby joins Kathy and, together, they decide to expand their criminal empire.

The film re-evaluates the most important established motifs connected with the Irish gangster figure. Firstly, the male gangster figure is deemed obsolete, with the three women stressing numerous times that they have no use for their husbands. This is also stressed on the symbolic level because Claire, the quickest to embrace male violence, is the only one of them who dies, while Kathy, the only one who does not personally kill anyone, is victorious. Through Kathy, the film addresses the established view of Irish American women as intimate with violence, but ultimately non-violent themselves. Her actions are not destructive. She unites the Irish community and gains the support of the Italians. Like *Little Annie Rooney*, it is femininity that ultimately prevails in the gangster world. Secondly, the father figure is replaced by a mother figure. Kathy's father pleads with her to abandon the life of crime but she does not listen. Also, she tells her children that one day they will inherit her position in the mob. Ruby learns from her mother that she was beaten as a child to make her stronger. In other words, she was taught to be violent by her mother. As the film ends, the two women are presented as strong and successful. Therefore, despite its flaws, the film is an interesting look at the classical Irish gangster stereotype.

As the oldest Irish character in American cinema, the gangster seems especially well-developed. The narrative patterns used in the representation are well-established and attractive to contemporary filmmakers. Amongst gangster films, Martin Scorsese's oeuvre deserves particular attention. In four of his gangster films analyzed in this subchapter, the Italian American auteur returns to the figure of the Irish mobster. Although the Irish and Italians in American were similarly downtrodden, and have gone through a similar transformation from rejection to acceptance in American society, they differ greatly in organized crime traditions. The Italian Mafia appears as a highly-structured organization with a clear hierarchy and long traditions. Italian violence is more methodical, targeted, and purposeful. The Irish mob, on the other hand, stems from old Irish tribe-like gangs characterized by no particular well-defined hierarchy. This is also reflected in the representation of Irish violence as wilder and more spontaneous. While Italian gangsters in Scorsese's films are in control and can rise through the ranks of the Mafia, the Irish are outsiders in the criminal underworld who will never be completely accepted by their better organized and more powerful Italian counterparts. While Italians represent power, the Irish stand for the violent element, sometimes controlled and directed by their Italian bosses. This contrast is also visible in high-profile mobsters; Scorsese's Italian Mafia bosses resemble Francis Ford Coppola's *Godfather*, who controls the criminal activity of his organization without engaging directly in violent actions. By contrast, even Scorsese's more prominent Irish gangsters, such as mob boss Frank Costello, do not just control organizations but also are personally violent. Scorsese seems to be particularly interested in the contrast between the Irish and Italians, which he must have observed growing up in a multiethnic neighborhood in New York.[84]

The motif of religion is explored in all but one of the Scorsese films analyzed in this subchapter. In *Gangs of New York*, the Irish are deeply religious, strengthened by their faith. The confrontation between the Irish and the Natives takes place in front of a church. The Irish, with women and children among them, feel unafraid of brutal armed men marching in their direction with burning torches. The Catholicism presented in the film is militant. A priest incapacitates a man who has been shouting at him. The importance of religion is also underscored in the character of Amsterdam's father, whose pseudonym is "Priest" and who carries a Celtic cross when he leads his men to a fight. In *The Departed*, though, religion is mocked by Costello—a devilish Irish American gangster—suggesting the role of faith in shaping the community has declined. Costello's monologues show Catholicism as the faith of the weak, of people who do not think you should just take what you need. He shows no respect for religion and mocks two Catholic priests and a nun. Interestingly, as the corrupter of young Colin, Costello is seen as the devil. In such a view, the *Non serviam* quotation, attributed by Colin to Joyce, may also be attributed to Milton's Lucifer from *Paradise Lost*.[85] Finally, in *The Irishman*, Frank Sheeran returns to the Church near the end of his life, when he asks for and is granted absolution from his sins.

---

84 Wernblad, 15.
85 Wernblad, 205.

4   Irish American Vigilantism

Violence associated with the Irish has arguably found its most explicit incarnation in Irish American vigilante films. According to William C. Culberson, vigilantism was brought to America as early as in the seventeenth century by Scotch-Irish, "who were instilled with a tradition of summary justice."[86] As the Scotch-Irish were used to violence and the lack of well-organized legal institutions, they understood justice in a more personal context. Thus, they began organizing themselves into groups that served their idea of justice. The Irish associated established legal structures with British lords and had only a direct personal response to injustice at their disposal. Although initially seen as a positive feature of society, American vigilantism degenerated into a tool used by some groups and individuals for personal gain and acquired a decidedly pejorative meaning.[87] The films analyzed in this section present a fictional contemporary vision of Irish American vigilantism, offering either a positive or an ambiguous view of the phenomenon and, it follows, of Irish vigilantes themselves. Since one of the films examined is a continuation of another, this section abandons the chronological order of presenting the primary sources.

The McManus brothers, Connor (Sean Patrick Flanery) and Murphy (Norman Reedus), are the main characters of *The Boondock Saints*, a 1999 film and its 2009 sequel *All Saints Day*, both directed by Troy Duffy. The brothers are poor Irish American Catholics living in Boston and working in a meat processing plant. Celebrating St. Patrick's day with their friends, they come into conflict with some members of the Russian mob. The humiliated mobsters return the next day to exact revenge on the brothers, who fight back and kill the armed criminals. After spending a night at the hospital, Connor and Murphy go to the police station where they explain what happened to FBI Special Agent Paul Smecker (Willem Dafoe) and the detectives investigating the case of the dead mobsters. The brothers are met with admiration and are considered heroes. Moreover, agent Smecker is surprised by their knowledge of foreign languages as the brothers seem to be able to communicate in various tongues.

For their safety, they decide to spend a night in a police station cell. At night, they experience an epiphany: both hear the voice of God telling them to fight crime. They embark on a quest to eradicate organized crime from Boston, starting by eliminating the Russian mob bosses during a meeting in a hotel. Experienced with firearms, they easily overpower a group of armed criminals.

---

86   William C. Culberson, *Vigilantism: Political History of Private Power in America* (New York: Greenwood Publishing Group, 1990), 39.

87   Culberson, 39.

Soon, aided by their friend, Rocco (David Della Rocco), a former member of the Italian Yakavetta Mafia, they target the Yakavetta family underboss, whom they find in a strip club, which they consider a place of depravation as it is filled with gangsters. The brothers promptly kill all the criminals within but they spare the dancer. Next, the brothers and Rocco kill a violent criminal said to have worked for the Yakavetta family as a contract killer. However, this time they find a worthy adversary in the mysterious "Il Duce" (Billy Connolly), whom the Yakavettas free from prison specifically as a countermeasure to the threat posed by the McManus brothers. Connor, Murphy, and Rocco are wounded but they manage to escape, leaving dead gangsters and a mystery that agent Smecker is determined to solve. Their last target is the head of the Yakavetta family, "Papa Joe" (Carlo Rota), whom they attempt to kill in his mansion. However, they are captured and held prisoner. "Papa Joe" personally shoots Rocco in the head, while the brothers can only watch their friend die.

Unknown to them, agent Smecker, dressed as a woman, enters the mansion in an attempt to save the brothers, whom he considers heroes. He is knocked unconscious by "Il Duce," who is about to kill the brothers as they pray over Rocco's body. It is revealed that "Il Duce" is Noah McManus, the brothers' long-lost father. A few months later, the brothers kill "Papa Joe" in the courtroom where he is being tried; this time they are aided by their father, agent Smecker, and a group of police officers that initially pursued them as criminals. As the credits roll, seemingly random people are asked whether the brothers are ultimately good or evil. Their opinions are divided. The story is continued in the sequel, *All Saints Day*, which sees the brothers returning from Ireland on a mission to clear their good name and pursue the remnants of the Yakavetta family.

Although the films gained a cult following, they were both disparaged by critics. Many criticized the films for their violence, with some saying that especially the first film was "more interested in finding fresh ways to stage execution scenes than in finding the meaning behind the human urge for self-appointed righting of wrongs,"[88] calling it perhaps too harshly "less a proper action-thriller than a series of gratuitously violent setpieces strung together with only the sketchiest semblance of a plot."[89] It was also pointed out that "Duffy's models are clearly snarky, ultraviolent Tarantino-esque crime pictures, but this movie's cleverness is never quite on a par with its bloodlust."[90] Positive

---

88   Robert Koehler, "Review: 'Boondock Saints,'" *Variety*, January 20, 2000, http://variety. com/2000/film/reviews/boondock-saints-1117775584/.

89   Nathan Rabin, "Review: The Boondock Saints," A.V. Club, January 21, 2000, http://www. avclub.com/review/the-boondock-saints-19871.

90   Maitland McDonagh, "The Boondock Saints Review," TV Guide, 2000, http://movies. tvguide.com/boondock-saints/review/134582.

THE IRISH AS OUTLAW HEROES

reviews were in the minority and the two parts of the *The Boondock Saints* now hold average scores of 20% and 23% respectively on the *Rottentomatoes* review aggregator. Although some reviews were probably unduly harsh, the films are incredibly violent, which, in connection with the Irish, creates an exciting opportunity to explore a recent development in the Irish stereotype in contemporary American cinema.

The McManus family are, by any definition, criminal, ruthless murderers who find their purpose in life when they begin to kill. However, they target criminals and are careful not to hurt the innocent. More importantly, they are motivated by compassion, and, in their view, they do not kill to satisfy their urges but to conform to the will of God. They are portrayed as positive characters. Their violence, although extreme and volitional, is precise and serves a higher purpose. In other words, it is not violence for its own sake and as such, the viewer can overlook or justify it. The acceptability of the Saints' violence is also linked to the comical portrayal of the gangsters. The criminals are grotesque, constructed with basic narrative motifs, and lack any depth. One exception is Louie (Peter Fonda), the mastermind behind all the events of the two films. He used the young Noah's desire for vengeance to eliminate his competition and rise to power, and then attempted to use Connor and Murphy in a similar way.

Virtually all the characters in the films are stereotypical. National and ethnic stereotypes abound but there are also stereotypes related to sexual orientation. The McManuses are referred to as Irish rather than American and are constructed with the use of various stereotypically Irish features. To begin with, they are devout Catholics. During a mass at the beginning of the first film, the brothers walk to the altar and kiss the crucifix. When one priest tries to react, another one stops him, as if acknowledging the brothers' unique status among the congregation. The brothers' Catholicism carries a hint of mysticism and has features that go beyond Catholic beliefs. Whenever Connor and Murphy murder a criminal, they recite a prayer passed down in the family:

> "And shepherds we shall be.
> For Thee, my Lord, for Thee.
> Power hath descended forth from Thy hand.
> That our feet may swiftly carry out Thy command.
> So we shall flow a river forth to Thee.
> And teeming with souls shall it ever be.
> In Nomine Patris, et Filii, et Spiritus Sancti."

The prayer shows the importance of religion to the McManus family, their adherence to family values, and, by extension, the unique role of the Irish in general in bringing people to God. The significance of the prayer is seen in a ritual followed by the brothers. They recite it before killing criminals, after which they put coins on the eyes of the dead and give them absolution. Their brand of Catholicism is a mixture of authentic beliefs and practices such as those shown during the Catholic Mass scene, and mystic practices connected with Greek mythology and idiosyncratic to the brothers. This makes the ritual almost pagan rather than Catholic, but consistent with elements of folk religion. Catholicism is depicted as a religion that is simultaneously close to and yet very distant from American society: out of place in the WASP world of American cities. This, in turn, is reminiscent of the view of the religion prevalent in the times of the first Irish immigrants to the USA.

Their performance of rituals makes them reminiscent of priests. However, the classical incarnation of the Irish American Catholic priest is unmistakably anti-violent: fighting crime by educating the youth and taking them off the streets. They genuinely care for people. Surprisingly, some care is also visible in the brothers' rituals as they absolve the criminals and pray for them; in their own understanding, they offer the criminals peace, tearing them away from the violent world in the only way possible. Therefore, on the basic level of their construction, they are an amalgam of the violent Irish cop fighting crime while adhering to the idea of retributive justice, and a priest caring for those who have lost their way in the world and embarked on a life of crime.

Adherence to the stereotype is visible also in the McManuses' living and working conditions. They work in a meat processing plant: a rather low-paid blue-collar job. They live in a miserable flat in an unkempt and insular Irish neighborhood. This, again, proves Troy Duffy used stereotypes associated with Irish immigrants to America. Menial jobs and insular neighborhoods were associated with Irish Americans until at least the first half of the twentieth century.

The most important Irish stereotype visible in the brothers and their father is violence. Even before the brothers receive the message from God and embark on their mission, they are shown to be violent. When Russian mobsters trouble the owner of an Irish pub the brothers frequent, they are not afraid to ridicule and hurt the gangsters. Afterward, when the gangsters come back to Murphy and Connor in order to exact their revenge, the brothers kill them. They are proficient with a variety of weapons. They immediately know how to use the various kinds of firearms they come across, as if using them was a part of their nature, or, perhaps, a result of earlier training. Either way, it indicates the two Irish Americans' extreme intimacy with violence. Their prowess in armed combat is shown when they allow Rocco to kill two criminals. The police investigators immediately note that judging by the trajectory of bullets, some shots

THE IRISH AS OUTLAW HEROES 207

were fired by highly proficient marksmen, while another person shooting the criminals was an amateur.

The films present the Irish at various stages of assimilation into American society. Apart from the Saints, the Irish are represented by various Irish pub patrons and the owner of the pub, police detectives investigating the deaths of various criminals throughout Boston, an arms dealer, and a Catholic priest. The pub patrons and Doc, the publican, appear just once, serving only as background fillers, while Doc's function is entirely humorous. It is difficult to speculate on their level of assimilation. The arms dealer is probably based on the stereotype of an Irish American trafficker sending weapons to Ireland or Northern Ireland. Virtually nothing is known about him, other than that he owns a storeroom filled with various weapons and accessories. He is also, apparently, an Irish patriot and a devoted Catholic, as one storeroom wall is decorated with the Irish tricolor painted under an inscription reading: "While the wicked stand confounded, call me with Thy saints surrounded." The tricolor, apart from being the flag of the Republic of Ireland, is used by Irish republicans in Northern Ireland. The inscription comes from the sixteenth stanza of a thirteenth-century hymn *Day of Wrath, O Day of Mourning* (*Dies Irae*) by Thomas da Celano.[91] The inscription further emphasizes the role played not only by the brothers but by the Irish in general in God's plan, as they are different from "the wicked" others. However, the most interesting observation concerns the Boston Police Department detectives who, initially, investigate the case of dead mobsters. Detectives Greenly (Bob Marley), Dolly (David Ferry), and Duffy (Brian Mahoney) are never referred to as Irish, although they are labeled with Irish surnames. Unlike typical Irish American police officers, they are rather incompetent and play a supporting role to agent Smecker, who openly mocks their theories concerning the crimes they investigate. As representatives of a well-established Irish minority, they have lost their Irish prowess and intuition regarding violent situations. However, they too understand their shortcomings and begin helping the Saints. In doing so, they revert to the idea of retributive justice which their ancestors followed and which they had hitherto been unable to put into effect themselves.

Like the films analyzed earlier, *The Boondock Saints* and its sequel stress the motif of family values. Of particular importance is the father. The McManus brothers are always presented together and it seems they are two halves of one person. This is also emphasized by the matching tattoos (Veritas—Aequitas) on their hands. Their attachment to one another is stressed every time one of

---

91   Charles C. Nott, ed., *The Seven Great Hymns of the Mediaeval Church* (New York: Edwin S. Gorham, Publisher Church Mission House, 1902), 44.

them is in danger: the other one can immediately sense it and respond. When they have their epiphany, it takes place simultaneously for both of them, and when Connor, in a trance, utters the words: "Destroy all this which is evil...", Murphy finishes "... so that which is good may flourish." The brothers are also shown arguing and even fighting with each other, underlining their immaturity and further emphasizing their status as outlaw heroes. This, however, is another way in which their brotherhood is emphasized, as these quarrels show the viewer that these two killers on a mission from God are just two regular men—brothers who sometimes have to resolve their conflicts by fighting, similarly to the two firefighting brothers in *Backdraft*. However, like such characters as John Sullivan in *Frequency*, they are incomplete without their father, Noah. Only when Noah appears in their lives can they overcome the most dangerous criminals. What is more, their father seems to be the only person they are unable to hurt physically. Despite all their skill, they cannot shoot him during the showdown in the street before they recognize him. He, however, can hurt them. Their mother is present only in stories and her influence on the brothers' lives is limited to the fact that she urged them to learn foreign languages, making them proficient in at least a few.

In the portrayal of the Irish American brothers, the most important thing is the vision of the law they represent. The Saints are, at first, pursued by the police and agent Smecker as they epitomize the idea of retributive justice, rejected as vigilantism. However, when Smecker discovers the Saints are the brothers he considers heroes he is torn between his membership of the police and the realization that society needs the Saints. He knows the law he upholds often allows criminals to walk free and continue their activity. This idea that the established law is incompetent is emphasized by the humorous portrayal of the police officers investigating the Saints' murders. Smecker, the only capable law enforcer, decides to help the brothers. Together with the three police officers working on the case, he brings the Saints to court in a police van during Papa Joe's trial in order for them to kill the Mafioso, since he is going to be acquitted. When helping the brothers, the police officers seem well-organized and proficient. The Saints leave the van, enter the courtroom and kill the head of the Yakavetta family. Cameras film the whole event, and agent Smecker closes his eyes when he hears the shot ending Papa Joe's life and marking Smecker's departure from the ideals of the established law.

What is more, in the sequel to *The Boondock Saints*, it is revealed that there is a whole organization, composed of law enforcement officials and priests, whose aim is to aid the Saints in their quest and which is headed by agent Smecker. Disillusioned, they have turned into vigilantes, the only people able to stop crime. The outlaw heroes, the Saints, have persuaded official heroes

THE IRISH AS OUTLAW HEROES   209

that outlaw methods and, more importantly, vigilante law, is superior to the established law and order.

Another cinematic representation of Irish vigilantism in America is rooted in a comic book. *Daredevil* (2003) by Mark Steven Johnson is based on a character created by Stan Lee and Bill Everett in the 1960s.[92] The film explores several Irish stereotypes familiar to American cinema. To begin with, Matt Murdock's (Ben Affleck) father, Jack (David Keith), is a boxer, the stereotypically Irish profession. Additionally, he has a low-paid blue-collar job, which he abandons to join an Irish gang. Jack Murdock is therefore reminiscent of the first groups of Irish immigrants, often employed in low grade professions, often criminal, and sometimes professional boxers. Jack worries about his son's future and knows Matt must be able to use the opportunities America offers, which means forsaking his innate Irish violence. Matt is determined to fulfill his father's wishes and applies himself to his studies, pointing up the importance of the father in the main character's life. Losing his father is the most important event in Matt's life, even overshadowing his own accident: when Jack is murdered by Wilson Fisk (Michael Clarke Duncan), known as the Kingpin, Matt decides his future.

One important motif explored primarily in films about Irish republicanism, but also present in *Daredevil*, is the juxtaposition of a well-established member of the Irish minority in America and an Irish newcomer. The corresponding contrast in *Daredevil* is based on the characters' approach to violence. As a member of the assimilated Irish minority, Matt Murdock only uses violence when the situation demands it—when an innocent person is in danger. This is consistent with representations of other well-established members of the Irish minority, like police officers and firefighters. The newcomer—a professional killer, Bullseye (Colin Farrell)—is violent whenever he likes. Psychopathic, he murders anyone who stands in his way or insults him, including a bartender who offends his Irish pride, an older woman on a plane, whom he finds annoying, the owner of a motorcycle he steals, and even Kingpin's guard, who presumably tried to prevent him from entering Fisk's office. His intimacy with violence allows him to use everyday objects as lethal projectiles.

Just as Frankie McGuire, an Irish newcomer in *The Devil's Own*, is not afraid to show disrespect to Burke, a powerful criminal, so too is Bullseye unafraid of Kingpin. He highlights his militant Irish identity by wearing a T-shirt with a Celtic cross on it. Finally, as in IRA films, the title character of *Daredevil* has to embrace his violent nature in order to defeat the newcomer. However, unlike

---

92   Stan Lee, *Daredevil Masterworks Vol.1* (New York: Marvel Entertainment, 2010), 4.

the main characters in films about republicanism, whose ability to use violence surfaces in the final confrontation with the Irish newcomer, Matt Murdock's struggle to control his innate violence begins long before he meets his nemesis.

Violence is the main driving force behind the actions of most characters in *Daredevil* and one of the film's main themes is Matt Murdock's struggle to control his violent tendencies. As a young boy, he obeys his father's wishes and rejects violence, becoming an easy target for bullies. When he sees his father committing a violent crime and suffers an accident, Matt finds himself, apparently, even more vulnerable: he is blinded and exposed to the world of violent bullies and criminals roaming the streets. All he can do is escape from the harsh reality and he spends most of his time studying on a rooftop, far above the streets of Hell's Kitchen. He discovers the accident that took his sight also gave him something valuable: training with his father's speed bag he discovers he has gained incredible reflexes. He also finds his heightened senses allow him to develop agility and dexterity. With his superpowers, he can respond with violence when bullies attack him but he remembers the promise he made to Jack to forsake violence and become a valuable member of society.

From this time on, Matt is torn between this promise and his innate propensity to use violence. Vital in the construction of the character is his altruism and willingness to protect the innocent and the weak who have no chance against the everyday brutality of Hell's Kitchen. To protect the innocent by peaceful means, according to his father's wishes, he becomes a lawyer and is known for working *pro bono* or accepting payment in the form of, for example, food. To protect them by violent means, he creates a new identity. He becomes a masked vigilante, adopting a name that reflects his attitude but is also a reference to his father's boxing pseudonym. The dissonance between his two identities is best seen when violent behavior is considered. As Daredevil, he seems not to feel pain and is capable of withstanding multiple blows from gangsters.

What is more, though wounded by Elektra, he forgets his injury when he fights Bullseye, completely ignoring the fact that he might need medical attention. The wounds, cuts, and bruises seem to affect his other identity, i.e., Matt Murdock. When Daredevil returns home after stopping a group of armed criminals and killing the one he was pursuing, he sheds the skin of the unstoppable superhero. He becomes a blind lawyer, Matt Murdock, again, with all the vulnerabilities of a normal person. Therefore, Matt is shown bearing the scars from many injuries sustained as Daredevil; he has cuts on his face and loses a tooth. Thus, there is a clear differentiation between the two identities: the violent Daredevil, who is, to some extent, immune to brutality and the vulnerable, non-violent Matt Murdock.

Admittedly, this division in the construction of the main character's two identities is not clear cut. This is shown in the scene in which Elektra (Jennifer

THE IRISH AS OUTLAW HEROES   211

Garner), Matt's love interest, and the young Murdock fight during their first meeting. Although Matt displays Daredevil's skills in martial arts, he ultimately has to accept Elektra's victory in hand-to-hand combat. When they fight again, Daredevil loses as Matt is unable to hurt the woman he loves. Finally, the two identities become one when Matt refuses to murder Wilson Fisk, although, as Daredevil, he did murder a gangster in cold blood earlier in the film. It is Matt's non-violent personality that suppresses Daredevil's violence at this moment, which is emphasized by the fact that he leaves his mask behind on the floor and walks away; the character is wearing Daredevil's costume, but with Matt's face visible.

The dissonance in the construction of the main character's two identities is interesting in the context of the perception of justice characteristic of the representation of Irish characters on the screen. Matt Murdock is a lawyer, devoted to upholding and working within the established legal system. However, whenever he becomes aware that the criminals he is opposing in court are going to walk free, he pursues them as a vigilante believing in retributive justice, which is characteristic of Irish representations. Therefore, although Matt Murdock acknowledges his American identity, his Irishness seems to dominate his nature.

An important aspect of the film, ignored in the theatrical release of the film but present in the director's cut, is Matt's struggle with his Catholic identity. Religion is a part of Matt's life as a boy. The walls of the apartment in which he lives with his father are literally covered by religious symbols, such as a crucifix and pictures of the Holy Mary. Matt's father does not seem to be a devout Catholic, which is emphasized by his boxing pseudonym, "The Devil," so it is perhaps Matt's late mother that was a religious person. One scene from the film, adopted from John Romita Jr.'s version of Daredevil's origins, shows a mysterious Catholic nun who visits Matt when he is in hospital following his accident; the boy finds comfort in holding a crucifix she is wearing. When he becomes an adult, he finds similar comfort in visiting the church. However, he only does so when the church is almost empty, abstaining from religious observance. An important role is played here by Father Everett, who cares about Matt and invites him to take part in masses and confess his sins, offers Matt does not take up. However, when Everett, a first-generation immigrant from Ireland, judging by his Irish accent,[93] learns Matt's secret identity, he supports him, understanding the need for vigilante justice.

The Boondock Saints, its sequel, and *Daredevil* project a similar vision of Irish vigilantism in America. Firstly, they acknowledge the appropriateness of Irish

---

93   Derrick O'Connor, who plays the part of Father Everett, is an Irish actor.

retributive justice whenever the established legal system fails. Retributive justice is exacted on criminals in its most extreme form, the death penalty. Irish vigilantes are presented as judges and executioners, similar to the New Hollywood vision of the violent Irish cop, although different from Harry Callahan in that they do not function within the established legal system. Secondly, Irish vigilantism is connected with militant Catholicism, characteristic of early generations of Irish immigrants. The Saints' religious function is stressed and acknowledged by Catholic priests who actively support them. Similarly, Matt Murdock is aided by a Catholic priest who acknowledges his dual identity. This runs counter to the classical image of the anti-violence Irish priest. Finally, other motifs used in the construction of Irish vigilantes are consistent with representations of other characters of Irish origin in American cinema, mainly outlaw heroes.

•••

As the present chapter is only a part of the analysis of contemporary Irish representations, the following summary focuses on the portrayal of the Irish as outlaw heroes. This, in turn, may be used as a measure of the character's acceptability to the viewer since outlaw heroes are not merely acceptable but actually attractive to viewers.[94] Nevertheless, such a criterion of attractiveness should be used cautiously and may serve only as a suggestion that a given character's actions are acceptable to the viewer.

The majority of Irish characters in contemporary American cinema seem to be outlaw heroes. In most cases being an outlaw status does not mean being unsympathetic. True, there are characters, such as Ryan Gaerity of *Blown Away* or Sean Miller of *Patriot Games*, who are outlaws but hardly heroes. Nevertheless, even an IRA fighter like Frankie McGuire may be considered a hero because he is faithful to his ideals, even if those ideals run counter to the American vision of the law. What is more, the unambiguously positive presentation of McGuire and the PIRA in *The Devil's Own*, together with the vaguely ambiguous-to-positive status of the IRA in the three remaining films analyzed in the same section, prove that the IRA itself may have been given the status of the outlaw hero.

Although gangsters fluctuate between the outlaw and the outlaw hero, it is possible to qualify at least some of them as the latter. Arguably the best example of the outlaw hero among Irish gangsters is Amsterdam Vallon of *Gangs of New York*. Amsterdam rejects American law, choosing justice based

---

94   Ray, *A Certain Tendency of the Hollywood Cinema, 1930–1980*, 59–60.

on retribution. Initially an immature young man blindly following the path of revenge, he strives for society's acceptance of himself and his compatriots. Therefore, *Gangs of New York* may be seen as the story of the outlaw hero coming of age and moving in the direction of the official hero. As such, Amsterdam is readily accepted by the viewer.

A compelling case regarding the boundary between the outlaw hero and villain is presented in *The Departed*. His selfishness and corruption unmistakably mark Frank Costello as a villain. To infiltrate Costello's organization, Billy Costigan must become an outlaw hero: he must acquire some of the villain's features but remain a defender of the social order. When he completes his mission, he wants his status as official hero restored but is thwarted in this by Colin Sullivan, a villain in the disguise of the official hero.

Whether Tom Reagan of *Miller's Crossing* and Henry Hill of *Goodfellas* are outlaw heroes or villains is debatable. It can be argued that Tom Reagan's status is undeveloped at the beginning of the film and that through his violence he reluctantly acquires the position of the outlaw, though not necessarily a hero, by the end of the film. Henry Hill, on the other hand, begins as a villain and acquires a vague status of neither hero nor villain at the end of the film.

Finally, Irish vigilantes seem to epitomize the outlaw hero ethos. They openly reject the law as inadequate for stopping crime but they serve society, protecting people and even risking their own lives. Their status as outlaws is further emphasized by the fact that American law enforcement agencies pursue them.

The most important feature of the Irish outlaw heroes and villains in the films analyzed here is that all of them seem unable or unwilling to become assimilated into American culture. Their distance from American culture is emphasized by the fact that they refer to themselves as Irish—not only that, but they are considered Irish by other characters. As more Irish than American, or even purely Irish, they are presented as fiercer and more savage than the official heroes. However, whereas violence associated with villains is more likely to be deemed unacceptable by the viewer, the outlaw heroes' brutality is acceptable because it is used for altruistic reasons.

In this respect, Irish cops, labeled as Irish with the use of Irish last names, form a different category of outlaw heroes. Although they work as police officers, they consider the established law inadequate. Therefore, when fighting crime, they use their own sense of justice, rather than directives provided by their superiors. However, unlike the outlaw heroes analyzed above, they do not consider themselves Irish. Instead, they are the descendants of the classic American western heroes who combine the ethos of a gunslinger protecting a frontier town with the violent Irish stereotype.

CHAPTER 5

Contemporary Hollywood: The Irish as Official Heroes

Official heroes are defined by Robert Ray as mature characters who accept the society in which they live, also embracing the rule of law as the mechanism guarding its proper functioning.[1] Thus, such characters contrast with or are in direct opposition to the outlaw heroes analyzed in the previous chapter. Irish screen representatives of official heroes include police officers and federal agents, firefighters, and boxers.

1   Irish American Law Enforcement

The previous chapter included a description and analysis of Irish characters serving in various law enforcement agencies, including the police. Their function in the films under discussion, however, is to provide contrast to characters representing Northern Irish republicans, gangsters, and vigilantes. In all three cases, the Irish American law enforcers are official heroes. Some of them, such as Tom O'Meara (*The Devil's Own*), Jack Ryan (*Patriot Games*), Jimmy Dove (*Blown Away*) and Captain Queenan (*The Departed*) keep their status as official heroes throughout the film, remaining positive father figures and proving their attachment to the ideals of American law. As such, they are fully integrated into American society and assimilated into American culture, even though they do not forget their Irish roots. However, some of the secondary characters who are initially official heroes seem to lose this status in the course of the film. For example, there is the team of Irish American police officers in *The Boondock Saints* who decide to support the vigilante outlaw heroes, thus affirming the inadequacy of established American law in comparison to the natural law represented by the outlaws.

There are several other representations of Irish American police officers. In most cases, however, these representations do not offer a new perspective on such figures, instead showing that Irish Americans are stereotypically seen as police officers, among other professions. Some of these films, however, carry

---

1   Ray, *A Certain Tendency of the Hollywood Cinema, 1930–1980*, 59–61.

© KONINKLIJKE BRILL NV, LEIDEN, 2021 | DOI:10.1163/9789004467972_007

THE IRISH AS OFFICIAL HEROES   215

an important message concerning the Irish, which should be mentioned in this study.

Some of these representations seem to indicate that intimacy with violence corrupts, as shown in Sidney Lumet's 1990 drama *Q&A*, in which Mike Brennan (Nick Nolte) is a violent NYPD cop whose excessive use of violence causes his downfall and death. His adversary, Al Reilly, a Deputy Attorney, is a righteous and non-violent character who is, nevertheless, haunted by the fact that his father, a decorated police officer, was a bigot and an outspoken enemy of other ethnic minorities.

Only the Lonely, a 1991 romantic comedy by Chris Columbus, is notable for presenting an Irish mother as an important controlling character. Danny Muldoon (John Candy) is unhappy because he is controlled by his overprotective mother, Rose (Maureen O'Hara). Danny, a police officer, and his girlfriend, Theresa (Ally Sheedy), are victims of the psychological aggression Rose uses to keep his son by her side. The film also shows the Irish in opposition to other ethnic minorities: Rose rejects Theresa because she is Sicilian and Polish, not Irish.

Another example is the Irish American police officer Detective Sean Devine (Kevin Bacon) in Clint Eastwood's critically acclaimed *Mystic River* (2003). The film focuses on an Irish community in which violence is ubiquitous and killing seems to be a natural response to injustice. This is underlined by the police officer being the least violent of the film's three main characters. The film explores the question of retributive justice, which it presents ambiguously. Firstly, retribution seems to be presented as an appropriate way of dealing with dangerous criminals preying on the innocent. Thus, when Dave Boyle (Tim Robbins), a blue-collar worker who was sexually abused as a child kills a child molester, the action is considered a crime by Sean but is presented in opposition to a crime involving the murder of a young girl. Resorting to retribution, which consists in ignoring the rules of the established law, leads to false accusations and the escalation of violence. Retribution also pushes Jimmy Markum (Sean Penn) to hunt the person who murdered his daughter, as this is all he can do after failing to protect her in the first place.

In all this, Sean is a police officer who does not accept justice based on retribution and does his job protecting the community while adhering to the established law and order. When Jimmy murders Dave, Sean has to choose between their friendship and his duty. As the film ends, he signals to Markum that he will arrest him, at the same time emphasizing his rejection of the retributive justice that characterizes his community. His choices are rewarded by stability in his personal life as he reunites with his estranged wife.

216   CHAPTER 5

A somewhat ambiguous character, who ultimately remains an official hero, appears in Ben Affleck's 2007 neo-noir crime thriller, *Gone Baby Gone*. The film tells the story of an Irish American private detective, Patrick Kenzie (Casey Affleck). When a four-year-old girl, Amanda McCready, is kidnapped from her home in the Boston neighborhood of Dorchester, Patrick and his partner, both professionally and privately, Angie Gennaro (Michelle Monaghan), begin investigating. They learn that Amanda's parents work for a drug lord, Cheese (Edi Gathegi) and, with two Boston Police Detectives, Remy Bressant (Ed Harris) and Nick Poole (John Ashton), they quickly conclude that the Haitian criminal is behind the kidnapping. This is corroborated by Capt. Jack Doyle (Morgan Freeman) of the Boston Police Department, who takes the case personally because he lost his own daughter some years earlier. They approach Cheese and the criminal is killed in a gunfight. Amanda's doll is found in a pond and the child is believed drowned.

A few months later, Patrick and Angie are investigating another child abduction. Patrick learns that the person responsible is a drug addict and child molester, Corwin Earle (Matthew Maher), and he asks Nick and Remy for help in rescuing the child. Patrick and the detectives are attacked by a woman who, with her husband, lives with Earle. Nick is mortally wounded and Patrick hides in Corwin's room, where he finds the criminal and the child's lifeless body. Unable to accept another tragic end of a child he was trying to rescue, Patrick resorts to retributive justice and kills Earle, while Remy shoots the woman and promises to cover for Patrick.

Thus, it might appear that Kenzie is an outlaw hero, since he punishes the child molester and murderer himself. However, there is a twist. Inspired by these events, he returns to Amanda's case, learning that Bressant and the girl's uncle, Lionel (Titus Welliver) organized the kidnapping. While he is questioning Lionel in a pub, a masked Remy appears, planning to kill the two men. However, the bartender shoots the corrupt detective in the back. Bressant escapes to the roof where he succumbs to his wounds and dies. While being questioned by the police, Patrick learns that Doyle, who quit his job after the failure to solve the Amanda case, lied to him when he confirmed Cheese's responsibility for the kidnapping. Together with Angie, they visit Doyle and find Amanda, now living happily, far from her parents. Doyle and Angie try to reason with Patrick but he is adamant that in the eyes of the law, Doyle is a kidnapper and the child should return to her mother. He informs the police of the girl's whereabouts; as a result, Doyle is arrested and Angie, unable to accept Amanda's fate, leaves Patrick.

Like most official heroes belonging to the category under discussion, Patrick Kenzie is forced to choose between what may be perceived as right and what

THE IRISH AS OFFICIAL HEROES

217

is legitimate according to the law. His decision effectively deprives Amanda of the chance of a happy childhood, since she returns to a clearly neglectful mother, but Kenzie cannot act against the law. At the same time, his killing of the child molester and agreeing to let Remy cover up his guilt is a contradiction that makes him a boundary example of the category.

In 2014's *Non-Stop*, an action thriller directed by Jaume Collet-Serra, Liam Neeson plays a U.S. Federal Air Marshall, Bill Marks, who is assigned to a plane from New York to London. During the flight, Bill receives a message on his phone: an unidentified person on board threatens to kill a passenger every twenty minutes and demands $150 million. Marks begins investigating the passengers, trying to find the terrorist. He confronts another Air Marshall on board, Jack Hammond (Anson Mount) and is attacked by his colleague. The two men fight in the toilet and Bill kills Hammond exactly twenty minutes after the threat was issued. It turns out that the account to which the money is to be transferred belongs to Bill and he becomes the main suspect. A news report says that Marks comes from Belfast, Northern Ireland, prompting speculation that he is in the IRA.

Bill's origins are used as evidence—almost conclusive proof—of his guilt. His alcohol abuse and psychological state after the loss of his daughter are also counted against him. His past as a decorated New York City police officer is completely dismissed by those who associate Northern Ireland with terrorism. The same stereotype is activated earlier when Bill begins his investigation. One of the first passengers he approaches for questioning is a Muslim doctor, Fahim Nasir (Omar Metwally). As more people die, including the captain of the plane, other passengers rebel against Marks and, although he fights, he is overwhelmed and subdued. He shares his story with the passengers, saying that he is not a good man, but he will save them, stressing the importance of his duty over any personal issues. When it turns out that there is a bomb onboard the plane, Marks orders the plane to descent to 8,000 ft., where the pressure of the explosion will not tear the fuselage apart. Now aided by other passengers, including Dr. Nasir, an Irish American New York police officer, Austin Reilly (Corey Stoll), and a woman who has believed him from the start, Jen Summers (Julianne Moore), Marks identifies the terrorists. One of them tells Bill that his father died on 9/11 and their aim is to show the incompetence of Air Marshals and inadequacy of security on airplanes. Marks fights the terrorists and shoots one of them as the plane descends to the safe altitude. The other one is killed in the explosion as the bomb detonates. The second pilot manages to land the crippled plane in Iceland and, while the machine rolls violently and uncontrollably down the runway, disintegrating, Bill saves a girl from falling through the damaged fuselage.

Marks is undoubtedly an official hero, who disregards his own safety to do his duty and help others. He adheres to the established American law and, even though his origins and unhappy life make him a suspect, he never stops his investigation. At one point, he tells the officials to apprehend him as soon as the plane lands, but he must save the passengers. At the end of the film, a news reporter announces that the suspected terrorist turned out to be the hero. Marks's superior, who also suspected him of the hijacking, admits his error to him. Bill talks to Jen and it is implied that they will develop a relationship. Thus, adherence to high values, American law, and the sense of duty allows a rejected man, stereotyped as a terrorist, to become a hero and achieve personal success.

As official heroes, Irish American police officers and federal agents are unbreakable and incorruptible. They are devoted to their duty, which they understand as helping and rescuing those in peril. Like Peter Casey of *Three Cheers for the Irish*, they are ready to sacrifice their own happiness if it means that the law will triumph.

2   Firefighters in the Irish American *Bildungsroman*

A firefighter is another typically Irish profession that found its way into Hollywood films. Firefighters in American cinema have long been associated with the Irish American minority, as "[l]arge number [of Irish] found work as firefighters and police officers"[2] when the children of immigrants from Ireland began to establish themselves as Americans. In *Firefighters*: *Their Lives In Their Own Words*, Dennis Smith gives the following account:

> In the old days, especially in the big cities, the fire service was basically an Irish club, and everybody came predominantly from the same background. The Irish dominated the fire service I grew up in. I would say that seventy-five percent of the people I knew as a kid in the fire department were Irish. It was a very cohesive group. Those days are gone. The fire service today is made up of everyone.[3]

The reality may have changed but the stereotype of Irishmen working as firefighters has become deeply entrenched in Americans' vision of their country. As such, it has surfaced in film. Film plots need Irish firefighters in the same

---

2   Margaret J. Goldstein, *Irish in America* (Minneapolis: Lerner Publications, 2004), 45.

3   Dennis Smith, *Firefighters: Their Lives in Their Own Words* (New York: Crown Publishing Group, 2010), 122.

THE IRISH AS OFFICIAL HEROES   219

way they need violent Irish police officers; they need their "perfect outsiders" who bridge the gap between their society, their civilization, and the violent reality trying to destroy the equilibrium.

The Irish firefighter, like the Irish police officer, is a man risking his life for the greater good. The latter exists in-between society and, due to his intimacy with violence, the world of crime that threatens civilization. Since such a character possesses the features of two opposing forces, he can resolve conflicts based on simple binary oppositions whose central part is violence. The firefighter also bridges the gap between two worlds: civilized society and destructive elements. In such a view, the firefighter must also possess the features of both worlds in order to mediate between them and, ultimately, emerge victorious. In this case, the Irish firefighter seems to be characterized by a kind of unique intimacy with fire, specific knowledge of how its destructive power works. However, the firefighter is undoubtedly a part of society and accepts its rules. Therefore, although such a character possesses the features of the outlaw hero, he is instead a non-prototypical example of the official hero.

In Ron Howard's *Backdraft* (1991), the ability to fight fire seems to run in the family of two Irish American brothers, sons of a firefighter. Stephen "Bull" McCaffrey (Kurt Russell) and his younger brother, Brian (William Baldwin), work together in the Chicago Fire Department. The film begins in 1971 with the two brothers as children quarreling in the fire department building where their father works. When a call for help comes, Brian goes with his father to see him in action. The boy is proud, especially since he knows his brother can only envy him. The mood of the scene, emphasized by the lofty score, shows how heroic the father is in his son's eyes. He saves a child from the fire and smiles and waves to Brian. The mood changes suddenly when a gas line bursts and Brian can only watch as his father is consumed by the explosion that follows. In one moment, he loses his father and hero.

Twenty years later, Brian is celebrating his graduation from a firefighter academy. In a conversation with a bartender, it is revealed that he has already tried to become a firefighter in the past and that he has had various jobs. Later, he admits to his colleague that he bribed his captain to be assigned to a particular "engine," as the firefighting teams are known, number 15. He meets his former girlfriend, Jennifer (Jennifer Jason Leigh), and her grandmother, who genuinely despises him, obviously for something he has done to her granddaughter. While watching firefighters extinguishing a fire, he meets his brother, who tells him that he has assigned him to Engine 17, "the toughest company in the city," commanded by Stephen.

Stephen is an experienced and dedicated firefighter. His dedication is the direct cause of his failure as a husband and a father: he is divorced and rarely sees his son, Sean. Therefore, he criticizes his younger brother for becoming a firefighter not because he wants to follow a family tradition, but because he has no other choice. During their first assignment together, the brothers enter a burning factory with the rest of the squad. As their leader, Stephen appears as a fierce warrior, walking fearlessly through the flames. The fire itself seems to be presented as a monster rather than a mindless element. It can assume various forms, withdraw, and hide in walls; this is emphasized by sound effects reminiscent of roaring and howling. When the fight is over, Stephen openly criticizes Martin Swayzak (J.T. Walsh), an alderman in Chicago responsible for cutting costs and reducing the number of fire engines.

During a firefighter's retirement party, Stephen's ex-wife's current partner mocks Brian in front of his older brother. Stephen hits him in the face and, in the ensuing brawl, he defends his brother's honor, cheered by some of the firefighters present. The brothers bond and Brian begins to develop his skills, encouraged by Stephen. They also take part in various assignments and appear to have developed a kind of mutual respect, although sometimes the tension between them is visible with Stephen believing Brian is not right for a firefighter, and Brian determined not to quit. During one assignment, the brothers are alone on a burning staircase. The fire recedes as if afraid of them. The sentient, monster-like quality of the fire is emphasized by the fact that it roars and closes the door, barring the brothers from one of the flats in the building. Stephen forces the door open and enters while Brian hesitates and falls as the flames engulf the inside of the apartment. Brian is sure his brother has perished. However, Stephen appears in the doorway, holding an ax in one hand and a child he has saved in the other. He denies he is a hero, saying he is only doing his duty, like his father. This is a reference to two aspects of the Irish stereotype in American cinema: the importance of duty and the importance of tradition.

Disillusioned with his abilities as a firefighter and unable to compete against his brother, Brian decides to become an assistant to an arson investigator, Donald Rimgale (Robert De Niro). They begin investigating a series of arson attacks whose victims are random people. Brian consults an imprisoned arsonist, Ronald Balter (Donald Sutherland), who suggests a firefighter might be the culprit. For Brian, Stephen becomes the prime suspect but he quickly identifies the real arsonist: John Adcox (Scott Glenn), a firefighter working with Stephen and a friend of their father.

The brothers confront Adcox on the roof of a burning factory. Before they can subdue him the roof partially collapses. Brian nearly dies in flames but is saved by Stephen. As they are running to the exit, Adcox reappears and incapacitates Brian. Another explosion sends Adcox flying off a catwalk but Stephen grabs him and refuses to let his fellow firefighter fall. They fall together

THE IRISH AS OFFICIAL HEROES

and Adcox dies instantly while Stephen is injured. Brian rushes to bring help for his brother and is suddenly able to fight the fire almost single-handedly. Stephen succumbs to his wounds in the ambulance but not before asking Brian not to tell anyone about Adcox. After his brother's funeral, Brian decides to pursue a career as a firefighter.

The film is based on a contrast between the two Irish American brothers. It shows how different their attitudes become when they are deprived of a male role model, i.e., their father. From the first scenes, the viewer is shown how important the father was for the two boys. Stephen, who was a teenager when the tragedy happened, becomes a living copy of their father; Brian, on the other hand, struggles, unable to find his role in the world. An important aspect of the contrast between the McCaffreys is the way they are presented in terms of their masculinity. While Stephen is a strong, adult man, Brian is still a boy, emphasized by the frequent reappearance in the film of a photograph of him taken immediately after the explosion that killed his father and showing a helpless child clinging to his father's helmet. As an aspiring father figure, Stephen tries to be a substitute for his father also in Brian's life but he is torn between being a role model and an older brother, playing pranks, and competing against his younger sibling. He is also unable to accept Brian's irresponsible approach to duty and family tradition.

The tradition itself plays a vital role in the film. The brothers are presented within the framework of a longer and larger tradition. This is especially clear in the funeral scene, in which a long column of marching firefighters bid farewell to their fallen comrades. What is more, some Irish themes, such as music and Irish dancing, are on view during a retirement party for a firefighter. The Irish seem to be predisposed to fight fire. This is seen in several scenes but is clearest when Brian attempts to save his dying brother. Although a trained firefighter, he often shows complete ignorance rather than expertise when fighting fire. However, when his brother's life is in direct danger, he suddenly starts acting instinctively, allowing him to overcome the flames. Stephen, impressed by Brian's actions, exclaims, "Look at him! That's my brother, goddammit!", underlining not only their brotherly ties but also Brian's Irish firefighting prowess.

The Irish firefighting tradition seems well-established in other characters too. Trying to win Brian's support, Martin Swayzak says: "I want someone from a real traditional firefighting club." McCaffrey responds: "Yeah, we got all kinds of traditions. Like dying young." The "real traditional firefighting club" seems to be a direct reference to Irish Americans in one of their traditional occupations. Finally, the Irish firefighting tradition is presented as unbroken, as the camera briefly focuses on Stephen's son looking at his father's coffin, in a parallel with the photograph of Brian mentioned above. The camera then switches to Brian, who will undoubtedly become a father figure and role model for his nephew: in the final scene, his actions suggest that he has become a living image of his late brother. Therefore, the film is Brian's coming-of-age story.

The violence in the film appears mainly in connection with the fire. As stated, the fire seems to be a sentient, malevolent force whose aim is to kill people and destroy their buildings. In this reading, firefighters appear to be warriors standing between society and fire. The Irish, living between the world of creation, attributed to society, and the world of violence and destruction, attributed to fire, are the best at fighting fire. Various characters refer to fire as if were sentient. Donald Rimgale, the arson investigator, tells Brian how the fire "eats, breathes and hates." The arsonist, Ronald Bartel, asks Brian if the fire saw him and, carefully observing Brian's reaction, adds: "It did." The firefighters' warrior-like qualities—Stephen's in particular—are illustrated by their use of axes as weapons taken into the flames.

The standard representation of Irish American firefighters uses motifs similar to those from *Backdraft*. Firstly, they rely heavily on stereotypes. The plot of *Frequency*, a science-fiction thriller directed by Gregory Hoblit and released in 2000, centers on an Irish American family with stereotypically Irish jobs. John Sullivan (Jim Caviezel) is a homicide detective, his father, Frank (Dennis Quaid), was a heroic firefighter who died in a warehouse fire, trying to save a girl, and his mother, Julia (Elizabeth Mitchell), is a nurse, an occupation traditionally associated with Irish women. Although the main character is a police officer, the film's motifs and patterns are similar to *Backdraft*. John Sullivan is at one point reminded by his father that, had he not become a policeman, he would have become "a third-generation firefighter." This touches upon an essential motif, prominent in *Backdraft*, i.e., tradition as a factor determining the life of Irish characters. The choice of the Irish American family's professions seems to facilitate the reception of the story: John contacts his father in the past and alters the timeline, saving Frank. With this fantastical plot, it seems the film's makers wanted to make the main characters appear as regular as possible. The Irish American family's stereotypical occupations may have been intended to give the American viewer something thoroughly familiar.

Jay Russell's *Ladder 49* (2004) is a post 9/11 celebration of firefighting that draws heavily on stereotypical Irish representations. The story of Jack Morrison (Joaquin Phoenix) begins when he graduates from the fire academy. Nothing is known of his earlier life. Assigned to Engine 33, he is subjected to several shenanigans, which constitute a peculiar rite of passage but are also designed to mark Irish American stereotypes. Firstly, he is sent to his captain, Mike Kennedy (John Travolta), who appears to be a disheveled drunk, welcoming his new subordinate while dressed in boxer shorts and drinking. He is

THE IRISH AS OFFICIAL HEROES

then led to another part of the firehouse where he is asked if he is a Catholic. When he affirms that he is, one of his new colleagues suggests that he should confess, as most of his colleagues do before going into action. Jack starts his confession, becoming increasingly startled as the priest's questions become more and more inquisitive and focused on sexuality. He then looks behind the curtain and, instead of the priest, he sees a group of firefighters laughing at him. Among them is Kennedy, now sober and uniformed. Most of the firefighters in the group are Irish, including Morrison, and his friend and mentor, Captain Mike Kennedy, but there is one African American. The sequence of scenes seems to show that some stereotypes about the Irish—mainly their Catholicism and tendency to overuse alcohol—are not grounded in reality, at least not when they are on duty.

In the context of the study, it is vital to note how important Irish themes seem to be in creating the archetypal firefighter in *Ladder 49*. On the level of production, Irish themes are present in the film's score, with traditional Irish music often heard in the background. The apparent connection between being a firefighter and attachment to Irish culture is expressed in several ways, the most important of which is that the firefighters, both Irish and non-Irish, socialize in a traditional Irish pub, where they also celebrate important events, including St. Patrick's Day.

Like *Backdraft*, other films about Irish American firefighters also stress the importance of the father figure in the shaping of the son's masculinity and the success in life which it entails. In *Frequency*, the father-son relationship is the single most potent force and can literally affect reality through the alterations of the timeline. Having grown up without his father, John is unsuccessful in his personal life. He seems a proficient police officer but his existence is bleak and pointless and the state of his family home reflects the disarray in his life. How John and Frank reach through time to contact each other is never fully explained but it seems some kind of psychic or spiritual connection between the father and his son plays a vital role in the sudden appearance of the phenomenon. John needs his father to be able to realize himself as a man and he contacts him on the radio. Although Julia is a loving mother, it is Frank's task to prepare John for the violent reality he is bound to live in, considering the stereotypical career path he has to choose as an Irish American. In the scenes set in the past, Frank is shown playing with his son, teaching him how to compete with others (baseball), and how to ignore bruises and setbacks, for example when learning to ride a bicycle. When John alters the timeline so that his father is alive in the present, he becomes successful both in his private and professional life.

Ladder 49 also relies on the motif of the importance of a father. Although nothing is known about Jack's parents, he finds a father figure in Mike Kennedy, who accompanies him on his first assignment. When Jack has to climb the stairs in a burning building, it is Mike who encourages him to proceed. Later, the two of them emerge from the building with Mike cheering on Jack's first victory. Kennedy is present during the most important events in Jack's personal life as well. When Jack invites Linda to the Irish pub for the first time, he introduces her to Kennedy in the first place; Mike is then present at their wedding. It is also Kennedy who offers Morrison an administrative position, as he cares not only for his young subordinate but also for his family. Finally, it is Kennedy who bids farewell to his fallen comrade. Thus, Captain Mike Kennedy performs the role of the father in Jack Morrison's coming of age as a firefighter.

There are differences in the amount of violence explored as an Irish feature in films about Irish American firefighters. In *Frequency*, violence is a destructive force that undermines the foundations of society, as it destroys families. Additionally, like the other films studied here, it presents violence as the domain of men. John has to realize his masculinity in order to be able to stop a serial killer threatening his mother but it is his father, presented throughout the film as a strong male role model, who can do that. This fits well in with the set of characteristic features observed in other films analyzed here.

On the other hand, an almost complete lack of physical violence between characters in *Ladder 49* seems to suit the film's overall attempt to put aside the negative elements of the Irish stereotype in America while preserving the positive ones. The only violent event takes place in a pub and involves Jack and one of his colleagues. Jack hits the other man, showing that, like every stereotypical Irishman, he is intimate with violence but he is not violent to others in his professional life. This quite modern approach to the Irish stereotype seems characteristic of films connected with firefighting Irish Americans, with *Frequency* as an exception because of the plot involving a police officer solving a crime.

The three films discussed above are not the only ones with American firefighters. Other Hollywood films have firefighter characters of explicitly Irish origins, while the ethnic identity of others cannot be determined. The former group is represented by Patrick Sullivan (Jeffrey Dean Morgan), one of the main characters of a 2008 romantic comedy entitled *The Accidental Husband*, directed by Griffin Dunne. The film's mood is lighter and, therefore, free from violence, due to the romantic comedy's generic conventions but Patrick shares the apparently carefree attitude of Brian McCaffrey and John Sullivan. A father-son relationship typical of Irish American representations is present in a 2007 family film, *Firehouse Dog* by Todd Holland, between Captain Connor Fahey and his son, Shane. Firefighting characters who are not Irish or whose identity cannot be determined can be found in films such as *Bad Day on the Block* (1997), directed by Craig R. Baxley and starring Charlie Sheen,

THE IRISH AS OFFICIAL HEROES   225

Quarantine (2008), a science-fiction horror directed by John Erick Dowdle, and
a 2008 Christian drama, *Fireproof*, by Alex Kendrick. What seems to differentiate these films from those in which the characters are explicitly of Irish origin
is the fact that the previous films do not employ the narrative schemas and
motifs which may be observed in the latter.

What seems to be the most critical underlying feature of the films analyzed
here is the fact that they are coming-of-age stories. In *Backdraft*, Stephen and
Brian lose their father at two different stages of their lives. Stephen grows up
and becomes a successful firefighter but fails as a father and a husband. His
brother, Brian, is only a child when the father dies, and thus he fails both in his
personal and professional life. It is only when he turns to Stephen, and when
his older brother becomes a role model for him that Brian succeeds in both
aspects of his life. John Sullivan of *Frequency* is also unable to succeed professionally or personally without the presence of his firefighting father, Frank.
When he succeeds in saving Frank, his life changes immediately as he becomes
a father and a police officer who manages to track down a serial killer. As for
Jack Morrison, the main character of *Ladder 49*, he is transformed from a man
afraid of rats on his first assignment to a firefighter who willingly sacrifices
his life to save a stranger from fire and refuses help as any attempt to save him
might prove fatal to his friends and colleagues. In the films that are not analyzed here, a similar change may be observed, as Patrick Sullivan undergoes
a shift from a rather carefree person to a loving husband, and Shane Fahey,
initially a troubled teenager, becomes a decorated hero.

3   New Boxers in Irish America

Like gangsters, the Irish boxer returned to contemporary American cinema
after a period of decline in New Hollywood. Films focusing on boxers frequently
touch upon other topics, typically involving the Irish. In most cases, the Irish
identity of the characters appearing in such films is taken for granted. That is,
the characters are labeled with Irish last names and there is no explicit reference to their Irish identity. However, as the films explore typically Irish problems in connection with a typically Irish profession, they are quite different
from films such as the *Dirty Harry* or *Die Hard* series, in which the characters
are only labeled with Irish surnames but there is no focus on Irish problems.

Although not so numerous as Irish police officers and gangsters, Irish boxers
do appear in several films, both as primary and secondary characters. Generally, films about boxers can be divided into separate categories. Firstly, there
are films about individual boxers, both fictional and historical. An essential

feature of such films is the boxers' relations and attitudes to their trainers and promoters. Another category are films presenting boxing as an alternative to some other expression of violence, such as crime or terrorism. Finally, there are films in which boxing plays a secondary role and is presented as a feature of the Irish minority.

Representing the first category is *Streets of Gold*, a 1986 drama directed by Joe Roth, in which a talented Jewish ex-boxer comes from the Soviet Union to America and starts training two young American pugilists. Alek Neuman (Klaus Maria Brandauer) is unable to realize his potential in training the Soviet national boxing team because of his Jewish origins. Therefore, he emigrates to the USA, where he begins working with Roland Jenkins (Wesley Snipes), a cocky African American, and Timmy Boyle (Adrian Pasdar), an Irish American thug. The plot is rather simple and obvious. Alek works as a dishwasher, trying to adjust to the American way of life. When he meets the two rival boxers, he starts using the antipathy, or even hatred they have for each other in order to turn them into professional boxers. Soon, the young fighters turn professional and Alek gets a chance to show up his former colleagues from the Soviet Union when he wins a contract for a series of fights between his protégés and Soviet boxers. However, Roland is injured defending a Russian woman from Timmy's ex-manager and cannot fight in the upcoming tournament. The Irishman Timmy becomes Alek's only hope. Encouraged by both his coach and Roland, Timmy knocks his opponent out.

The film focuses on Alek's struggle to adjust to American life and Timmy Boyle is not a fully developed character. On the contrary, he is a stereotypical young Irish pugilist who has never had any formal training but is neverthe-less quite successful in underground boxing. He claims that he fights using his instinct, and he is confident that were he provided with adequate training, he would be a successful boxer. Initially, he is undisciplined and disrespects Alek because he is Jewish, although he later claims he is not prejudiced. This approach reflects the conflict between the Irish and other ethnic minorities in America.

Timmy suffers has an inferiority complex and does not trust Alek, convinced the coach does not treat him seriously, but only as an addition to Roland. This feeling of inadequacy in the best thing he can do puts a severe strain on his relationship with other people, particularly with Roland. However, ultimately, it is Roland who reminds the young Irishman that he is a fighter and that he should start believing in himself. Finally, the last shot in the film shows an Irishman, an African American, and their Jewish-Russian coach standing together as winners.

THE IRISH AS OFFICIAL HEROES   227

Streets of Gold presents boxing as a sport of underprivileged people from communities dominated by violence. When asked what kind of people devote so much time to training boxing, Timmy and Roland say poor people. Timmy's father works as a motorman for Brooklyn-Manhattan Transit, a job Timmy considers unrewarding. Boxing is therefore the only way for the young man to flee from a life he does not want to a better one. What is more, the sport is shown as a way of patching ethnic divisions. The focus of the film is undoubtedly on the Russian diaspora in America but the fact that Timmy and Roland become friends and learn respect for their Russian coach and his compatriots is also meaningful.

The film explores the classic opposition between America and Russia or the Soviet Union, and therefore, the final confrontation between Timmy Boyle and the Russian champion is shown as a duel between the two countries. Timmy is smaller than his opponent and the clash reminds the viewer of David and Goliath. The Russian smiles when Timmy hits him in the face, as if to underline the comparison. However, in this case, David is Irish, and the viewer is reminded of this when Timmy makes the sign of the cross before the fight and before the final round. However, the final shot reminds the viewer that the Irishman's victory and—it follows—the success of America, is possible only thanks to the cooperation between various ethnic minorities.

Split Decisions, a 1988 drama directed by David Drury, focuses on boxing as a part of family tradition. Dan McGuinn (Gene Hackman), an ex-boxer whose father was also a pugilist, has trained his two sons, Ray (Jeff Fahey) and Eddie (Craig Sheffer), to follow in his footsteps. The former is a professional boxer who moves out of his home in New York to pursue a career in the middle-weight division, signing a contract with his father's rival and encountering a mobster, Benny Pistone (James Tolkan). He inadvertently becomes involved in matches controlled by the mob and when he refuses to throw a fight against Julian "the Snake" Pedroza (Eddie Velez), a man known for killing an opponent in the ring, he is beaten and has his hand broken. When Ray punches Benny Pistone, he is severely beaten by Pedroza and thrown out of a window, falling to his death. Eddie, who has been prepared by Dan to take part in the Olympic Games, is informed by two teenaged members of his father's boxing club that Ray has been kidnapped but arrives too late to save his brother. After Ray's funeral, Eddie learns the killer's identity and considers revenge. He approaches Pedroza with a gun in his hand and threatens to kill him but he is unable to kill a man in cold blood. Knowing that Pistone is beyond the reach of the police, Eddie devises another plan of revenge: to face Pedroza in the ring. Trained by his father and grandfather, Eddie puts aside his plans of going to college and faces Pedroza. When it appears that he is going to lose, Pedroza starts mocking him, which allows Eddie to deliver a blow that disorients his opponent. After a series of fierce attacks, Eddie knocks Pedroza out. As family and friends cheer, the police arrive to arrest Pistone and "the Snake."

Split Decisions focuses on the relations between three generations of McGuinns. It is noticeable that the family seems to be composed only of males, portraying boxing as an unequivocally masculine sport. At the beginning of the film, Eddie, his father, and his grandfather are shown celebrating Eddie's admission to St. James's College. In their conversations, Ray appears as a prodigal son who left his family in order to pursue a boxing career. Despite Ray's apparent success, Dan, an NYPD officer, is proud only of his younger son, who is going to be the first educated McGuinn. The dynamic between the members of the family is based on their approach to violence. The father, apart from being an ex-boxer, has a stereotypically Irish job related to violence. The older son pursues a violent career and finally goes too far in a world controlled by brutality. The younger one is allowed to use his innate violence, inherited with boxing skills, in a sublime confrontation at the Olympic Games.

The film explores a set of standard motifs used to portray the Irish in American cinema. The most important ones are undoubtedly family values and the importance of the father, which are expressed through the characters' approach to boxing. Violence, as the foundation of boxing, is ubiquitous. Similarly to *Streets of Gold*, religious motifs are limited only to the scene of Ray's funeral and to Eddie praying before the fight against Pedroza. The funeral is, however, quickly contrasted with the wake, with family and friends drinking in a pub, singing and arguing violently. The family are working class but capable of upward social mobility thanks to Eddie's success in education. Their feud with Pedroza and Pistone corresponds to the conflict between the Irish and representatives of other ethnic minorities.

Boxing is shown as a family activity, epitomizing the values essential for the family. The McGuinns own a boxing club to which whole families come to watch matches between young boys. Boxing is also the only aspect of life the family members have in common. Benny Pistone's approach to boxing corrupts the discipline and, as a result, affects the McGuinn family values, which are honor, courage, and fighting spirit. Therefore, Ray cannot agree to be dishonest when it concerns the most fundamental aspect of his life and, although he is disillusioned, he refuses Pistone's conditions.

Ray does not lose his courage or fighting spirit, even when overwhelmed by Pistone's mobsters. On the contrary, he attempts to fight on, unable to accept defeat. Also, boxing is the only way to reclaim the lost values as the quest for revenge in the ring unites the three generations of the family. Eddie's victory

THE IRISH AS OFFICIAL HEROES 229

is, therefore, the triumph of the values cherished by the Irish American family of boxers.

The two films analyzed above, although presenting different stories, follow a similar pattern. In both of them there is a struggling young boxer, Timmy Boyle in *Streets of Gold* and Eddie McGuinn in *Split Decisions*, who has to overcome his weaknesses and various external obstacles on his way to the final fight with a stronger and more experienced opponent. Although the odds are initially against them, they win because of their innate talent, fighting spirit, and the help of their trainer, an older, very experienced boxer. The plots of such films are based primarily on Sylvester Stallone's character in *Rocky* (1976), whose financial success encouraged the production of a number of clones. The reception of *Streets of Gold* and *Split Decisions* has been lukewarm, and they illustrate very well the words of the producer of *Rocky*, Irwin Winkler, who said: "More money has been lost by people trying to imitate *Rocky* than was ever made by the original picture."[4] The Irish perspective on the story of a struggling young pugilist was not enough to make these films successful. However, it is interesting to see how their authors took a *Rocky*-like story as the core of the plot and wrapped it in various themes, including typically Irish ones. The similarity of narrative motifs in the two films to other films involving the Irish proves once again the existence of a deeply-rooted stereotype, based on the history of Irish immigrants to America and transformed into a modern myth.

More recently, Hollywood has used the stereotype of the Irish boxer to tell different stories, concentrating on contemporary issues such as homosexuality and women's empowerment. Homosexuality is the focus of an American independent (though made in Hollywood) film *Fighting Tommy Riley* (2004), directed by Eddie O'Flaherty with J. P. Davis, who also wrote the script, as the title character. At the beginning of the film, Tommy is preparing for a fight, and when he is about to get in the ring, he thinks back over the events of the previous seven months. He is presented as a person who lacks motivation, both in his private and professional life. He was a boxer before, and nearly became a member of the U.S. Olympic boxing team in 2000 in the middleweight division, but due to a hand injury he had to quit mid-fight. Up until now he has been working as a computer technician, laying computer cable, and as a sparring partner. His girlfriend has left him and he lives alone. One day, he impresses Marty Goldberg (Eddie Jones), a boxing trainer, and his business partner Diane (Diane Tayler), who convince him to work with them and go back to the ring and, after some training, he wins his first fight. For Marty,

---

4 Roger Ebert, "Streets Of Gold Movie Review & Film Summary (1986) | Roger Ebert," RogerEbert.com, November 14, 1986, http://www.rogerebert.com/reviews/streets-of-gold-1986.

whose former protégé left him right before an important fight, Tommy's talent presents an opportunity to become a recognized trainer.

Marty learns that Tommy was not injured during his fight before the Olympic Games. The real reason he withdrew from the Olympics was that he was mistreated and disrespected by his coach, who was also his stepfather. Marty encourages and motivates Tommy, putting him on the right track to success both in his private and professional life. Tommy is able to win back his ex-girlfriend and decides to face Leroy Kane, a middleweight contender who went to the Olympic Games instead of the young Irish American. In order to prepare for the fight, Tommy and Marty go to a secluded cabin in the woods, where Marty starts seducing Tommy, revealing that he is a homosexual. Tommy's reaction is fierce, and the two decide never to talk about the incident again. Tommy wins the fight against Kane, using the strategy devised by Marty. However, that night, Marty is taken to hospital and, when he is released, Tommy offers to stay at his place and watch over him.

Tommy learns that Marty was forced to quit boxing because of his homosexuality. In order to end his career on his own terms, he damaged his hand. When Bob Silver offers Tommy a contract worth a million dollars he also encourages him to leave Marty but Tommy staunchly refuses, even against the advice of Marty and Diane. Marty tries to discourage Tommy from working with him. When nothing works, he becomes sexually abusive, which causes Tommy to react furiously against his trainer. Feeling bad about what he said to Marty, Tommy visits him and proposes they spend a night together. Marty refuses vehemently and Tommy leaves. The next morning, Tommy and Diane learn that Marty has committed suicide. As the film returns to the first scene, Tommy is seen crying but he then looks into the mirror and sees an apparition of Marty standing behind him. He enters the ring dressed in Marty's old ring robe.

The film employs narrative motifs characteristic of the representations of the Irish in American cinema but these motifs are somewhat reworked. J. P. Davis plays with classic conventions of presenting boxers and with stereotypical representations of Irish Americans. He labels his main character with an Irish last name, and he chooses a Jewish identity for his trainer. This reversal of the classic historical Irish trainer-Jewish boxer juxtaposition might be a conscious decision on the part of the writer but it may also be based on several real-life and fictional Jewish boxing trainers, such as Mickey Goldmill (Burgess Meredith) from *Rocky*, who is widely considered to be based on the real-life Charley Goldman. What is more, instead of choosing a beginner as the main character, the writer decided to focus on a boxer who is given a second chance. The main reason for that seems to be related to the role of violence.

THE IRISH AS OFFICIAL HEROES   231

As a typical Irish boxer character, Tommy Riley does a rather low-paid blue-collar job. Boxing is a springboard to success for him. Therefore, due to his characteristically Irish intimacy with violence, expressed as a talent for boxing, Tommy is noticed by Mickey and Diane. As Tommy is not a beginner, but a competent boxer, his training is focused primarily on motivation. His loss of motivation can be attributed to the psychological violence Tommy was subjected to because of his stepfather. This, in turn, is an interesting development of the notion of Irish masculinity, as physical violence, the most important aspect defining an Irish man is deemed subordinate to psychological violence. In other words, it turns out that psychological violence can destroy a physically strong person. However, another motif seems to play an important role here.

The motif of the importance of the father is developed in an interesting way. Tommy's stepfather, instead of helping him develop his abilities, destroys his future. Still, the fact that he is able to do so signifies that he is, in fact, an essential person in his life. Quenching Tommy's motivation, the stepfather diverts him from the path to success. It is Marty who steps in and becomes a new father figure. However, Marty is gay, and sexually interested in his new protégé. This causes an initial violent reaction from Tommy, who nevertheless remains faithful to Marty as a role model. Tommy's subordination to Marty reaches its peak when the heterosexual Irish American pugilist offers himself sexually to his trainer. This, in turn, presents an unparalleled perspective on the notion of Irish masculinity, defined by intimacy with violence, with the main character appearing physically strong but psychologically weak.

Women's empowerment in connection with Irish stereotypes is, arguably, best expressed in Clint Eastwood's 2004 drama, *Million Dollar Baby*. The film offers a development of the now-classic narrative pattern involving a young aspiring boxer and his older, more experienced trainer but this time the young boxer is a woman. Maggie Fitzgerald (Hilary Swank) is a waitress who dreams of becoming a professional boxer. She asks Frankie Dunn (Clint Eastwood), an older, experienced Los Angeles trainer, who started training pugilists in the 1960s, to become her coach. Not wanting to train a woman, he refuses. Maggie is too determined to give up and comes to Dunn's gym every day to work out and show him her motivation. When Frankie's protégé, "Big" Willie (Mike Colter), decides to sign a contract with another manager, Dunn agrees to train Maggie, although he is still reluctant and only promises to teach her the basics of boxing.

However, after Maggie's first fight, Frankie has to admit she is a talented boxer and focuses on training her. His effort is not in vain as she becomes a star of women's welterweight boxing. Maggie is loyal to Frankie and does not

232   CHAPTER 5

abandon him when an opportunity to work with a more successful manager appears. Soon her fame spreads beyond America and, with Frankie, she travels to Europe, where she fights against a U.K. boxer. Dunn gives her an Irish pseudonym *Mo Chuisle* but refuses to tell her what it means. When they return to America, Frankie arranges for his protégée a one-million-dollar match against a WBA champion, a German ex-prostitute, Billie (Lucia Rijker). During the fight, Maggie is punched from behind and falls on a corner stool. Although Frank is not able to accept the diagnosis, the accident renders Maggie quadriplegic and unable to breathe unaided. Blaming himself for Maggie's accident, Frankie stays with her and looks after his former trainee.

Maggie's condition deteriorates and, due to bedsores, her leg is amputated. Unable to cope, she begs Frankie to help her commit suicide, so that when she dies she will remember who she was before the accident. Frankie refuses but asks a priest, Father Horvak (Brian F. O'Byrne), a priest who genuinely hates Frankie, for advice and is warned that euthanasia is a mortal sin and that he, as a Catholic, should not consider it. Meanwhile, Maggie attempts suicide by biting her tongue in order to bleed to death. She is, however, saved by medical staff. Having decided that Maggie is more important to him than his faith, Frankie visits Maggie one last time in order to help her. He tells her that her Irish pseudonym means "my darling and my blood" and he administers a lethal dose of adrenaline, before walking away.

Million Dollar Baby is an emotional and powerful movie that explores and develops several motifs characteristic of Irish representations. The most important aspect is, quite obviously, violence presented as both a creative and a destructive force. Maggie Fitzgerald, a young Irish American woman, is able to improve her life thanks to her talent for a violent sport. However, she is destroyed by violence just when she is about to reach the apex of her career. Violence is shown as a male characteristic, and a woman entering the gym to train is immediately mocked by the men. At first Frank will not even allow her to use his speed bag, for fear that somebody might think he is training her. He also calls women's boxing a "freak show," emphasizing that violence is not the domain of women. When he agrees to train her, he demands obedience and wonders if he can forget that he is preparing a girl to become a boxer.

Even when he starts helping Maggie, he does not treat her seriously, but only as a distraction he needs when he is abandoned by Willie. However, as he watches her first fight from a distance, he decides to honestly help her become a boxer, finally acknowledging her by saying, "This is my fighter."[5] As Maggie

---

5   Drucilla Cornell, *Clint Eastwood and Issues of American Masculinity* (New York: Fordham Univ Press, 2009), 189.

THE IRISH AS OFFICIAL HEROES   233

wins fights and progressively improves her innate talents, Dunn realizes that violence, epitomized by boxing, is not just the domain of men.

Maggie's skill and propensity for controlled violent behavior is actually an obstacle to her career. She has a tendency and the ability to knock out her opponents in the first round, depriving audiences of a good spectacle. Therefore, Frank has to bribe managers to allow her to fight with their protégées and soon he decides to move her up a class so that her opponents will be stronger and able to last longer in the ring. During her first fight, Maggie's nose is broken but she refuses to give up, displaying a real fighting spirit.

Family values are also explored in the film. Despite his initial reserve, Frankie soon begins to treat Maggie like a daughter. The two become foster family members to each other, as their biological families are dysfunctional. Dunn has lost contact with his biological daughter, who returns each letter he sends her, and Maggie "offers him a chance to repair what he cannot repair with his own daughter."[6] Maggie's family, consisting of her mother, sister, and brother, are selfish and only care about the money she wins. When she buys them a house, they are worried about losing their welfare money and mock her profession. When they visit her in hospital they try to make her sign documents allowing them to transfer all her money to their accounts. More importantly, the mother emphasizes the fact that Maggie lost. Dunn, on the other hand, genuinely cares about the young woman. He tries to keep Maggie from making the mistakes he has made in his life, and, as he is about to fulfill her last wish, he tells her the meaning of her pseudonym, affirming that he has considered her a daughter for some time. When he leaves the hospital he has nothing left in his life and never returns to the gym. It is left unstated whether the events shown in the film resulted in Dunn's mending the relationship with his own daughter, but the story, narrated by Dunn's friend, Eddie Dupris (Morgan Freeman), turns out to be a letter to her.

Maggie's family also breaks no stereotypes of the Irish, especially not the Irish in boxing films. Like all the characters in boxing films analyzed so far, she comes from a poor working-class background. However, her family is also dysfunctional. When she describes them to Dunn, she says: "The truth is, my brother's in prison, my sister is on welfare, pretending one of her babies is still alive. My daddy's dead and my mama weigh three hundred and twelve pounds." She says she has no prospects apart from boxing, her only way of escaping her family. Once again, this reflects the situation of Irish immigrants for whom boxing was sometimes the sole means of breaking free from the painful conditions of their everyday life.

---

6   Cornell, 189.

234 CHAPTER 5

Religion plays an essential role in Frankie's life. At the beginning of the film, he is shown praying before going to sleep. He attends mass every day, after which he usually torments Father Horvak with questions calculated to enrage him. In one early scene the priest responds to Frank's "doubts" by calling him a "fucking pagan." Nevertheless, Dunn is a devout Catholic. When Maggie is injured he goes to the church and prays and when asked by Maggie to assist her in suicide, "facing the ultimate ethical crisis,"[7] he goes to Father Horvak for advice. The priest tells Dunn to leave Maggie in God's hands, that only God can decide when someone dies. Frankie replies: "She's not asking for God's help. She's asking mine." Ultimately, the love for his "daughter" is stronger than the beliefs and convictions to which he has been shown faithful throughout the whole film. As a devout Catholic, he sacrifices his faith and his soul in order to help Maggie.

The Irish identity of the main characters is strongly emphasized throughout the film. Notwithstanding the set of motifs analyzed above, two major elements point to the Irishness of Dunn and Fitzgerald. Firstly, Dunn is seen reading Irish poets, such as Yeats. Conscious of his ancestry, he finds solace when he connects with Ireland through poetry. As he reads Irish versions of the poems—even those by Yeats, who is generally known not to have spoken the language—Dunn translates the poems for Maggie, as he wants her to experience the same calm evoked through the connection with Ireland. Secondly, the Irish nickname Frankie gives Maggie, *Mo Chuisle*, is written on her boxing robe below the harp, a symbol of Ireland. When Maggie enters the ring for her first European fight, a section of the audience starts chanting the pseudonym. More importantly, as Maggie's opponent is British, the Irish become euphoric when she wins by a knockout. The popularity of *Million Dollar Baby* increased interest in the Irish language among the film's audience.[8] Audiences chant *Mo Chuisle* whenever Maggie fights, which Dupris comments on as follows: "Seems there were Irish people everywhere. Or people who wanted to be." Thus, Maggie is presented as an Irish hero, cheered and applauded by her compatriots because of her talent for a stereotypically Irish sport.

Finally, the film presents Irishness in a decidedly positive light, despite the ubiquity of violence in this representation. This might explain the comment regarding people who wanted to be Irish. Firstly, Irishness is presented "as a metaphor for home, belonging, and connectedness—all the values perceived to be missing in an early-twenty-first-century world dominated by the

---

7   Cornell, 118.
8   Wes Davis, "Fighting Words," *The New York Times*, February 26, 2005, sec. Opinion, http://www.nytimes.com/2005/02/26/opinion/26davis.html.

THE IRISH AS OFFICIAL HEROES   235

homogenizing force of global capitalism."[9] This is emphasized especially by a very positive realization of the motif of the importance of the father and the motif of family values. Although the ending of the film is tragic, the characters are enriched through their connection with each other; this connection is emphasized with the Irish language and the literature used to describe it. Secondly, the Irish ethos is contrasted with white trash, represented by Maggie's family.[10] In this view, Irishness containing and epitomizing positive values—i.e., values connected with family, honor, fighting spirit, confidence, and trust—is presented as something to aspire to. Thus, the film can be understood as Maggie's "transition from white trash to Irishness."[11] Undoubtedly, the climax of the transformation comes when Maggie learns the meaning of *Mo Chuisle*, at the same time realizing that she has attained the qualities and values connected with Irishness and embodied by her father-daughter relationship with Dunn. Thus, her death, intertwined with Frankie's sacrificing himself in religious terms, is a final and compelling expression of the connection they have formed.

Similar rags-to-riches stories are presented in biographical films about Irish American boxers. Ron Howard's *Cinderella Man* (2005) tells the story of James Braddock, an Irish American boxer, portrayed in the film by Russell Crowe. David O. Russell's *The Fighter* (2010) tells the story of Micky "the Irish" Ward (Mark Wahlberg).

Another category of boxing film includes productions in which the violence of boxing is presented as an alternative to other forms of brutality. An example is a 1992 drama *Gladiator*, directed by Rowdy Herrington. In order to pay his father's gambling debts, Tommy Riley (James Marshall), a high-school student, engages in illegal underground boxing. He soon begins to win and attracts the attention of Jimmy Horn (Brian Dennehy), a boxing promoter who purchases Tommy's father's debts and blackmails the young man into fighting for him. Tommy befriends an African American, Lincoln Haines (Cuba Gooding Jr.), who fights in order to support his girlfriend and their child, and Romano (Jon Seda), whose aim is to earn enough money to send his father's body to Cuba. Although Tommy initially plans to earn money quickly and go to college, he becomes attracted to boxing and addicted to his success and, as a result, neglects school.

---

9   Aidan Arrowsmith, "Imaginary Connections? Postmemory and Irish Diaspora Writing," in *Irish Studies: Memory Ireland, Diaspora and Memory Practices*, ed. Oona Frawley (Syracuse, NY: Syracuse University Press, 2012), 12.

10   Hamilton Carroll, *Affirmative Reaction: New Formations of White Masculinity* (Durham, NC: Duke University Press, 2011), 132.

11   Carroll, 134.

Soon, Romano is seriously injured and declared brain dead after a fight with a gang member called Shortcut. Tommy avenges his friend, winning a fight against Shortcut. Subsequently, he has to face Lincoln and, finally, the enraged Horn, who wanted Lincoln or Tommy to die during the fight. Tommy wins, freeing his father from debt and himself from the world of illegal boxing.

The film presents boxing, although in a brutal underground form, as an alternative to gang violence. Even though the fights are controlled by ruthless promoters who want to see contenders die in the ring, Tommy stays faithful to the rules of the sport. What is more, both he and his friends engage in boxing for selfless reasons and are juxtaposed with Shortcut, a gang member who uses a blinding fluid smeared on his gloves in order to win and does not hesitate to kill his opponents. Shortcut represents gang violence, which is unacceptable and dishonorable, while Tommy and his friends represent honor and the ideals of fair play. Like all films focusing on Irish boxers, *Gladiator* explores the motifs of family values and the importance of the father: it is because of his father that Tommy begins to participate in underground fights.

Like firefighting, boxing is sometimes not central to films but only an addition that emphasizes Irish identity. An excellent example of this is *Daredevil*, analyzed in the previous section. However, boxing has found its way into a genre of film in which violence is not supposed to play a significant role, i.e., romantic comedy. *She's The One* (1996) is a collection of Irish stereotypes. To begin with, two brothers, Mickey (Edward Burns) and Francis (Mike McGlone), compete with each other. Secondly, the dominance of their father, Frank (John Mahoney), in their lives is emphasized by the fact that their mother never appears on the screen. Moreover, Irish masculinity is underscored by the fact that the father is a sexist who never allows women on board his motorboat. Finally, and most importantly, when the men quarrel, Frank gives them boxing gloves to settle the dispute. Mickey emerges victorious.

In general, films focusing on Irish boxers seem to emphasize the importance of family. They usually talk about traditionally Irish family values in the context of traditional Irish sport. Considering the specificity of boxing, the films usually show blue-collar workers or people with a working-class background as the main characters. Moreover, they focus on ethnic conflicts, usually juxtaposing an Irish boxer with one of another ethnic background, with the opponent usually more reliable and visibly more powerful than his or her Irish counterpart. Finally, they have educational value, as such films show that through determination and following the advice of more experienced members of the community, a person can achieve success.

What is essential, boxing films show acceptable violence juxtaposed with instances of unacceptable violence. In films focusing on a young boxer's

THE IRISH AS OFFICIAL HEROES   237

training, unacceptable violence is connected with criminals, common in the boxers' communities, or with dishonest contenders and unsportsmanlike behavior. When following a code of conduct connected with boxing, an Irish person is able to succeed. A similar view is presented in films showing violence as an alternative to other forms of violent behavior. Unlike the first classical boxers, who were often presented similarly to gangsters, contemporary on-screen boxers are honest athletes and their abilities are presented as a talent, rather than propensity to violence.

Finally, boxing films involving Irish characters present the abovementioned Irish themes in the context of a well-established formula, characterizing boxing films in general. Leger Grindon distinguishes six types of conflict that appear in boxing films. The first is the conflict between material and spiritual values. Secondly, there is the juxtaposition of success achieved individually due to "market forces"—for example, financial success—and success stemming from cooperation with others and altruism. Thirdly, there is the conflict between social mobility arising from the boxer's success and allegiance to the community to which he or she belongs. Fourthly there is conflict related to the discrepancy between masculine values followed in the ring and a woman's influence. Fifthly, there is conflict stemming from the boxer's inability to eradicate tyranny, and lastly, there is the emotional conflict that arises when discipline connected with harsh living conditions is juxtaposed with the boxer's sympathy for other people.[12] All these conflicts are present in the studied films. However, the clash between masculinity and woman's influence is usually limited since the role of women in the representation of the Irish is usually marginal.

4 Other Violent Characters

Representations of the Irish in contemporary American cinema are not limited to the categories analyzed above and violence in connection with the Irish sometimes appears when least expected. The 1985 science-fiction blockbuster, *Back to the Future* by Robert Zemeckis, as well as its sequels, feature Irish American characters. Marty McFly, a time-traveling teenager, resorts to violence whenever he is accused of lacking courage. His adversaries in various periods are members of the Tannen family, who are fierce and always ready to torment the McFly family. Moreover, the fortunes of Marty and his family

---

12   Leger Grindon, *Knockout: The Boxer and Boxing in American Cinema* (Jackson: University Press of Mississippi, 2011), 7.

change with a single act of violence when his father, George (Crispin Glover), punches Biff Tannen. This event gives George confidence thanks to which he becomes a successful writer and is no longer bullied by Biff.

Violent characters—both those merely labeled as Irish by their last names and those who are explicitly Irish—appear in comedies, some of which are worth attention. In the well-known Christmas-themed comedy *Home Alone* (1990), directed by Chris Columbus, Kevin McAlister (Macaulay Culkin) is accidentally left at home on his own by his parents. When two robbers assault him, he fights them using a variety of violent methods. The film also stresses the importance of family, which Kevin has to learn through his experiences. In *Celtic Pride* (1996), directed by Tom DeCerchio, two fans of the Boston Celtics basketball team, Mike O'Hara (Daniel Stern), a teacher, and Jimmy Flaherty (Dan Aykroyd), a plumber, kidnap Lewis Scott (Damon Wayans), a star of the Utah Jazz team in order to give the Celtics a better chance of winning a match. Finally, in Danny DeVito's *Duplex* (2003), a young couple, Alex (Ben Stiller) and Nancy (Drew Barrymore) try to get rid of their neighbor, Mrs. Connelly (Eileen Essell), a seemingly nice, fragile old Irish American woman, who is nevertheless ruining their personal and professional lives. At first, the couple try to send Mrs. Connelly to Ireland but when this fails they devise various ways of killing her. However, Mrs. Connelly seems impervious to violence and spends her time watching T.V., playing in a brass band, and dancing Irish dances. In the end, it is revealed that Mrs. Connelly is the head of a group of scammers who harass young couples living in the eponymous duplex in order to extort money.

Finally, the American fascination with the Irish resulted in horror films drawing inspiration from Irish culture. In a rather well-known series of eight horror films, *Leprechaun*, the first of which was released in 1993, various groups of people are tormented by a character inspired by Irish folklore, but transformed into a brutal monster, murdering people in order to find his pot of gold.

5 The Irish Ethnotype in Contemporary American Cinema

Unlike the New Hollywood period, which, probably due to its shorter time span, only dealt with Irish identity in passing, contemporary American cinema offers a host of Irish characters in a variety of usually stereotypical roles, social functions, and occupations. In terms of the variety of representations, contemporary American cinema seems to be a direct continuator of Classical Hollywood, in which Irish characters were frequently portrayed, often by Irish American directors. However, it also draws from New Hollywood's Irish characters, who were often labeled as Irish with the use of Irish surnames.

THE IRISH AS OFFICIAL HEROES   239

The category of labeled characters seems to be formed exclusively by stereotypical Irish cops, inspired by Dirty Harry Callahan, who himself is heavily based on the figure of an American gunslinger. The motifs used in the creation of such characters emphasize their intimacy with violence. The violent Irish cop is unable to escape from the world of violence either because of a deeply entrenched sense of duty or because he himself is the source of violence—the character whose appearance destroys the equilibrium and sets the story in motion. In both cases, he is the only person able to restore the balance. An interesting theme connected with the violent Irish cop is his inability to form a stable relationship or start a family due to his sense of duty. Such a representation of the Irish is noteworthy. The creators of characters such as John McClane or RoboCop may not have focused on their characters' Irish identity, but rather, when designing them as violent police officers, they decided to give them Irish surnames. Thus, unwittingly, they joined two different facets of the Irish stereotype, i.e., the stereotype of an Irish police officer and violence stereotypically associated with Irishmen in America.

The category of characters who are overtly Irish is represented by a significantly larger number of cinematic figures. Contemporary cinema is not afraid to emphasize the Irishness of film characters in various ways. Apart from Irish police officers, who are usually less violent than their counterparts who are only labeled with Irish last names, the selection of characters includes Irish republican fighters from Northern Ireland, gangsters, firefighters, boxers, and vigilantes. The films analyzed in this study vary widely in terms of the depth of their characters and in their cinematic value but they sometimes follow strikingly similar patterns of representation for Irish characters, whose lives are usually connected with violence which they sometimes use for personal gain, but most often to protect others, fight crime, or take action they see as just, even if they run counter to the established law and order.

Most of these films, regardless of genre and subject, focus on family values. Upholding family values is one of the Irish characters' most important aims. It is rivaled by a sense of duty—mainly duty understood as patriotic responsibility for the freedom of Ireland. The importance of family is stressed in the majority of the films analyzed, and if there is no real family present in the life of the main character, he or she finds substitute family members. The most important figure in an Irish family is the father, which stems from the traditional view of the Irish father-son relationship. The Irish formed a mostly patriarchal society and the father took on the role of breadwinner. Thus, a vital function of the father was to teach his child, primarily a son, to become a breadwinner for his future family. Therefore, Irish sons on screen are taught by their fathers to eventually substitute them in their profession, which generally happens when the father is no longer able to work.[13] Similarly, in contemporary Hollywood, the Irish father's role is to shape his ward's life. This is achieved in three primary ways; firstly, a young person may follow the instructions or advice provided by the father figure. What is interesting is that if the instructions are present, the father figure giving them is usually not a biological parent of the main character, but rather someone chosen by the character as the substitute father. A variety of characters may perform this function, such as a higher-ranking officer in the case of police officers and firefighters, a boxing trainer, or a leader of the mob. This representation of father figure-child relations is represented in the majority of films featuring the Irish. In *The Kitchen*, the function of the mother figure replaces that of the father, but the overall character of the relationship between the child and the parent remains the same.

Another common way of portraying the relationship between the father figure and the main character is through the loss of the father. This usually happens in dramatic circumstances and influences the main character to follow the father's example or try to avenge him. In both cases, it is usually a biological parent who dies, and this makes the life of the main character difficult. As such, he or she cannot be successful either in private or professional life. It is only when a substitute father figure appears that the main character is able to become successful personally or professionally, although the two kinds of success do not have to be achieved simultaneously. The least common way of portraying father figure-child relations in "Irish films" is through negative influence, when the child does not want to follow the pattern established by the father. This may be seen in *Goodfellas* and in *The Departed*, in which the main characters are prepared to go to great lengths just to avoid repeating some of their fathers' traits, such as being hardworking but poor. Finally, if the father figure is the main character in a film, his function is to protect the child figure. In all of the abovementioned contexts, the father figure may be substituted by an older brother.

Contemporary Hollywood also pays more attention to the religious life of the Irish. However, the importance of religion varies from film to film and seems most clearly marked as a universal aspect of life in the case of Irish vigilantes. However, the limited number of films about Irish vigilantism makes the above statement a tentative one and the issue must be studied further when other such films are produced. One interesting feature of Catholicism displayed in the films studied is its aggressive nature. Catholicism is connected with violence and, in some cases, encourages the belief that violence in the

---

13   Michael Hout, *Following in Father's Footsteps: Social Mobility in Ireland* (Cambridge, Mass.: Harvard University Press, 1989), 242.

THE IRISH AS OFFICIAL HEROES   241

Irish is an acceptable countermeasure to the brutality of the contemporary world. Finally, some characters are shown as being opposed to the Catholic Church, for example Frankie McGuire in *The Devil's Own* and Frank Costello in *The Departed*. In both cases, the rejection of the faith also carries a religious significance. Frankie McGuire does not reject Satan during the Confirmation ceremony of Tom O'Meara's daughter, which is another way of marking a contrast between him and the religious police officer. At the same time, Frank Costello's anti-religious stance, expressed in his *Non serviam* motto, makes him a devil-like character himself, especially when one considers the corrupting influence he has on Colin Sullivan.

The most important aspect of the films about the Irish, and the one that connects all the productions analyzed, is the ubiquity of violence. Regardless of their function, social role, or occupation, the Irish characters are presented in connection with violence. This violence is predominantly presented as an acceptable reaction to the brutality present in the world. This, however, depends on the category of film. Firstly, in the case of violence, the extreme brutality with which Irish cops fight crime is justified as being the only reliable reaction to violence perpetrated by criminals. Violence is also present in other representations of Irish police officers, but it is somewhat more generic and shown as connected with the profession, although, admittedly, indicates the existence of a deeply rooted stereotype of police officers being Irish. However, when an Irish police officer, a representative of a well-established and assimilated Irish community, is confronted with an Irish republican newcomer, as seen in IRA films, the police officer is usually less violent or non-violent, which puts him in direct opposition to the brutal newcomer. Virtually the only act of violence used by such a police officer is shown at the end of the film and directed against the newcomer, as violence is the only way to stop a violent opponent. This is done to show that violence should be a last resort and, to some extent, showcases the American vision of the law, which is not based on brutality and retribution and is superior to the retributive justice of the republican Irish. However, the ambiguous-to-positive vision of the IRA in such films seems to suggest that, for the Irish, a violent response is the only way to deal with the structural violence used by the British.

In the case of gangsters and boxers, violence is also connected to the roles performed by the characters. Obviously, in the case of gangsters, it is rather unacceptable, but when used by the main characters, it is sometimes shown positively. The best example of such a portrayal of gang-related Irish brutality is perhaps *Gangs Of New York*, in which the downtrodden Irish respond with violence against the brutal Natives. Importantly, virtually all representations of the Irish gangsters are based on the history of the first Irish immigrants who, rejected by American society, organized themselves into gangs in order to gain respect and prosperity. In the case of boxers, violence is acceptable not only because it is used for competing in sport, but because the main Irish character usually uses violence honorably or for a noble reason. This is generally contrasted with an opponent, typically an outsider or belonging to a different ethnic minority, whose association with unacceptable violence is expressed by his or her disregard for the rules of honorable fighting or by fighting for a cause that is not noble.

In firefighter films, aggression against other people is almost absent. However, this does not mean that violence is missing from such films, as it is expressed as the innate capacity of the Irish to understand the destructive element and fight it. This seems to be an expression of the motif of the intimacy of violence.

Finally, Irish vigilantes seem to be an amalgam of the violent Irish cop, who uses extreme violence to fight crime, and a twisted incarnation of the Irish American Catholic priest, who, guided by religious zeal and legitimate care for society, eradicates violence. Connecting virtually all the stereotypical elements of the representation of the Irish, the Irish vigilante, which is the newest type of character in the context of this study, uses extreme violence but is nevertheless accepted by the community. In the creation of Irish vigilantes, the motifs associated with higher values, such as family relations, responsibility, and honor, help the viewer accept a character whose crime fighting methods are not concordant with the rules of the established American law. More importantly, the vigilante offers an acceptable vision of the Irish law based on retributive justice, which involves seemingly uncivilized methods of fighting criminals. Thus, although not represented in a large number of films, the Irish vigilante is fascinating in the context of this study and provides a new, positive look at the Irish stereotype in America.

In conclusion, the representation of violence as an element of the Irish stereotype in contemporary American cinema is decisively more favorable than in the Classical period of American filmmaking and less controversial than in New Hollywood. This is, admittedly, connected with the growing acceptability of cinematic violence. However, the panoply of overtly Irish characters shown in stereotypically Irish roles and usually connected with violence also shows an increasing acceptance of the image of the violent Irishman by filmmakers, and, consequently, by the public. With the end of the Troubles in Northern Ireland, the growing significance of Ireland, an economically prosperous country, and the success of Irish Americans in securing a respectable position within American society, the representations of the Irish have become decidedly more positive. What is more, as these representations are definitely based on inveterate stereotypes concerning the Irish in America, the stereotype of a violent Irishman has also lost its negative undertone. More than a hundred years after the Irish, like the notorious Typhoid Mary, were scapegoats, blamed for the plagues and tribulations that affected the otherwise perfect American society, the Irish have become heroes of American popular culture.

Conclusion

One of the first films analyzed in this book is *The Public Enemy*, released in 1931 and designed to be watched in a cinema. It is black-and-white and employs sound, then a quite recent and groundbreaking addition to moving images. Chronologically, one of the latest ones is *The Irishman*, which premiered in 2019 and, following a limited cinematic release, has been distributed by Netflix. As I write this, the film is available for streaming at any time and in any place with broadband Internet access. It uses a novel digital de-aging technique, which allowed Martin Scorsese to show his characters at various stages of their lives. The eighty-eight years separating the two films are a vast and rich period, encompassing numerous technical advances, as well as social and political changes that have affected the way films are made and watched. However, the two films share a reliance on the Irish stereotype, which was present at the very beginning of American cinema and is still visible today.

The Irish, both in Ireland and in America, have undergone a profound transformation. They entered the 20th century as a nation deprived of their freedom, with wounds still fresh from the unspeakable tragedy of the Great Famine, and a constant hemorrhage of people escaping the island in search of a new home. In America, they were unwelcome immigrants, considered too savage and brutal to integrate into American society. In the 20th century, they became a proud nation whose success is truly enviable. Thanks to their perseverance, they regained their long-lost independence and achieved economic success in Ireland: rapid growth lasting until the financial crisis in the late 2000s earned them the moniker of the Celtic Tiger. Moreover, they have also reached the highest positions in American society, becoming heroes and leaders in culture and politics. Interestingly, the Irish have never abandoned the qualities that made them so different from their British neighbors and initially unwelcome among the American WASP elite. They have remained Catholic and kept their signature Irish nonconformity. Although divided over willingness to become assimilated into American culture, it can hardly be denied that their success in the USA is an American dream come true.

The improving situation of the Irish diaspora in America resulted in the steady evolution of their ethnotype in American cinema. The first classical films openly mocked the Irish for their perceived violent nature, establishing this characteristic as the kernel of their representation in cinema. In the 1930s, Classical Hollywood divided the Irish into two groups, based on their relationship with violence. Male gangsters and, initially, boxers used violence for personal gain, whereas women and Catholic priests understood the destructive

CONCLUSION   245

nature of violence and were able to reject it and guide others to success. As the dominant motif in the representation of the Irish, violence was ubiquitous in films and initially used to emphasize the negative impact of the Irish on American society. All the Classical Hollywood films featuring Irish gangsters addressed serious social problems, such as juvenile delinquency, alcoholism, poverty, and violence against women. Importantly, in all such films, the life of crime was shown as seductively appealing to Irish people since it allowed them to enjoy a temporary sense of achievement. This ethnotype served as a good explanation of the perceived behavior of the Irish community: rejected by society, deprived of the possibility of success, and inherently intimate with violence, they resorted to crime. However, it was the violence they embraced that was the main obstacle to achieving real, long-term success. The vision of the gangster was pessimistic and it always led to the character's downfall, which could not be averted. Thus, the work of Irish American Catholic priests was aimed at keeping youth far from the world of violence. Irish boxers in America were in a slightly better position. Although they used violence for selfish reasons, they were redeemable and could be integrated into American society. However, a personal tragedy or a difficult, cathartic life-changing situation was necessary for them to succeed. A similarly ambiguous portrayal of Irish trade unions focused on individual choices connected with the acceptance or rejection of violence. Thus, in classical Hollywood, a basic dichotomy between negative-violent and positive-non-violent characters was visible, with the non-violent ones epitomizing the values desirable for American society.

This view changed in the 1940s, during World War II. Although Ireland did not fight in the war, the Irish in American were among the most famous and readily recognizable combatants. Real-life war heroes were represented on the screen along with similarly portrayed fictional characters, attesting to the changing view of the Irish. Thus, the negative selfish violence represented by gangsters and boxers was replaced by positive violence employed as a defensive measure in order to protect the country. At the same time, the Irish were no longer presented as violent for the sake of violence. The focus now shifted towards other features traditionally associated with them, such as family, devotion to duty, and Irish American romanticism, probably best expressed and confronted with violent Irish reality in John Ford's *The Quiet Man*.

The tendency to portray violence connected with the Irish in a positive way was dominant in New Hollywood. Gangsters and boxers, the villains and ambiguous characters of the classical era, started to be portrayed as old and tired, indicating that they had lived past their prime and had to be replaced by new Irish characters. However, despite the already high position of the Irish in American society, such characters were more violent than ever before. The first

Irish cop to appear in New Hollywood was Don Siegel's Dan Madigan—a New York detective trying to lead a successful life in a world of violence. Ultimately, Madigan must die, emphasizing the impossibility of his attempt to unite his private and professional life. As such, Madigan filled the gap between the Irish police officer of Classical Hollywood and the violent Irish super cop of New Hollywood, represented by "Dirty" Harry Callahan. Clint Eastwood's character epitomized the idea of retributive justice, often going against the established law and order, which made the character an outlaw hero. On the one hand, Callahan was constructed on the basis of a traditional American western hero, who stands between the social order and the world of crime because he possesses the qualities of both sides of the conflict. On the other hand, Dirty Harry represented a new quality in American cinema. He was a heroic police officer who could not afford to have a private life as he chose duty over personal happiness but he also displayed the qualities of a psychopath unable to exist without violence. This peculiar combination of a sense of responsibility and an inability to live without violence became one of the most important motifs in the representation of the Irish stereotype in New Hollywood and beyond.

New Hollywood was critical of the typically Irish idea of union violence. In *The Molly Maguires* Irish miners were presented on the one hand as terrorists who acted against the rightful owner of the enterprise where they worked; on the other hand, they were a brave though downtrodden minority who had the courage to rise against voracious American capitalism. The ambiguity was the result of director Martin Ritt's communist sympathies.[1] Nevertheless, it fitted well in the climate of countercultural social changes and the tendency to represent the Irish in the context of trade unions. When they resorted to violence, they were immediately rejected—and betrayed by one of their own—but their motives seemed to be acknowledged and, at some level, understood.

The representation of the Irish stereotype in contemporary American cinema draws from the rich tradition of the previous eras. The cast of Irish characters in contemporary American cinema includes official heroes, who adhere to the ideals of American law, as well as outlaw heroes, including extremely popular gangsters, but also figures modelled on Dirty Harry—violent Irish cops and vigilantes, who cross the boundary between what is legal and illegal in order to fight crime. Their violent response to crime is deemed necessary or even desirable. They operate outside the boundaries of the law to protect the innocent, but pay a high price; they remain outside society—pariahs, lonely heroes unable to make a meaningful connection to other members of society.

---

1   Katz, *The Film Encyclopedia*, 1159.

Irish gangsters have also returned in contemporary American films. The popularity of such characters results in a variety of their representations on the screen. Some of them see a life of crime as the only viable alternative to poverty and lack of success. Others have an established position within criminal organizations. In the case of the latter, they often work for the Italian Mafia as hitmen and henchmen. Frank Costello of *The Departed* is in charge of a powerful and dangerous criminal organization. Regardless of their position, violence connected with Irish gangsters in America is still destructive and inescapable and leads to the inevitable downfall of such characters. Gangster films, particularly those directed by Martin Scorsese, explore the motifs of the importance of the father figure, who usually has a negative influence on the main character, ultimately corrupting the male gangster. A recent twist on the cinematic representation of the Irish gangster figure is *The Kitchen*, which replaces male gangsters with female ones, while employing numerous well-known tropes and narrative patterns.

Northern Irish republicans, ignored in the New Hollywood era, have made a comeback to the cinema in contemporary films. Notably, those belonging to the IRA tend to be represented ambiguously or in a straightforwardly positive way as patriots and freedom fighters. They are outlaw heroes, since what they do is illegal, but their actions seem to be understood. They are usually contrasted with the Irish living in America, represented as official heroes, i.e. upholders of American law. The contrast lies in the construction of the characters and their approach to violence. While Northern Irish newcomers are fierce and wild, using violence freely, the Irish living in America are usually calm and peaceful, refraining from violence until forced to protect their families.

A significant change took place in the case of Irish firefighters. Represented in New Hollywood by Steve McQueen's Mike O'Halloran in *The Towering Inferno* (1974), Irish firefighters have become quite frequently portrayed heroes in contemporary American cinema, which pays more attention to their private lives, stressing the difficulty they face trying to fulfill personal and professional duties: this is unlike *The Towering Inferno*, in which the emphasis was solely on firefighting. One of the most important motifs in the construction of Irish firefighters in contemporary American cinema is the importance of the father figure, as it is the father who is the carrier of traditional values that allow the main character to achieve personal or professional success. The focus on the young character's achievement of success after a series of misfortunes makes the plots of the films discussed in this section a type of cinematic *Bildungsroman*. The violence in these films is indirect, epitomized by fire. Thus, violence is a destructive element turning order into chaos. The Irish, being intimate with violence, can stand against the fire and win, often willingly sacrificing their lives. This is, arguably, best seen in *Backdraft* (1991), in which fire is presented almost as a sentient malevolent creature whose sole purpose is to destroy. The Irish are the only ones who can defeat it.

The final kind of Irish American character in contemporary American cinema is the boxer. In films about Irish boxers violence is used primarily for entertainment but boxing films have recently evolved from productions following a rather rudimentary *Rocky*-like scenario, about a trainer and his young male apprentice, into films commenting on issues of masculinity and femininity. Although plots inspired by *Rocky* are present, the most worthwhile films featuring Irish boxers deviate from the typical narrative pattern. Two such films are *Fighting Tommy Riley* (2004), addressing the issues of masculinity and homosexuality, and *Million Dollar Baby* (2004), showing the stereotype reversal when it comes to the Irish boxer's gender. Violence in boxing films is used primarily as a source of entertainment; however, there are some other qualities of violence presented in connection with boxing. Firstly, violence in the ring is an alternative for other, more severe expressions of brutality. Secondly, violence creates a bond between the trainer and the trainee; in some cases, the bond goes beyond the classical master-apprentice dependency and transforms into a parent-child relationship. In this way, boxing violence is creative rather than destructive.

Irish outlaw heroes are savage and brutal, ignoring constraints imposed on their nature by American society. Official heroes are, in general, tamed; their innate Irish intimacy with violence has been redirected and is no longer a threat to society. On the contrary, the Irish intimacy with violence is used either as protection against more serious and more violent threats, as in the case of police officers and firefighters or, in the case of Irish boxers, it as an alternative to more serious violence or at least a form of entertainment. Thus, the most critical symptomatic meanings produced by contemporary films featuring official heroes of Irish origin seem to be, firstly, that embracing American culture is enough to change even the most negative characteristic features; secondly, that American society can put these negative features to good use, making even stereotypical Irish violence a desirable quality in the right circumstances.

At the same time, contemporary American cinema explores numerous well-established patterns of cinematic representation, which apply to Irish characters regardless of the category they represent. The most important one seems to be the importance of the father figure, or—as in *The Kitchen*—the mother figure. This shows not only the value of the family but also the vitality of tradition associated with the Irish. They are also represented in the context of the importance of duty, which may be serving family, community, society, or gang, and they are very unlikely to betray their values. These largely positive motifs in their construction correspond to their positive reception. Even the most despicably violent Irish outlaws are unquestionable heroes of American cinema, proving how far they have come from *Levi and Cohen, Irish Comedians*, who were rejected by their audience for their violent behavior.

The cinematic Irish did not have to change to be accepted. They remained violent but at the same time their other, more desirable features and histories came to prominence, which allowed society to see their violence in a different light. Even though they tend to be presented in terms of a hetero-image, with their national identity stressed as Irish rather than American, this hetero-image is, nevertheless, familiar. Contemporary representations of the Irish in American cinema still rely heavily on stereotypes and well-established narrative patterns, some of which have existed since the dawn of the American film industry and are deeply rooted in the American subconscious. As stated in the introduction, the image of the Irish is contradictory in many ways, combining violence with acceptable and desirable features. At the same time, violence connected with them is not necessarily a negative feature. However, it remains a stereotypical constant, an expected ingredient that must be added to the ethnotype. Many Irish characters appeared on screen between *The Public Enemy* and *The Irishman*. Just as there were Irish characters before Tom Powers, there are bound to be a lot more of them after Frank Sheeran. To paraphrase Timothy J. Meagher's introduction to *The Columbia Guide to Irish American History* quoted in the first chapter, the first violent Irishmen appeared in American cinema in 1903 in a short comedy *Levi and Cohen, Irish Comedians*. The last violent Irish man or woman has not yet appeared and probably never will because few things have been as constant in the history of American cinema as the presence of violence connected with the Irish.

Filmography

In Chronological Order

Early American Films and Classical Hollywood

Levi and Cohen, Irish Comedians
Director: G.W. Bitzer. Screenplay: Unknown. Cast: Unknown. American Mutoscope, 1903.

Tess of the Storm Country
Director: Edwin S. Porter. Screenplay: B.P. Schulberg. Cast: Mary Pickford, Harold Lockwood, Olive Golden (Olive Carey). Famous Players Film Company, 1914.

Hold Your Horses
Director: E. Mason Hopper. Screenplay: Gerald C. Duffy. Cast: Tom Moore, Sylvia Ashton, Naomi Childers. Goldwyn Pictures Corporation, 1921.

Conductor 1492
Directors: Frank Griffin, Charles Hines. Screenplay: Johnny Hines. Cast: Johnny Hines, Doris May, Dan Mason. Warner Bros., 1924.

Little Annie Rooney
Director: William Beaudine. Screenplay: Mary Pickford, Hope Loring. Cast: Mary Pickford, William Haines, Walter Dames, Gordon Griffith. Mary Pickford Company, 1925.

Underworld
Director: Josef von. Sternberg. Screenplay: Charles Furthman and Ben Hecht. Cast: George Bancroft, Clive Brook, Evelyn Brent. Paramount Pictures, 1927.

The Racket
Director: Lewis Milestone. Screenplay: Bartlett Cormack. Cast: Thomas Meighan, Louis Wolheim, Marie Prevost, George E. Stone. The Caddo Company, 1928.

The Public Enemy
Director: William A. Wellman. Screenplay: Kubec Glasmon, John Bright, Harvey F. Thew. Cast: James Cagney, Edward Woods, Jean Harlow, Mae Clarke (Uncredited). Warner Bros., 1931.

The Champ
Director: King Vidor. Screenplay: Frances Marion. Cast: Wallace Beery, Jackie Cooper, Irene Rich. MGM, 1931.

The Life of Jimmy Dolan
Director: Archie Mayo. Screenplay: David Boehm, Ervin Gelsey. Cast: Douglas Fairbanks Jr., Loretta Young, Aline MacMahon, Guy Kibbee. Warner Bros., 1933.

Come on Marines!
Director: Henry Hathaway. Screenplay: Joel Sayre. Cast: Richard Allen, Ida Lupino, Roscoe Karns. Paramount Pictures, 1934.

The Informer
Director: John Ford. Screenplay: Dudley Nichols. Cast: Victor McLaglen, Heather Angel, Preston Foster. RKO Radio Pictures, 1935.

The Irish in US
Director: Lloyd Bacon. Screenplay: Earl Baldwin. Cast: James Cagney, Pat O'Brien, Olivia de Havilland, Mary Gordon. Warner Bros., 1935.

Beloved Enemy
Director: H.C. Potter. Screenplay: John Balderston, Rose Franken. Cast: Merle Oberon, Brian Ahere, Karen Morley. The Samuel Goldwyn Company, 1936.

The Milky Way
Director: Leo McCarey. Screenplay: Grover Jones, Frank Butler. Cast: Harold Lloyd, Lionel Stander, William Gargan. Paramount Pictures, 1936.

Submarine D-1
Director: Lloyd Bacon. Screenplay: Frank Wead, Warren Duff. Cast: Pat O'Brien, George Brent, Wayne Morris. Warner Bros., 1937.

Angels with Dirty Faces
Director: Michael Curtiz. Screenplay: John Wexley, Warren Duff. Cast: James Cagney, Pat O'Brien, Humphrey Bogart, The Dead End Kids. Warner Bros., 1938.

Boys Town
Director: Norman Taurog. Screenplay: John Meehan, Dore Schary. Cast: Spencer Tracy, Mickey Rooney, Henry Hull. MGM, 1938.

FILMOGRAPHY   253

East Side Kids
Director: Bob Hill. Screenplay: William Lively. Cast: Leon Ames, Dennis Moore, Joyce Bryant. Sam Katzman Productions, 1940.

The Fighting 69th
Director: William Keighley. Screenplay: Norman Reilly Raine, Fred Niblo Jr. Cast: James Cagney, Pat O'Brien, George Brent. Warner Bros., 1940.

Three Cheers for the Irish
Director: Lloyd Bacon. Screenplay: Richard Macaulay, Jerry Wald. Cast: Priscilla Lane, Thomas Mitchell, Dennis Morgan. Warner Bros., 1940.

Yankee Doodle Dandy
Director: Michael Curtiz. Screenplay: Robert Buckner, Edmund Joseph. Cast: James Cagney, Joan Leslie, Walter Huston. Warner Bros., 1942

Air Force
Director: Howard Hawks. Screenplay: Dudley Nichols. Cast: John Ridgely, John Garfield, Harry Carey. Warner Bros., 1943.

Going My Way
Director: Leo McCarey. Screenplay: Frank Butler, Frank Cavett. Cast: Bing Crosby, Barry Fitzgerald, Frank McHugh. Paramount Pictures, 1944.

Roger Touhy, Gangster
Director: Robert Florey. Screenplay: Jerry Cady. Cast: Preston Foster, Victor McLaglen, Lois Andrews. Twentieth Century Fox, 1944.

The Fighting Sullivans
Director: Lloyd Bacon. Screenplay: Mary C. McCall Jr. Cast: Anne Baxter, Thomas Mitchell, Edward Ryan, John Campbell, James Cardwell, John Alvin, George Offerman Jr. Twentieth Century Fox, 1944.

The Bells of St. Mary's
Director: Leo McCarey. Screenplay: Dudley Nichols. Cast: Bing Crosby, Ingrid Bergman, Henry Travers. Rainbow Productions, 1945.

The Valley of Decision
Director: Tay Garnett. Screenplay: John Meehan, Sonya Levien. Cast: Greer Garson, Gregory Peck, Donald Crisp, Gladys Cooper. MGM, 1945.

FILMOGRAPHY

They Were Expendable
Director: John Ford. Screenplay: Frank Wead. Cast: John Wayne, Robert Montgomery, Donna Reed. MGM, 1945.

The Lady from Shanghai
Director: Orson Welles. Screenplay: Orson Welles. Cast: Rita Hayworth, Orson Welles, Everett Sloane. Mercury Productions, 1947.

I Wouldn't Be In Your Shoes
Director: William Nigh. Screenplay: Steve Fisher. Cast: Don Castle, Elyse Knox, Regis Toomey. Walter Mirisch Productions, 1948.

Champion
Director: Mark Robson. Screenplay: Carl Foreman. Cast: Kirk Douglas, Arthur Kennedy, Marilyn Maxwell, Ruth Roman. Stanley Kramer Productions, 1949.

The Quiet Man
Director: John Ford. Screenplay: Frank S. Nugent. Cast: John Wayne, Maureen O'Hara, Victor McLaglen, Barry Fitzgerald. Argosy Pictures, 1952.

Island in the Sky
Director: William A. Wellman. Screenplay: Ernest K. Gann. Cast: John Wayne, Lloyd Nolan, Walter Abel. Wayne -Fellows Productions, 1953.

On the Waterfront
Director: Elia Kazan. Screenplay: Budd Schulberg. Cast: Marlon Brando, Karl Malden, Lee J. Cobb. Horizon Pictures, 1954.

To Hell and Back
Director: Jesse Hibbs. Screenplay: Gil Doud. Cast: Audie Murphy, Marshall Thompson, Charles Drake. Universal International Pictures, 1955.

The Long Gray Line
Director: John Ford. Screenplay: Marty Maher. Cast: Tyrone Power, Maureen O'Hara, Robert Francis. Columbia Pictures, 1955.

A Terrible Beauty
Director: Tay Garnett. Screenplay: Robert Wright Campbell. Cast: Robert Mitchum, Richard Harris, Anne Heywood. D.R.M. Productions, Raymond Stross Productions, 1960.

FILMOGRAPHY

Mad Dog Coll
Director: Burt Balaban. Screenplay: Leo Liebermen. Cast: John Chandler, Kay Doubleday, Brooke Hayward. Thalia Productions Inc., 1961.

The Cardinal
Director: Otto Preminger. Screenplay: Robert Dozier. Cast: Tom Tryon, John Huston, Romy Schneider. Otto Preminger Films, 1963.

New Hollywood Films

Madigan
Director: Don Siegel (as Donald Siegel). Screenplay: Howard Rodman, Abraham Polonsky, Richard Dougherty. Cast: Richard Widmark, Henry Fonda, Inger Stevens. Universal Pictures, 1968.

The Molly Maguires
Director: Martin Ritt. Screenplay: Arthur H. Lewis, Walter Bernstein. Cast: Sean Connery, Richard Harris, Samantha Eggar. Paramount Pictures, 1970.

Dirty Harry
Director: Don Siegel. Screenplay: Harry Julian Fink, Rita M. Fink. Cast: Clint Eastwood, Andrew Robinson, Harry Guardino. Warner Bros., 1971.

French Connection
Director: William Friedkin. Screenplay: Ernest Tidyman, Robin Moore. Cast: Gene Hackman, Roy Scheider, Fernando Rey. D'Antoni Productions, Schine-Moore Productions, 1971.

Fat City
Director: John Huston. Screenplay: Leonard Gardner. Cast: Stacy Keach, Jeff Bridges, Susan Tyrell, Candy Clark. Columbia Pictures, 1972.

The Friends of Eddie Coyle
Director: Peter Yates. Screenplay: George V. Higgins, Paul Monash. Cast: Robert Mitchum, Peter Boyle, Richard Jordan. Paramount Pictures, 1973.

Magnum Force
Director: Ted Post. Screenplay: John Milius, Michael Cimino. Cast: Clint Eastwood, Hal Holbrook, Mitchel Ryan, David Soul. Warner Bros., 1973.

256 FILMOGRAPHY

The Towering Inferno
Director: John Guillermin. Screenplay: Stirling Silliphant. Cast: Steve McQueen, Paul Newman, William Holden, Faye Dunaway. Twentieth Century Fox, Warner Bros., 1974.

French Connection II
Director: John Frankenheimer. Screenplay: Alexander Jacobs, Robert Dillon, Laurie Dillon. Cast: Gene Hackman, Fernando Rey, Bernard Fresson. Twentieth Century Fox Film Corporation, 1975.

The Enforcer
Director: James Fargo. Screenplay: Stirling Silliphant, Dean Riesner. Cast: Clint Eastwood, Tyne Daly, Harry Guardino. Warner Bros., 1976.

New York, New York
Director: Martin Scorsese. Screenplay: Earl Mac Rauch, Mardik Martin. Cast: Liza Minelli, Robert De Niro, Lionel Stander. Chartoff-Winkler Productions, 1977.

The Champ
Director: Franco Zeffirelli. Screenplay: Walter Newman. Cast: Jon Voight, Faye Dunaway, Ricky Schroder. MGM, 1979.

Contemporary Hollywood Films

Bad Boys
Director: Rick Rosenthal. Screenplay: Richard Di Lello. Cast: Sean Penn, Reni Santoni, Jim Moody. Emi Films, Solofilm, 1983.

Sudden Impact
Director: Clint Eastwood. Screenplay: Joseph C. Stinson, Earl E. Smith, Charles B. Pierce. Cast: Clint Eastwood, Sondra Locke, Pat Hingle. Warner Bros., 1983.

Back to the Future
Director: Robert Zemeckis. Screenplay: Robert Zemeckis, Bob Gale. Cast: Michael J. Fox, Christopher Lloyd, Lea Thompson. Universal Pictures, 1985.

Streets of Gold
Director: Joe Roth. Screenplay: Dezsö Magyar, Heywood Gould, Richard Price, Tom Cole. Cast: Klaus Maria Brandauer, Adrian Pasdar, Wesley Snipes. Roundhouse, 1986.

FILMOGRAPHY

RoboCop
Director: Paul Verhoeven. Screenplay: Edward Neumeier, Michael Miner. Cast: Peter Weller, Nancy Allen, Dan O'Herlihy. Orion Pictures, 1987.

Die Hard
Director: John McTiernan. Screenplay: Roderick Thorp, Jeb Stuart, Steven E. de Souza. Cast: Bruce Willis, Alan Rickman, Bonnie Bedelia. Twentieth Century Fox Film Corporation, 1988.

Split Decisions
Director: David Drury. Screenplay: David Fallon. Cast: Gene Hackman, Graig Shaffer, Jeff Fahey. New Century Entertainment Corporation, 1988.

The Dead Pool
Director: Buddy Van Horn. Screenplay: Steve Sharon, Durk Pearson, Sandy Shaw. Cast: Clint Eastwood, Liam Neeson, Patricia Clarkson. Warner Bros., 1988.

Die Hard 2
Director: Renny Harlin. Screenplay: Steven E. de Souza, Doug Richardson. Cast: Bruce Willis, William Sadler, Bonnie Bedelia. Twentieth Century Fox, 1990.

Goodfellas
Director: Martin Scorsese. Screenplay: Nicholas Pileggi, Martin Scorsese. Cast: Robert De Niro, Ray Liotta, Joe Pesci. Warner Bros., 1990.

Home Alone
Director: Chris Columbus. Screenplay: John Hughes. Cast: Macaulay Culkin, Joe Pesci, Daniel Stern. Twentieth Century Fox, 1990.

Miller's Crossing
Directors: Joel Coen, Ethan Coen. Screenplay: Joel Coen, Ethan Coen. Cast: Gabriel Byrne, Albert Finney, John Turturro. Circle Films, Twentieth Century Fox Film Corporation, 1990.

RoboCop 2
Director: Irvin Kershner. Screenplay: Frank Miller, Walon Green. Cast: Peter Weller, Belina Bauer, John Glover. Orion Pictures, Tobor Productions, 1990.

Backdraft
Director: Ron Howard. Writer: Gregory Widen. Cast: Kurt Russell, William Baldwin, Robert De Niro. Imagine Films Entertainment, Trilogy Entertainment Group, 1991.

Only The Lonely
Director: Chris Columbus. Screenplay: Chris Columbus. Vast: John Candy, Maureen O'Hara, Ally Sheedy. Twentieth Century Fox, 1991.

Patriot Games
Director: Philip Noyce. Screenplay: Tom Clancy, W. Peter Iliff, Donald Stewart. Cast: Harrison Ford, Sean Bean, Anne Archer. Mace Neufeld Productions, Paramount Pictures, 1992.

RoboCop 3
Director: Fred Dekker. Screenplay: Frank Miller, Fred Dekker. Cast: Robert Burke, Mario Machado, Remy Ryan, Nancy Allen. Orion Pictures, 1993.

Blown Away
Director: Stephen Hopkins. Screenplay: John Rice, Joe Batteer, Jay Roach. Cast: Jeff Bridges, Tommy Lee Jones, Suzy Amis. Metro-Goldwyn-Mayer (MGM), Trilogy Entertainment Group, 1994.

Die Hard: With a Vengeance
Director: John McTiernan. Screenplay: Jonathan Hensleigh, Roderick Thorp. Cast: Bruce Willis, Jeremy Irons, Samuel L. Jackson. Cinergi Pictures Entertainment, Twentieth Century Fox Film Corporation, 1995.

Celtic Pride
Director: Tom DeCerchio. Screenplay: Judd Apatow. Cast: Damon Wayans, Daniel Stern, Dan Aykroyd. Caravan Pictures, Hollywood Pictures, 1996.

She's The One
Director: Edward Burns. Screenplay: Edward Burns. Cast: Edward Burns, Jennifer Aniston, John Mahoney. Good Machine, Marlboro Road Gang Productions, South Fork Pictures, 1996.

Sleepers
Director: Barry Levinson. Screenplay: Barry Levinson. Cast: Robert De Niro, Kevin Bacon, Brad Pitt. Astoria Films, Baltimore Pictures, Polygram Filmed Entertainment, Propaganda Films, Warner Bros., 1996.

The Devil's Own
Director: Alan J. Pakula. Screenplay: Kevin Jarre, David Aaron Cohen, Vincent Patrick. Cast: Harrison Ford, Brad Pitt, Margaret Colin. Columbia Pictures Corporation, 1997.

FILMOGRAPHY

The Jackal
Director: Michael Caton-Jones. Screenplay: Kenneth Ross, Chuck Pfarrer. Cast: Bruce Willis, Richard Gere, Sidney Poitier. Alphaville Films/Universal Pictures, 1997.

The Boondock Saints
Director: Troy Duffy. Screenplay: Troy Duffy. Cast: Willem Dafoe, Sean Patrick Flanery, Norman Reedus. Franchise Pictures, Brood Syndicate, Fried Films, 1999.

Frequency
Director: Gregory Hoblit. Screenplay: Toby Emmerich. Cast: Dennis Quaid, Jim Caviezel, Shawn Doyle. New Line Cinema, 2000.

Gangs of New York
Director: Martin Scorsese. Screenplay: Jay Cocks, Steven Zaillian, Kenneth Lonergan. Cast: Leonardo DiCaprio, Cameron Diaz, Daniel Day-Lewis. Miramax, 2002.

Daredevil
Director: Mark Steven Johnson. Screenplay: Mark Steven Johnson. Cast: Ben Affleck, Jennifer Garner, Colin Farrell. Marvel Enterprises, New Regency Pictures, Horseshoe Bay Productions, 2003.

Duplex
Director: Danny DeVito. Screenplay: Larry Doyle. Cast: Ben Stiller, Drew Barrymore, Eileen Essell. Miramax, 2003.

Mystic River
Director: Clint Eastwood. Screenplay: Brian Helgeland. Cast: Sean Penn, Tim Robbins, Kevin Bacon, Laurence Fishburne. Warner Bros., Village Roadshow Pictures, 2003.

Fighting Tommy Riley
Director: Eddie O'Flaherty. Screenplay: J.P. Davis. Cast: Eddie Jones, J.P. Davis, Christina Chambers. Visualeyes Productions, 1st Chance Productions, 2004.

Ladder 49
Director: Jay Russell. Screenplay: Lewis Colick. Cast: Joaquin Phoenix, John Travolta, Jacinda Barrett. Touchstone Pictures, Beacon Pictures, Casey Silver Productions, 2004.

Million Dollar Baby
Director: Clint Eastwood. Screenplay: Paul Haggis, F.X. Toole. Cast: Hilary Swank, Clint Eastwood, Morgan Freeman. Warner Bros., Lakeshore Entertainment, 2004.

A History of Violence
Director: David Cronenberg. Writer: Josh Olson. Cast: Viggo Mortensen, Maria Bello, William Hurt, Ed Harris. BenderSpink/New Line Cinema, 2005.

Cinderella Man
Director: Ron Howard. Screenplay: Cliff Hollingsworth, Akiva Goldsman. Cast: Russell Crowe, Renée Zellweger, Craig Bierko. Universal Pictures, Miramax, 2005.

The Departed
Director: Martin Scorsese. Screenplay: William Monahan. Cast: Leonardo DiCaprio, Matt Damon, Jack Nicholson, Mark Wahlberg, Martin Sheen. Warner Bros., 2006.

Live Free or Die Hard
Director: Len Wiseman. Screenplay: Mark Bomback. Cast: Bruce Willis, Timothy Olyphant, Justin Long, Maggie Q. Twentieth Century Fox, 2007.

Gone Baby Gone
Director: Ben Affleck. Screenplay: Ben Affleck, Aaron Stockard. Cast: Casey Affleck, Morgan Freeman, Ed Harris, Michelle Monaghan. Miramax, 2008.

The Boondock Saints II: All Saints' Day
Director: Troy Duffy. Screenplay: Troy Duffy. Cast: Sean Patrick Flanery, Norman Reedus, Billy Connolly. Stage 6 Films, CB Productions, 2009.

The Fighter
Director: David O. Russell. Screenplay: Scott Silver, Paul Tamasy. Cast: Mark Wahlberg, Christian Bale, Amy Adams. The Weinstein Company, 2010.

The Town
Director: Ben Affleck. Screenplay: Peter Craig, Ben Affleck. Cast: Ben Affleck, Rebecca Hall, Jeremy Renner, Jon Hamm. Warner Bros., Legendary Entertainment, GK Films, 2010.

FILMOGRAPHY

A Good Day to Die Hard
Director: John Moore. Screenplay: Skip Woods. Cast: Bruce Willis, Jai Courtney, Sebastian Koch, Mary Elizabeth Winstead. Twentieth Century Fox, 2013.

Non-Stop
Director: Jaume Collet-Serra. Screenplay: John W. Richardson, Chris Roach. Cast: Liam Neeson, Julianne Moore, Scot McNairy, Corey Stoll. StudioCanal, Anton, Silver Pictures, 2014.

RoboCop
Director: José Padilha. Screenplay: Joshua Zetumer, Edward Neumeier, Michael Miner. Cast: Joel Kinnaman, Gary Oldman, Michael Keaton, Abbie Cornish. MGM, Columbia, 2014.

The Irishman
Director: Martin Scorsese. Screenplay: Steven Zaillian. Cast: Robert De Niro, Al Pacino, Joe Pesci, Harvey Keitel. Tribeca Productions, Sikelia Productions, Winkler Films, 2019.

The Kitchen
Director: Andrea Berloff. Screenplay: Andrea Berloff. Cast: Melissa McCarthy, Tiffany Haddish, Elisabeth Moss, Domhnall Gleeson. BRON Creative, New Line Cinema, 2019.

Works Cited

Andrew, Geoff. "The Public Enemy Review." TimeOut, November 4, 2012. https://web.archive.org/web/20121104223009/https://www.timeout.com/film/reviews/71552/the_public_enemy.html.

"Angels with Dirty Faces (1938)." Rotten Tomatoes. Accessed January 22, 2021. https://www.rottentomatoes.com/m/angels_with_dirty_faces.

Arendt, Hannah. *Crises of the Republic: Lying in Politics; Civil Disobedience; On Violence; Thoughts on Politics and Revolution*. New York, NY: Harcourt Brace Jovanovich, 1972.

Arrowsmith, Aidan. "Imaginary Connections? Postmemory and Irish Diaspora Writing." In *Irish Studies: Memory Ireland, Diaspora and Memory Practices*, edited by Oona Frawley. Syracuse, N.Y.: Syracuse University Press, 2012.

Baker, Brian. *Masculinity in Fiction and Film: Representing Men in Popular Genres, 1945–2000*. London: Continuum International Publishing Group, 2006.

Basinger, Jeanine. "Translating War: The Combat Film Genre and Saving Private Ryan." *Perspectives on History*, October 1, 1998. https://www.historians.org/publications-and-directories/perspectives-on-history/october-1998/translating-war-the-combat-film-genre-and-saving-private-ryan.

Berliner, Todd. *Hollywood Incoherent: Narration in Seventies Cinema*. Austin: University of Texas Press, 2010.

Beyer, Cornelia. *Violent Globalisms: Conflict in Response to Empire*. London; New York: Routledge, 2013.

Biskind, Peter. "Any Which Way He Can." In *Clint Eastwood: Interviews, Revised and Updated*, edited by Robert E. Kapsis and Kathie Coblentz. Jackson: Univ. Press of Mississippi, 2012.

Biskind, Peter. *Easy Riders Raging Bulls: How the Sex-Drugs-And Rock 'N Roll Generation Save*. Simon and Schuster, 2011.

Blake, John W. *The Ulster American Connection*. Ulster: New University of Ulster, 1981.

Bondanella, Peter E. *Hollywood Italians: Dagos, Palookas, Romeos, Wise Guys, and Sopranos*. New York: Continuum, 2004.

Booker, M. Keith. *Alternate Americas: Science Fiction Film and American Culture*. Westport, Conn: Praeger, 2006.

Bordwell, David. *The Way Hollywood Tells It: Story And Style in Modern Movies*. Berkeley: University of California Press, 2006.

Bordwell, David, Janet Staiger, and Kristin Thompson. *The Classical Hollywood Cinema: Film Style & Mode of Production to 1960*. London New York: Routledge, Taylor & Francis Group, 2015.

Bordwell, David, and Kristin Thompson. *Film Art: An Introduction*. 8th ed. Boston: McGraw Hill, 2008.

WORKS CITED

Boyce, David George. *Nineteenth-Century Ireland: The Search for Stability*. Dublin: Gill & Macmillan, 2005.

Bureau, U. S. Census. "American FactFinder - Results 2013." Accessed June 23, 2015. http://factfinder.census.gov/faces/tableservices/jsf/pages/productview.xhtml?pid=ACS_13_5YR_DP02&src=pt.

Butters, Gerald R. *Banned in Kansas: Motion Picture Censorship, 1915–1966*. Columbia: University of Missouri Press, 2007.

Byrne, James Patrick, Philip Coleman, and Jason Francis King. *Ireland and the Americas: Culture, Politics, and History : A Multidisciplinary Encyclopedia*. Santa Barbara, Calif: ABC-CLIO, 2008.

Byron, Reginald. *Irish America*. Oxford Studies in Social and Cultural Anthropology. Oxford: Oxford University Press, 1999.

Carroll, Hamilton. *Affirmative Reaction: New Formations of White Masculinity*. Durham, NC: Duke University Press, 2011.

Carter, Cynthia, and C. Kay Weaver. *Violence And The Media*. Buckingham: Open University Press, 2003.

Central Statistics Office of Ireland. "CSO Quicktables: Population 1901–2011." Accessed June 24, 2015. http://www.cso.ie/multiquicktables/quickTables.aspx?id=cna13.

Cettl, Robert. *Terrorism in American Cinema: An Analytical Filmography, 1960–2008*. Jefferson, Car. du N.: McFarland & Co., 2009.

Clancy, Tom. *Patriot Games*. New York: Penguin Books Group US, 1988.

Cornell, Drucilla. *Clint Eastwood and Issues of American Masculinity*. New York: Fordham Univ Press, 2009.

Crowther, Bosley. "' Air Force,' South Sea Thriller, Arrives at the Hollywood – 'Immortal Sergeant' Is Newcomer at the Roxy." *The New York Times*, February 4, 1943, sec. Archives. https://www.nytimes.com/1943/02/04/archives/air-force-south-sea-thriller-arrives-at-the-hollywood-immortal.html.

Culberson, William C. *Vigilantism: Political History of Private Power in America*. New York: Greenwood Publishing Group, 1990.

Davis, Wes. "Fighting Words." *The New York Times*, February 26, 2005, sec. Opinion. http://www.nytimes.com/2005/02/26/opinion/26davis.html.

Dinello, Daniel. *Technophobia!: Science Fiction Visions of Posthuman Technology*. Austin: University of Texas Press, 2005.

Eastin, Matthew S. *Encyclopedia of Media Violence: One-Volume Set*. Thousand Oaks: SAGE Publications, 2013.

Ebert, Roger. "Streets Of Gold Movie Review & Film Summary (1986) | Roger Ebert." RogerEbert.com, November 14, 1986. http://www.rogerebert.com/reviews/streets-of-gold-1986.

Ebert, Roger. "The Jackal Movie Review & Film Summary (1997) | Roger Ebert." Accessed August 13, 2013. http://www.rogerebert.com/reviews/the-jackal-1997.

Eliot, Marc. *American Rebel: The Life of Clint Eastwood*. New York: Harmony Books, 2009. http://search.ebscohost.com/login.aspx?direct=true&scope=site&db=nlebk&db=nlabk&AN=720456.

Eliot, Marc. *American Rebel: The Life of Clint Eastwood*. New York: Harmony Books, 2009.

English, Richard. *Armed Struggle: The History of the IRA*. London: Pan Books, 2008.

Erickson, Hal. "Submarine D-1 (1937) Synopsis." AllMovie. Accessed February 6, 2021. https://www.allmovie.com/movie/submarine-d-1-v112135.

Fee, Gayle, and Raposa. "Tough Guy's Tattoo Is Talk of 'The Town.'" *Massachusetts Film Office* (blog). Accessed February 17, 2021. https://mafilm.org/2010/09/19/tough-guy%e2%80%99s-tattoo-is-talk-of-%e2%80%98the-town%e2%80%99/.

Fisher, James T. *On the Irish Waterfront: The Crusader, the Movie, and the Soul of the Port of New York*. Ithaca: Cornell University Press, 2011.

Flynn, Roderick, and Patrick Brereton. *Historical Dictionary of Irish Cinema*. Lanham, Md.: Scarecrow Press, 2007.

Foster, Thomas. *The Souls of Cyberfolk: Posthumanism as Vernacular Theory*. Minneapolis: University of Minnesota Press, 2005.

Fox, Margalit. "Henry Hill, Mobster of 'Goodfellas,' Dies at 69." *The New York Times*, June 13, 2012, sec. N.Y. / Region. http://www.nytimes.com/2012/06/14/nyregion/henry-hill-mobster-of-goodfellas-dies-at-69.html.

Slang.ie. "Frankie." Dictionary of Irish Slang. Accessed August 11, 2013. http://www.slang.ie/index.php?county=all&entry=Frankie&letter=F.

Galtung, Johan. *Peace by Peaceful Means: Peace and Conflict, Development and Civilization*. Los Angeles: SAGE, 1996.

Garbowski, Christopher. *Pursuits of Happiness: The American Dream, Civil Society, Religion and Popular Culture*. Lublin: Maria Curie-Sklodowska University Press, 2008.

Gilpatric, Katy. "Violent Female Action Characters in Contemporary American Cinema." *Sex Roles* 62, no. June 2010 (March 7, 2010). https://doi.org/10.1007/s11199-010-9757-7.

Goldstein, Margaret J. *Irish in America*. Minneapolis: Lerner Publications, 2004.

Gray, Gordon. *Cinema: A Visual Anthropology*. Oxford; New York: Berg, 2010.

Griffin, Patrick. *The People with No Name: Ireland's Ulster Scots, America's Scots Irish, and the Creation of a British Atlantic World, 1689–1764*. Princeton, N.J: Princeton University Press, 2001.

Grindon, Leger. *Knockout: The Boxer and Boxing in American Cinema*. Jackson: University Press of Mississippi, 2011.

Hardy, Phil. *The BFI Companion to Crime*. London: Cassell, 1997.

Hayden, Tom. *Irish on the Inside: In Search of the Soul of Irish America*. Irish on the Inside: In Search of the Soul of Irish America.: Verso, 2003.

Heller-Nicholas, Alexandra. *Rape-Revenge Films: A Critical Study*. Jefferson: McFarland, 2011.

WORKS CITED

Herling, Bradley L. "Ethics, Heart and Violence in MIller's Crossing." In *The Philosophy of the Coen Brothers*, edited by Mark T. Conard. Lexington: University Press of Kentucky, 2009.

Hey, Kenneth R. "Ambivalence as a Theme In." In *Hollywood as Historian: American Film in a Cultural Context*, edited by Peter C. Rollins. Lexington: University Press of Kentucky, n.d.

Hoffman, Ronald. *Princes of Ireland, Planters of Maryland: A Carroll Saga, 1500–1782*. Williamsburg: UNC Press Books, 2002.

Hout, Michael. *Following in Father's Footsteps: Social Mobility in Ireland*. Cambridge, Mass.: Harvard University Press, 1989.

Howell, James C. *Gangs in America's Communities*. Thousand Oaks: SAGE Publications, 2011.

Hughes, Howard. *Aim for the Heart the Films of Clint Eastwood*. London; New York; New York: I.B. Tauris ; Distributed in the United States and Canada exclusively by Palgrave Macmillan, 2009. http://site.ebrary.com/id/10424526.

Hurley, John W. *Shillelagh: The Irish Fighting Stick*. Lulu.com, 2007.

Ignatiev, Noel. *How the Irish Became White*. New York; London: Routledge, 1995.

Isenberg, Michael T. *John L. Sullivan and His America*. Urbana: University of Illinois Press, 1994.

Jeffords, Susan. *Hard Bodies: Hollywood Masculinity in the Reagan Era*. New Brunswick, N.J.: Rutgers University Press, 1994.

Jenkins, Philip. *Decade of Nightmares : The End of the Sixties and the Making of Eighties America: The End of the Sixties and the Making of Eighties America*. New York: Oxford University Press, USA, 2006.

Johnston, Jessica R. *The American Body in Context: An Anthology*. Wilmington: Rowman & Littlefield, 2001.

Kael, Pauline. *5001 Nights at the Movies*. New York: Henry Holt and Company, 1991.

Katz, Ephraim. *The Film Encyclopedia 5e: The Most Comprehensive Encyclopedia of World Cinema in a Single Volume*. New York: HarperCollins, 2005.

Kehr, Dave. *When Movies Mattered: Reviews from a Transformative Decade*. Chicago: University of Chicago Press, 2011.

Kenny, Kevin. *The American Irish: A History*. London: Routledge, 2014.

Koehler, Robert. "Review: 'Boondock Saints.'" Variety, January 20, 2000. http://variety.com/2000/film/reviews/boondock-saints-1117775584/.

Krämer, Peter. *The New Hollywood: From Bonnie And Clyde To Star Wars*. New York: Columbia University Press, 2005.

Kreng, John. *Fight Choreography: The Art of Non-Verbal Dialogue*. Cengage Learning, n.d.

"La Mamma Italiana: Interrogating a National Stereotype | Research Network Funded by the Arts and Humanities Research Council." Accessed November 22, 2014. http://lamammaitaliana.wordpress.com/.

Lagel, Laremy. "Infernal Affairs vs. the Remake, The Departed - Film.Com." Film.com, October 5, 2006. http://www.film.com/movies/infernal-affairs-vs-the-remake-the-departed.

Larkins, Bob, and Boyd Magers. *The Films of Audie Murphy*. Jefferson, N.C.; London: McFarland, 2009.

Lavin, Chad. *The Politics of Responsibility*. University of Illinois Press, 2008.

Lee, Stan. *Daredevil Masterworks Vol.1*. Marvel Entertainment, 2010.

Leerssen, Joep. "Imagology: On Using Ethnicity to Make Sense of the World." In *Les Stéréotypes Dans La Construction Des Identités Nationales Depuis Une Perspective Transnationale*, edited by Géraldine Galéote, Vol. 10. Paris: Revue Iberic@l, 2016.

Leerssen, Joep. "Nationality: Irish." Imagologica. Accessed May 2, 2020. https://imagologica.eu/ethnotypology.

Leerssen, Joep. "The Rhetoric of National Character: A Programmatic Survey." *Poetics Today* 21, no. 2 (June 1, 2000): 267–92. https://doi.org/10.1215/03335372-21-2-267.

Lengel, Edward G. *The Irish Through British Eyes: Perceptions of Ireland in the Famine Era*. Greenwood Publishing Group, 2002.

Lichtenfeld, Eric. *Action Speaks Louder: Violence, Spectacle, and the American Action Movie*. Wesleyan University Press, 2007.

Lloyd, Christopher. "Air Force (1943)." *The Film Yap* (blog), January 16, 2012. https://www.thefilmyap.com/movies/air-force-1943/.

LoBrutto, Vincent. *Martin Scorsese: A Biography*. Westport: Praeger, 2008.

Lourdeaux, Lee. *Italian Irish Filmmakers in America*. Philadelphia: Temple University Press, 1990.

Malanowski, James. "Abraham Lincoln: The President as Outlaw." In *Lincoln: A President for the Ages*, edited by Karl Weber. New York: PublicAffairs, 2012.

Maltby, Richard. "The Production Code and the Mythologies of 'Pre-Code' Hollywood." In *The Classical Hollywood Reader*, edited by Stephen Neale. Abingdon, Oxon; New York: Routledge, 2012.

Mannion, James. *The Everything Mafia Book: True Life Accounts of Legendary Figures, Infamous Crime Families, and Chilling Events*. Avon, MA: Adams Media Corp., 2003.

Mattern, Joanne. *Audie Murphy*. Hockessin: Mitchell Lane Publishers, Inc., 2015.

McBride, Joseph. *Searching for John Ford*. Jackson: University Press of Mississippi, 2011.

McDermott, Scott. *Charles Carroll of Carrollton: Faithful Revolutionary*. Scepter, 2002.

McDonagh, Maitland. "The Boondock Saints Review." TV Guide, 2000. http://movies.tvguide.com/boondock-saints/review/134582.

McGarty, Craig, Vincent Y. Yzerbyt, and Russell Spears. "Social, Cultural and Cognitive Factors in Stereotype Formation." In *Stereotypes as Explanations: The Formation of Meaningful Beliefs about Social Groups*, edited by Craig McGarty, Vincent Y. Yzerbyt, and Russell Spears. Cambridge: Cambridge University Press, 2002.

Meagher, Robert Emmet, and Elizabeth Neave. *Ancient Ireland: An Explorer's Guide*. Northampton, Mass: Interlink Books, 2004.

WORKS CITED

Meagher, Timothy J. *The Columbia Guide to Irish American History*. The Columbia Guides to American History and Cultures. New York: Columbia University Press, 2005.

Middleton, Richard, and Anne Lombard. *Colonial America: A History to 1763*. Malden, MA: John Wiley & Sons, 2011.

Miller, Kerby A. *Emigrants and Exiles: Ireland and the Irish Exodus to North America*. Oxford: Oxford University Press, 1988.

Monaco, Paul. *A History of American Movies: A Film-by-Film Look at the Art, Craft, and Business of Cinema*. Lanham, Md: Scarecrow Press, 2010.

Monaco, Paul. *The Sixties, 1960–1969*. Berkeley: University of California Press, 2003.

Moran, Daniel. "Printing the Legend of John Ford's 'The Informer.'" *New Hibernia Review / Iris Éireannach Nua* 15, no. 4 (2011): 127–43.

Moser, Joseph Paul. *Irish Masculinity on Screen: The Pugilists and Peacemakers of John Ford, Jim Sheridan and Paul Greengrass*. Jefferson: McFarland, 2013.

Mossman, Jennifer, ed. "Will Hays." In *Encyclopedia of World Biography*. Detroit: Gale Research, 1998.

Nash, Jay Robert. *Almanac of World Crime*. Garden City, N.Y.: Anchor Pr./Doubleday, 1981.

Neeson, Eoin. *Myths from Easter 1916*. Aubane: Aubane Historical Society, 2007.

Neibaur, James L. *James Cagney Films of the 1930s*. Lanham: Rowman & Littlefield, 2015.

Nott, Charles C., ed. *The Seven Great Hymns of the Mediaeval Church*. New York: Edwin S. Gorham, Publisher Church Mission House, 1902.

Oakland, John. *British Civilization: An Introduction*. London ; New York: Routledge, 2010.

O'Brien, Patrick. "Irish Americans." In *The Social History of Crime and Punishment in America: An Encyclopedia*, edited by Wilbur R. Miller. Thousand Oaks: SAGE Publications, 2012.

Padden, Michael, and Robert Sullivan. *May the Road Rise to Meet You: Everything You Need to Know about Irish American History*. New York: Plume, 1999.

Paulson, Timothy J., and Robert Asher. *Irish Immigrants*. New York: Facts on File, 2009.

Potrero Hill Archives Project., and Peter Linenthal. *San Francisco's Potrero Hill*. Charleston SC: Arcadia, 2005.

Potter, W. James. *On Media Violence*. Thousand Oaks: SAGE, 1999.

Prince, Stephen. *Classical Film Violence: Designing and Regulating Brutality in Hollywood Cinema, 1930–1968*. New Brunswick(N.B.); New Jersey; London: Rutgers University Press, 2003.

Rabin, Nathan. "Review: The Boondock Saints." A.V. Club, January 21, 2000. http://www.avclub.com/review/the-boondock-saints-19871.

Rafter, Nicole. *Shots in the Mirror : Crime Films and Society*. Oxford University Press, USA, 2000.

Rajan, Amol. "Fury as Actress Tells Film Festival 'I Would Have Joined the IRA.'" *Independent*, 12 2008. http://www.independent.co.uk/arts-entertainment/films/news/fury-as-actress-tells-film-festival-i-would-have-joined-the-ira-927097.html.

Ray, Robert Beverley. *A Certain Tendency of the Hollywood Cinema, 1930–1980*. Princeton, N.J: Princeton University Press, 1985.

Rayback, Joseph G. *History of American Labor*. New York: The Free Press, 2014.

Redmond, Patrick R. *The Irish and the Making of American Sport, 1835–1920*. Jefferson: McFarland, 2014.

Rekawek, Kacper. *Irish Republican Terrorism and Politics: A Comparative Study of the Official and the Provisional IRA*. London: Routledge, 2011.

Robinson, Philip S. *The Plantation of Ulster: British Settlement in an Irish Landscape, 1600–1670*. Ulster Historical Foundation, 2000.

Rocca, Alexander. "The History Page: Down the Mines. A 19th-Century Union, a Charismatic Businessman and an Alleged Conspiracy." *The Daily*, 2011.

Rowell, Erica. *The Brothers Grim: The Films of Ethan and Joel Coen*. Lanham: Scarecrow Press, 2007.

Salt, Barry. *Film Style and Technology: History and Analysis*. 3. & Biggest ed. London: Starword, 2009.

Seal, Graham. *The Outlaw Legend: A Cultural Tradition in Britain, America and Australia*. Cambridge: Cambridge University Press, 1996.

Seary, E., and William Kirwin. *Family Names of the Island of Newfoundland*. Montreal: McGill-Queen's Press - MQUP, 1998.

Shahidullah, Shahid M. *Crime Policy in America: Laws, Institutions, and Programs*. Lanham: University Press of America, 2008.

Singer, Merrill. *Introduction to Syndemics: A Critical Systems Approach to Public and Community Health*. San Francisco: John Wiley & Sons, 2009.

Smith, Dennis. *Firefighters: Their Lives in Their Own Words*. New York: Broadway Books, 2010.

Smith, Paul. *Clint Eastwood: A Cultural Production*. Minneapolis: University of Minnesota Press, 1993.

Storey, John. *Cultural Theory and Popular Culture: An Introduction*. New York: Routledge, 2015.

Streeter, Michael. "Princess Tries to Defuse Row over Trip to IRA Film." The Independent. Accessed August 13, 2013. http://www.independent.co.uk/news/princess-tries-to-defuse-row-over-trip-to-ira-film-1257620.html.

Suid, Lawrence H. *Sailing on the Silver Screen: Hollywood and the U.S. Navy*. Annapolis: Naval Institute Press, 1996.

Świderska, Małgorzata. "Comparativist Imagology and the Phenomenon of Strangeness." *CLCWeb: Comparative Literature and Culture* 15, no. 7 (2013).

Teays, Wanda. *Seeing the Light: Exploring Ethics Through Movies*. John Wiley & Sons, 2012.

The Public Enemy (1931). Accessed January 22, 2021. https://www.rottentomatoes.com/m/1016885-public_enemy.

WORKS CITED

The Public Enemy (1931) - IMDb. Accessed January 16, 2021. http://www.imdb.com/title/tt0022286/fullcredits.

Thomas, Kevin. "Mechanical 'RoboCop 3' in Need of Policing." *Los Angeles Times*, November 5, 1993. http://articles.latimes.com/1993-11-05/entertainment/ca-53331_1_original-robocop.

Vasquez Jr., Felix. "Bad Boys (1983)." *Cinema Crazed* (blog), June 12, 2012. http://cinema-crazed.com/blog/2012/12/06/bad-boys-1983/.

Vraukó, Tamás. "Changing Stereotypes – The Altering Role of the WASP Hero," n.pag. Katowice: University of Silesia, 1999.

Wernblad, Annette. *The Passion of Martin Scorsese: A Critical Study of the Films*. Jefferson: McFarland, 2010.

U.S. Naval Institute. "What Is the Most Realistic Submarine Movie Ever Made?," October 1, 2019. https://www.usni.org/magazines/proceedings/2019/october/what-most-realistic-submarine-movie-ever-made.

Whiteley, Chris. "The Public Enemy (1931)." Hollywood's Golden Age: 30 Years of Brilliance 1930–59. Accessed January 17, 2021. http://www.hollywoodsgoldenage.com/movies/the_public_enemy.html.

Wilkinson, Desi. "Euro-Paddy Land." The Journal of Music. Accessed May 9, 2020. https://journalofmusic.com/focus/euro-paddy-land.

Wright, Will. *Six Guns and Society: A Structural Study of the Western*. Berkeley: University of California Press, 1975.

Young, Alison. *The Scene of Violence: Cinema, Crime, Affect*. London: Routledge, 2010.

Zelizer, Julian. "Opinion: How Nixon's Scandal Still Hurts America - CNN.Com." *CNN.Com*, July 7, 2014. http://edition.cnn.com/2014/07/07/opinion/zelizer-watergate-politics/.

Index

Affleck, Ben 190, 192, 209, 216
Affleck, Casey 216
African American 18, 19, 48, 118, 125, 141, 152, 154, 155, 186, 189, 199, 223, 226, 235
Aherne, Brian 96
Air Force 103, 104
Albright, Lola 84
alcohol 18, 44, 50, 55, 58, 59, 66, 217, 223
alcoholism 39, 52, 85, 100, 140, 142, 185, 245
Allen, Nancy 160
Allen, Woody 111
Allgood, Sarah 37
All Saints' Day (Boondock Saints II) 203, 204
Alvin, John 104
Ames, Leon 72
Amis, Suzy 180
Anatomy of a Murder 63
Ancient Order of Hibernians, The 30, 137
Angel, Heather 93
Angels with Dirty Faces 64, 71–74, 108, 184, 195
Anglican Church 12, 13
anti-violence 2–4, 8, 70, 72, 81, 96, 101, 206, 212
Archer, Anne 172, 180
Arendt, Hannah 63
Arnold, Gary 151
Asbury, Herbert 185
Ashton, John 216
assimilation 8, 9, 37, 39, 171, 173, 176, 207, 209, 213, 214, 241, 244
auto-image 5, 6, 46, 109
Aykroyd, Dan 238

Backdraft 208, 219, 222, 223, 225, 248
Back to the Future 237
Bacon, Kevin 185, 215
Bacon, Lloyd 62, 75, 81, 102
Bad Boys 181, 184, 194
Bad Day on the Block 224
Balaban, Burt 63
Baldwin, Alec 198
Baldwin, William 219
Ball, Lucille 37
Bancroft, George 52, 66

Barrymore, Drew 238
Barrymore, Lionel 98
Bauer, Belinda 161
Baxley, Craig R. 224
Baxter, Anne 104
Bean, Sean 172
Beatty, Warren 111
Beaudine, William 47
Bedelia, Bonnie 154
beer 55, 58, 91, 199
Beery, Wallace 85
Belfast 16, 168, 170, 171, 174, 217
Bells of St. Mary, The 71
Beloved Enemy 96, 97
Benet, Marianne 97
Bergman, Ingrid 71
Berloff, Andrea 199
Biskind, Peter 110, 111, 124
Black and Tans 32, 93, 95
Blade Runner 159
Blissert, Robert 24
Blown Away 172, 174–76, 178–80, 212, 214
Bobb, Jeremy 199
Bogart, Humphrey 64, 66
Bolling, Angie 163
Bond, Ward 91
Bonnie and Clyde 110–12, 143
Bookwalter, DeVeren 130
Boondock Saints, The 72, 203, 205, 207, 208, 211, 214
Boru, Brian 15
Boston 22, 38, 172, 185, 187, 188, 190, 191, 203, 207, 216
Boston Celtics 238
Bostonians 189
Boston Massacre 15
Boyle, Peter 139
Boys Town 70, 71
Brandauer, Klaus Maria 226
Brando, Marlon 100
Brandt, Charles 192
Breen, Joseph 44, 45
Brent, Evelyn 52
Bridges, Jeff 140, 172, 173
Brook, Clive 52

INDEX 271

Bryant, Joyce 73
Bulger, Whitey 189
Burke, Robert John 161
Burns, Edward 236
Byrne, Gabriel 182

Cagney, James 45, 55, 57, 62, 64, 81, 92, 102, 109
Calvert, George 13
Cameron, James 159
Campbell, John 104
Canavale, Bobby 192
Candy, John 215
Canvale, Bobby 192
Cardinal, The 71
Cardwell, James 104
Carr, Patrick 15
Carrey, Harry 103
Carrigan, Bill 38
Carrolls of Annapolis 13, 14
Caruso, David 37
Catholicism 12, 24, 202, 205, 206, 212, 223, 240
Caton-Jones, Michael 175
Celtic Pride 238
Champ, The (*1931*) 85, 92
Champ, The (*1979*) 92, 142
Champion 85
Charlestown, Boston 190–92
Chase, Alden 74
chauvinism 121, 131
Chester, Hal E. 74
Chicago 38, 53, 55, 84, 181, 219, 220
Childers, Naomi 49
Cimino, Michael 112
Cinderella Man 235
Civil War (Irish) 11, 32, 33, 92
Clancy, Tom 174
Clannad 174
Clan na Gael 29, 30
Clark, Candy 141
Clarke, Mae 59
Clements, Stanley 71
Cline, Maggie 37
Cobb, Lee J. 100
Coen, Ethan and Joel 182
Cohan, George M. 37
Cokes, Curtis 140
Colasanto, Nicholas 141

Colin, Margaret 180
Collet-Serra, Jaume 217
Collins, Michael 32, 33
Colter, Mike 231
Columbus, Chris 215, 238
Come on Marines! 101
Comiskey, Charles 38
Conductor 1492 50, 54, 77, 89, 108
Connaughtmen 22
Connery, Sean 136
Connolly, Billy 204
Connolly, James 27
Cook, Donald 57
Cooper, Gary 121
Cooper, Gladys 99
Cooper, Jackie 85
Coppola, Francis Ford 113, 194, 202
Corbett, James "Gentleman Jim" 38, 92
Corkonians, the 22
Corridan, John M. 101
Courtney, Jai 159
Cox, Ronny 160
Crawford, Joan 37
Crisp, Donald 98
Cronenberg, David 187
Crosby, Bing 37, 71
Crowe, Russell 235
Crudup, Billy 185
Culkin, Macaulay 238
Curtis, Tony 107
Curtiz, Michael 64, 72
Cusack, John 37

d'Arcy James, Brian 199
Dafoe, Willem 203
Dáil Éireann 32
Dale, James Badge 189, 199
Dalton, Kristen 198
Daly, Tyne 130
Damon, Matt 187
Danheim, John 83
Daredevil 209–11, 236
Dashielle, G. W. D. (Cmdr.) 102
Davis, J. P. 229, 230
Davitt, Michael 29
Day-Lewis, Daniel 185
Dead End Kids, the 64, 65, 72, 74, 108
Dead Pool, The 150, 153, 166
Death Wish 151

DeCerchio, Tom   238
Declaration of Independence
   (American)   14
Deer Hunter   112
Defenders, the   16
de Havilland, Olivia   81
Dekker, Fred   161
delinquency (juvenile)   64, 65, 67, 69, 70, 72,
   181, 245
Della Rocco, David   204
De Niro, Robert   142, 184, 192, 220
Dennehy, Brian   235
Departed, The   185, 187, 189–92, 196, 198, 202,
   213, 214, 240, 241, 247
Depp, Johnny   37
Detroit   22, 98, 160, 161, 163, 165
de Valera, Eamon   31–34
Devil's Own, The   167, 171, 174–80, 209, 212,
   214, 241
DeVito, Danny   238
Devoy, John   29–31
DiCaprio, Leonardo   185, 188
Die Hard   122, 153, 154, 162, 166, 225
Die Hard 2: Die Harder   158
Die Hard With A Vengeance
   (*Die Hard III*)   154, 155, 157, 162
Dillman, Bradford   129
Dirty Harry   3, 111, 114–16, 121, 122, 124, 125,
   129, 132, 133, 135, 150–54, 157, 159, 162, 166,
   225, 239, 246
Douglas, Kirk   82
Dowdle, Erick John   225
Downey Jr., Robert   37
draft riots, New York City   186
Drake, Peter   151
Drury, David   227
Dublin   15, 16, 24, 25, 30–32, 89, 93
Duffy, Troy   203, 206
Dunaway, Faye   111
Duncan, Michael Clarke   209
Dunne, Griffin   224
Duplex   238
Duryea, Dan   98
D'Orsay, Fifi   77

Eagle Wing   11
Easter Rising, the   24, 30, 31
East Side Kids   72

Eastwood, Clint   37, 114, 122, 124, 215, 231, 246
Ebert, Roger   175, 229
Edwards, Jack   74
Eggar, Samantha   137
Eisenhower, Dwight D.   106
Eldard, Ron   185
Ellis, Patricia   62
Enforcer, The   124, 129, 130, 145, 166
Essell, Eileen   238
ethnotype   3–6, 8, 41, 46, 47, 52, 54, 86, 115,
   174, 238, 244, 245, 249
Everett, Bill   209

Fairbanks Jr., Douglas   77
Famine of 1740, the   12, 17
Fargo, James   124
Farley, Jim   74
Farmiga, Vera   188
Farrell, Colin   209
Fat City   140, 142
father figure   8, 56, 62, 170, 177, 194–98, 201,
   221–23, 231, 240, 247, 248
FBI   36, 133, 135, 156, 173, 175, 176, 188, 191,
   199, 203
Feeney, Martin   92
femininity   4, 143, 198, 201, 248
Fenian Brotherhood (Fenians)   23, 25, 28, 29
Fenton, Leslie   58
Ferry, David   207
Fighter, The   235
Fighting 69th, The   71, 102
Fighting Sullivans, The   104, 105
Fighting Tommy Riley   229, 231, 248
Fink, Rita M.   114
Fink. Harry J.   114
Finney, Albert   182
Fireproof   225
Flanagan, Edward J.   70, 71
Flanery, Sean Patrick   203
Florey, Robert   63
Flynn, Errol   37, 92
Flynn, Rita   60
Fonda, Henry   113
Fonda, Peter   205
Ford, Harrison   37, 168, 172
Ford, John   38, 45, 86, 92, 105, 106, 110, 189,
   245
Ford, Wallace   93

INDEX

273

Foster, Preston   94, 98
France   15, 16, 134
Frankenheimer, John   132
Freeman, Morgan   216, 233
French Connection, The   112, 131, 133, 162
French Connection II, The   134, 162
Frequency   208, 222–25
Fresson, Bernard   134
Friedkin, William   131, 132
Friends of Eddie Coyle, The   138–40, 146
Friends of Irish Freedom, the   30, 32
Friske, Robert   74

Gallina, Lucy   193
Galtung, Johan   7, 177, 179
Gangs of New York   185–87, 195, 202, 212, 213, 241
Gardner, Leonard   140
Garfield, John   103
Gargan, William   82
Garland, Judy   37
Garner, Jennifer   211
Garnett, Tay   96, 97
Garrett, Edward   123
Garson, Greer   97
Gassman, Vittorio   184
Gathegi, Edi   216
Gentleman Jim   92
George, Lloyd   32
Gere, Richard   175
Germans   30, 31, 34, 41, 107
Gladiator   235, 236
Glenn, Scott   220
Glover, Crispin   238
Godfather   182, 194, 202
Godunov, Alexander   155
Going My Way   71
Goldman, Charley   230
Gompers, Samuel   28
Good Day to Die Hard, A   154, 158, 159
Goodfellas   184, 187, 192–94, 213, 240
Gooding Jr., Cuba   235
Gordon, Mary   81
Grahame, Margot   93
Great Famine, The   12, 17, 20–24, 26, 27, 37, 244
Great Guy   92
Greek   48

Grey, Shirley   77
Grey, Virginia   75
Griffin, Frank   50
Guardino, Harry   113
Guinness   175

Hackman, Gene   132, 227
Haddish, Tiffany   199
Hall, Rebecca   191
Hamm, Jon   191
Hanlon, Ned   38
Harlin, Renny   154
Harlow, Jean   59
Harolde, Ralf   62
Harrigan, Edward "Ned"   37
Harris, Ed   216
Harris, Richard   97, 136, 165, 174
Harrison, George   36
Hart, Tony   37
Harvey, Irene   75
Hathaway, Henry   101
Hawks, Howard   103
Hays, Will   43, 44
Hayworth, Rita   37
Heaven's Gate   112, 113
henchman   187, 191, 192, 197, 247
heroism   23, 103, 107, 108, 122, 172, 178, 219, 222, 246
Herrington, Rowdy   235
hetero-image   5, 6, 8, 46, 105, 109, 192, 249
Heywood, Anne   96
Hibbs, Jesse   106
Hickman, Bill   133
High Noon   121, 156
Hill, Robert F.   72
Hines, Johnny   50
Hispanic Americans   118
History of Violence, A   187, 197
Hoblit, Gregory   222
Hoffa, Jimmy   192–94
Hold Your Horses   49
Holland, Todd   224
Home Alone   238
homosexuality   110, 198, 199, 229, 230, 248
Hopkins, Stephen   172
Hopper, E. Mason   49
Howard, Ron   219, 235
Hughes, John (Archbishop)   22

Hunt, Marsha 99
Huston, John 140

I Heard You Paint Houses 192
Ihnat, Steve 113
imagology 4, 5
Informer, The 92, 95–97, 146
IRA (Irish Republican Army) 32, 33, 35, 36, 86, 92–97, 167, 168, 172–75, 179, 189, 209, 212, 217, 241, 247
Irish Free State, the 26, 32, 34
Irish immigrants 1, 14, 15, 21, 22, 24–28, 35–39, 49–51, 76, 136, 185, 189, 206, 209, 212, 218, 241
Irish immigration to America 5, 10, 13, 17, 19, 21, 34, 35, 39
Irish independence 2, 11, 25, 29–34, 39, 41, 86, 92, 96, 111, 244
Irish Italian 183
Irishman, The 192–94, 198, 202, 226, 244, 249
Irish Republican Brotherhood 24, 30
Irons, Jeremy 155
Island in the Sky 106
Italian 113, 118, 132, 182–84, 190, 192–95, 198, 201, 202, 204, 247
I Wouldn't Be In You Shoes 63

Jackal, The 175, 176, 178–80
Jackson, Andrew 17, 18
Jackson, Samuel L. 155
Jaws 112
Jazz Singer 42
Jenkins, Allen 81
Jewish 48, 76, 182, 200, 226, 230
Johnson, Mark Steven 209
Jones, Eddie 229
Jones, Tommy Lee 172
Jordan, Richard 139

Kael, Pauline 124
Kazan, Elia 100
Keach, Stacy 140
Keaton, Buster 37
Keats, Steven 139
Keenan, Sean 36
Kehoe, John 136–38
Keighley, William 71, 102
Keith, David 209
Kelly, Gene 37

Kelly, Grace 37
Kelly, Michael J. "King" 38
Kendrick, Alex 225
Kennedy, Arthur 83
Kennedy, John F. 37, 110, 193
Kerrigan, J. M. 94
Kershner, Irvin 161
Kibbee, Guy 78
Kinnaman, Joel 162
Kinnell Murray 57
Kitchen, The 199, 247, 248
Kubrick, Stanley 111

Ladder 49 222–25
Lady from Shanghai , The 63
Lane, Priscilla 75, 253
Lean, David 110
Lee, Stan 209
Leigh, Jennifer Jason 219
Lesley, Maxine 74
Levi and Cohen, Irish Comedians 46, 249
Life of Jimmy Dolan, The 77, 79, 80, 82, 83, 85, 92
Liotta, Ray 183
Little Annie Rooney 47, 54, 56, 57, 61, 62, 64, 75, 108, 144, 201
Live Free or Die Hard 154, 158, 159
Lloyd, Harold 82
Loach, Ken 32
Locke, Sandra 151
Long Gray Line, The 106
Lord, Daniel J. (Rev.) 44
Los Angeles 83, 154, 156, 231
Lucas, George 112

MacArthur, Douglas (Gen.) 105
Mack, Helen 82
MacMahon, Aline 78
Mad Dog Coll 63
Madigan 113–15, 121, 124, 246
Mafia (Italian Mafia) 183, 184, 192–95, 200–202, 204, 247
Magnum Force 123–25, 127, 129, 145
Maher, Matthew 216
Mahoney, Brian 207
Malden, Karl 100
Marley, Bob 207
Marshall, James 235
Maryland 13, 14

INDEX

masculinity 4, 119, 143, 146, 198, 221, 223, 224, 228, 231, 236, 237, 248
Massachusetts 22, 188, 191
Masterson, Thomas 24
Maxwell, Marilyn 83
Mayo, Archie 77
McCarey, Leo 38, 71, 82
McCarthy Melissa 199
McCourt, Malachy 37
McElhone, Natascha 168
McGarrity, Joseph 32
McGlone, Mike 236
McGraw, John J. "Mugsy" 38
McGuire, P.J. 28
McHenry, James 16
McHugh, Frank 81
McLaglen, Victor 86, 93
McLaughlin, Dennis 191
McQueen, Steve 143, 247
McStiofain, Sean 36
McTiernan, John 154, 155
Meek, Donald 57
Meeker, George 78
Menjou, Adolphe 82
Mercer, Beryl 56
Meredith, Burgess 230
Metwally, Omar 217
Mexican 24, 25, 40, 85, 141, 181
Milestones, Lewis 52
Milky Way, The 82, 92
Miller, Frank 161
Miller's Crossing 182, 213
Million Dollar Baby 231, 232, 234, 248
Minelli, Liza 142
Mitchell, Elizabeth 222
Mitchell, Thomas 75
Mitchum, John 129
Mitchum, Robert 138
mob (Irish) 40, 66, 67, 84, 139, 140, 145, 182, 187, 188, 191, 197, 199–202, 240
mobster (Irish) 63, 145, 187–89, 194
Molly Maguires, The 136–38, 165, 246
Monaghan, Michelle 216
Montgomery, Ray 103
Montgomery, Robert 105
Moore, Dennis 73
Moore, John 154
Moore, Julianne 217
Moore, Tom 49, 154

Morales, Esai 181
Morgan, Dennis 75
Morgan, Jeffrey Dean 224
Morris, Wayne 102
Mortensen, Viggo 187
Moss, Elisabeth 199
mother 47, 56, 60, 71, 77, 78, 81, 93, 95, 96, 99, 103, 104, 107, 183, 184, 191, 195, 198, 201, 208, 215, 222, 223, 236, 240, 248
Motion Picture Production Code 3, 43, 45, 106
Mount, Anson 217
Munstermen 22
Murphy, Audie 106
Murray, Bill 37
Mystic River 215

nationalism 25, 28, 29, 31, 35
Natwick, Mildred 90
Neeson, Liam 24, 153, 185, 217
Netflix 192
New York, New York 142
Nicholson, Jack 188, 189
Nigh, William 63
Nolte, Nick 215
non-violent 2, 4, 7, 8, 47, 67, 109, 112, 146, 169, 182, 201, 210, 211, 215, 241, 245
Noonan, Tom 161
NORAID (Northern Aid Committee) 36, 168
North, Sheree 113
Northern Ireland 2, 8, 32, 35, 36, 96, 109, 167, 168, 170, 171, 174–76, 179, 207, 217, 239, 242
Northern Irish republicans 3, 36, 149, 150, 167, 170, 172, 214, 247
Noyce, Philip 172

O'Brien, Dave 73
O'Byrne, Brian F. 232
O'Connell Daniel 25
O'Connor, Julia 28
O'Connor, Thomas "Terrible Tommy" 52
O'Hara, Maureen 86, 215
O' Herlihy, Dan 97
O'Mahony, John 24
O'Riordan, Dolores 171
Oberon, Merle 96
Offerman, George 104
One from the Heart 113
Only the Lonely 215

On the Waterfront 100, 101, 146
Orange and Green Riots 25
O'Brien, Pat 45, 64, 71, 73, 75, 102
O'Connor, Derrick 211
O'Connor, Robert 62
O'Connor, Una 93
O'Flaherty, Eddie 229
O'Flaherty, Liam 93
O'Reilly, Leonora 28

Pacino, Al 192
Padilha, José 162
Pakula, Alan J 154, 167
Paquin, Anna 193
Pasdar, Adrian 226
Patric, Jason 185
Patriot Games 171–76, 178–80, 212, 214
Patton, George 106
Peck, Gregory 37, 97
Pell, Joshua (Capt.) 15
Penn, Arthur 111
Penn, Sean 37, 181, 215
Perrino, Joe 184
Pesci, Joe 184, 192
Philadelphia 25, 31, 38, 187, 193
Phoenix, Joaquin 222
Pileggi, Nicolas 183
Pitt, Brad 167, 168, 185
Pittsburgh 91, 97
Plunkett, Jerry 102
Polito, Jon 182
Popwell, Albert 130, 152, 182
Porter, Edwin S. 47
Post, Ted 124
Postlethwaite, Pete 191
Potter, H.C. 96
Pratt, Purnell 56
Production Code Administration (PCA) 44, 45
Provisional Irish Republican Army (PIRA) 35, 36, 167–72, 174–78, 180, 212
pub 6, 66, 75, 86, 89, 91, 139, 171, 174, 175, 189, 199, 206, 207, 216, 223, 224, 228
Public Enemy, The 55, 56, 59–62, 64, 244, 249

Quaid, Dennis 222
Quiet Man, The 86, 92, 109, 245
Quigley, Martin 44
Quinn, Anthony 37

Racket, The 52–54, 72, 73, 75, 144
Raleigh, Walter 10
Ray, Robert 8, 103, 122, 148–50, 214
Reedus, Norman 203
religion 202, 205, 206, 211, 234, 240
Renfro, Brad 184
Renner, Jeremy 190
retributive justice 3, 123, 136, 138, 144, 150, 151, 184, 206–8, 211, 212, 215, 216, 241, 242, 246
revenge 59, 101, 122, 151, 162, 172, 176–78, 184, 189, 195, 196, 198, 203, 206, 213, 227, 228
Rey, Fernando 132
Rich, Irene 85
Rickman, Alan 154, 167
Ridgely, John 103
Rijker, Lucia 232
Riley, John 25
Ritt, Martin 136, 246
Robbins, Tim 215
RoboCop (the original film and character) 159–66, 239
RoboCop (2014) 162
RoboCop 2 161
Robocop 3 162
Robson, Mark 82
Roger Touhy, Gangster 63
Roman, Ruth 83
Romano, Ray 192
Romita Jr., John 211
Rooney, Patrick 37
Roscoe, Karns 101
Rosenthal, Rick 181
Rota, Carlo 204
Roth, Joe 226
Rourke, Mickey 36, 37
Russell, David O. 235
Russell, Jay 222
Russell, Kurt 219
Ryan, Edward 104

Saint, Eva Marie 101
San Francisco 22, 24, 103, 114, 116, 133, 135, 143
Scheider, Roy 132
Schroder, Ricky 142
Scorsese, Martin 142, 183, 185, 187, 192, 194, 201, 202, 244, 247
Scotch-Irish 11, 24, 25, 31, 39, 129, 157, 203
Scots 11, 12, 15

INDEX 277

Scott, Ridley 159
Seda, Jon 235
Sheedy, Ally 181, 215
Sheen, Charlie 224
Sheen, Martin 188
Sheffer, Craig 227
Sheridan, Ann 64
Shields, Arthur 89
Siegel, Don 111, 113, 115, 122, 124, 125, 246
Sinn Féin 31, 174
Sleepers 184, 195
Smith, Gladys 47
Smith, Kurtwood 160
Snipes, Wesley 226
Society of the United Irishmen, the 16–18, 23, 28, 39
soldiers 25, 33, 61, 71, 101, 102, 106–8, 145, 171, 174
Split Decisions 227–29
Stallone, Sylvester 140, 229
Steiger, Rod 100
Stein, Sammy 79
Stephens, James 24
stereotype activation 3, 114, 161
Stern, Daniel 238
Stevens, Inger 113
Stewart, Paul 83
Stiller, Ben 238
Stoll, Corey 217
Stone, George E. 53
Streets of Gold 226–29
Submarine D-1 102
Sudden Impact 150, 151, 153, 166
Sullivan, John L. 38
Sutherland, Donald 220
Swank, Hilary 231

Talbot, Lyle 78
Tandy, Jessica 99
Taurog, Norman 70
Tayler, Diane 229
Terrible Beauty, A 96
terrorism 23, 178, 179, 217, 226
Tess of the Storm Country 47
The Irish in US 75, 81
They Were Expendable 105
Three Cheers for the Irish 75, 218
To Hell and Back 106
Tolkan, James 227

Towering Inferno, The 142, 143, 247
Town, The 190, 198
Tracy, Spencer 37, 70
Travolta, John 222
Troubles, The 34, 36, 242
Tuker, Jonathan 184
Turturro, John 182
Tyrell, Susan 140

Ulster 11, 12, 15, 16, 21, 31, 167, 174
Ulster Orangemen 16, 17, 25, 31
Underworld 52, 53

Valley of Decision, The 97
Van Horn, Buddy 150
van Rooten, Luis 84
Velez, Eddie 227
VelJohnson, Reginald 154
Verhoeven, Paul 159, 163
Voight, Jon 142
von Sternberg, Joseph 52

Wahlberg, Mark 188, 190, 235
Walsh, Maurice 86
Walsh, Raoul 92
Washington, George 15, 16
Waterloo Bridge 59
Watford, Myk 199
Wayans, Damon 238
Wayne, John 37, 79, 86, 105, 106
Wead, Frank 102
Weller, Peter 160
Welles, Orson 63
Welliver, Titus 216
Wellman, William 55, 106
Weston, Doris 102
White, De'voreaux 154
White Anglo-Saxon Protestant (WASP) 1, 5, 121, 122, 134
Widmark, Richard 113
Willis, Bruce 122, 153, 175
Wilson, Woodrow 31
Wind that Shakes the Barley, The 32
Winkler, Irwin 229
Winstead, Mary Elizabeth 159
Wise, Robert 110
Wiseman, Len 154
Wolheim, Louis 53
women's empowerment 229, 231

women (Irish) 2, 4, 18, 26–28, 35, 37, 44, 47, 49, 52, 62, 96, 101, 114, 180, 198, 199, 201, 202, 222, 244
Woods, Edward 55, 57
working-class 98, 168, 233, 236

Yankee Doodle Dandy 109

Zeffirelli, Franco 142
Zemeckis, Robert 237
Zimmerman, Fred 74, 121